AF522303

AN ENCYCLOPEDIC DICTIONARY OF
POLITICS

AN ENCYCLOPEDIC DICTIONARY OF POLITICS

M. Mahmood
Reader in Political Science
Aligarh Muslim University
Aligarh

ANMOL PUBLICATIONS PVT. LTD.
NEW DELHI - 110 002 (INDIA)

ANMOL PUBLICATIONS PVT. LTD.
H.O.: 4374/4B, Ansari Road, Darya Ganj,
New Delhi-110 002 (India)
Ph.: 23278000, 23261597

B.O.: No. 1015, Ist Main Road, BSK IIIrd Stage
IIIrd Phase, IIIrd Block,
Bangalore - 560 085 (India)
Visit us at: www.anmolpublications.com

An Encyclopedic Dictionary of Politics

First Published, 2006

ISBN 81-261-3046-6

PRINTED IN INDIA

Printed at Mehra Offset Press, Delhi.

Preface

To cater to reference needs of students and general readers a subject dictionary must collate authentic, authoritative, up-to-date and optimal information on topics selected, preferably in parsimonious and simple language. The present work is a comprehensive compendium of some 1400 brief entries on a wide range of political ideas and ideologies, institutions and structures, and events and facts. It must prove to be a rich source of political knowledge, indeed.

While all possible care has been taken to ensure the accuracy of data a few errors here and there cannot be ruled out. Such errors, if any, will be rectified in future editions.

An asterism (*) placed on a term occurring in the text of this work indicates that it is included herein as a regular entry.

M. MAHMOOD

Department of Political Science
Aligarh Muslim University
Aligarh 202002 India

A

A Posteriori (from Latin *a* = from and *posteriori* = after) from what comes after, i.e. empirical or inductive reasoning; from the effects to their causes, not from assumed axioms or self-evident truths.

A Priori/A Priorism (Latin *a* = from and *prior* = before) means abstract or philosophical reasoning from causes to effects or from assumed axioms to their consequences. Apriorism or deductivism is the use of *a priori* reasoning,

ABM Treaty (1972) or the five-year Treaty to Limit the Intercontinental Ballistic Missiles signed between the erstwhile USSR and the USA as a first step to halt the nuclear arms race between the two was a child of the east-west *deténte.* This treaty on defensive missile systems limited the number of anti-ballistic missiles to 100 for each side to be deployed in two areas of a radius of 150 square kilometers, one of them being the national capital of the two countries. Another Interim Agreement on Offensive Missiles was signed in 1974 which imposed numerical limitations on deployment of different types of offensive nuclear weapons--the ICBM's, nuclear submarines and nuclear submarine launchers.

Act of God is in Anglo-Saxon law an accidental act resulting from a cause that is beyond human interference or control e.g. natural disasters or earthquakes. Unless stipulated to the contrary in a contract a party is not liable to pay for damages caused by an act of God; also called an inevitable or unpreventable incident.

Act of Parliament or a legislative act is a law or statute passed by a parliament or legislative assembly and assented to by the head of the state.

Act of State. In international law the doctrine of the act of state emanates from a state's sovereign equality and means that the courts of one state do not, as a rule, question the validity of the official acts of another sovereign state or the official acts of its agents, provided they are not derogatory to principles of international law (Oppenheim).

Act of Proclamations, 1539 (England) empowered the king to legislate by ordinance but its repeal later barred the king from legislation except on a bill presented by Parliament.

Act of Settlement, 1701 (UK) was, along with the Bill of Rights,* an important foundation of constitutional government in Great Britain. It settled the Crown on Sophia, the Princess of Hanover in Germany, a grand-daughter of King James I, and her descendants. Sovereigns of the United Kingdom were to be Protestant; they could not leave the Kingdom without the consent of Parliament; no foreigner was entitled to receive a grant from the Crown nor could hold any civil or military office under the Crown; ministers of the Crown became accountable for the acts of their sovereigns taken on their advice; and the judges were to hold office during "good behaviour", i.e. for life and could not be removed by the Crown except on an address presented by Parliament for their removal.

Act of War is any act, like border crossing or unauthorized entry into the air space of a state or any other move, declared to constitute an act of war which may invite retaliatory action by the affected state.

Act of Supremacy, 1534 (Britain) appointed the King of England and his successors as the Protector and Only Supreme Head of the Church and Clergy of England. The Act marked the final break of England with the Roman Catholic Church and the beginning of English Reformation.

Act, Appropriations is that part of the annual budget by which a parliamentary assembly approves the demands for grants submitted by the executive and empowers it to *appropriate* (take out) the sanctioned amounts from the consolidated fund (the public exchequer) and spend them for approved purposes. The appropriations act consolidates all the demands for grants made by the ministries/departments of the government. The Act carries a schedule indicating separately the amount sanctioned against each demand for grant.

Act, Consolidation is a parliamentary act which consolidates or puts together all separate laws dealing with the same subject in a single instrument.

Act, Finance is that part of an annual budget which consolidates the proposals for taxation presented by the government in a single act authorizing the government to levy and collect the approved taxes. In a constitutional democracy no tax can be levied or collected without the authority of parliament.

Accountability and Responsibility. In common parlance the terms are used interchangeably but there is a subtle difference between the two. While accountability of a subordinate means his liability to account for his actions before his superiors, responsibility of a person for something implies his moral culpability. Accountability involves legal relationships between levels of a hierarchy and is diffused throughout an organization while responsibility is personal. Responsibility is shared but accountability cannot be shared. Failure to give an account may invite legal penalties but moral lapses may attract only disapproval or reprobation or censure.

Acculturation is the process by which groups and communities acquire the cultural characteristics of other groups or communities through direct contacts and intermingling.

Ad Referendum (subject to reference). If an international treaty or agreement is signed *ad referendum* it will not come into force unless ratified by the constitutional machinery of the respective signatories.

Adhocracy is a model of organization which does not believe in rigid hierarchism, absolute rules and standardized procedures and practices. It rather prefers fluid and flexible administration. It is akin to an informal organization with attendant flexibility and preference to innovative teamwork. Adhocracy is advocated as an antidote to the "iron cage" of Weberian bureaucracy.

Administrative Reforms Commission (India) was set up by the Government of India as a commission of inquiry on 5 January 1966 under the chairmanship of Morarji Desai. On his appointment in 1967 as deputy prime minister and finance minister of the Government of India he was succeeded by K. Hanumanthaiyya. The Commission was asked to look into the organization and functioning of all branches of the Indian administration at the central, state and local levels as well as the whole gamut of the union-state relations and suggest appropriate reforms. The Commission completed its work in 1970 and submitted 20 reports containing some 378 recommendations which were implemented during the next decade.

Administrative Tribunals consist of persons that exercise judicial or quasi-judicial functions outside the hierarchy of ordinary courts. Such tribunals are concerned with application of specialized administrative law in specialized sectors of public administration. They differ from ordinary courts in that their procedures are less complicated and less time-consuming. In India the central and state administrative tribunals, the income tax appellate authority and sales-tax tribunals are some examples. They should not be confounded with the administrative courts existing in continental Europe. The latter apply the administrative law in respect of disputes between private individuals and state authorities.

Advocate-General (India) is the principal law officer of the state government in all states of the Indian Union. He is appointed by the state governor during his pleasure. His term is coterminous with the term of the ministry which recommends his appointment. He must be a person qualified to be appointed as a judge of the high court. He is responsible for tendering legal advice on matters referred to him by the state government. He also performs such other legal duties as are assigned to him by the state governor. He is entitled to attend the proceedings of the state legislature and to express his views but without a vote.

Affirmative Action refers to time-bound action-plans for equalization of opportunity for minorities and deprived groups who suffer from disabilities in the present because of discrimination practised against them in the past by the dominant community. Affirmative action takes many different forms such as preferential treatment, positive or protective discrimination, reverse discrimination or the quota system in public service. In the USA blacks, Amerindians, Chicanoes, Jews and women have been recognized as disadvantaged groups eligible for affirmative action benefits. The Civil Rights Acts of 1964 and 1991 ensured equal rights for the blacks and the Equal Employment Opportunities Act of 1972 provided for equality of opportunity in the private sector on a voluntary basis. In Europe the European Court of Justice in a ruling delivered in 1997 upheld as legal affirmative action programmes for women in the public sector thus clearing the way for implementation of such policies in the whole of the European Union. In India reservation of jobs in public services and of seats in educational institutions is constitutionally guaranteed for members of the scheduled castes, scheduled tribes and other backward classes.

Afghan Revolution (1978). The feudal monarch of Afghanistan, King Muhammad Zahir Shah, who reigned from 1933 to 1973, was deposed from throne by his cousin and former prime minister Sardar Muhammad Daoud Khan in 1973 when the king was vacationing in Rome, Italy. Daoud declared Afghanistan a republic and proclaimed himself as president, prime minister, and minister for defence and foreign affairs. Daoud in turn was overthrown and killed in a Marxist - led *coup d' etat* in April 1978 which event came to be known as the "Thaur Revolution" (Thaur being the native equivalent of the month of April). Thereafter. Nur Muhammad Taraqqi, the imprisoned leader of the outlawed Marxist Khalq Party (the People's Democratic Party of Afghanistan), was made president and prime minister. The moderate Taraqqi was ousted by his hardline Marxist colleague Hafizullah Amin in September 1979. Amin's harsh policies antagonized the entire Afghan population. The USSR is, therefore, understood to have got him killed and sent about 80,000 Soviet troops into Afghanistan with a view to making it a Soviet socialist republic. The exiled communist leader Babrak Karmal was brought from Prague and installed as president. That started the Afghan *jihad* with the aid of the USA and the Arab countries. The Soviets were forced to withdraw their one lac troops in 1988. On 25 April 1992, surrounded by Afghan Mujahideen from all sides, the puppet communist regime in Kabul collapsed and was replaced by the Mujahideen. That was the end of the Afghan communist revolution.

African Development Bank--ADB was established by the Economic Commission for Africa (ECA) in 1964 to provide long-term developmental assistance at concessional rates to countries of the African continent. Its headquarter is in Abidjan, Ivory Coast.

African Union (formerly the Organization of African Unity founded in 1963) is a regional intergovernmental organization which now includes all states of the African continent as members. The African Union was launched on 9 July 2002 in pursuance of a Constitutive Act signed by all the member-states of the erstwhile Organization of African Unity (OAU) in 2001. Its headquarters is in Addis Ababa, Ethiopia.

Aga Khan is the title of the spiritual head (*Imam*) of the Nizari Ismaili sect whose members reside in countries of the Indian subcontinent and parts of East Africa and engage in trade and commerce. Hasan Ali Shah (1800-1881), who claimed to be a descendant of Ali, the son-in-law of the Prophet

Muhammad, through the Fatimid dynasty of Egypt, was an Iranian chieftain. He acquired great influence in the court of the Qajar king Fateh Ali Shah, who made him governor of Qum, Mahallat and Kirman provinces and conferred upon him the title of Aga Khan. However, aggrieved at indifference shown towards him by the next Qajar king, Muhammad Shah, he unsuccessfully tried to overthrow him, then fled Iran and sought refuge in British India. He helped the British forces during the first Afghan War (1839-1842) and the conquest of Sind (1842-1843). As a reward the British made him prince entitled to be addressed as "His Highness" and granted him political pension for life. He then settled in Bombay and died there in 1881. His eldest son, Shah Ali Shah (1830-1885) succeeded him as Aga Khan II and died in Poona. Sir Sultan Muhammad Shah Aga Khan III (1877-1957) was the lone son of Aga Khan II. He was a loyal supporter of the British in India. He led the Simla Deputation of the Muslim notables who waited upon the Viceroy on 1 October 1906. He was the president of the All-India Muslim League* during 1908-1911. He served as the president of the Assembly of the League of Nations* during 1937-1938 and represented the Indian Muslims in the Round Table Conference* on the Indian constitutional problem held in London during 1930-1932. Prince Karim al-Husaini Aga Khan IV (1936) is a renowned philanthropist who established the Aga Khan Foundation, the Aga Khan University, the Central Asian University and the Institute of Islamic Studies.

Agency for International Development-- AID was created in pursuance of the Foreign Assistance Act, 1961, passed by the US Congress to administer, normally on a bilateral basis, American economic assistance programmes for developing countries. It is an autonomous agency within the US Department of State.

Agent Provocateur (a:zhen provokater) or a provoking agent is somebody planted by an adverse foreign power or group into a target country or group to incite the people to commit illegal acts like murder, arson or destruction of property that may justify retaliatory or punitive action against them.

Aggression was defined in a Resolution passed by the UN General Assembly on 14 December 1974 as "the use of armed force by a state against the sovereignty, territorial integrity or political independence of another state, or in any other manner inconsistent with the Charter of the United Nations."

Agitation means a state of turbulence and activism on the part of a particular group or movement as a means of self-articulation. Although there is no agreement either on the meaning or content of this term it generally depicts that phase of a movement when its ideas are universally accepted by its adherents and it is crystallized into an organization to struggle for the attainment of the desired ends. Some instances are the agitations launched by the Constitutionalists, the nationalists, the democrats, the workers and the women's movements.

Agrément (French for "agreement") is in diplomatic usage a written communication from one state to another state conveying the acceptability of a person as a diplomatic envoy. As a matter of courtesy the sending state seeks prior approval of the receiving country before accrediting a person as an envoy to that country.

Ahinsa (Sanskrit *a* = without + *hinsa* = violence) is a passive condition of non-use of force in interpersonal, intergroup and interstate relations that is a necessary concomittant of peaceful coexistence. The ancient Indian religious principle of non-violence against and non-killing of living beings was transferred, along with the concept of *Satyagraha,* to the political realm by M.K. Gandhi (1869-1948) as a means of resistance to British imperialism and attainment of *Swaraj.*

Aid-India Consortium. Led by the International Bank for Reconstruction and Development* a number of aid-consortia were formed by the developed countries to provide aid to the developing countries. Each consortium met to determine and pledge the quantum of official development assistance (ODA) to the target developing country in a given financial year. Started in 1958, the Aid-India Consortium was the biggest foreign-aid programme during the cold-war era. The Consortium included thirteen donor countries namely the USA, the UK, Canada, Western Germany, Japan, Italy, Austria, Denmark, Sweden, Netherlands, France, Belgium and Norway besides seven multilateral aid-giving agencies including the IBRD*, IMF* and the OECD*. The 23rd meeting of the Consortium was held in 1989. On 2 June 2003 the finance ministry of the Government of India announced that India will discontinue receiving developmental assistance from donors other than the USA, UK, the European Union, Japan and Russia.

Air Space, National is the air space surrounding the national territory and the territorial waters of a state over which it exercises its sovereign jurisdiction under international law. Other states can use this space only with the consent of that state and in accordance with the rules of international law and the regulations of the International Civil Aviation Organization (ICAO).

Akali Dal. The Shiromani [central] Akali Dal is a political party of the Sikh community formed in Panjab in 1921. *Akali* means a worshipper of God and the Akalis rose as a monotheist, puritan and reformist sect within the mainstream Sikhism. During the second decade of the twentieth century the Akalis launched a powerful movement to wrest the control of their *gurudwaras* (temples) and sacred shrines from the *Udasa* priests who were semi-Hindu and semi-Sikh. Thereafter, they formed the Shiromani Gurudwara Parbandhak Committee [the central gurudwara management committee] in 1920. The crowning glory of the Akalis was the passage of the Central Gurudwaras Act, 1925, by the central legislature which conferred on the Shiromani Gurudwara Parbandhak Committee the sole right to manage their religious places as a representative of the Sikh community.

Akhil Bharatiya Vidiyarathi Parishad-- ABVP (All-India Students Council) was established in 1948 as an affiliate of the RSS* to organize the Hindu students and teachers on a platform of Hindu nationalism and to realize the ideal of "Hindu, Hindi, Hindustan". It combats particularly liberal, secularist and leftist tendencies. It has a countrywide network of branches in schools, colleges and university campuses and takes part in student-union elections.

Aksaichin is a subdivision of the Ladakh district of the Indian-controlled State of Jummu and Kashmir bordering the Xinjiang province of China. In 1958 the Chinese built a road linking Lhasa in Tibet to Urumqi in Xinjiang passing through Aksaichin. In 1959 the Chinese troops killed an Indian police party on patrol in this area and during the 1962 India-China war occupied it by claiming it as part of the Xinjiang province.

Aldermen is same as "elder men"; they are members chosen by a municipal body to act as a sort of an upper chamber.

Alien is a foreigner or non-national permitted to reside for the time-being in another country without enjoying the status and political rights of the citizens of that country.

Alienation means a state of apathy, indifference, isolation, or lack of inducement to act. In Marxist theory alienation means the separation of the worker from the product of his labour because capitalistic production reduces him to the status of a mechanical instrument. *Political* alienation means the tendency of an individual or a group to keep aloof from the political process.

Aligarh Movement (India) was launched by Sir Syed Ahmad Khan (1817-1898) a nobleman who retired from the service of the British East India Company*, and the like-minded scholars, educationists and litterateures during the 1870's for the rehabilitation of the post-Mughal Muslim feudal class which had suffered most from the consequences of the Indian Revolt* of 1857 and was going down because of its anti-British attitude, obscurantism and aversion to modern education. The main objectives of the movement were the religious and cultural reform, promotion of modern secular eduction, rapprochement with the British for securing a better deal for the community, and keeping away from agitational politics against the government of the day. The crowning glory of the movement was the establishment of a modern school at Aligarh City (erstwhile United Provinces) in 1875 which later developed into the **Muhammedan Anglo-Oriental College** in 1877, which was incorporated as the Aligarh Muslim University by an Act of the Central Legislative Assembly in 1920. One year after the formation of the Indian National Congress, Syed Ahmad founded the Mohammedan Educational Congress (later renamed as the **All India Muslim Educational Conference**) with its headquarters at Aligarh, holding its annual sessions in different cities of India to advance the cause of modern education among the Muslims..The Aligarh Movement succeeded in attracting the Muslims towards modern education and launching them on the path of modernization.

Algerian Civil War (1991-99) resulted from the military-backed regime of the Algerian National Liberation Front abrogating the results of the first round of national elections held on 26 December 1991 in which the Islamic Salvation Front obtained a majority of seats. The President of the Republic resigned and dissolved the National Assembly and handed over the government to the military. The Islamic Salvation Front was banned and subsequently one-party rule was reinstituted. During 1991-99 about 1,50,000 Algerians were reported to have been killed.

Alliance. In international relations an alliance is a grouping of two or more states formed by means of an intergovernmental treaty committing the allies to come to each other's help in case any one of them was attacked. The necessity for alliance formation arises from the fact that no single power howsoever strong can meet all the military challenges singlehandedly.

Alliances have existed throughout human history. Alliances are formed not only for military defence but also for any other subsidiary purpose or purposes. A contemporary example is the North Atlantic Treaty Organization (NATO), a collective self-defence organization of the countries of north America and Western Europe. Coalitions of political parties in democratic countries are also loosely called alliances.

Alliance for Progress was the biggest development assistance programme for Latin America created under a charter approved by a conference of twenty Latin American states convened In 1961 in Penta Del Est, Uruguay, to counteract the appeal of Castroism and communism in Latin America by accelerating economic development and social change with financial and technical assistance from the Organization of American States (OAS)*, International Development Association (IDA), the UN Commission for Latin America, and the United States Agency for International Development (USAID). At the time it was called the "Marshall Plan for Latin America" because the United States agreed to contribute as much as a sum of $ 20 billion for Latin American development. The decline of the appeal of Fidel Castro after the Cuban Missile Crisis* of 1962 coupled with growing American involvement in the Vietnam war was responsible for reduction of American commitments for Latin America. Moreover, most of the beneficiary states were not interested in implementing the much needed social, economic and democratic reforms. The results of the programme during the ten years of its operation were found to be dismal. The OAS therefore disbanded the permanent committee created to implement the alliance programme in 1973.

Alternate Vote is also called preferential vote but should not be confounded with proportional representation (PR) or the quota system of voting. In electoral systems following the method of alternate votes each voter is given a single ballot paper on which he may indicate his preferences for candidates contesting that seat in a numerical order as 1, 2, 3, and so on. In case no candidate obtains the clear majority of votes cast the name of the candidate securing the least number of votes is eliminated from the contest and the second preference votes shown on the ballot papers cast in his favour are distributed among the rest of candidates. Suppose a seat is contested by three candidates the winner will be declared in the second counting. But if there are more than three candidates then after the counting of the second preference votes the name of the candidate securing the least votes is eliminated and third preference votes indicated on ballots cast in his favour are distributed among the rest. This process is repeated till a candidate obtains a clear majority.

American Civil War (1861-65). In the months following Abraham Lincoln's election as the President of the USA in 1860 Seven southern states of the Union declared their secession from the Union on the plea that they had joined the union by their free will and they were free to leave it at will. The seceding states then formed the *Confederated States of America.* The civil war between the confederate and federal forces started in 1861 when the federal government launched a military campaign to bring back the seceding states into the Union. The civil war ended on 9 April 1865 with the defeat of the confederacy. Lincoln had threatened the southern states that if they do not rejion the union he will issue a Proclamation of Emancipation (to free the negroes of the southern states from slavery which he did on 1 January 1863. Subsequently, the XIII Amendment to the US Constitution was ratified in 1865 which freed the negroes throughout the United States.

Amesterdam Treaty was signed by the member-states of the European Union in October 1997 and came into force on 1 May 1999. It added a new Article 6 into the Treaty on the European Union (Maastricht Treaty*) which states that the European Union *is founded on the principles of liberty, democracy, respect for human rights and freedoms and rule of law, principles which are common to the Member-States''.

Member-states violating these principles and the European Convention on Human Rights* will be liable to suspension of certain of their rights deriving from the application of the union treaty. In pursuance of this objective the European Union adopted a Charter of Fundamental Rights in December 2000. The Amesterdam Treaty also extended the scope of qualified majority voting and the powers of the European Parliament. It gave additional powers to the European Court. It also authorized the appointment of a High Representative for European Common Foreign and Security Policy. Certain amendments to the treaty were introduced by the Nice Treaty, 2001.

Amicus Curiae (Latin for ''friend of the court'') is an informed or interested person or an interest group or a body who may at the discretion of a court be granted permission or requested by the court itself to appear before it as an *amicus curiae* to help it dispose of a particular case being heard by it.

Amnesty International is a transnational nongovernmental organization founded in 1961 in London to defend the cause of human freedom throughout the world. It tries to secure the release of prisoners of conscience, who are imprisoned not because of any offence or crime committed by them but because of their political convictions, race or religious belief. It secures its objectives by sending petitions to the constitutional authorities of the states concerned and by making appeals to thc world public opinion. The Amnesty is opposed to detention without trial, all forms of torture, executions and the death penalty in general. It was awarded the Nobel Peace Prize in 1977. In 2005 it had about one million members and 6000 volunteer groups in 74 countries.

Anand Marg is a semi-secret cultist order founded by Prabhat Ranjan Sarkar (died in 1990) in 1955 at Anand Nagar, Purulia district of West Bengal, its political wing is the Proutist Bloc of India which takes part in provincial elections in West Bengal.

Anandpur Sahib Resolution was passed by the working committee of the Shiromani Akali Dal* at its session held in Anandpur Sahib town in Panjab in 1978 which demanded a federal set-up in India, redivision of powers and functions between the union and the constituent states and grant of maximum autonomy to the states. The resolution was believed to have contributed to the rise of a secessionist movement in Panjab.

Anarchism (from Greek *anarchia* = non-rule) is a theory that denies the necessity of both government and property. The philosophical anarchists advocate the maximization of human freedom in a federation of self-governing communities supplanting the centralised state by doing away with its armed forces, police and bureaucracy. One such philosopher was Michael Bakunin (1614-1876). The revolutionary anarchists on the other hand stand for violent overthrow of both the government and property seen as inimical to human freedom. One such philosopher was Peotr Koropotkin (1842-1921). There is, however, no uniform doctrine or method of anarchism. As a political movement it was dead long ago.

Andean Community or properly the Andean Community of Nations was formed in 1997 in supersession of the former Andean Group (founded in 1969). The Community aims at regional integration in the Andean region. A free-trade area between the Andean bloc and the Mercosur* (Southern American Community) is visualized. The member-states are: Bolivia, Colombia, Ecuador, Peru and Venezuela.

Angary, Right of is the right of a belligerent under inter-national law to use or destroy the material, equipments, arms depots or military installations of a neutral state, if necessitated by the exigencies of the war. Such a right was exercised during the Franco-Prussian War of 1870.

Anschluss (German for integration) refers to forcible integration of German-speaking Austria with Germany by the Nazi regime on 11 March 1938. The union of Austria and Germany was prohibited by the Versailles Treaty of 1919. Austria, the largest German state after Prussia, was a constituent unit of the German Confederation from 1848 to 1866. In 1945

Austria was occupied by the Allied Powers. The occupation was ended by the signing of the Austrian State Treaty in 1955 between the allies which neutralized Austria and forbade its future union with Germany.

Antarctica is the southern icy continent surrounding the South Pole. The sections of the South Atlantic, Pacific, and Indian Ocean surrounding the Antarctica are known as the Antarctic Ocean.

Antarctica Treaty was signed on 1 December 1959 by twelve original signatory states in Washington, D.C., and came into force in 1961. The original signatories were: Argentina, Australia, Belgium, Chile, France, Japan, New Zealand, Norway, Russia, South Africa, the UK, and the USA. Provision was made for accession of other states later. In 2002 there were 27 members including ten consultative members. The Treaty commits the signatories to keep the Antarctic as a demilitarized and neutralized Zone for 30 years. The treaty was to be revised after the expiry of 30 years. In 1998 the treaty was renewed for another 50 years. The original treaty recognizes the right of all states to explore and exploit the resources of the Antarctic regions for peaceful purposes only. It prohibits carrying out of nuclear explosions and dumping of nuclear waste there. The Antarctic waters are declared as open seas but some countries have proclaimed their sovereignty on specied areas. Such territorial claims are controversial. The treaty does not deal with such territorial claims. The 1998 revision has also banned mining, oil exploration and mineral extraction in the region.

Anti-Clericalism refers to opposition to the clerical or religious class or the Roman Catholic Church.

Anti-Corruption Convention (2003). The Convention Against Corruption (CAC) was signed initially by 95 countries at a 120-nation conference convened in Merida, Mexico, on 9-12 December 2003. By 2005 the CAC had 146 signatories and 36 states had ratified it. It was to come into force after required ratification by 30 states. The Convention binds the ratifying countries to declare corrupt practices in international dealings as criminal acts and to take appropriate preventive and punitive measures against corruption. Illegal worldwide transactions per annum were estimated as worth some one thousand billion US dollars and money-laundering became a common phenomenon.

Anti-Defection Law (India) refers to the Constitution (52nd Amendment) Act, 1985, which is incorporated in the Constitution as the Tenth Schedule (popularly known as the anti-defection law). The law authorizes the presiding officers of the Lok Sabha and state legislative assemblies to terminate the membership of individual members of parliament/state legislators if they defect from parties on whose ticket they were elected. It provides for the status of members expelled from their parties and cases of splits in and mergers of legislative parties. The constitutional amendment affected Articles 101, 102 and 190 of the Constitution. To put further curbs on the evil practice of defection the Constitution (91st Amendment) Act, 2003 was passed which deleted the dubious paragraph 3 of the Tenth Schedule. It barred a defector from becoming a minister or holding any remunerative public office for at least the duration of the remaining term of the concerned house or until the next elections. The Act also limited the size of ministries at the centre and in the states to 15 per cent of the total strength of the Lok Sabha and the elected houses of state legislative assemblies. But no ministry has to have less than twelve members.

Anti-Genocide Convention Genocide means extermination of a racial, national, ethnic or religious community. The practice of genocide is outlawed by the UN Convention on the Prevention and Punishment of the Crime of Genocide. It was adopted by the UN General Assembly on 9 December 1948. The national courts as well as the International Criminal

Court (ICC)* have jurisdiction of trying and punishing persons accused of committing the crime of genocide.

Anti-Mines Convention (1999) refers to the Convention on the Prohibition of the Use, Stockpiling, Production and Transfer of Anti-Personnel Mines and on their Destruction; was signed on 18 September 1997 in Oslo, Norway, and came into force in 1999. By 2004 it had been ratified by 141 states.

Anti-Semitism means prejudice and discrimination against the Jews who settled in European countries after their expulsion from Palestine at the hands of the Romans 1000 years ago. The anti-Jewish feeling is attributed to their particular religion (Judaism) and their particular race (Semitism) which were different from the Christian religion and Aryan race of the Europeans. Anti-Semitism, however, should not be confounded with anti-Zionism. Zionism* is a political ideology as well as a movement which regards Zion (Palestine) as the homeland of all Jews of the world and advocates their return to Palestine to the detriment of the native Arab inhabitants. Anti-Zionism is merely opposition to the racist ideal of a Zionist state and does not imply hatred of the Jewish people.

Anti-Torture Convention (1984). The Convention Against Torture, and Other Cruel, Inhuman or Degrading Treatment or Punishment was adopted by the UN General Assembly on 10 December 1984. As at 31 December 2005, 127 states were parties to it. Articles 21 and 22 of the Convention require the signatories to recognize the competence of a ten-member UN Committee Against Torture (created in 1984) to receive and consider communications from any party claiming that another party was not fulfilling its obligations under the Convention and also to receive complaints from, or on behalf of, individuals claiming to be targets of torture. The Committee is competent to call upon the accused parties to submit a report to it underlining measures taken to prevent and punish acts of torture within three territories.

Anti-Trust Laws are enacted to curb formation of monopolies, mega trusts, cartels, conglomeration of businesses, mergers and acquisitions and many restrictive trade practices that hinder competition in a free-market economy.

Antyodaya (Sanskrit for sustenance) is the principle of helping and uplifting the poorest of the poor in the population as advocated by M. K. Gandhi through his speeches and writings. The principle was incorporated in the developing policy of the Government of India during the 1970's leading to the launching of poverty alleviation and unemployment assistance programmes such as Food-for-Work Programme and supply of foodgrains to the people living below the poverty line at nominal prices.

ANZUS (acronym for Australia-New Zealand-US) was a cold-war era tripartite military alliance for the defence of the Far East against communist aggression created by the ANZUS Treaty of for Mutual Assistance in Canberra, Australia, on 1 September 1951. The ANZUS (Pacific) Council was created by a tripartite agreement signed on 4 August 1952 with its headquarters in Canberra.

Apartheid (Afrikaans for keeping apart) refers to the racist and segregationist policy of the white regime in South Africa which was opposed to integration of the black majority in the South African political system. The white ruling minority, therefore, evolved a policy of separate political, social and economic development of the two races. The policy was implemented by creating separate black homelands called Bantustans* with limited self-government. Thus apartheid became an instrument for maintaining white supremacy in South Africa. Apartheid ended with the transfer of power to the black majority in 1994.

Appeasement is submission to or making undue concessions to an aggressor. It is akin to expediency and opportunism. The

Munich Agreement is often cited as a classic case of appeasement.

Aqaba, Gulf of is the northeaster arm of the Red Sea, 190 kms long and 16.1 to 24.1 kms wide located between the Sinai and the Arabian peninsula. It is an international waterway. The Port of Aqaba is under Jordanian sovereignty while the adjoining Port of Eilat is under Israeli control. The Jordanian village of Eilat was captured by Israelis after the signing of the armistice agreements with the Arab states in 1948.

Arab Ba'ath Socialist Party. An Arab Party was founded by Syrian Arab leaders Slahuddin Bitaar and Michel Aflaq in Damascus in 1941. It adopted the word *Ba'ath* (resurgence) to its name during 1950's. The party struggled to realize its ideals of secularism, socialism, Arab nationalism and Arab unity. The Party's Syrian wing has ruled Syria since 1963. Its Iraqi wing came to power in Iraq in 1968. The Ba'athist regime in Iraq came to an end with the American invasion and occupation of Iraq in March 2003.

Arab Maghreb Union was founded in 1989 by Algeria, Libya, Mauritania, Morocco and Tunisia to boost political cooperation and regional development in north Africa. Its headquarters is at Rabat, Morocco.

Arab Socialist Union (Egypt) was originally formed in 1957 by Egyptian dictator Jamal Abdun Nasir as the National Union as a single official party under his personal command, after banning all other political parties and groups. It was renamed as the *Arab Socialist Union* in 1961. It was dissolved by Nasir's successor Anwar El-Sadat who restored the multiparty system.

Arabism (*Uruba* in Arabic) means promotion of an Arab ethnic identity and solidarity based on Arab blood and the Arabic language and culture to the exclusion of all distinctions based on religion, sect, tribe or locality.

Arbitration, International. According to the Hague Convention for the Pacific Settlement of International Disputes of 1899, as amended in 1907, international arbitration is "the settlement of disputes between states by judges of their own choice and on the basis of respect for law". Recourse to arbitration implies an agreement to accept in good faith the award of an arbitrator or arbitration tribunal.

Archipelago/Archipelagic State. Article 46 of the UN Convention on the Law of the Sea (UNCLOS) defines *archipelago* as a group of islands, parts of islands, interconnecting waters and other natural features which are so closely interconnected that such islands, waters and other natural features form an intrinsic geographical, economic and political entity, or which historically have been regarded as such. It is a geographical term. Examples are Polynesia and Micronesia An *archipelagic state,* on the other hand, is constituted wholly by one or more archipelagos and may include other islands. It is a political term. Examples are Indonesia and Maldives.

Aristocracy means government by the *aristos* or the best people. Aristocracy may either be rational, that is, based on merit and excellence (though there is no universal criterion of either merit or excellence) or hereditary, that is, based on birth in a noble family. It was the hereditary type of aristocracy that existed in Europe from the ancient times till the eighteenth century.

Armed Force (Special Powers) Act, 1958 was an emergency-power act passed in 1958 to deal with insurgency in Nagaland. It may be promulgated in any disturbed area at the discretion of the Government of India. The act empowers the armed forces to arrest suspected people and enter property without a warrant and to shoot to kill even in circumstances when they are not in imminent danger.

Armistice in international law is a temporary suspension of hostilities as agreed to by the belligerents.

Articles of Confederation. The thirteen British colonies of north America which declared their independence in 1776 soon concluded an intergovernmental treaty. The ''Articles of Confederation'') to form a confederation or loose association with a central organ by the name of the Congress of the United States, composed of delegates deputed by the states. The Articles remained in force from 1781 till 1789 when a new federal constitution framed at the Philadelphia Constitutional convention came into force converting the confederation into a modern federal union.

Arya Samaj was a religious-revivalist movement launched in 1875 by Swami Dayanand Saraswati (1824-1883) who is called a saviour of Hindu religion. In his magnum opus *Satyarth Prakash* (Light of Truth 1875) he articulated the basic principles of the Arya Samaj creed as: the belief in one God, the identification of the Vedas as the embodiment of complete truth, and the logical inference that the age of Vedic religion constituted the golden age of Hinduism. He called for a return to pure and pristine Vedic religion, condemned idolatory, untouchability, child marriage and prohibition of widow-remarriage. He rejected the hereditary caste system in favour of a meritocratic *varna* system. He advocated the union of Vedic religion with modern science as a way of regeneration of the Hindu society. At the same time, he was staunchly opposed to both Islam and Christianity. The Arya Samaj strove for shudhdhi i.e. purification or reconversion of such Indians as were converted to other religions to the Vedic fold. The Arya Samaj movement gained most adherents in Panjab from where it spread to the rest of north India. It materially contributed to the rise of religion-based nationalism and growth of exclusivist organizations; like the All-India Hindu Mahasabha* and the Rashtriya Swayam Sevak Sangh (RSS)*. The Arya Samaj operates through a network of local, provincial and all-India samajs (societies). Local units elect their representatives to the provincial and central units. Arya Samajists created a large number of Dayanand Anglo-Vedic (DAV) schools and colleges besides other philanthropic institutions.

ASEAN Free Trade Area-- AFTA is visualised to come into being by 2008 in pursuance of an agreement signed by the member-states of the ASEAN in 1992. But AFTA came into being in respect of six core member-states (Brunei, Indonesia, Malaysia, Philippines, Singapore and Thailand) with effect from 1 January 2002. For the rest different dates were prescribed for joining the AFTA.

ASEAN Regional Forum--ARF was created in 1993 as an informal consultative forum to engage in intraregional consultations on matters of security cooperation and to engage in dialogues with extraregional powers on matters of economic development. Since 1994 ARF holds annual meetings at foreign ministers' level. Participants: Australia, Canada, European Union, India, Japan, South Korea/North Korea, Mayanmar, Mongolia, New Zealand, USA, China, Laos, Papua New Guinea, Russia and Vietnam.

Asian Development Bank--- ADB was established in 1966 in Bangkok, Thailand, by the UN Economic Commission for Asia and the Far East (ECAFE), renamed as the UN Economic and Social Commission for Asia, and the Pacific (UNESCAP). The Bank has 35 regional and 14 extraregional states as its members. It provides developmental assistance to the regional states at concessional rates and works in close cooperation with the UN specialized agencies to boost economic and social development in the region. The headquarters of the ADB is in Manila, Philippines.

Asia-Pacific Cooperation-- APEC was founded in 1989 in Canberra, Australia, as an informal consultative forum to facilitate economic cooperation, trade and investment liberalization and business development in the Asia-Pacific region. Member-States: Australia, Brunei, Canada, Chile, China. Hong Kong, Indonesia, Japan, South Korea, Malaysia, Mexico, New Zealand, Papua New Guinea, Peru, Philippine, Russia, Singapore, Taiwan, Thailand, USA and Vietnam. Headquarters: Singapore.

Assam Accord (1985) was signed on 14 August 1985 between the home secretary of the Government of India and the All-Assam Students Union (AASU) and the All-Assam Gana Sangram Parishad (AAGSP) at the height of the agitation launched by them for the expulsion of the east Bengali (mostly Muslim) Settlers in Assam designating them as foreigners. Under the pact it was decided that east Bengali immigrants who came to Assam after 1 January 1966 and up to 25 March 1971 would be detected and their names would be deleted from the electoral rolls. Immigrants who came on or after 25 March 1971 (emergence of Bangladesh) would be deported to the country of their origin after determining their status as illegal migrants. Accordingly, an amendment to the Indian Citizenship Act, 1955, was passed allowing the east Bengalis who migrated to Assam between 1966 and 1971 to have all citizenship rights except the right to vote in elections for a period of ten years. Thereafter the Indian Parliament passed the Illegal Migrants (Determination by Tribunal) Act, which came into force on 15 October 1985 to detect and deport the illegal migrants from Assam.

Assam Rifles is the oldest paramilitary force of the Indian Union established in 1835 with its headquarters in Shillong. It is responsible for maintaining internal security in the northeast region of India under the operational control of the Indian Army.

Assimilation is the process of making or becoming similar. It is the process of absorbing the minorities into the majority community socially and culturally. Assimilation may be forced such as the Sinification of the natives in Tibet and Xinjiang or spontaneous such as in the American melting pot.

Association of Southeast Asian Nations--ASEAN is a regional economic cooperation forum of ten southeast Asian states formed in 1967. Member-states: Brunei, Darussalaam, Cambodia, Indonesia, Laos, Malaysia, Mayanmar, Philippines,

Singapore, Thailand, and Vietnam. Headquarters: Jakarta, Indonesia.

Asylum (from Greek *asylon*-freedom from seizure) means refuge. Persons fleeing from persecution or for whatever cause may seek asylum or refuge in another country Asylum may be either *diplomatic* i.e. taking refuge in an embassy, legation, consulate or warship or any other venue of a foreign country; or *territorial* i.e. a refugee should cross into the territory of a foreign country and seek asylum. Asylum may or may not be granted. The practice of granting diplomatic asylum to the persecuted is regulated by the 1961 Vienna Convention on Diplomatic Relations* and that of territorial asylum by the 1967 UN Declaration on Territorial Asylum.

Atlantic Alliance is synonymous with the North Atlantic Treaty Organization (NATO)*. The word Atlantic is derived from Atlas, a mountain on the Libyan coast which symbolises the Atlantic Ocean. The Atlantic Ocean spreads between Europe and America in the west (called North Atlantic Ocean) and between Europe and Africa in the east (called the South Atlantic Ocean). The Atlantic alliance includes countries of north America and Europe only.

Atlantic Charter was drawn up in the middle of World war II By the British Prime Minister Sir Winston Churchill and the American President Franklin D. Roosevelt on 14 August 1941. Its eight points summed up the basic principles of a new world order after the war. The Charter was subscribed to by the United Nations (countries that were supporting the Allies against the Axis powers). It was the forerunner of the Charter of the UNO* adopted in 1945. The eight points declared in the Atlantic Charter were: non-admissibility of aggrandisement territorial or other; no territorial changes without the consent of the people concerned; restoration of sovereign rights and self-government to subject people; freedom of trade and access to markets and raw-materials to all nations; improvement of labour standards, social security and economic development; establishment of peace and freedom from fear and want; freedom of navigation through the high seas; and disarming the aggressor nations; creation of a system of collective security, and reduction of armaments.

Attaché is the junior-most diplomatic rank in the diplomatic service. It should not be confounded with the post of military attach or the special attaches like cultural, press, commercial or other attached with foreign embassies and missions. They may or may not hold a diplomatic status. Their function is not diplomatic; they gather information in their respective fields for the benefit of the home country.

Autarchy/Autarky means (i) self-rule or absolute sovereignty; or (ii) absolute national self-reliance and self-sufficiency. As an economic doctrine it calls for producing everything at home and dispensing with imports. Such a policy was adopted by Nazi Germany before the second World War to withstand a possible economic blockade by its enemies and by Mao's China in the face of Western quarantine. However, autarky is absolutely impracticable in an era of interdependence and globalism.

Authoritarian Personality. An authoritarian personality is an illiberal and anti-liberal personality which displays certain authoritarian or anti-liberal tendencies and attitudes, e.g. irrationalism, anti-intellectualism, dogmatism, prejudice, intolerance of the views and beliefs of opponents, superstitiousness, aggressive temper, toughness and cynicism, etc. Cf. T.W. Adorno, E. Frankel-Brunswick, D. Livinson and N. Sanford, *The Authoritarian Personality* (New York: Norton, 1950).

Authoritarian Regime is one which is not founded on constitutionalism and rule of law. The regime exercises authority unlimited and unrestricted by constitutional rules and parliamentary and public opinion. Those who wield authority are neither representative of the people nor responsible to them.

Authoritarianism is just the opposite of constitutionalism. It means belief in or exercise of or submission to absolute authority.

Traditional dictatorships, modern oligarchies, Communism, Fascism, Nazism and racialism are different forms of authoritarianism.

Autocracy is opposite of democracy and synonymous with dictatorship. Autocracy whether of one person or a group or a class or a party does not rest on the consent of the governed nor is it responsible to them.

Auto-Emancipation was a social reform movement among the European Jewry during the nineteenth century. It is synonymous with self-emancipation or self-liberation.

Autonomy is a Greek term meaning self-rule. In government and politics it refers to a limited or specified measure of self-government, short of complete independence, enjoyed by a province of an empire or a local or regional subdivision of a unitary or federal state, defined by an administrative order, or a legislative act or the constitutional law.

Axis Powers during World War II were Nazi Germany, Fascist Italy and militarist Japan. They were at war with the Allied Powers, namely the USA, USSR, UK and France.

B

Bab al-Mandab (Arabic term meaning "entrance of tears") is the name of a narrow strait that links the Red Sea with the Gulf of Oman and the Indian Ocean. It is the only outlet from the Gulf af Aqaba* to the Arabian Sea and the Indian Ocean.

Backbencher. Those members of parliamentary bodies whether belonging to the government or the opposition party who do not hold any portfolio or official position, sit on the back benches are called "backbenchers". Their role is to follow the party whip, be present in the house and vote in favour of the party motions. The front benches on the government side are occupied by the ministers and are called "treasury benches". On the opposition side the front benches are occupied by the party leaders and members of the shadow cabinet. Unlike the backbencher a *crossbencher* is a partyless member in the British House of Lords who votes at will sometimes in favour of one party and sometimes in favour of the other party.

Backward Areas are those regions, subregions, districts or large tracts in Indian states which are economically underdeveloped and suffer from mass poverty and unemployment. They include tribal belts, hill areas, drought-prone areas, desert area, flood -affected areas, and much of the northeastern region. The Government of India makes special grants for speedy development of these areas and tax incentives are provided to induce the private businessmen to locate their businesses and industries there.

Backward Classes Commission. The egalitarian Constitution of India has made special provisions for the upliftment of the Scheduled Castes* (SC's), the scheduled Tribes* (ST's), and other Backward classes* (OBC's). While the Government of India undertook the task of identifying and notifying the scheduled castes and scheduled tribes and provided them the benefit of reservation of jobs in government and public sector services, the responsibility of identifying and notifying the other socially and educationally backward classes entrusted to a commission to be appointed by the President of India in terms of Article 340 of the Indian Constitution. Accordingly, the first Backward Classes Commission, headed by Kakasaheb Karlelkar, was appointed by the Government of India in 1955 which submitted its report in 1956. The Commission identified 2,394 communities as backward but laid no specific criterion for a definition of backwardness. The responsibility of providing welfare benefits to them was assigned to state governments. .This arrangement continued till 1978. Concerned with the plight of the other backward classes which constituted a 54 per cent majority of the Indian population, the Janata Party government at the centre appointed a second backward classes commission under the chairmanship of Bindeshwari Prasad Mandal in 1978 which submitted its report in 1980. It identified 3,743 backward classes on the basis of the traditional backward castes. A backward caste was *ipso facto* a backward class. The Commission recommended a 27 per cent reserved quota for them in the public services and public undertakings of the central and state governments. The Commission's recommendation was implemented through an office memorandum of the Government of India issued on 13 August 1990. A Supreme Court judgment delivered on 16 November 1992 excluded the "creamy layer* of the backward classes from the benefit of reservations. A National Commission on the Backward Classes was created under an Act of Parliament passed in 1993 to investigate and report on the implementation of the safeguards for the backward classes. On the recommendation of the National Commission on Backward Classes the Government of India on 4 February 2004 raised the income limit for the "creamy layer" (socially advanced) among the OBC's from the existing Rs. 1,00,000 per annum to Rs. 2,50,000 per annum. Persons earning up to this limit shall continue to enjoy the benefit of reservation in direct recruitment for civil posts and services.

Baghdad Pact (1954) was one of the cold-war era alliances of the Western bloc directed against the USSR. Following the refusal of the Arab countries to join the so-called "Middle East Defence Organization* proposed by the Western Powers in 1950, the latter turned to countries situated on the northern tier of the Middle East. Thus treaties of mutual assistance were signed between Turkey, Pakistan, Iran, Iraq and the UK in 1954. The US did not join the arrangement formally. The Baghdad pact Council held its first meeting in Baghdad on 21-22 November 1955. The US joined its Military and Economic Consultative Committees in 1957 and provided military and economic assistance to the partners. On 5 March 1959 the US signed bilateral security cooperation agreements with Turkey, Iran and Pakistan in Ankara, Turkey. Following the overthrow of the Iraqi monarchy in July 1958, Iraq withdrew from the Baghdad Pact in March 1959 and in May cancelled her military and economic cooperation agreements with the US. On 18 August the Baghdad Pact was renamed as Central Treaty Organization (CENTO) and in October its headquarters was shifted to Ankara. The CENTO was formally dissolved in 1979.

Bahujan Samaj Party--BSP is a regional political party in north India founded in 1985 by Kanshi Ram to articulate the interests of the bahujan (majority) i.e. the Scheduled Castes*, the scheduled Tribes* and the Other Backward Classes*, who together constituted the majority of the Indian population.

Bailiff is a keeper or superintendent attached to a sheriff*. The jurisdictional area of a bailiff is called bailiwick.

Balance of Payments refers to the difference between payments received by a country from other countries and payments made by it to other countries over a given period of time. These payments include both the visible and invisible receipts and disbursals. Visible payments include all types of goods, commodities and precious metals while invisible payments refer to insurance, transportation and transit charges, the money spent by the tourists, interest paid on the borrowed capital and charges on transfer of money, etc. All current receipts and disbursals of a country make its "balance of payments on current account" while the inflow and outflow of the capital constitutes the "balance of payments on capital account". A country's final balance of payments is calculated by taking into consideration both its current and capital accounts. If the balance results in a surplus the balance of payments' is called favourable. If it shows a deficit it is regarded as unfavourable. In the former case money comes into the country, in the case of the latter money goes out of the country.

Balance of Power is equipoise or equilibrium of power existing at a given time; a policy or process of maintaining in such a distribution of power at the international level through alliances and counteralliances that no single power or a group of powers is allowed to threaten the survival of others. The opposite concept is collective security*.

Balance of Terror designates a nuclear stalemate or a nuclear balance of power wherein no nuclear power can dare launch a first strike against an adversary without risking a retaliatory strike and *mutual assured destruction.* Thus all are deterred from launching a first strike while all are capable of launching a retaliatory strike.

Balance of Trade refers to the difference between the values of a country's visible imports and exports. If the value of imports is greater than the value of exports the balance of trade is regarded as unfavourable because it implies country's indebtedness; conversely if the value of exports a is greater than the value of imports the balance of trade is considered *favourable* as it implies pecuniary gain for the country.

Balfour Declaration (1917) was made, as a reward for Jewish cooperation with the British during World war I, by James Balfour, the British foreign secretary on behalf of the British government, in a letter addressed to a leader of the World Zionist Congress Baron Rothschild which reads: The British Government favours the establishment in Palestine of a national home for the Jewish people and will use their best endeavours to facilitate the achievement of that object, it being clearly understood that nothing shall be done which may prejudice the civil and religious rights of existing non-Jewish communities in Palestine

Balkan Pact (1954) was signed between Greece, Turkey and former Yugoslavia in August 1954 with the express purpose of coming to the aid of any one of the signatory parties if attacked by a non-signatory power. The pact was concluded for a term of 20 years and was not formally abrogated thereafter.

Balkan/Balkanization. Balkan is a Turkish term for mountain. The mountain is a range which starts from the east and crosses Bulgaria towards the west. The Balkan Peninsula forms part of southeastern Europe. The region was part of the Ottoman Empire during the nineteenth century, at present, it is divided into eight independent countries. The region is famous for having a long history of military conquests, border disputes, ethnic and religious feuds, emigrations and wars. Hence *Balkanization* came to be used for division of a country or region into feuding or warring units.

Ballot (from Italian *ballotta*). In old times little coloured balls were used to indicate choice. Hence ballot came to be used as a vote as well as the ballot paper on which choice is indicated. Nowadays in addition to the ballot paper a number of mechanical, electrical and electronic devices (such as the electronic voting machines) are used for voting purposes. Ballot is said to have been first used in Athens in 500 B.C.

Bandung Conference. The first ever conference of 29 Asian and African nations was held at Bandung City in Indonesia on 18-24 April 1955. It was jointly sponsored by Indonesia, Burma, Ceylon (Sri Lanka), India and Pakistan. The Bandung Declaration on World Peace and Cooperation reiterated the principles of the UN Charter as well as the *Panchsheel** advocated by Jawaharlal Nehru. A second Asian-African conference of heads of state or government or foreign ministers from 105 countries was held in Jakarta on 22-23 April 2005 to commemorate the 50th anniversary of the Bandung Conference of 1955. The final communique stressed the need of strengthening Asian-African solidarity and cooperation in an eral of globalization.

Bangladesh War (1971). East Bengal which was a separate province of British India during 1905-11 became East Pakistan on 15 August 1947 as the eastern province of the Dominions of Pakistan as a result of partition of British India into the Dominions of India and Pakistan. East Pakistan became the sovereign Republic of Bangladesh on 16 December 1971 as a result of a civil war between the two wings of Pakistan the subsequent military intervention by India in the crisis, and eventual defeat of the Pakistani army. East Bengal is surrounded from all sides by the Indian territory except for a short southern-eastern frontier with Myanmar and a southern coast fronting the Bay of Bengal. Nothing was common between the two wings of Pakistan except their common religion and they were geographically separated by 1000 miles of intervening Indian territory. The first expression of East Bengali nationalism was made in 1952 when a number of Bengali students agitating against the declaration of Urdu as the official language of Pakistan were killed in police firing. In response Bengali was made the second official language of Pakistan in 1954. In 1955 Pakistan was converted into two units of East and West Pakistan with equal representation to each in the National Assembly. But Bengali grievances against the central government grew day-by-day and a separatist movement was spearheaded by the Awami League, headed by Sheikh Mujeebur Rahman. The party fought the national elections held in December 1970 on a six-point formula for maximal autonomy for East Pakistan which fell short of independence. The Awami League won an overwhelming majority of seats in the eastern wing and became the majority party in the National Assembly. However, under pressure from the West Pakistani politicians, the military dictator General Yahya Khan, the successor of dictator field Marshal Ayub Khan, refused to invite the leader of the majority. Sheikh Mujeebur Rahman, to form the government and in March 1971 postponed the convening of the National Assembly indefinitely. The Awami League retaliated by declaring the secession of East/from Pakistan and its proclamation as the People's Republic of Bangladesh. The central government ordered a military crackdown against the secessionists which sent an estimated 9.5 million east Bengalis into the Indian territory as refugees. On 4 December, making an excuse of the refugee burden, India intervened militarily on behalf of the secessionists. After a brief war the Pakistani army surrendered to the Indian army and India took more than 90,000 Pakistani troops as prisoners of war who were not released until Pakistan agreed to recognize the independence of Bangladesh and convert the cease-fire line in the state of Jạmmu and Kashmir into a Line of Control i.e. a *de facto* border between the two parts of the State.

Bank for International Settlements was founded in 1930 at Basel, Switzerland, under an agreement signed between the representatives of the central banks of Belgium, Britain, Germany, Italy and Japan with partial participation of the USA. The BIS is known as the bank of the central banks because it plays a big role in facilitating international financial settlements.

Bantustans were derived from the Bantu tribes are ethnic and linguistic groups of Africa numbering about 120 million, mainly concentrated in South Africa. *Bantustans* were the names given to the homelands of the Bantu people enjoying limited self-government under the South African Bantu Home Rule Act, 1959, to give effect to the racist policy of apartheid*. Bantustans were dissolved with the transfer of power to the black majority in 1994.

Bar-At-Law/Barrister. Barristers (properly "the barristers-at-law") are members of the legal profession who belong to one of the four Inns of Court in England and wales. Lincoln's Inn, Gray's Inn, the Inner Temple and the Middle Temple -- or the Inn of Court of Northern Ireland. Those aspiring to become practising lawyers have to undergo a period of training in the Inns of Courts School of Law and after completing the prescribed course satisfactorily are *called to the bar.* They must then serve as an apprentice with a qualified barrister for at least one year before they are admitted to the General council of the Bar and enter legal profession. The corresponding lawyers in Scotland are called *advocates.*

Bay of Bengal is an extension of the Indian Ocean 2,090 kms long and 1,610 kms wide. It is bounded by Bangladesh, India, Myanmar (Burma), Thailand and Sri Lanka. The islands of Andaman and Nicobar separate it from the Andaman Sea its eastern extension.

Bedouins (anglicized form of Arabic *badawi* = an inhabitant of wilderness) are unsettled nomads who live in the deserts of Arabia, Jordan, Syria and Egypt. *Badawi* is the opposite of *hadhari* (settled city-dwellers).

Behaviouralism is the scientific study of the political behaviour of individuals and groups within and without the political institutions. The aspire to build a positive science of politics like physics and chemistry to explain political life in the society. It should not be confounded with *behaviourism* which is a branch of psychology concerned with analysis of human behaviour in terms of stimulus and response.

Belgaum Dispute (India). Belgaum Taluqa is a Marathi-speaking enclave within the Kannada-speaking State of Karnataka. After the division of the State of Bombay into two separate linguistic states of Maharashtra and Gujarat in 1960, the government of Maharashtra called for the integration of Belgaum and the adjoining Marathi-speaking areas with Maharashtra. With the concurrence of both the states the Government of India referred the claim to a Commission of Inquiry headed by Justice Mehar Chand Mahajan. The Commission recommended for retention of this area within Karnataka. However, Maharashtra did not accept the decision of the Commission and decided to raise the issue before the Supreme Court.

Belligerency in international law refers to a state of armed conflict between or among states or rival forces in a civil war.

Bench and Bar. The bench designates the body of judges and the bar the body of advocates.

Benelux Union was a customs union formed by Belgium, Netherlands and luxembour on 5 September 1944. The union came into being in 1948. The three countries later joined the European Economic Community (EEC).

Benevolent Despotism refers to a policy of benevolence adopted by a despotic regime towards its subjects such as that claimed by the British authorities to be pursued in relation to native Indians after the Indian Revolt of 1857.

Benevolent Neutrality is the policy of a state which proclaims its neutrality in an international war but nevertheless pursues a policy of aid and assistance to the friendly belligerent countries by non-military means such as provision of financial and economic assistance to Britain and France during World War I and the Lend-Lease assistance during World War II given to the friendly countries by the USA.

Benthamism is same as utilitarianism advocated by Jeremy Bentham (1748-1832). He discarded the fictitious notions of natural rights, natural law and social contract and made the principle of utility, i.e. ''the greatest happiness of the greatest number'' the criterion of morals, legislation and social policy.

Bering Sea. is the northward extension of the Pacific Ocean between Siberia and Alaska.

Bering Straits a strategic sea-passage between the Pacific Ocean and the Arctic Sea.

Berlin Crisis (1948/1961). After the defeat of Nazi Germany in 1945 the Allied Powers--the USA, the USSR, Britain and France, agreed among themselves to carve out Germany into four military occupation zones until a final settlement regarding the future of Germany was reached. Similarly, the capital city of Berlin too was divided into east and west zones, the eastern part being allotted to the Soviet Union and the western part to the western powers. Since Berlin was located within the territory of east Germany which became the Soviet occupation zone, the Soviets later felt uneasiness over the presence of western forces in west Berlin. With the objective of easing out the western powers from west Berlin the Soviets closed all the road links between west Berlin and the west German territory just before the winter of 1948 on the pretext of carrying necessary repairs. Thus a crisis was created endangering the lives of west Berliners. The western powers, however, responded to the Soviet challenge by supplying all the necessities for west Berliners throughout the winter by erecting an air-bridge between west Germany and west Berlin. When the Soviet tactic failed the blockade was lifed in 1949. Another crisis was created in 1961 when the Soviet Union pressed the western powers to negotiate a final settlement, of the German problem otherwise they will transfer sovereignty the German Democratic Republic (east German communist regime) in which case the western powers shall have to negotiate with the GDR regarding the future of west Berlin. The western powers led by the USA declared their intention to defend west Berlin at all costs. Failing in their objective the Soviets erected a wall to separate east from West Berlin to prevent the exodus of east Germans to West Germany. That wall became a symbol of the east-west cold war.

Berlin Wall. At the end of the second World War the Allies divided Germany into Western-occupied and Soviet occupied zones. The capital city Berlin which was located within the Soviet occupied zone was also divided among the four powers. West Berlin was occupied by the Western Powers and east Berlin by the Soviet Union. The Soviets tried twice in 1948 and 1958 to force the Western powers to evacuate west Berlin but failed in view of the advance of the Western Powers. Eventually the Communist regime of east Germany in 1961 erected an invincible wall around east Berlin to insulate it from west Berlin and to prevent the flight of east Germans to west Berlin and from there to other Western countries. At the height of *detente* the German people of both sides forcibly dismantled this on 9 November 1989. This event was followed by the signing of the German Reunification Treaty in 1990.

Berlin-Rome-Tokyo Axis. In October 1936 the Berlin-Rome axis was formed by an agreement between Nazi Germany and Fascist Italy to oppose the democratic government in Spain and the USSR. This nexus was further strengthened by the signing of a bilateral in May 1939 on mutual security, japan joined the Axis as a result of signing of tripartite agreement in September 1940 on collaboration of the three powers during World War II.

Bharat is the land of Bharat, that is India. The 1950 Constitution of the Indian Republic declares in its Article I that "India, that is Bharat, shall be a Union of States". The adoption of the name Bharat (land of Bharat, an ancestor Lord Rama) was adopted to appease the revivalist forces. "India" is an anglicized form of Arabic *Hind* and the country was known throughout centuries as Hind or Hindustan.

Bharatiya Jana Sangh (Indian People's Front) was a right-wing Hindu nationalist political party founded by a former leader of the All-India Hindu Mahasabha* Shyama Prasad Mukerji (1901-1953) October 1951 in Calcutta. The BJS merged in the Janata Party* in 1977. When the JP disintegrated in 1980 the former BJS-RSS elements came out to form a new right-wing party by the name of Bharatiya Janata Party*.

Bharatiya Janata Party (Indian People's Party) is a right-wing Hindu nationalist party founded by the BJS-RSS elements who came out of the Janata Party in 1980 to pursue a Hindu nationalist agenda. Being the single largest parliamentary party the BJP was invited to form a ministry at the Centre on 15 May 1996. A ministry headed by Atal Behari Vajpayi was sworn in on 16 May and asked to prove its majority by 31 May. Anticipating its defeat the ministry resigned on 28 May and was succeeded by the United Front ministry headed by H.D. Dewe Gowda backed by the outside support by the Indian National Congress. The Congress withdrew its support from this ministry on 30 May 1997 and the United Front ministry was defeated on the floor of the Lok Sabha on 11 April 1997. Then I.K. Gujaral was elected as, leader of the United Front on 19 April and was sworn in next day as the prime minister. However, in the parliamentary elections held in 1998 the BJP formed the National Democratic Alliance with a number of regional parties and the NDA was returned to a majority in the Lok Sabha. It formed a ministry with Atal Behari Vajpayi as prime minister and won the vote of confidence on 28 April. The NDA lost its majority in parliamentary elections held in 2004 and was succeeded by a Congress-led United Progressive Alliance ministry.

Bharatiya Lok Dal --BLD was formed in 1974 as a result of merger of seven political parties of the time: Bharatiya Kranti Dal, Samyukt Socialist Party, Swatantara Party and four small groups as an electoral front to provide an alternative to the ruling congress (Indira) Party. The BLD was merged in the Janata Party* formed in 1977.

Bhoodan/Gramdan Movement was a movement launched during the 1950's by Acharya Vinayak (Vinoba) Bhave (1895-1994), an associate of Mahatma Gandhi. *Bhoodan* (giving of land as charity) meant that big landlords in a village voluntarily surrender their surplus land for redistribution among the landless. Similarly *gramdan* (giving of a village as charity) meant that all landholders in a village first voluntarily surrender all their land to the *sarvodaya** workers who will then redistribute it equally among the villagers so that all the landless got a share. The movement failed to achieve its objective because only a Bhave could be a holy man not all the Indian villagers.

Bhumiputra is Sanskrit for the sons of the soil.

Biafra was the name given to the eastern region of Nigeria which was inhabited by the Christian Ibo tribals and rich in oil whose military governor, allegedly under western instigation declared its independ from Nigeria on 30 May 1967. The breakaway forces were crushed by the federal forces in an year-long civil war.

Bicameralism is a principle of having a legislative assembly composed of two chambers. While a directly elected house, called the first or lower house, should be vested with the controlling power over government, legislation and finance, there should be a nominated or indirectly elected second or upper chamber to revise the legislation passed by the first or lower chamber and to delay for some time the hasty or ill-considered legislation passed by the first chamber so that it is duly reconsidered.

Bicephalous Executive means double-headed executive in France introduced by the Constitution of 1958 under which the executive is headed by a directly elected president of the republic as well as a prime minister nominated by him as head of the government. The president is not responsible to the national assembly but the prime minister along with the ministry is responsible to parliament although members of the government are barred from membership of parliament.

Big-Stick Policy (US) refers to the policy of highhandedness and bullying practised by successive US administrations towards the countries of Latin America. The term is derived from President Theodore Roosevelt's dictum: ''Speak softly, but carry a big stick''.

Bill of Attainder is an act of parliament holding somebody guilty of committing a crime and prescribing punishment for it without a judicial trial. The practice is considered contrary to rule of law. Article 1, Sections 9 and 10 of the US Constitution, therefore, expressly forbids the Congress from passing bills of attainder and ex post facto laws.

Bill of Rights (UK), The Bill of Rights was passed by the Convention Parliament in October 1689. It established constitutional monarchy and parliamentary sovereignty in England. It marked the culmination of the so-called glorious or constitutional revolution of 1688-89. The Whigs and Tories had united against James II for his arbitrary rule and Catholicism in 1688. They invited Prince William of Orange (of Protestant faith) to proceed to England to liberate her from the hated king. William arrived in England in November 1688. James II finding himself deserted by Parliament, Church and army fled to France. William was requested to issue writs for a ''Convention'' to meet on 22 January 1689. The houses of this Convention declared the abdication of James II and invited Prince William and Princess Mary of Orange to become King and queen of England on acceptance of the conditions laid down in the Declaration of Rights drafted by the Convention and presented to William and Mary on 13 February 1689. The monarchs accepted both the crown and the attached conditions. Thereupon the Convention converted itself into a parliament (hence ''Convention Parliament''). This parliament enacted the terms of the Declaration of Rights as the Bill of Rights in October 1689. The Convention Parliament was dissolved on 29 January 1791. The Bill of Rights governs the institution of constitutional monarchy in England. After William and

Mary the crown was vested in Princess Sophia of Hanover and her heirs for ever. Every king on his accession must testify to the Anglican Church to be a Protestant. Catholics and those marrying with Catholics were excluded from succession. The Bill after confirming the abdication of James II enacted the following: (l) the king shall not have the power of suspending or executing the law without consent of parliament; (2) the king shall not dispense with existing laws and their enforcement; (3) the levying of taxes without authority of parliament shall be illegal; (4) subjects shall have the right to petition the king; prosecutions for such petitioning shall be illegal; (5) raising or keeping of a standing army in peacetime without the authority of parliament shall be illegal; (6) the protestant subjects shall be entitled to bear arms for self-defence; (7) emergency laws snail not be imposed in peacetime; and (8) parliament shall be convened in session periodically.

Bill of Rights (US) is an informal designation for the first ten constitutional amendments incorporated in the Constitution of the USA in 1791. These became necessary because the original document prepared at the Philadelphia Constitutional Convention did not contain any guarantees of fundamental rights and freedoms.

Biological Weapons Convention (1972). Biological weapons are counted among thc weapons of mass destruction and considered dangerous for the existence of the mankind and, therefore, sought to be eliminated. The latest international measure is the Convention on the Prohibition, the Development, Production, and Stockpiling of Bacteriological and Toxic Weapons and their Destruction, which was signed by the member-states of the UN in 1972 and which came into force in 1975. In 2001 the US withdrew from talks over the question of concluding verification protocols. An earlier attempt at banning the biological weapons was the Geneva Protocol for Prohibition of the Use in War of Asphyxiating, poisonous or other Gases and of Bacteriological

Methods of Warfare, signed in 1925 by the member-states of the Council of the of Nations.

Biosafety Protocol was signed by 150 states on 31 January 2000 in Montreal, Canada. It is a first protocol to the UN Convention on Biodiversity signed in 1992. The protocol regulates the trade in genetically modified (GM) foods and crops. The right of importing countries to seek information about GM organisms in advance and to refuse entry to such products has been recognized.

Bipartisan Foreign Policy refers to foreign policy of the USA which is formulated with complete agreement between the Republican and Democratic Parties in the Congress. The parties may differ in respect of mechanics of policy but display a common approach to foreign policy issues whether security or economic.

Bipolarity refers to a structure of international politics existing between 1945 and 1991 marked by struggle between tow poles of power or power-blocs called east and west led respectively by the former USSR and the USA. After the collapse of the USSR in 1991 the USA remained as the sole superpower and the hegemony of this single power came to be described as *unipolarity*. Its opposite *multipolarity* may not be far away.

Black Muslims (US). The Black Muslim movement in the US is a social liberation movement among certain segments of the black community who suffer from racial discrimination, exploitation and abject poverty. The movement has no ideological affinity with the mainstream Islam or the Muslim community. It represents merely a black attempt at self-identification and self-assertion. The movement is said to have been started by an Arab named Wali Farad born in Mecca, in 1977. He migrated to America in 1930 and established a mosque in Detroit and another in Chicago for the blacks who regarded him as their prophet. Farad was succeeded on his death in 1934 by Elijah Muhammad (formerly Elijah Pool), a Christian converted to black Muslim faith. He was succeeded by Stockley Carmichael. The Black Muslims are opposed to both Christianity and white domination.

Black Power was a slogan first raised by Stockley Carmichael in 1965 to achieve black empowerment and autonomy. He rejected the grant of civil rights and racial integration as useless for the blacks because of inherent racialism if the white society. The blacks, therefore, demanded representation in proportion of their population in all walks of life and provision of basic amenities of civic life in all cities with black concentration.

Black Rod, Usher of. The Gentleman Usher of the Black Rod is an officer of the British House of Lords, appointed by the Crown. His deputy is called the Yeoman Usher. Both are official messengers of the House of Lords. Any one of them summons the Commons to the Lords when the Royal Commissioners assemble to signify royal assent to the bills, executes orders for commitment of parties for a breach of privilege or contempt of the house, and assists in performance of ceremonies.

Black Sea is an inland sea located between southeast Europe Asia. It is connected with the Mediterranean Sea by the Bosporus*, Sea of Marmara and the Dardenelles. Its area is 413,360 sq kms.

Black Sea Economic Cooperation Group was formed in 1992 with headquarters at Istambul, Turkey by Albania, Armenia, Azerbaijan, Bulgaria, Georgia, Greece, Moldova, Rumania, Russia, Turkey, Ukrain. Nine other countries take part in its deliberations as observers.

Black Sea Powers are Russia, Ukraine, Georgia, Turkey, Bulgaria and Rumania.

Blackmail means transgression, particularly extortion of money or some other benefit from a victim by means of (1) threatening him of disclosing some personal information which might be damaging to his reputation; or (2) threatening the life and property of the victim or somebody connected with him. In civilized societies blackmail is regarded as tantamounting to moral assassination. Maximum punishment under British law is life imprisonment.

Blitzkrieg (German for a lightning strike) is abbreviated in English as Blitz to describe a sudden and massive attack against an enemy target.

Bloc/Block. A *bloc* is either a group of states having similar social, economic or political systems like the communist bloc or the capitalist bloc or a group of individuals and parties organized around some particular interest or purpose like the leftist bloc or the rightist bloc.) *Block*, on the other hand, means a group of things forming a unit like a block of seats in a representative assembly or a theatre; or a residential complex made of blocks of houses.

Bloc Politics refers to conflictual relationship between rival power-blocs or mutually antagonistic military alliances.

Block Grants or lump sum grants or opposite of matching and conditional grants. A block grant is made by a donor to a done without categorization or conditions or specifications regarding the manner and method of its use.

Blockade Problem. means encirclement. In international law a belligerent state has a legal right to encircle and block the ports or coast of an enemy country for outward communications. In peacetime too states impose trade embargo or economic and military sanctions as punitive or coercive measures.

Bodoland The Nalbari Division of the Indian State of Assam is inhabited by a tribe called Bodo. During the 1990's the Bodo youth launched a violent movement for the creation of a separate state of Bodoland, which demand was rejected by the Government of India.

Bolshevik Revolution (1917) refers to the violent overthrow of the democratic government in Russia and establishment of a communist dictatorship on 17 October 1917. A popular revolt against the Tsar in 1905 had forced him to restore civil liberties and convene a *duma* (parliament). But very soon the Tsar reneged on his promises and reverted to despotism. Meanwhile Russia became pitted against Germany in World war I. The defeat of the Russian army at the hands of the Germans early in 1917 triggered great unrest and revolt by the soldiers and workers forced the Tsar Nicholas II to abdicate. The *Duma* was convened which appointed a provisional government headed by Prince Luov. At the same time, a workers *soviet* (council) spontaneously sprang up in St. Petersburg which took over the local administration. Similar Soviets sprang up in Moscow and other big cities and assumed control of local affairs. In July Luov government resigned and was succeeded by a democratic coalition headed by Kerensky. The Bolsheviks did not join the government but under Lenin's direction (who had returned to Russia in April after living in exile in Europe since 1905) hatched a conspiracy to overthrow the provisional government. Thus a few days before the inauguration of the constituent assembly the Bolsheviks overthrew the Kerenski government by force, dissolved the constituent assembly, killed the Tsar and his family and imposed Bolshevik dictatorship.

Bolshevik/Menshevik in Russian mean respectively majority minority. The Russian Social Democratic and Labour Party split in 1903 into two factions. The Bolsheviks under V.I. Lenin's leadership were revolutionary Marxists believing in violent revolution and the dictatorship of the proletariat. The Mensheviks, on the other hand believed in parliamentary democracy and evolutionary socialism. Lenin continued to call his faction Bolshevik even enough it ceased later to be a majority. The split became permanent in 1912. The Bolsheviks captured power in Moscow on 17 October 1917. They changed their name to All-Russian Communist Party (Bolshevik) in 1925; again to the Communist Party of the Soviet Union (Bolshevik) in 1936; and finally they dropped the word Bolshevik from the name of the party in 1952. The CPSU ceased to be the sovereign authority of the former USSR in 1991.

Bolshevism refers to theory and practice of Leninism as made up of the doctrines of a vanguard party of professional revolutionaries; strict secrecy, unity and discipline within the party; concentration of the authority in central leadership; subordination of the majority to the minority; dictatorship of the communist party over the proletariat; use of intrigues, force and fraud to gain political power; and reliance on coercion and terror to keep the people under control.

Bona Fides/Bona Fide. Latin Bona fides "good faith" It implies absence of fraud and deceit. *Bona fide* means true or authentic e.g. *bona fide* citizen. Converse terms are *fides* (bad faith) and *mala fide* (untrue/malicious).

Bonapartism is derived from *Bonaparte,* family name of Napoleon I, the emperor of France, and his nephew Louis Philippe Bonaparte Napoleon or Napoleon III (1830-1848). Bonapartism stands for heroic ideas as well as dynamic and heroic leadership of extraordinary individuals like Napoleons with a stress on strong authoritarian state, aggressive pursuit of power and an adventurist course of political and military action.

Bonn Constitution refers to the Basic Law of the Federal Republic of Germany adopted by a Parliamentary Assembly elected by the people of West Germany and approved and promulgated by the Occupying Powers in 1949 which became the constitution of the Federal Republic of Germany. On reunification of the two parts of Germany in 1991 the Basic Law was amended suitably and the capital was shifted to Berlin, the Germany's capital before 1945.

Borda Ballot. As a variant of the preferential ballot, the borda ballot is based on the assumption that the second, third or fourth preferences shown on a ballot paper should not carry the same weight and value as the first preference. So the first preference is allotted a given number of points, then the second preference is given less points than the first preference then the third preference is given less points than the second one and so on. The winning candidate is one who obtains the largest number of cumulative points.

Border Security Force--BSF is a paramilitary force of the Indian union to guard India's international borders. It is sometimes also deployed in areas affected by civil strife or insurgency.

Borough, Pocket (borough = town) pocket boroughs were boroughs in England which since the middle ages had been receiving royal writs to return their members to the parliament at Westminster in London, in due course most of these boroughs became depopulated but their magnates continued to declare and certify their nominees as elected to parliament. They were also called "rotten" boroughs. They were opposed by the Chartist Movement* and eventually replaced by parliamentary constituencies having equal population under the first Representation of the People Act, 1832.

Bosnian Crisis (1993-95). Bosnia Herzegovina is since 1 March 1992 an independent state in south-eastern Europe with Serajevo as its capital. The Provinces of Bosnia and Herzegovina were parts of the Ottoman (Turkish) Empire for almost 400 years before they were annexed to Austria-Hungary in 1878. Later they became part of the Kingdom of Serbs, Croats an d Slovenes formed in 1918. This Kingdom was renamed as Yugoslavia in 1929. In 1945 Bosnia Herzegovina became one of the six autonomous republics of the Federation of Yugoslavia. Under the federal constitution the three ethnic communities inhabiting the republic namely the Serbs, the Croats and the Slav Muslims (Bosniks) shared political power and lived amicably. Then started the disintegration of Yugoslavia with Slovenia and Croatia declaring their independence in 1991. Following a referendum Bosnia Herzegovia too declared its independence on 1 March 1992. This was opposed by the Bosnian Serbs who then resorted to "ethnic cleansing" i.e., liquidation of Muslim enclaves with a view to establish a "greater Serbia". In the resulting strife more than 200,000 Muslims were believed to have been massacred and about one million displaced. The NATO and EU intervened to restore peace. In accordance with the American brokered General Framework Agreement for Peace in Bosnia Herzegovina, signed between the leaders of the three ethnic groups at Dayton, Ohio, USA, in December 1995, Bosnia Herzegovina was Preserved as a single sovereign state but territorially divided into a autonomous Bosnian Serb Republic, occupying 51 per cent of the territory, and a autonomous Federated Muslim-Croat Republic, occupying 49 per cent of the territory, with a central government vested only with the power to control foreign affairs and foreign trade. On 20 December 1995 power was formally transferred to an international NATO-led Implementation Force (IF), which was superseded in December 1996 by the NATO-led Stabilization Force (SFOR) to supervise the implementation of the peace agreement and maintain peace. The mandate of the SFOR was extended by the UN Security Council from time to time until it was decided in 2005 to replace it by a reduced peacekeeping deployed by the European Union.

Bosporus and Dardenelles. The strait of Bosporus links the Sea of Marmara (an inland sea in Turkey) with the Black Sea and the strait of Dardenells links the Sea of Marmara with the Aegian sea and the Mediterranean Sea. Both the straits are of great strategic and economic importance for the Black sea powers. Under the Montreax Convention of 1938 both straits are placed under Turkish sovereignty and control but other nations are guaranteed freedom of passage in peace and war. However, in case Turkey feels a threat to her national security it may restrict the passage of warships during war-time.

Bourgevois/ Bourgevoisie. Both are derived from *bourg* = city. In common usage a *bourgevois* is a member of the *bourgevoisie* i.e. the urban middle class. But strictly the *bourgevoisie,* as opposed to the *proletariat* (industrial working class), is a class of city-dwelling, capital-accumulating industrialists, manufacturers, businessmen, traders, merchants, corporate managers, bankers, insurers and financiers, etc.

Boxer Rebellion (1900) was spearheaded in China against the foreigners by a secret anti-foreigner organization known as the *Boxers.*

Brahmo Samaj (Divine Society) was a socio-religious reform movement within the *sanatan Dharma*, strongly influence by the teachings of Christianity and Islam launched by Raja Ram Mohan Roy in Calcutta in 1828. Until 1830 it was little more than an informal weekly gathering of the enlightened Brahmins of the city in a private residence. Then a permanent Brahmo building was constructed, a trust-deed drawn and a board of trustees appointed to run the affairs of the Brahmo samaj. This sect believed in monotheism and equality of all human beings. It rejected idolatory, untouchability, all superstitions, the doctrine of *karma* and transmigration of souls, child marriage and prohibition of widow-remarriage. Its influence in the Bengali society had almost died down by the beginning of the twentieth century. By 1950 its followers were believed to constitute merely 0.2 per cent of the Indian population.

Brainwashing means to compel a person to give up his old ideas and embrace new ideas either through persistent indoctrination or by exerting upon him constant psychological and/or physical pressure.

Brest-Litovsk Treaties (1918) were armistice treaties signed during the closing year of World War I between Bolshevik Russia and ukrain on the one side and the Central Powers (Austria-Hungary, Germany and Turkey) on the other. Faced with military defeat Russia ceded Estonia and Latvia to Germany and Kars, Ardanan and Batum provinces of Armenia to Turkey Besides Russia undertook to pay 300 million gold rubles in war reparations, These agreements were concluded at the behest of Lenin keeping in view the military vulnerability of Russia. But the Bolsneviks repudiated these treaties soon after the defeat of the central powers.

Brettonwoods Conference/System. A Conference of leading nations consider the postwar monetary, financial and trade arrangements was held in July 1944 in Brettonwoods, New Hampshire, USA. The three-weak conference started on 1 July 1944 and ended with the signing of an agreement to establish the IMF* and the IBRD. By the Brettonwoods system is meant the set of institutions-- the IBRD*, IMF*, and the (abortive) ITO* (replaced by GATT* in 1948 and then by the WTO* in 1995).

Brezhnev Doctrine of limited sovereignty of the member-states of the Soviet Bloc was propounte by Leonid Brezhnev, the General Secretary of the Communist Party of the Soviet Union, in 1968 to deal with internal reform movement in Czechoslovaki, accordingly, Russian troops invaded and occupied that country and overthrew the reformist communist regime which was accused of undermining the communist ideology.

Budget is the statement of estimated revenue and expenditure for a given financial year. A budget may be either surplus or deficit or balanced. A balanced budget in the past was considered to be a sign of sound financial management. However, Jon Maynard Keynes, in the wake of the Great Depression*, showed budget supluses or deficits could be used to regulate the economy. A deficit budget implies more public spending that is conducive to economic growth. Conversely a balanced budget tends to maintain the status quo. An *incremental* budget is one which assumes the underlying policies and allocations made to execute them in the previous years as givens. Hence no major changes are contemplated. Only incremental (minor) auditions or deletions here and there can be considered. Conversely a *zero-based* budget is a radical approach to public-budget making. It requires that for the sake of economy, efficiency and productivity each item of expenditure a fresh justification of the contemplated activities and a pertinent summary of cost and benefit has to be provided.

Buffer State is a small sovereign state located between two rival great powers. A buffer state usually adopts neutrality towards its neighbours. Some examples are Switzerland between east, and west Europe, Belgium and Luxembourg between Germany and France, and Nepal between India and China.

Bureaucracy is a form of hierarchical, centralized organization characteristic of both the public and private sectors. All bureaucracies follow principles of centralization, unity of command, chain of command, rationality, legality, accountability, professionalism and efficiency.

Bushido (Japanese for honour) is the Japanese code of honour including, among other things, a strong sense of personal honour, dignity and integrity, filial loyalty and an intense feeling of patriotism and nationalism. For instance, if a Japanese is ashamed or dishonoured he commits *harakiri* (suicide by rupturing one's belly) to vindicate his honour.

Buxar, Battle of (1764) was fought on 23 October 1764 at Buxar (Bengal) between the forces of the East India Company led by Sir Hector Monro and the combined forces of Mir Qasim (installed as the Nawab of Bengal by the Company in 1760 and deposed in 1763), Shujauddaula, the Nawab of Awadh and the Rohillas. This was the last Indian attempt to dislodge the Company from Bengal. The Indian forces were defeated. The Nawab of Awadh agreed to become a vassal of the Company. On 12 August 1765 Robert Clive obtained the grant of *Diwani* (land revenue administration) of Bengal, Bihar and Orissa from the Mughal Emperor Shah Alam II. Although nominally agents of the Mughal Empire the grant of Diwani made the Company a *de facto* sovereign territorial power in east India from where they spread their rule over the rest of the mainland.

By-election is midterm election to fill a seat in an elective body which has been vacated by a member by resignation, or dismissal or death before the expiry of his term.

By-laws (from Saxon *by* or *bye* = twin). A by-law originally was a twin law. In modern times, however, bylaws are framed by corporate bodies and registered societies to regulate their own internal affairs. Bylaws are required to be reasonable and legal and should not be violative of or derogatory to the law of the land.

C

Cabal (1) as derived from cabale it refers to persons acting in concert to achieve their ends by deceitful means; (2) as composed of initials of the names of Clifford, Ashley, Buckingham, Arlington and Landerdale who were ministers of Charles II and called ''cabal ministry'' who exercised executive authority to the exclusion of the Privy Council which was the constitutional executive. Cabal thus means an inner cabinet and has a sinister meaning.

Cabinet is drawn from French *cabinet* meaning a closed chamber. It came to be used for a body of select ministers and advisers who deliberate secretly over matters of state in a closed chamber. In England it originated from the Cabinet Council which was a small body of select and most trusted privy councillors appointed by Charles II to run the government.

A **ministerial cabinet** in France is entirely different from the Council of Ministers. Each ministry/department of the French government has a ministerial cabinet at the top, headed by a *chief of the cabinet* or a director of cabinet to advise the minister concerned on matters of policy and administration. This cabinet has no standing outside the ministry concerned.

A **parliamentary cabinet** or council of ministers is composed of principal leaders of the majority party in the popular chamber of parliament under the leadership of a prime minister (or first minister or chancellor) who is the head of government and the leader of the house. Parliamentary cabinets are also known as ''government'', ''ministry'' or ''political'' or ''parliamentary'' executive. Parliamentary cabinets are collegium which exercise collective authority on behalf of parliament and own collective responsibility for their actions before parliament and the people.

A **presidential cabinet** of the American type, on the other hand, is neither a collective executive nor does it exercise collective authority. In the USA, the cabinet is an extraconstitutional body with an advisory and coordinative role, wholly subordinate to the president. The cabinet is composed of the President, Vice-president, and all the heads of the 16 executive departments. All the heads are nominated by the president and appointed by him after the approval of the Senate. Other officials with cabinet rank are the chief of the staff to the president, the Director of the Office of Management and Budget the IPS Trade Representative the Administrator of the Environmental protection Agency and the Director of the Office National Drug Control Policy.

Cabinet Committees (India). The union cabinet in India has a number of committees to reduce the workload of the cabinet. These are: the Cabinet Committee on Political Affairs, the Cabinet Committee on Security, the Appointments Committee of the Cabinet, the Cabinet Committee on Economic Affairs, the Cabinet Committee on Prices, which monitors prices, the Cabinet Committee on the WTO, and the Cabinet Committee on Infrastructure.

Cabinet Mission Plan (1946) was the last plan presented by the British Government to the Indian political parties to preserve the political unity and territorial integrity of India while accommodating the demand of the All-India Muslim League* for regional autonomy. The Plan envisaged (1) creation of an All-India Union vested with powers over defence, foreign affairs, and communications; the residuary powers were, to be vested in the provinces; (2) election of a constituent

Assembly to frame the constitution of the All-India Union; (3) soon after the inauguration of the constituent Assembly the members belonging to groups A, B, and C, were to split into three separate groups to frame the respective constitutions for three regional federations-one for the northwest, one for the east and one for the rest of India; and (4) installation of an Interim Government to work till such time as the Constituent assembly framed the constitution. The constituent Assembly was elected early in 1946. The Muslim League joined the interim government in October 1946 but boycotted the constituent Assembly which convened on 9 December 1946. The Congress had initially accepted the plan so the League too accepted it; later the Congress repudiated the plan so the League too rejected. The collapse of the Cabinet mission Plan led to the partition settlement between the Congress, the League and other parties, Accordingly the Indian Independence Act, 1947 was passed by the British parliament which provided for the transfer of power to the Dominions of India and Pakistan on 15 August 1947.

Cabinet Secretariat (India) is a department of the Government of India meant to provide secretarial assistance to the central cabinet and its committees. It is headed by a Cabinet Secretary who is the senior-most secretary to the Government of India and head of the civil service. It operates under the direction of the prime minister. It is responsible for preparing and circulating the agenda and minuter of the meetings of the cabinet and cabinet committees. It transmits particular decisions concerning particular agencies or departments to the concerned agencies and departments. It is also responsible for framing rules for the transaction of the business of Government of India and allocation of work among the ministries/departments of the Government of India under the direction of the prime minister and with the approval of the President of India.

Cadre (French for ''frame'' or ''framework''; means (1) sanctioned posts in a military regiment or airforce squadron which can be filled when required; (2) the approved strength of positions or a sanctioned category of posts in civil services, hence *service cadre* or *cadre* post; (3) full-time party workers of communist, fascist or militia-type organizations, hence *party cadres;* and (4) a cadre in the Indian administration refers to the allotted state or a group of states where an officer of an All-India Service (the Indian Administrative service, the Indian Police service and the India Forest Service) has to serve after completing his training till his retirement (except periods of deputation to the central government}. To curb provincialism and encourage a national outlook every state of the Indian Union gets only one-third of its requirement for officers of an all-India service from among candidates belonging to that state and remaining two-third requirement from candidates belonging to other states. No officer can refuse to join the cadre allotted to him and once allotted a cadre cannot be changed except through marriage with a spouse belonging to another cadre.

Caesarism (from caesar, the emperor of the Roman Empire) is synonymous with absolute rule and imperialism.

Calvo Clause in an intergovernmental agreement concerns the application of the Calvo Doctrine enunciated by Carlos Calvo (1824-1906), an Argentinian diplomat and historian, who advocated that foreign governments should not intervene diplomatically to settle private claims of their citizens or corporations against Latine American governments unless judicial remedies available through local courts are exhausted. The Calvo doctrine was also incorporated in Article I of the second Hague Convention.

Canon (from Latin *canna* = cane or rule) is a rule pertaining to matters ecclesiastical i.e. the rule or law of the Christian Church. Hence *canon law* is a collection of rules and ordinances governing the internal functioning of the Roman Catholic Church.

Capitol Hill (US) is the name of the place where the two houses of the US Congress are located. Symbolizes the legislative branch in the USA.

Capital Punishment is the death sentence pronounced by a legally competent authority with due process of law. Though still prevalent in many countries it is generally opposed in most civilized countries.

Capitalism is an economic system in which the means of production, distribution and exchange for the most part lie in private hands and goods and services are bought and sold according to prices determined by a free market in which the aim of producers and providers is to make a profit. Capitalism is based on the idea of private property as the natural right of human beings. Some of the basic elements of capitalism are the right to acquire, hold and dispose of private property; freedom to engage in an enterprise or occupation of one's choice; profit-mating as an incentive to production; freedom of competition as a regulating mechanism of economic activities; freedom of contract; a wage system; monetary value as a mechanism of exchange, and a Policy of "rationalism" i.e. systematic efficiency in the conduct of business.

Capitulationism refers to a policy of military surrender or political submission to a superior power. *Career* means road or pathway; a profession or public service which a person adopts as a full-time, life-long vocation, e.g. a civil-service, diplomatic, military or a professional career.

Capitulations (to capitulate = to surrender) refer to treaties signed between unequal partners (e.g. the militarily and economically dominant European powers on the one hand and the weak and vulnerable Asian and African countries on the other) whereby the weaker or dependent parties surrender part of their sovereign rights in favour of the dominant partner. Thus colonial powers obtained extraterritorial rights in such countries as the Ottoman Empire, China, japan and Iran. Extraterritoriality meant that their functionaries or settlements or trade zones or naval and military bases became exempt from operation of local laws and jurisdiction of local courts.

Career Service. A career service in government is a public service which is so organized and conducted as to encourage careers. The concept has overtones of protectionism as well as professionalism.

Careerism is a pejorative term to describe the dedication of a post-holder in public service solely to the enhancement of his own personal prospects; hence a *careerist* .

Caribbean Community CARICOM was founded in 1973 by the Treaty of Chaguaramas for greater regional integration and creation of a Caribbean common market which came into being in July 2001 Headquarters: Georgetown, Guyana. Member-States: Antigua & Barbuda, Bahamas (did not join the common market}, Barbados, Belize, Dominica, Grenada, Guyana, Haiti, St. Lucia, St. Vincent & the Grenadines, Suriname, and Trinidad and Tobago. There are five associate members and seven territories have the status of observers with the CARICOM.

Caribbean Sea, is an extension of the Atlantic Ocean, in its north and east are situated West Indies, in the west Central American isthmus and in its south is located the South American continent.

Cartel is a form of monopoly association created by an agreement/ understanding among a group of countries engaged in a particular sector of industrial, commercial or extraction activity whether at the national or international level to control production, distribution, technologies, raw-materials or markets to ensure arbitrary price-fixing and profit-making

Caste (*Jati* in Hindi) is the traditional block of the Indian society. It is defined as an hereditary, endogamous social group associated with a traditional occupation and occupying a particular superior or inferior rank in the hierarchy of castes. Caste differs from both traditional tribe and the modern class. Both caste and tribe are hereditary but while caste is an endogamous closed group carrying a ritual status of purity or pollution in relation to other castes the tribe is not so. Modern classes are a product of socioeconomic inequalities in modern capitalist society. They are neither hereditary, nor closed nor static groups.

Casteism is a tendency of according primacy to one's own caste-group and making it the focus of his political loyalty to the exclusion of other caste-groups or the national community,

Castroism refers to radical revolutionary ideas and policies of Fidel Castro (born 1906) who came to power in Cuba in 1958 after ousting the longtime pro-American dictator Fulgeucio Batista. Castro opposed US domination of Latin America, called for expulsion of foreign companies and advocated socialistic reconstruction to eradicate poverty in Latin America. No other country in Latin America underwent a socialist revolution because of American policy of containment of Castro and Castroism.

Casus Belli is Latin for the cause of war; any action which triggers a war.

Caucasus is a geographical term used for both the Caucasus mountain range and the Caucasian region. The mountain range extends about 1,210 kms from the mouth of Kuban River on the Black sea to the Apsheron Peninsula on the Caspian sea. It forms the dividing line between Europe and Asia. The Caucasus region is divided into two subregions -- North Caucasia and Transcaucasia. North Caucasia lies entirely within the Russian Federation and includes the provinces of Daghestan, Chechenya, Ingushtia and Osetia. Trans Caucasia includes the independent states of Georgia, Armenia and Azerbaijan (which were up to 1991 constituent republics of the former USSR).

Census is counting of persons, livestock, households and establishments, etc. The first census in the world is stated to have been held in Rome in 432 B.C. The first census in the United Kingdom was held in 1801. The first census in India was initiated in 1871 and completed in 1872. Decennial census in India has regularly been held since 1884. The last Indian census was held in 2001. The responsibility for collecting, collating, analysing and publishing census data is vested in the Registrar-General of India under the Ministry of Home affairs.

Central Administrative Tribunal -- CAT was created by the Government of India on 1 November 1985 under the administrative Tribunals Act, 1985. It had its principal bench at New Delhi and 17 regional benches located in different parts of India. The CAT was composed of a Chairman (who must be a judge), a Vice-Chairman, one Judicial Member and one Administrative Member. It was meant to hear and dispose of service-related cases and complaints of central government employees expeditiously and inexpensively. Following the example set by the Centre most state governments also established State Administrative Tribunals under the 1985 Act. However, the central cabinet in its meeting held on 21 April 2005 was reported as having decided in principle to amend the Administrative Tribunals Act to provide for abolition of the Central and State Administrative Tribunals.

Central America is the southernmost geographical region of North America lying between Mexico and South America, and comprises the countries of Panama, Costa Rica, Nicaragua, Honduras, El Salvadore, Guatemala and Belize.

Central American Free Trade Agreement -- CAFTA was signed by the USA, El Salvadore, Guatemala, Honduras and Nicaragua on 17 December 2003 in Washington, D.C. It provides for duty-free exports from the CAFTA countries to the USA. Reciprocally, 80 per cent of industrial exports from the USA to the CAFTA countries would be duty-free and the tariffs on the rest of trade would be eliminated within ten years. Similarly, 50 per cent of US agricultural exports to the CAFTA countries would be duty-free and tariffs on the rest of trade would be eliminated within ten years. The Dominican Republic signed a free-trade agreement with the USA in 2004 and thereby integrated itself with CAFTA.

Central Asia refers to a geographic region comprising the countries of Tibet, xinjiang, Afghanistan, Turkemenistan, Uzbekistan, Kirghyzia, Kazakhastan and Tajikistan.

Central Bank is the financial institution entrusted with the function of issuing currency for a nation and safekeeping its foreign-currency and gold reserves besides other functions relating to money, banking and finance. It is also called the of banks because it keeps the balances of the national banks and is the lender of the last resort. In the UK the Bank of England (founded in 1794), in the US the Federal Reserve system (founded in 1913) and in India the Reserve Bank of India (originally founded as the imperial Bank of India under an act of the central legislature and renamed as the RBI in 1955; are some examples of a central bank.

Central Board of Direct Taxes (India) was created within the Department of Revenue, Ministry of finance of the Government of India under the Central Board of Revenue Act, 1963. In 1964 the Board was spilt into a Central Board of Direct Taxes and a Central Board of Excise and customs. The former enforces laws concerning income tax, wealth tax, state duty and service tax while the latter enforces excise and custom laws. Under the Customs Act, 1962, it is the Chief Customs Authority of India.

Central Bureau of Investigation CBI was created by a resolution of the Ministry of Home Affairs, Government of India in 1963 to detect and investigate misuse of central government funds and offences committed by central government employees as well as cases referred to it by central government employees.

Central Industrial Security Force-- CISF was created under the Central Industrial Security Force Act, 1969 to protect the industrial undertakings of the central government; public sector enterprises; airports and government buildings.

Central Intelligence Agency--CIA is an intelligence agency of the US government created under the National Security Act, 1947, and located in the Executive Office of the President*. It is headed by a director appointed by the President with the consent of the Senate. He reports directly to the President. It operates secretly. Its activities are carried on by a network of case officers (American citizens who have served with the CIA for at least 20 years) who recruit spies and agents from among the nationals of foreign countries for collecting information regarding activities subersive of American national security and detrimental to the American national interests. The CIA provides an important intelligence input to the foreign and defence policy-making in the US government.

Central Pay Commissions. To compensate for the rise in the cost of living since the end of the second world war, the Government of has appointed periodically central pay commissions for upward revision of the pay-scales and emoluments of its employees. The first commission was appointed in 1947 and reported in 1950; the second was appointed in 1957 and reported in 1960; the third in 1970 and reported in 1973; the fourth in 1983 and reported in 1986; and the fifth was appointed in 1991 and reported in 1998 and its recommendations were implemented retrospectively from 1 January 1996. The sixth was appointed in 2006.

Central Powers during World War I were Austria-Hungarh, Bulgaria, Germany and the Ottoman Empire. They were confronted by the Allied Powers -- Britain, France, Russia and the USA.

Central Reserve Police Force -- CRPF was originally raised by the British Indian government under the Crown Representative's Police Force Law, 1939 to aid and assist the rulers of the Princely States in maintaining law and order, dealing with internal disturbances and controlling political agitations. The Law lapsed with the lapse of British paramountcy on 15 August 1947. It was replaced by the Central Reserve Police Force Act, 1949 and the Central Reserve police Force was raised as an armed force of the Union to be deployed in aid of the civil authorities of the states, and union territories during internal disturbance, insurgencies and to perform such other functions as assigned to it by the central government. In 1992 the Government of India raised a Rapid Action Force (RAF) to deal with inter-community disturbances in riot-prone areas.

Central Secretariat (India) is the conglomeration of various ministries/departments of the government or India. It is the Drain-rust of the Indian administration. It works as a single unit with collective responsibility as in the case or the central Ministry, Each secretariat ministry/department is headed by a minister/minister/minister of state on the political side and by a Secretary to the GOI on the administrative side. It may have one or more additional secretaries, According to the principle of specialization and division of work each department is divided into wings; the wings are divided into divisions; and the divisions into sections. A wing is headed by a joint secretary; a division by a deputy secretary and a section by an under-secretary. The secretariat part of the government is responsible for advising and assisting the political executive in the formulation of policy and taking of decisions; for administering the central subjects through the executive departments/agencies; for intra-departmental and inter-department coordination; and for supervision and control of the entire administrative system from the highest level.

Central Treaty Organization--CENTO was a Western-sponsored military alliance of the countries located on the northern-tier of the former USSR (Turkey, Iran, Iraq and Pakistan) for defence against communist expansionism. It originated as the Baghdad Pact signed between Turkey and Iraq in 1955 in Baghdad. It was joined later by Iran, Pakistan and the UK. Its military headquarters was at Baghdad. The

USA did not join formally but became a member of its defence, economic and anti-subversion committees. After the overthrow of the pro-western monarchy in 1958 Iraq withdrew in 1959. Then its headquarters was shifted to Ankara, Turkey, and its name was changed to CENTO. It was formally disbanded in 1979.

Central Vigilance Commission (India) was created by a Resolution of the Government of India in 1964 to look into charges or corruption against central government employees in accordance with the Prevention of Corruption Act, 1958. It became a statutory body under the Central vigilance Commission Act, 2003. It is compose of a number of vigilance commissioners and headed by a chief Vigilance Commissioner.

Certiorari, Writ of (Latin *Certeriori* = to be informed). A writ of *certiorari* is issued by a superior court to an interior court or tribunal asking it to transfer the record or proceedings in a given case under its consideration to the directing court. The purpose of such transfer is either that the judgment of the inferior court is reviewed and corrected or the superior court itself conducts the proceedings to the end and delivers the judgment.

Chancellor. (1) Designation of the head of the federal government in the Federal Republic or Germany, equivalent of a prime minister. His office is Known as chancellory. (2) the administrative head of the federal Chancellory in Switzerland who is elected by the Federal Assembly and works under the direction of the Federal Council.

Chancellor of the Duchy of Lancaster is a member of the British cabinet responsible for the affairs of the Cabinet office.

Chancellor of the Exchequer is a member of the British cabinet and occupies the same place and plays the same role as the minister of finance elsewhere.

Chancellor, Lord is an ancient office under the British crown. The Lord chancellor is appointed by the sovereign. He is the presiding officer of the House of Lords both as a legislative chamber as well as the supreme court of appeal; he is also the presiding judge of the Lord Chancellor's Court (also Known as the Chancery which is a division of the High Court of Justice); and he is also a member of the British cabinet with full-time charge of the Lord Chancellor's Department (equivalent to a justice ministry). According to constitutional reforms enacted in 2005 the office of the Lord chancellor was retained with an additional title of the Secretary of State for Constitutional Affairs and his appointing power was transferred to a Judicial Appointment Council.

Charge d' Affaires is the designation of a foreign service officer who is given the charge of an embassy or legation during the absence of a regular ambassador or minister. When placed temporarily he is called *charge d' affaires ad interim* but if his placement is on a permanent basis he is called *charge d' affaires en titre.*

Charisma/Charismatic Leader (Greek charisma = gift or grace). It refers to purely personal as distinct from institutional) power of a gifted person. As defined by Max weber, *charisma* is applied to a certain quality of an individual personality by virtue of which he is set apart from ordinary men and treated as endowed with supernatural, superhuman, or at least specifically exceptional power or qualities. These are such as are not accessible to the ordinary person, but are regarded as of divine origin or as exemplary, and on the basis of them the individual concerned is treated as a leader.

Charter is derived from Latin *charta* meaning writing material made of papyrus and hence came to be used for the text written on the sheet. The term is variously used to designate public instruments issued by a sovereign authority or a legislature to incorporate societies, companies, professional associations, municipal bodies and universities; it is also used for deeds, contracts and founding instruments (constitutions) of international bodies like the charter of the

UNO, its specialized agencies, and other regional and intergovernmental international organization.

Charter of Economic Rights and Duties of States was adopted by the UN general Assembly on 12 December 1974 with a view to establishing a new international economic order (NIEO). It was signed by 120 member-states but opposes by Belgium, Denmark, Germany, Luxembourg, the UK and the USA.

Charter of Paris for a New Europe (1990) was signed on 21 November 1990 in Paris by heads of state or government of 32 European countries of the Conference on Security and Cooperation in Europe (Helsinki Conference) plus the USA and Canada to herald a new era of security and cooperation in Europe. Its signature along with the signing of the Treaty on Reduction of Conventional Weapons in Europe marked the final end of the cold war in Europe. Thereafter, the CSCE was made a permanent arrangement as the OSCE.

Charter of the UNO was drawn up by the representatives of 50 countries at the United Nations Conference on International Organization held in San Francisco, USA, from 25 April to 26 June 1945. The Charter was signed on 26 June by 50 countries plus one country which signed it later and came into force on 24 October 1945.

Chartist Movement arose out of the dissatisfaction of the British working class with the first Representation 01 the People Act, 1832. The movement had its origin in the workingmen's Association founded in 1836 in London. They submitted their demands in the form of a charter to the British Parliament and launched countrywide agitation for their acceptance. Their demands included (1) introduction of universal adult franchise; (2) voting by ballot; (3; abolition of property qualification for contesting parliamentary elections; (4) payment of a salary to members of parliament residing in London to enable the working class MP's to stay in London full time and take part in parliamentary proceedings; (5)

demarcation of parliamentary constituencies of equal size; and (6) making compulsory annual sessions of parliament. These demands were accepted in gradual steps over a period of 100 years through the various representation of people acts.

Chauvinism is after Nicholas Chauvin, soldier of napoleon's army who became famous for keeping the standard aloft and marching ahead on the battlefield despite being seriously wounded. As a tendency it depicts an extreme and aggressive form of nationalism. It is an admixture of patriotism, nationalism, militarism and expansionism. It has more to do with popular emotion than with reason.

Chechenya Problem Chechenya or the Chechenya Republic is a region with an area of 1,58,000 Skms in southeast Russia located in the North Caucasus. It is a petroleum-producing region inhabited by Muslim Chechens. Before 1991 Chechenya and Ingushetia formed a combined Checheno-ingushetia Autonomous Republic of the former USSR. In November 1991 the Chechens unilaterally declared their independence of Russia and formed the Chechen Republic. In 1992 Ingushetia was recognized as an autonomous republic of the Russian Federation, in 1993 armed hostilities broke out between the Russian-installed government of the Checnen Republic and the Chechen nationalists who wanted separation from Russia. In 1995 Russian forces occupied Chechenya and since then the country is ruled by Russian-installed puppet regimes.

Checks-and-Balances is an essential mechanism of constitutionalism or constitutionally limited government. It is based from the thesis of John Locke that concentration of authority in a single person or institution is the very condition of absolute rule and tyranny. The legislative, executive and judicial powers of government, therefore, should be Kept separate and lodged in different institutions and authority be divided among them in such a way that if one outsteps its constitutional limits the others should check and limit it to its constitutional domain. The result would be balanced government tree from arbitrariness and tyranny. The classical example of the embodiment of this theory of separation of powers and constitutional checks is the 1789 federal constitution of the USA.

Chemical Weapons Convention (1993) was signed in 1993 and came into force in 1997 which not only bans the use of chemical weapons but goes beyond it to obligate the signatories to eliminate the stockpiles of their chemical weapons and dismantle the related production facilities over a ten year period. By 2005 the Convention had 174 signatories. It was the most significant international agreement: to prevent the proliferation of the weapons of mass destruction since the signing of the Nuclear Non-Proliferation Treaty (NPT) in 1968. The ban on chemical weapons is to be supervised by an International Organization for Prostitution of Chemical weapons to be established at the Hague, Netherlands.

Chinese Revolution (1911/1949). China underwent two revolutions during the twentieth century the first was a democratic one in 1911 when the Chinese Nationalist Party (Kuomintang) under the leadership of Sun Yat Sen overthrew the Manchu dynasty and proclaimed the Republic of China. The Republic was governed by the Kuomintang till the second revolution--the communist revolution of 1949. The Chinese Communist Party was established in 1920 and its influence grew gradually among the Chinese people. By 1930's it had become a political force in parts of China. The Chinese communists fought side by side with the nationalists against the Japanese who had occupied Manchuria in 1930 and again against the Japanese occupation of China during World War II. However, after the end of the war the struggle for supremacy between the two forces started in 1946 which developed into a full-fledged civil war. The Communist Party backed by the Chinese masses routed the armies of the Kuomintang regime and proclaimed the People's Republic of China in Beijing on 1 October 1949.

Citizenship. A citizen or national of a country is one, whether natural born or naturalized, who enjoys the rights of citizenship and discharges its obligations under the law of the land. Non-citizens residing in a country are called aliens in India anybody who was a resident of India at the time of coming into being of the Constitution of India (26 January 1950); or who was born in India; or one who was residing in India for five years before the commencement of the constitution is recognized as a citizen of the Indian Republic, besides Indian returnees from abroad and the naturalized persons. The Indian Citizenship Act, 1955, deals with matters connected with acquisition and termination of Indian citizenship. In 2005 the Act was amended to grant dual citizenship to persons of Indian origin except those from Pakistan and Bangladesh.

Civic Culture is a particular variety of the democratic political culture that is characteristic of the mature democracies of Britain, France, USA and the Scandinavian countries, It is a mixed culture which combines deference to authority with political participation. It is conducive to political legitimacy and stability.

Civil Code. A civil code means a collection of laws governing the personal and family matters of citizens such as marriage and divorce, adoption and succession, inheritance, charities and religious endowments, etc. In France, a predominantly Roman Catholic country, the civil Code or the Napoleonic Code, as distinct from the Canon Law*, was the first modern, secular, legal code promulgated by napoleon I in 1804. Subsequently it was borrowed by other European countries and the Kemalist Turkey. In contemporary India there is no uniform civil code for all citizens. In ancient India Manu's code prevailed, in medieval India the Islamic and Vedic communities were governed by the Shariat law and the customary code respectively British rule in India continued the same practice by enacting the personal laws of various religions communicates to govern the personal and religious matters Hindus, Muslims, Christians and Parsis. After independence the Constitution of the Indian Republic aid not abolish the personal laws and replace them by a uniform civil code but rather gave a direction under article 44 to the effect that the Indian state shall strive to promulgate a uniform civil code for all citizens in India. This directive later raised a lot or controversy as it conflicted with the constitutional guarantee of religious freedom under Articles 25-28 which also includes the right of all citizens to be governed by their respective personal laws in respect of their personal and family matters. However, a uniform or common civil code may be conveniently used as a device for cultural assimilation of the religious minorities. A precedent was set by the French colonialists in Algeria during the nineteenth century. A precondition for the extension of political rights to the native Algerians, Muslim by faith, was that they accept the Napoleonic Code. This failed because no true follower of Islam could abandon the law of the *shariat* in favour of an irreligious civil code.

Civil Defence refers to the sum total of measures that become necessary during a war to protect the cities and towns which become an easy targets of air-raids by the enemy, besides the defensive action of the regular armed forces on the front. The examples are operating air-raid warning systems, building air-raid shelters, providing emergency relief to the affected population, etc. In India a civil defence organization has been created under the Civil Defence Act, 1968. Besides, the Home Guards and the Territorial Army* also play a role.

Civil Disobedience and/or passive resistance against injustice was a doctrine first preached by Henry David Thoreau in North America in 1869, applied by M.K Gandhi in South Africa and in British India, and followed by Ram Manohar Lohia in independent India. As a form of direct action* it means that a group of people or the people at large have a moral right to defy, resist, disobey or break a public law or policy on the ground that they believe such law or policy to be illegal, immoral, unjust or injurious to the public. Acts of civil disobedience must constitute open and clear breaches or law or at least the authorities should consider them as unlawful. Instances are Gandhi's symbolic breaking of the salt law on 6 August 1930 or the ''Quit India'' movement launched by the Indian National Congress on 8 August 1942.

Civil Liberties or basic political freedoms, along with free and fair elections, are an essential requirement of democracy, without these freedoms in the civil (public) sphere nobody can either be a free citizen or participate in the political process freely. Most important civil liberties are: protection of life and personal security; freedom of speech and expression; freedom of faith, belief and worship; freedom or movement and residence; freedom of association and peaceful assembly; and freedom to choose any occupation or profession, etc. Civil liberties are guaranteed either by the constitution or the law of the state or by mere absence of state restrictions and/or interference.

Civil Rights mean (1) rights of citizens created by the positive or state-made law, rather than by divine law or natural law; and (2) in the USA the term is used to describe the political rights of ethnic minorities, particularly the black Americans.

Civil Rights Act, 1976 as passed by the Indian parliament is a revised version of the Untouchability (Offences) Act, 1955. Article 17 of the 1950 Constitution of India outlawed the age old practice of untouchability and declared any disabilities arising out of this practice as offences punishable under a law to be made by Indian parliament, Accordingly, the Untouchability (Offences) Act, 1955 was passed to define offences related to the practice of untouchability and prescribed a maximum punishment of six months' imprisonment and a fine of Rs. five hundred for persons found guilty of acts oral or physical abuse or discrimination against the former untouchables (now members of the scheduled castes*), in view of rising cases of atrocities against this class and ineffectivity of the law to prevent them, the untouchability law of 1955 was amended in 1976 to remove the legal loopholes and provide more stringent punishments for offenders and terminated the benefit of compounding of the untouchability offences cases under the former i

Civil Service In the United Kingdom and the countries of the commonwealth the civil service refers to those servants of the Crown, other than political or judicial office-holders, who are employed, in a civil capacity, and whose remuneration is paid out of money provided by Parliament. The civil service is characterized by (1) recruitment on the basis of merit as determined through open, competitive examinations; (2) relative security of tenure from entry till retirement; (3) professionalism; and (4) anonymity and political neutrality.

Civil Service Neutrality. The classical theory of British- style parliamentary democracy vests supreme power of policy-making in the political executive (the responsible ministry) and subordinates the permanent executive (the civil service) to the political executive. The civil servants therefore required to be non-political, non-partisan and politically neutral. In modern times however this theory appears to have broken down. The civil servants no longer play a passive role of policy advisors but themselves are involved in setting political priorities and making of decisions. In almost all political systems the civil servants have been recognized as a political force. The civil servants are not automatons but human beings. It is but natural that they will be influenced by their personal political preferences as well as by the cultural and political context.

Civil Society is the non-state part of the society or the sum total of social interests and institutions existing autonomously of the political state. In a democracy the civil sphere is considered as immune from the regulation or intervention of state authorities.

Civil War is a struggle for sovereignty between more or less equal parties or rival governments within the same state. A civil war is a state of internal armed conflict between two rival forces aspiring for supremacy, examples are American civil war of the nineteenth century and the Russian, Spanish and Chinese civil wars of the twentieth century.

Clash-of-Civilizations Thesis. According to Samuel P. Huntington *The clash of civilizations (1988),* the sources of conflict in the post-Cold war era will not be primarily power-political or economic but rather ideological and cultural, Nation-states will stay in their place but the struggle for power shall take place between civilizational blocs. The thesis appears to be grounded not so much in the (fictitious) irreconcilability of the western with the non-Western civilization as in the perceived necessity of finding an alternative enemy (the Islamic world) after the demise of the communist world to sustain the dynamism, drive and growth of the Euro-American power-bloc.

Class is a social stratum or a category of persons differentiated from other classes or categories by virtue of its socioeconomic status in the society. A modern capitalist society is broadly stratified into upper, middle and lower classes. Each of these is further differentiated into upper-upper, upper-middle, middle-middle, lower-middle and the lower-working classes.

Class Struggle refers to a state of antagonism or conflict between different classes in the society whose interests may be mutually incompatible or contradictory. According to Marxist theory, class struggle between the proletariat and the bourgeoisie in a capitalist society is inevitable because their class interests are irreconcilable and the contradiction cannot be removed except under socialism.

Classical Liberalism refers to liberal preferences and tendencies during the early phase of capitalist revolution as represented by John Locke, Adam Smith and J.S. Mill. Classical or old liberalism may be summed up in three basic themes: (1) the moral emphasis affirms the natural rights of the individual to life, liberty, property and pursuit of happiness. Justice is based on fair and equal treatment of all individuals whose personal rights are immutable and inviolable and must be protected from infringement of other individuals and the authorities. (2) the economic emphasis calls for economic freedom of the individual from all state-imposed restraints and/or intervention in economic matters. Liberal economists advised that free market, free competition and enlightened self-interest are best regulators of economic activity; and (3) the political emphasis favoured limited government with an night-watchman role, based on contractual consent of the individuals and on free democratic competitive participation within a framework of representative government.

Classless Society is a Marxist formulation which means that in a mature socialist society classes are abolished because differences in the origins of incomes are eliminated. This implies that either all workers have become owners or that all have become wage wage-earners. In a sense both hypotheses are true. Every member of a socialist society has his share in ownership since the mean of production belong to the whole community and everyone at the same time is a wage-earner because all incomes are derived from work.

Clausewits Doctrine refers to the famous dictum that "war is a continuation of diplomacy by other means" or the doctrine of the primacy of the political over the military means as presented by the Prussian general Karl von Clausewits (1780-1831) in his treatise entitled *On* war. If politics has, precedence over war then generals ought to work under the direction of the statesmen.

Coalition is same as an alliance, e.g. military or electoral or parliamentary coalitions. A grand coalition in a parliamentary system means coalescence of all parliamentary parties and groups in support of the government in office.

COCOM is an acronym for the Coordinating Committee for Multilateral Export Controls. It was a semi-official committee made up of the representatives of the Western bloc countries formed in 1950 to monitor, control and prevent the transfer of advanced technology to the Soviet bloc and communist countries. With the end of the cold war it was formally wound up in 1994. It was succeeded by the so-called Wassenaar arrangement, a grouping of 28 developed countries that was inaugurated in Vienna, in 1996. It aims at preventing the transfer of advanced technology to the developing countries.

Code of Civil Procedure (India) was first enacted in 1308 and has since been revised from time to time.

Code of Criminal Procedure (India) was first enacted in 1908 and was entirely revised in 1973.

Codetermination is synonymous with workers* participation in corporate decision-making and management, for instance, the German Workers' Codetermination Act, 1976, gave the employees the right of codetermination and participation both on the Shop-floor level and the decision-making i.e. the board-of-directors level. The same right has been given to workers engaged by public services.

Cohabitation In the where the President of the republic and the National Assembly are elected directly by the people for separate terms and where the President of the Republic has the prerogative of appointing and dismissing the prime minister and his cabinet but where, at the same time, the prime minister and the cabinet are collectively responsible to the National Assembly the President of the Republic may enjoy the prerogative of appointing the ministry so long as his own party controls the majority in the National Assembly. But in case the Presidency and the Assembly are controlled by different parties a working arrangement between the two is arrived at whereby the President or the Republic appoints the nominee of the parliamentary majority as the prime minister and acts like the constitutional monarch of Great Britain.

Cold War as against hot war means a state of neither war nor peace but of endemic tension and fear. The term particularly applies to East-West relations during the period 1946-1991 when the two power-blocs led by the USA and USSR were locked in an ideological and political struggle for supremacy over the world; each bloc lived in constant fear of a sudden by the other; and each used all means available to it except an all out war to achieve its objectives. Cold was follower by *detente* .

Collective Bargaining is a legally recognized democratic right of the trade unions to freely bargain with their employers or employers' association in respect of their wages, hours ox work, service conditions and peaceful settlement of disputes. Failure of collective bargaining may lead either to conciliation or arbitration or strike action.

Collective Goods are those benefits, facilities and services that are useful for the whole community. Collective goods cannot be taken care of by private individuals or the private sector because they are motivated by private gain Since activities like national defence or public education or social services and public utilities have no profit angle therefore they are more effectively managed by the state.

Collective Leadership is an organizational Principle enunciated by Vladimir Lenin for the Communist party and state. Leadership function should nut be performed by a single individual but by a collegium of leaders exercising decision-making authority collectively. For example the politburo of the party or the presidium of parliament or presidium of the council of ministers.

Collective Measures refer to such preventive or punitive or compulsive actions taken by two or more member-states of the United Nations, in conjunction with regional or international organizations, or by the security, Council of the United Nations, to contain a threat to or actual breach of international peace and security in a region or repel the aggression committed by one member-state against another, in accordance with the Charter of the United Nations.

Collective Security. The principle of collective security was formulated by President Woodrow Wilson of the USA as an antidote of power politics and has been operationalized through the Covenant of the League of nations and the charter of the UNO. It means that the security of each member of the community of states is the responsibility of all other states. If one is attacked all others are bound to repel the attacker. Whereas before 1919 states sought their security in alliances and counter-alliances in an eral of an international organization the whole body-politic is responsible for maintaining international security.

Collective Security Organization--CSO had its origin in a five-year collective security agreement signed by the heads of state of the Commonwealth of Independent States (CIS) in Moscow in May 1992. In April 1999 Armenia, Belarus, Kazakhastan, Kyrghyzia, Russia, Tajikistan and the Ukraine signed a protocol extending their collective security pact for another five years. In April 2003 the signatories to the protocol decided to create a permanent collective Security Organization (CSO) which was inaugurated in September of the same year. The CSO is meant to deal with intraregional conflicts and emerging threats to the security of the CIS region. The last meeting of the foreign ministers of the CSO was held in Moscow on 30 November 2005.

Collectivism or collectivist ideologies refer to all economic and political ideologies which subordinate the human individual to the human collective and aim at realizing collective goals through collective (or state) action and centralized planning, management and control. Example are communism, fascism, nazism, syndicalism, guild socialism and authoritarian corporatism.

Colombo Plan for Collective Economic and Social development in Asia and the pacific was launched in 1950 by seven developed member-states of the commonwealth to assist in the socioeconomic development of the poor countries of the region, in the beginning the Plan was conceived for a term of six years. Later it was extended for a number of five-year terms, Then in 1980 it was put on a permanent looting. Now 24 countries participate in this plan. The Headquarters is at Colombo, Sri Lanka.

Colonialism refer to the process or policy of conquest of the economically and militarily weak countries of Asia and Africa during the nineteenth century by the economically and militarily developed countries of tester Europe and converting them into colonies by establishing their direct or indirect rule there with a view to exploiting their human and material resources for the benefit of the colonial powers. Thus colonies became a source of supply of raw materials to the industrialized countries and a captive market for the consumption of their manufactured goods. The distinctive feature of colonialism is economic exploitation of the colonized people. Otherwise, it is a form of imperialism.

Colony (from Latin *colo* = to cultivate the land). Originally a colony was a place where people were brought from another place or country and given land for cultivation. These were called *coloni* (settlers or colonizers). From sixteenth century onwards the term came to be applied to settlements in virgin lands or territories acquired by sovereign countries abroad such as Australia, Canada and New Zealand. During the nineteenth and twentieth centuries the term was used for foreign dependencies of the European empires, such as India, Ceylon, Malaya, Nigeria and Algeria. The process of granting national independence to colonial peoples came to be known as *decolonization*.

Comity of Nations (*Comitas gentium* = international comity) refers to "rules of politeness, convenience and goodwill observed by states in their mutual intercourse without being legally bound by them'' (Oppenneim).

Commissioner for Linguistic Minorities (India). The reorganization of states in India, mainly on the linguistic basis, took place under the states Reorganization Act, 1956*. The Act was framed in accordance with the recommendations of the States Reorganization Commission appointed by the Government of India in 1954. While recommending for the linguistic reorganization of states the Commission had visualized that in the reorganized states certain pockets of linguistic minorities may remain shall require certain constitutional safeguards in respect of the mother tongues. The constitutional safeguards by the commission were incorporated as Articles 350-A and 350-B, in the Constitution of India through the Constitution (Seventh) Amendment Act. 1956 while Article 350-A provides safeguards for provision of facilities for imparting of primary education to the children belonging to linguistic minorities through their mother tongue, Article 350-B (1) provides for the appointment by the President of India of a Special Officer for the Linguistic Minorities to investigate all matters pertaining to the implementation of constitutional safeguards in respect of linguistic minorities and to report to the President upon such matters at such intervals as the President may direct, and the President shall cause all such reports to be laid before the two houses of parliament for debate and its recommendations sent to the governments of concerned state governments and union territories for follow up action. This officer was assigned the role of an investigating agency rather than an administrative machinery for enforcement of the safeguards for the linguistic minorities. The Special Officer for the Linguistic minorities was appointed on 30 July 1957. He submitted his first report in 1958. His office was later renamed as the Commissioner Linguistic Minorities. Up to 2004 the CLM had submitted 38 reports to the Government which have been laid before Parliament and published. The Office of the CLM has been lying vacant since 1977 and his functions are performed by a Deputy Commissioner for Linguistic Minorities. The headquarters of the CLM is in Allahabad, Uttar Pradesh with regional offices in Belgaum (Karnataka), Calcutta (West Bengal) and. Chennai (Tamil Nadu).

Committee on Public Undertakings is a standing committee of Indian parliament meant to scrutinize the reports and accounts of the public undertakings as well as the reports of the comptroller and Auditor-General of India, if any, in this respect. The Committee also oversees the general functioning of these undertakings.

Committee on Subordinate Legislation is a standing committee of Indian Parliament meant to scrutinize and approve the rules, regulations, sub-rules and by-laws formulated by the ministries/ departments of government under rule-making authority delegated by parliament through its acts. It is also known as delegated legislation.

Common Law. The laws of England fall under two categories: (1) written, e.g. acts of parliament, royal charters and proclamations and treaties; and (2) unwritten, e.g. usages and customs including principles or equity. In England Common law is the body of custom rules customs, rules and maxims that evolved daring the Middle Age, have force of law and regarded as binding upon the courts in consequence of long usage and not by reason of parliamentary enactment, The rules of Common law are not found in a codified from but are scattered in the form of judicial precedents (also known as case law). The principle of *stare decisis** requires that legal aspects of judgments delivered by the courts are binding upon courts of equal or lower status if facts are similar. In an era of parliamentary sovereignty Common Law survives by the leave of Parliament, parliament is competent to abolish it but neither the king nor Parliament is competent to create new rules of Common Law.

Common Market is formed by integration of separate markets of contracting countries into a single regional market minus custom duties, tariffs, quotas and other restrictions on trade resulting in economic benefits to all partners are the European common market, the Caribbean Community or the Andean (Community and common market.

Commonwealth of Independent States--CIS is a friendly association of Russia and eleven other independent states which were up to 25 December 1991 constituent republics of the former USSR. Anticipating the collapse of the USSR the heads of state of Belarus, Russia and the Ukraine singed the so-called Minsk Declaration on 8 December 1991 providing for the creation of a Commonwealth of Independent states which shall be open for accession to other countries. On 21 December 1991 a further declaration was signed with eight former republics of the USSR namely Armenia, Azerbaijan, Kazakhastan, Kyrghyzistan, Moldova, Tajikistan, Turkeministan and Uzbekistan which recognized the independence and national sovereignty of the signatories. On 26 December 1991 the USSR Supreme Soviet formally abrogated the 1922 Treaty of Union and thereby dissolved the USSR. Georgia joined the CIS in 1993. The CIS adopted the so-called Minsk Charter, on 22 January 1993. Under it there is a council of heads of state which meets twice a year and a council of heads of government which meets every three months. There is an executive committee to coordinate the activities of the organization The headquarters is at Minsk, Belarus. At a CIS summit held on 18-19 September in Yalta, Ukraine, the Presidents of Russia, Belarus, Kazakhstan and Ukraine signed a treaty visualizing first the creation of a single economic zone of the CIS countries with uniform tariffs and customs and then a free trade are and then an economic community, other countries were minted to accede to the treaty.

Commonwealth of Nations is a free and voluntary association of 55 independent states in Asia, Africa and the Caribbean.

Some of them have retained the status of British dominions* while others were formerly colonies, dependencies or protectorates of the United Kingdom and have their own constitutional heads of state. There is no formal organization or constitution. Its activities are informally governed by the Declaration of Commonwealth Principles adopted in 1971. There is a Commonwealth Secretariat located in London and headed by a Secretary General to coordinate cooperative arrangements among the member-states under the umbrella of the Commonwealth. The Commonwealth Heads of State or Government Meeting (CHOGM) is held every two years in the territory of one of the member-states. It is inaugurated by the British monarch. Its resolutions and recommendations are non-binding upon the participating governments. The political entity which existed as the British Empire from the year 1600 until World War I was rechristened as the British Commonwealth in 1919. It was composed of the dominions which acknowledged the British Crown as their constitutional head. However, with the independence of India and Pakistan in 1947 and their insistence on joining the Commonwealth as independent republics the British Commonwealth was converted into the present Commonwealth of Nations entailing no obligation on the part of its members to acknowledge the British Crown as their constitutional head.

Communal Award (1932) is also known as MacDonald Award, after British Prime Minister Ramsay MacDonald, who, after the conclusion of the second session of the Round Table Conference* on the Indian constitutional problem, made an announcement on 1 December 1931, later endorsed by the two houses of British Parliament, to the effect that "If the communities in India were unable to reach a settlement acceptable to all parties on the communal question. . . . His Majesty's Government were determined that India's constitutional advance should not on that account be frustrated and that they would remove this obstacle by devising and applying themselves a pro visional scheme". The Indian leaders failed to agree among themselves upon a scheme of distribution of seats among different communities in the third session so the RTC. The British Government then unilaterally announced the Communal Award (the scheme of representation of different communities in the legislatures of British India) on 16 August 1932. The Communal Award originally provided for communal quotas in the provincial legislatures only. Separate electorates were provided for Muslims, Sikhs, Indian Christians, Anglo-Indians and resident Europeans. Further, special representation was provided for the Depressed classes (the untouchables) for a period of twenty years. However, M.K. Gandhi went on fast-unto-death against special electorate for the untouchables as he regarded it as a move to separate them from the Hindu community. As a result of a pact signed between B.R. Ambedkar, the leader of the untouchables, and M.K. Gandhi, as the leader of the Indian National Congress, signed in Poona (Poona Pact*) Special electorate for the untouchables was replaced by a scheme of reservation of seats for them in the general constituencies. The Communal Award was amended accordingly Subsequently, the British Government on 24 December 1932 announced that 33.3 per cent of British Indian seats in the Central Legislative Assembly is 11 be allocated to the Muslim community, with these modifications the Communal Award became an integral part of the Government of India Act, 1935, and formed the basis of general elections held in 1937 and 1946.

Communalism is used in two senses. In a positive sense communalism or communitarianism is synonymous with love of the community as against egotism and preference of a communal approach to social problems over an individualistic approach. In a negative sense, which developed in British India communalism or rather religious communalism is synonymous with sectarianism and sectarian discrimination.

Commune designates (1) self-governing municipal ties in medieval France established by royal charters; (2) communal governments established by French revolutionaries in Paris in 1793, 1794 and 1879; (3) territorial units below the cantons in Switzerland; and (4) collectivized agricultural villages in China created in 1958 and abolished in 1979. A commune is also an exclusive settlement whose members opt to live a cooperative and communal life. A *communard* is a member of a commune.

Commune of Paris (1871) was the first Community of the world created by the French workers after their uprising against the bourgeoisie in Paris on 18 March 1871. The Commune was suppressed by the bourgevois regime by the force of arms.

Communism or Marxist-Leninst socialism is an ideology and system which prescribes abolition of private property and enterprise and its replacement by collective (state) ownership of all means of production, distribution and exchange in the society within a centrally planned and managed economy under the dictatorship of a monopolist and omnicompetent communist party.

Communist International/Comintern was an international union of pro-Soviet national communist parties. It was founded in Moscow in 1919. Its activities were guided by the Communist Party of the Soviet Union. It was replaced by the communist Information Bureau (COMINFORM) in 1947.

Communist Manifesto (1848) was a political pamphlet written jointly by Karl Marx (1818-1833) and Friedrich Engels (1820-1895). It declared: ''A spectre is haunting (capitalist) Europe--the spectre of Communism''. The history of all hitherto existing human society is the history of class struggles. The modern capitalist society which succeeded the feudal society is also split into two hostile classes the bourgevoisie and the proletariat whose interests are irreconcilable. The theory of communism may be summed up in a single sentences abolition of private property because it is the root cause of antagonism of capital and wage-labour and the basis of the exploitation of the working class. Justice cannot be established without the common ownership of the means of production. The communists therefore stand for a revolutionary overthrow of the present order. ''The proletarians have nothing to lose except their chains''. They have a world to conquer. The *Manifesto* ended with the slogan: ''workingmen of all countries, unite''.

Communist Party of India-- CPI was founded in 1925. For most time up to World war II it suffered from persecution on the part of the British Indian government for its pro-Soviet leanings. However, when Nazi Germany attacked Russia in 1940 and the USSR joined the Western powers as an ally the ''imperialist'' war became a holy crusade in defence of the communist motherland and the CPI supported the British in their war efforts. After independence it entered electoral politics and gained some seats in national parliament, The Sino-Soviet rift after 1958 had its impact on the international communist movement and the CPI too became divided into a pro-Moscow and a pro-Beijing factions. The 1962 India-China border war intensified internal dissension in the party and in 1964 the pro-Beijng broke away from the CPI to form the Communist Party of India (Marxist). The CPI (M) got a foothold in West Bengal and Kerala states. In the aftermath of the embourgevoisment of the People's Republic of China since 1977 and the collapse of the USSR in 1991 the two parties shed their ideological differences and entered into political collaboration while keeping their separate organizations. Both are partners in the left fronts in West Bengal and Kerala. A third communist outfit in India is the Communist Party of India (Marxist-Leninst) which was formed in 1969. It believes in class struggle and opposes the ''revisionist'' policies of both the CPI and the CPI (M).

Communitarianism is a philosophy that accords supreme importance to community and common good as against individualism and individual self-interest.. It stresses the importance or communities and social responsibility.

Community Development refers to ''processes by which efforts of the people are united with those of the governmental authorities to improve the economic, social and cultural conditions of communities in the life of the nation and enable them to contribute fully to national progress''. The distinctive feature of community development is that a single agency begins to deal with groups of communities on a general or multi-functional basis with the objective of helping them to solve their problems on the basis of self-help and mutual assistance.

Community Development Programme The community development Programme was launched in India on 2 October 1952 with 55 pilot projects with technical assistance from the Ford Foundation of the USA. On 1 April 1958 the countryside was demarcated into community development block with extension officers and village level workers to implement the programme. In 1959 the CDP was transferred to the newly created *panchayati raj* bodies (a system of rural local self-government) in 1969 the CDP was converted into an integrate Rural Development Programme (IRDP) with agricultural production as the main focus of developmental effort.

Comparative Politics is a branch of political science that studies political systems on global, regional, national and local levels but deals particularly with the politics of non-western countries by the application on systems and/or structural-functional or cultural approaches. Of particular interest are problems of nation-building, state-building, political development, political legitimacy and stability and human rights.

Comprador (Spanish for collaborator). A comprador class in the less developed countries of Asia, Africa and Latin America is a local elite (politicians, businessmen and brokers, etc.) which collaborates with foreign governments and multinational corporations to serve its own economic interests at the cost of the national interest.

Comprehensive Test Ban Treaty--CTBT was signed by the five declared nuclear-weapon powers (the USA, Russia, UK, France and China} on 24 September 1996 at the UN headquarters in New York. It will come into force when all the 44 countries known for possessing nuclear capability have signed it. The CTBT failed to get US Senate's approval when it was submitted to its vote on 14 October 1999.

Comptroller and Auditor-General of India is an independent officer of the Indian Union appointed by the President of India under Articles 148-151 of the Indian Constitution. His function is to audit and scrutinize the public accounts of both the union and state governments each year and present his reports to the President of India and state governors which acre then laid before the two houses of Indian Parliament and state legislative assemblies.

Compulsory Voting Australia is the lone democratic country which has prescribed compulsory voting in federal and state elections, After completion of polling each non-voter is given a form to state the reason for abstention. If the stated reason is not considered as valid the non-voter has to pay a prescribed fine.

Concert of Europe was a directorate or consultative forum of great powers created in 1815 for joint management of international political affairs in Europe. It gradually extended its interest to non-European affairs as well. Initially it included Russia, Austria, Prussia, Britain and France. Italy was admitted in 1867. Then China and Japan were invited to take part in its deliberations. It was for the first time that the USA took part in its deliberations over the Moroccan question. The concert ceased to exist by World War I and its role was taken over by the council of the League of Nations in 1919.

Conciliation is one of the methods of pacific settlement of disputes It means referring a dispute to an impartial committee or commission of inquiry which after due investigation of facts and reconciling the conflicting claims formulates proposals for settlement which are non-binding. Parties concerned are free to accept or reject them.

Concordats mean agreements, conventions or treaties A *conçordat* between the Holy See and a Christian state is Christian state an undertaking whereby the offers the Vatican special privilege to manage the churches and benefices within that state and in return the Vatican extends political support to that state and promises non-interference in its internal affairs. In Switzerland *concordats* (inter-cantonal conventions or treaties) were entered into to regulate matters of common concern. The practice was allowed by the federal constitutions of 1848, 1874 and 1999. Article 48 of the Swiss constitution allows the cantons to enter into concordats to create common organizations and institutions to fulfil tasks of regional interest. Such conventions should not be contrary to the law or rights of the Confederation, nor to the rights of other cantons and the Confederation must be notified of such agreements.

Concurrent Majority or the rule of unanimity means that decisions should not be made by numerical majority alone as it may result in the domination of the minority by the majority. As a safeguard, equal weight must be given to the interests as well as the numbers. Each interest should be given a concurrent voice in the making of policy and a veto on its execution.

Condominium means joint rule over a territory by two or more sovereign states whose respective rights and obligations are laid down in a treaty.

Confederation (from Latin *foedus* = pact) is an alliance or association or league of sovereign states created for some specific purpose, e.g. defence against common enemies. Before the adoption of the federal constitution of the USA in 1789 the words confederation and federation had the same meaning. But since the American union differed fundamentally from the earlier confederation in important respects the two terms acquired different meanings. A confederation is not a sovereign state under international law as it is created by a treaty signed by sovereign states. Conversely, a federation or a federal union is a sovereign state under international law as it is created by means of a supreme constitution adopted in the name of the sovereign people of the union which is the result of a merger of separate sovereignties. Similarly the general government of a confederation is neither vested with independent authority nor can it operate directly upon the people of the confederating states. But in a federation both the general and regional governments derive their powers from a supreme constitution and operate directly upon their people in their respective jurisdictions. Finally, a confederation is revocable by its constituents whereas the right to secession is not available to any federating unit nor is the union revocable. Examples are the Swiss Confederation (1296-1848); German Confederation (1867-1878); and American Confederation (1783-1789).

Congress-League Pact (1916) or the "Lucknow Pact" between the Indian National Congress and the All-India Muslim League to launch a joint struggle for the implementation of a scheme of constitutional reforms agreed to by the two organizations in their joint session held in Lucknow in 1916. The main points of the scheme were immediate introduction of self-government; four-fifth members of the provincial legislative assemblies to be elected by the people on the basis of universal adult sufferage; separate electorate for Muslims to continue and one-third of seats in the imperial Legislative Council to be reserved for them, provincial revenues to be separated from Central revenues; provinces to be given full autonomy; fully responsible government to be installed in both centre and provinces; and the council for the Secretary of State for India to be abolished After the War the (Congress-league Scheme was relegated to the background with the radicalization of the Indian National under M.K. Gandhi and the practice of holding annual sessions of the two organizations in the same place was discontinued from 1923.

Conscientious Objection means an objection made by somebody to rendering compulsory military service or performing any other duty which in the opinion and belief of the objector will be contrary to his conscience or religious faith.

Conseil d' Etat (France) or the Council of State is the highest administrative court in the hierarchy of administrative courts in France. It not only hears and disposes of cases brought before it under the administrative law but also advises the government on administrative and legal matters and scrutinizes the drafts of government bills and decrees.

Conseil de l' Entente (The Entente Council) was founded in 1959 with its headquarters in Abidjan, Ivory Coast, to promote to promote economic cooperation among the member-states. The Council signed a Convention of Assistance and Cooperation to further intensify regional cooperation in 1996. It operates through its annual meetings. Members: Benin, Burkina Fasu, Ivory Coast, Niger, and Togo.

Conservatism. In general parlance a conservative is one who tends by temperament to conserve the old and eschew the new. Conservatism, however, means preservation of the existing social status quo and opposition to any sudden or radical change. It is a philosophy of the privileged classes who want to maintain their privileged position and preserve their vested interests. Just as liberalism arose in reaction to feudalism and despotism so was conservatism a response to the excesses of liberalism and radicalism, Conservatism was derived from the French term *conservateur* that was applied to those who advocated the restoration of the prerevolutionary order after the downfall of Napoleon I. The term became a vogue after the publication of Edmund Burke's *Reflections on the Revolution in France* (1790). F.J.C. Hearnshaw in his *Conservatism in England* (1933) summarized the main tenets of conservatism as: reverence of the past; the organic conception of society; communal unity; opposition to revolution; cautious and evolutionary reform; the religious basis of the state; the divine source of legitimate authority; priority of duties to rights; the prime importance of character and integrity; loyalty to superiors and respect for authority; and commonsense, realism practicality.

Consolidated Fund was first instituted in Britain by the Younger Pitt in 1787 as an account with the Bank of England into which all revenues and proceeds of public loans were paid and from which money for public expenditure was withdrawn under authority of Parliament. In India the Consolidated fund is an account maintained with the Reserve Bank of India who are the bankers of the Government of India. Separate consolidated funds are maintained for the Union of India and each of the States of the Union. General revenues are paid into them and no money can be withdrawn except under Parliament's authority. For non-revenue receipts like security deposits a separate public account is maintained withdrawal from which does not require parliamentary authorization.

Conspiracy (from Latin *conspirare* = to plot) is an act of plotting or planning in secret of something to inflict damage upon an individual or groups or government. The term is also used for the plot or plan thus hatched.

Constitution or the fundamental law lays down the structure of government and defines the powers, functions and inter-relationships of the different organs of the government. Most democratic constitutions also include a bill of rights, A constitution is also defined as that primary law from which all secondary laws are derived.

Constitutional Amendment refers to a modification in the text of a constitution or the fundamental law by way of alteration, addition or deletion through the legal procedure laid down by the constitutional law. Different methods of amendment are adopted in different countries.

Constitutional Autocracy refers to system of government which although neither representative of nor responsible to the people over whom it rule is nevertheless bound to operate in accordance with the law as law as laid down by the supreme authority. For example the colonial administration in British India.

Constitutional Bureaucracy means a system of bureaucratic government such that prevailed in British India which is bound to act in accordance with the laws, rules, regulations and directions as laid down by colonial authorities.

Constitutional Democracy is a democratic society where rule of law and civil liberty prevail and where powers and jurisdictions of the governmental authorities are defined and delimited by a constitution and the government is accountable under the law.

Constitutional Dictatorship is synonymous with constitutional emergency regime which is established under a proclamation of emergency for a temporary period to deal with a crisis or emergency situation. It is terminated as soon as the crisis is overcome. It is *constitutional* because it is proclaimed under constitutional provisions and it is dictatorship because the legislative and executive authorities are vested with extraordinary powers free from normal constitutional restraints.

Constitutional Monarchy is a system of government where monarchy is limited by the customs, conventions and the law of the constitution and is bound to act only in accordance with the advice given by a popular ministry.

Constitutional Review. see Judicial Review.

Constitutionalism or constitutional government is a system in which powers of the government are defined and limited by a set of constitutional rules, written or unwritten. Constitutionalism implies supremacy of regular law as opposed to the arbitrary will of the rulers. The objective is to ensure rule of law, limited and responsible government and civil liberties. Some devices of constitutionalism are a written and supreme constitution, federalism, internal separation of powers and checks and balances, an independent and impartial judiciary and a constitutionally guaranteed bill of rights.

Constituent Assembly is the assembly or body which is elected by the vote of a people to frame a constitution or fundamental law of their state. The function of such a body is to adopt and enact a constitutional document for the country in the name of the sovereign people. The Constituent Assembly of India was elected indirectly from the legislative assemblies of the provinces in 1946 and finished its work of constitution-making on 26 November 1949.

Constituent Power means the power of making, amending or repealing a constitution or fundamental law through the prescribed legal procedure. The constituent power may be exercised by a constitutional convention or a constituent assembly or by a parliament or by parliament and electorate together i.e. a constitutional amendment is approved by parliament and ratified by the people in a national referendum.

Consul/Consular Service. The consular service is a branch of diplomatic service which is specifically concerned with the conduct of commercial relations with foreign countries. Consuls possess neither the diplomatic status nor enjoy the diplomatic immunities unless specifically provided for in a bilateral treaty. A consul cannot start his work unless granted an exequatur* by the host country. Sometimes an honorary consul is appointed from among the national of the host country. The recognized consular ranks are consul-general, consul, vice-consul and consular agent. The difference of rank does not have an impact on the status or privileges of a consul. Their privileges and immunities have been codified under the Vienna Convention on Consular Relations, 1963. The residence/office of a consul/consul-general is called a consulate/consulate-general akin to a diplomatic corps a consular corps is also organized in the port or commercial centre of a host country composed of all consular functionaries stationed there. It is headed by the highest-ranking and senior-most consul who is called the dean of the consular corps. He is the guardian of the privileges and immunities of the consular staff and represents on their behalf to the authorities of the host government. The Vienna Convention on Consular Relations allows the states to expand or modify its provisions by mutual consent.

Consular Exequatur is a permit granted by a host state to a consular officer of another state allowing him to engage in his consular functions. Pending grant of an exequatur the concerned officer may be allowed to function temporarily, An exequatur may be denied or withdrawn anytime.

Consular Patent is a document issued by the appointing government confirming that a particular person is appointed to a particular consular post and containing the details about the post and the incumbent, the consular district to which assigned and the seat of the consulate. A consular patent is transmitted to the host government through diplomatic channels.

Consular Shield is an emblem displayed at the entrance of a consulate containing the national emblem of the state represented and the name of the consulate.

Consultative Committees of Parliament (India) were created by the Government of India in 1954 as Informal consultative Committees of Parliament, then 25 in number. They are quite distinct from parliamentary committees. Their members are nominated by political parties represented in parliament but the power to convene their meetings and fix the duration of the meetings is vested in the concerned ministers. The word ''informal'' was dropped from their designation by the Government of India in April 1969.

Containment describes the general trend of American foreign policy towards the former USSR in particular and communism and communist movements in general. In the post-world War II era the American administration perceived that Soviet power is inherently expansive. Its expansionist drive is buttressed by its communist ideology. Since Soviet Communism was perceived as a threat to the freedom of the non-communist world the Americans formulated and pursued a policy of "containing" Soviet power within the lines dividing the free world from the communist world. The result was the cold war between the Soviet and Western power-blocs that persisted during 1947-1991.

Contingency Fund of India was created by an Act of Parliament into which are paid from time such sums as are determined by the said Act to enable the government to take advances from this fund to meet unforeseen expenditures pending necessary appropriation by the Parliament.

Contraband of War are under international law prohibited goods that cannot be exported by the neutral states to any one of the belligerent in a war, because they can be used for military purposes. Countries at war also issue proclamations listing items which they regard as transit.

Convention on Elimination of the Threat of Nuclear Terrorism was sponsored by Russia and approved by the UN General assembly in April 2005. It was to come into force after requisite ratification by 122 states.

Conventional Forces in Europe Treaty--CFE (1990) was signed between the member-states of the NATO and member-states of the former Warsaw Treaty Organization in 1990 for drastic reduction of conventional weapons and war material in Europe; was revised in 1991 after the collapse of the USSR; came into force in 1992 after ratification by the CSCE*. The signing of the CFE along with the signature of the Charter of Paris for a New Europe by the necessary of the CSCE marked the final end of the cold war in Europe.

Conventions of the Constitution. Conventions are the unwritten principles or practices surrounding a constitution, The British Constitution is distinguished by the fact it is composed largely of unwritten understandings which do not have the status of law nor they are enforceable through courts law. Nevertheless they are regarded as fundamental in the working of the constitution so much so that if any one of the fundamental conventions is broken the constitution itself breaks down. They are observed equally by the Crown, Parliament and parties. Their sanction lies in the force of habit and tradition, the force of public opinion, and their practical necessity.

Corporation was defined by Chief Justice John Marshall of the USA in 1819 as "...an artificial being, invisible, intangible, and existing in the contemplation of the law. Being the mere creation of law, it possesses only those properties which the charter of its creation confers upon it, either expressly or incidental to its existence".

Corporatism. A corporatist, as distinguished from a pluralist, regime is one in which government and private sector institutions are interlocked. The state intermediates between competing social interests to ensure social harmony and bring about desired policy outcomes. This is known as liberal or societal corporatism. Cooptation of organized interest groups in the policy-making process is a characteristic of the political economies of advanced industrial democracies, Conversely, totalitarian or state corporatism is associated with Fascist regimes and may be defined as "a system of interest representation in which constituent units are organized into a limited number of singular, compulsory, non-competitive, hierarchically ordered and functionally differentiated categories, recognized or licensed (if not created) by the state and granted a deliberate representational monopoly within their respective categories in exchange for observing certain controls on their selection of leaders and articulation of demands and supports" (Philippe C. Schmitter).

Cosmopolitanism (from Greek *Cosmopolis* = world city) is opposite of nationalism or rather repudiation of one's own patriotism, national loyalty and culture in favour of "universal brotherhood" or "unity of mankind". Thus a cosmopolitan person would transcend national boundaries and call himself the ''citizen of the world''.

Council for Mutual Economic Cooperation --COMECON was an economic community of the Soviet bloc countries created in 1949 in Moscow as a counterpart of the Marshall Plan* in Western Europe. It integrated the socialist economies of the USSR, Bulgaria, Poland, Romania and Albania. Albania broke away in 1961. Mongolia joined in 1962 and Cuba in 1972. With the disintegration of the Soviet bloc the COMECON was dissolved in 1991.

Council of Europe is an intergovernmental political organization of 45 European nations founded under a statute signed by the founding countries on 5 May 1949 in London. Its headquarters is in Strasbourg, France. It should not be confounded with the European Council (Council of Ministers) of the European Union*.

Counsel is an abbreviation of Counsellor. In England a counsel or counsellor is a barrister whose duty is to give advice on matters of law and to manage causes for his clients.

Countervailing Duty is an import duty imposed to protect the domestic business and industry against dumping and unfair competition.

Countervailing Power means that if one sector of the national economy accumulates preponderant power it may be counterbalanced by the power of the other sectors so that fair competition is maintained and the public saved from exploitation.

Coup d' Etat (French for ''political push'') is forcible takeover of a civilian government by a military dictator or junta. It differs from a political revolution in that it results merely in a change of government personnel and not in the overturn of the political system.

Court of First Instance means a court having original jurisdiction; the court that first considers a case or a trial court.

Court-Martial is a tribunal occasionally constituted by the military authorities for trial of members of the armed forces for committing offences affecting discipline in the ranks of the armed forces, for example mutiny, desertion, insubordination, and non-compliance with orders, etc.

Covenant of the League of Nations. The Covenant or the legal instrument constituting the League of Nations as an instrument of collective security was conceived and drafted by woodrow Wilson. It became an integral part of the Treaty of Versailles* signed in 1919. In place of prevailing power-politics and state of nature an international organization would be responsible for maintaining international peace and collective security by promoting disarmament, pacific settlement of international disputes, organizing collective measures against aggressors, and providing collective guarantees for national independence and territorial integrity of all member-states. The central defect of the Covenant lay in the fact that it placed the responsibility of taking collective measures against aggressors and peace-breakers on individual member-states represented in the Assembly of the League rather than on the great powers as represented in the Council of League who alone could enforce collective measures and maintain collective security.

Crimean War (1854-56) was fought jointly by Britain, France and Turkey to stop Russian advance towards Turkey and the Mediterranean. The war was ended by the Treaty of Paris (1856) which neutralized the Black Sea and obligated the signatories to respect the national independence and territorial integrity of Turkey.

Criminal Investigation Department--CID (India) was created as a department of Central and Provincial governments in British India to investigate criminal activities but more particularly to keep an eye on nationalist activities and political workers. After 1947 the central CID was converted into the Intelligence Bureau* (IB) while provincial CID's were retained with the same functions as under colonial rule.

Cripps Mission refers to the mission of Sir Stafford Crpps, a member of British Parliament, who was sent to India with constitutional proposals for promised transfer of power to Indian hands after World war II. He arrived in New Delhi on 22 March 1942. By 12 April negotiations broke down as the Indian National Congress insisted on immediate transfer of power. British callousness forced the Congress to pass the "(Quit India" resolution on 9 August 1942.

Crown in the UK political system is equivalent of the executive or executive state (as against Parliament and the judiciary). The Crown is a composed of the Sovereign* (reigning king or queen), the departments of state headed by ministers of the Crown, regional executives of Wales, Scotland and Northern Ireland, the armed forces of the Crown, and the civil services of the Crown including the regional civil services. The functioning of the Crown is governed by the conventions of parliamentary sovereignty and ministerial responsibility.

Crown Privilege is the privilege of the ministers and civil servants of the Crown during wartime (recognized by the courts) to refuse to produce a document before the court as evidence on the ground that public interest requires secrecy. However, in peace-time a judge is entitled to examine the withheld document in private to satisfy himself as to the veracity of the official claim to secrecy.

Crusades (crusade = taking the cross i.e. waging holy war) were military campaigns by the Christians of Europe under the leadership of the Church undertaken successively from the eleventh century down to the thirteenth century to wrest the control of the Holy Land (Palestine) from the Muslims. The first crusade was launched in 1095 by Pope urban II. Sometimes they regained Palestire and sometimes lost it. The crusaders were finally defeated by the Muslims during the thirteenth century. The term *Crusade* is also applied to militant struggle against some evil, or against bad people or bad institutions.

Cuban Revolution (1958) refers to the coming to power in Cuba of Fidel Castro (born 1906) in 1958 after overthrowing the longtime pro-American regime of dictator Fulgencio Batista. He denounced American imperialism in Latin America, abolished private property and established a communist system, confiscated foreign enterprises and made an alliance with the former USSR. Castro survived the CIA-Sponsored by of Pigs expedition by anti-Castro Cubans in 1961 and the Cuban Missile Crisis of 1962. How are despite the disappearance of the USSR and the American boycott and sanctions Castro was still in the saddle in 2005.

Cultural Pluralism is the opposite of cultural assimilation, A policy of cultural pluralism is directed towards preservation of ethnic, cultural, religious and linguistic diversities in a plural society and recognizing cultural autonomy of all minority groups.

Cultural Relativism is the opposite of ethnocentrism. The concept is derived from Melville Herskovits' dictum that "truth, goodness and beauty had as many manifestations as there were cultures". There is no universal culture and there are no universal norms and values. Therefore cultures of different societies should be studied objectively without applying the culture of any given society as the standard of judging other societies.

Cultural Revolution was launched by Mao Ze Dong, Chairman of the Communist Party of China in 1966 with the help of the Red Guards to eliminate bourgevois elements from the Chinese Party and state. The movement was aimed against Mao's opponents. It came to an end with Deng Xio Ping's coming to power in 1977.

Cyprus Problem. Cyprus is an island situated in the eastern Mediterranean Sea about 100 kilometers from Turkey. Its area is 9,251 sqkms. It is inhabited by Greek and Turkish communities. The island was conquered by Turkey in 1571. It was ceded by Turkey to Great Britain at the Congress of Berlin in 1878 Britain annexed it as a Crown colony in 1914. Under British rule the Greeks started a violent movement demanding merger of the island with Greece. In response the Turks demanded its partition into Greek and Turkish territories. Negotiations between Britain, Greece and Turkey were started in 1955 Settle the status of Cyprus. An agreement was reached in 1959 over granting independence to Cyprus in 1960 and the terms of Cypriot constitution. The treaties signed among the parties precluded both merger and partition. Cyprus became an independent republic on 16 August 1960. The Greek community again tried to stage a military ,coup for enosis (merger) of Cyprus with Greece. Exercising her right to protect the Turkish minority under the treaty of 1959, Turkey landed its forces on the island on 20 July 1974 and occupied nearly 30 per cent of northern Cyprus. In 1983 the Turkish community declared its independent Turkish Republic of Northern Cyprus. Negotiations for reunification of the two parts were started under the auspices of the UN in 1997. In 2004 Northern Cyprus became a member of the European Union.

D

Dalit (Sanskrit for the oppressed) is applied to members of the former untouchable castes in India which were categorized as the Depressed Classes under the Government of India Acts, 1913 and 1935, and as the Scheduled Castes under the Constitution of the Indian Republic. They are informally called *dalit* because in the past they were subjected to oppression, discrimination and exploitation at the hands of the upper castes. M. K. Gandhi christened them as *harijan* (the progeny of God).

Dandi March (1930). Also known as salt *Satyagraha,* the Dandi March was started by M. K. Gandhi along with his associates on 12 March 1930 from Ahmedabad and traversing some 388 kilometers of the route reached Dandi village on the Gujarat coast on 6 April. There taking a lump of dried salt from the beach (the making of salt by private individuals was prohibited by the salt Act 1882 he symbolically broke the law and started the civil disobedience movement against the British Empire the second since 1922. The Dandi march was reenacted by the India National Congress in April 2005 to communicated the salt Satyagraha.

De Facto/De Jure Government. A de facto (in fact) government is one which has come to power as a result of a *coup_* d' *etat* or a revolution. The same government becomes a de *jure* (in law) or legal government when other states recognize it as legitimate government.

De Facto/De Jure **Recognition.** Under international law de facto recognition of a government implies its temporary recognition as an existing fact. *De jure* recognition is incumbent on the permanence of the actual authority and its ability to discharge international obligations. Thus de *facto* recognition is a transitional phase before *de jure* or legal recognition is accorded which implies establishment of diplomatic relations with the government so recognized.

Declaration of Independence (1776) was a document signed by the leaders of thirteen British colonies of north America declaring their independence of Great Britain on the basis of their natural right to self-government and the right to rebel against unjust government.

Declaration of Rights (1689) was document presented by the Convention Parliament of England to William of Orange and his wife Mary containing terms and conditions on which the English Crown was to be conferred on them. Both accepted these terms and were installed as king and queen of England. Thereupon the Declaration was passed by Parliament, with minor changes, as the Bill of Rights*. The Bill of Rights of 1689 along with the Act of Settlement of 1703 became the legal basis of constitutional monarchy in England.

Declaration of Rights of Man and Citizen (1789) was passed by the National Assembly of Revolutionary France on 27 august 1789. Just as the Bill of Rights (1689) was a manifestation of constitutional revolution in England so was the French Declaration a manifestation of the democratic revolution in France. The Declaration is rooted in the philosophy of natural rights and declares the fundamental rights and liberties of the citizens as eternal, inalienable and inviolable. Since 1789 the Declaration has been an integral part of all French constitutions including the present constitution of the Fifth Republic adopted in 1958.

Declaration of War is a formality prescribed by classical international law before a state could exercise its sovereign right of resort to use of force to restitute its national rights or enforce its legitimate claims. Such a declaration ought to be issued by the constitutional authority of a state e.g. The head of the state or national parliament. The effect of such declaration is that the state of peace between the parties is replaced by a state of belligerency and all belligerents become bound by the rules of international law of war. A war is halted by a cease-fire, a truce or an armistice and terminated by the signing of a peace treaty.

Decree means either (1) a decision or order of a judge made in pursuance of a judgment delivered by him in a case; or (2) a legal instrument, as a counterpart of a parliamentary act, issued by executive authorities having the force of law

Deed refers to an instrument whether in writing or in containing terms of an agreement between parties able to contract, duly signed, sealed and delivered, e.g. a sale deed or a lease deed.

Defence of India Act. The first DIA, closely following the pattern of the British Defence of the Realm act, was passed in 1915 to deal with emergency arising out of World War I. The second Defence of India Act was passed in 1939 after the outbreak of World war II. The third DIA was passed in 1962 to deal with emergency arising out of India-China border-war. The fourth DIA was passed in 1971 after the outbreak of India -Pakistan war. It was amended in 1975 and lapsed in 1977.

Deficit Financing is an attempt on the part of government to spend more than its total revenue in all forms. It is only governments that can deficit-finance and spend resources they do not command because it is their prerogative to create money either directly or through the central bank. As money is accepted in exchange of goods and services governments can obtain for themselves all kinds of goods and services in exchange of created money. Deficit financing is used as an anti-cyclycal measure. It is also called *compensatory finance* or *pump* priming to stimulate demand and inject purchasing power into the economy. DF as a part of monetary policy was first advocates by John Maynard Keynes in his *The General Theory of Employment, Interest and Money* (1936). However, in India for some time DF was resorted to not as a temporary measure a to overcome recession and unemployment arising out of a cyclical crisis but as a means to finance development plans. Such DF represents an invisible tax on the public and leads to hyperinflation.

Delegated Legislation means rule-making power delegated in an act of parliament to the executive to give effect to the aims and objectives of that Act. Also called subordinate legislation.

Demarché is a diplomatic move undertaken by a state in relation to another state, conveyed by means of a diplomatic note, a memorandum, or a statement or the like to lodge a protest or demand some action or make some proposal. A demarche can be made in full observance of principles of international law.

Democracy means rule by the *demos* (people) or in the words of Abraham Lincoln " government of the people, for the people, and by the people". The essentials of democracy are: popular sovereignty, representative and responsible government, civil liberties and rule of law.

----, Basic was a political system devised by the martial-law regime of General Ayub Khan in Pakistan in 1958 as an alternative to the existing system of parliamentary democracy*. It provided for limited and controlled political participation of the through a hierarchy of councils running from the bottom to the top. At the base were the Union Councils (local councils) for which one Basic Democrat (member) was elected for each one thousand persons, Above it were the *thana* (police circle) and *tahsil* (revenue subdivision) councils composed of chairmen of the Union Councils and an equal number of official members appointed by the government. Above them Were the District Councils composed of one-halt civil servants and one-half Basic Democrats appointed by the divisional commissioners. Above them were the Divisional Councils composed in a manner similar, the district councils. The first elections were held in December 1959 and January 1960. With the promulgation of a new constitution prepared under ayub Khan's direction in 1962 these councils were made the vehicles for the election of the National Assembly and the Provincial Legislative assemblies. After the collapse of military rule in 1971 a new democratic constituuion was adopted which replaced basic democracy with parliamentary democracy.

----, Bourgevois or capitalist democracy is, in the Marxist view, not truly representative of the working class. All liberal democracies had held to be bourgevois democracies as they are controlled by the bourgevoisie and serve their class interests.

----, Consociational is an alternative to majoritarian democracy, Consociation means bringing about consensus. Consociational model is based on the belief that policies should not be decided by numerical majorities but by bargaining and consensus among the different communities, classes and interests for greater legitimacy. It stresses mutual accommodation and toleration as against competition and conflict. The examples are Austria. Finland and Switzerland.

----, Direct is the opposite of indirect or representative democracy. It means direct participation of the people in legislation and administration through initiative, referendum and recall. Director democracy was found in the ancient Greek city states. In modern times direct democracy prevails in the communes of Switzerland and some cities of New England in the USA. For most territorial states indirect or representative democracy is the rule.

----, Guided or tutelary democracy has been advocated by many post-colonial Asian and African countries on the ground that the native people were not prepared for running western-style democracy. They therefore needed a system of participation guided and controlled by the ruling elite.

The examples are Turkey under·Mustafa Kamal, Egypt under Jamal Abdun Nasir, Indonesia under Ahmed Sukarno and Pakistan under Ayub Khan.

----, **Parliamentary** is a system of representative and responsible government. The electorate elects a parliament, then the parliamentary majority forms the government and the parliamentary minority assumes the role of a constitutional opposition for the time-being. The government or ministry remains so long as the parliamentary majority does not withdraw its support and confidence in the ministry. The legislative and executive and legislative powers are fused and placed in the same hands.

----, **Pluralist** is opposite of majoritarian democracy. In a plural society diverse competing groups, communities, classes and interests should be provided a share in political power.

----, **Presidential** is the opposite of parliamentary form of democracy. If parliamentary democracy is based on the principle of fusion of legislative and executive powers presidential democracy is based on separation of the two powers. Thus a directly elected congress in the USA is the principal legislative organ while a directly elected president of the USA is the head of the administration. Both organs work together in a system of checks and balances but none can remove the other during its term of office.

----, **Socialist** is the opposite of bourgevois democracy. In the Marxist view if bourgevois democracy is marked by the dictatorship of the bourgevoisie the socialist democracy is workers' democracy organized, guided and controlled by their vanguard-- the communist party.

Democratic Centralism is a Leninst principle for the functioning of soviet-style communist parties and state. The *democratic* in this term means that members are free to express themselves so long as a decision is not taken by the majority. Once a decision is taken the minority must submit to the will of the majority. *Centralism* means strict subordination of the lower bodies to higher bodies and whole-hearted compliance with directions of the central authorities.

Denizen. In Britain a foreign-born person can be granted denizenship by letters of denization granted by the Crown through the home secretary. A denizen's status is midway between an alien and a natural-born or naturalized subject with lesser privileges.

Departmentally-Related Standing Committees (India) Modeled after the subject-related select committees of British Parliament, a set of 17 Departmentally-related Standing Committees were created on 8 April 1993. The jurisdiction of each of these committees covers one or more of ministries/ departments of the Government of India. Each committee is composed of not more than 45 members (30 nominated by the Lok Sabha Speaker from among the members of the Lok Sabha and fifteen nominated by the chairperson of the Rajya Sabha from among the members of the Rajya Sabha in proportion to strength of different political parties in the two houses). These committees are constituted for one year. Their function is to consider and report on the demands for grants of the related ministries, to undertake detailed scrutiny of the bills referred to them by the Speaker of the Lok Sabha or the Chairperson of the Rajya Sabha, after the first reading and to consider the annual reports of the related ministries/ departments and their long-term policies and programmes. These committees generally operate in a non-partisan manner, frame their reports by consensus with individual members having a right to append a note of dissent. However, these committees are barred from meddling in the day-to-day administration of the ministries/departments. Their reports are merely recommendatory in nature. The government may or may not accept their recommendations or amend them in the consideration stage of a bill in the full house.

Dependency Theory deals with conditions of political dependence and socioeconomic underdevelopment in the underdeveloped countries of Asia, Africa and Latin America, although there is neither an authoritative nor a coherent theory of dependence the dependency theorists generally hold that poverty and underdevelopment of these countries is not self-inflicted but results from their dependence upon the economies of the developed countries.

Depositary State or depositary intergovernmental organization is the state or IGO which keeps in safe custody the original document of a treaty or agreement or any other instrument as agreed to between the signatories. For example, the USA, Russia and Britain are the depositary states of the Nuclear Non-Proliferation Treaty (NPT). The depositary is responsible for safekeeping the document, for issuing its certified copies, for getting it registered with the UN Secretariat, and for notifying any occurrences or communications received relating to the document.

Despotism means "any state of affairs where law has disappeared and where the particular will as such, whether of a dictator or a mob, counts as law or rather takes the place of law" (F.W.G. Hegel), A despot is one who tramples upon the law and whose will is unrestrained by constitutional checks and the public opinion.

Detént (from French *detendre* = relaxation of the bow string after the release of the arrow). In general detente refers to relaxation of tension or reduction of conflict between two or more groups. In international relations the term was used vaguely to describe the thaw in east-west Cold War during the period 1962-70 as symbolized by the resolution of the Cuban missile crisis in 1962; the signing of the Partial Test Ban Treaty* in 1963, and of the Nuclear Nonproliferation Treaty in 1968, the convening of the European security conference in Helsinki in 1970; the Four-Power agreement recognizing the divided status of Berlin in 1971, and West German peace treaties signed with the former USSR, Poland

and east Germany recognizing the postwar borders *Detente* became a vogue to describe the particular phase in east-west relations during the period 1969-1991 when both the superpowers--the USA and USSR--realized the futility of continuing the cold War confrontation in an era of nuclear statement and agreed to resolve their disputes by means of negotiations, compromises and mutual accommodation of each other's interests. *Detente* in this particular sense marks an intermediate stage between the Cold War and full-fledged peaceful coexistence. It was a triangular process between the USA USSR and communist China. The process led to the end of the Cold War as symbolized by the peace settlement in Vietnam in 1974; the signing of the Final Act of the Helsinki conference in 1975; the strategic arms limitation treaties, reunification of Germany and the collapse of the USSR.

Deterrence is capability to prevent an enemy from attacking. Nuclear deterrence means the capability of the nuclear weapons to deter their possessors from launching a first strike because of the near certainty that a second strike by the attacked against; the attacker will result in the mutual destruction of both. Hence nuclear weapons are not to be used on the battlefield but to be Kept in store as a deterrent.

Devaluation/Revaluation. Devaluation of a national currency is effected when its capacity to purchase foreign currencies needed to finance its imports declines either because of inflation at home or deflation abroad. Conversely revaluation is effected when the value of the national currency rises in relation to foreign currencies because of the rising demand for its goods and commodities in foreign markets.

Developing Countries are the poor and backward countries or Asia, Africa and Latin America. They are also described as underdeveloped or less developed and the poorest among them are called the least developed. The developing countries are collectively designated as the *South**. They stand in contract with the developed countries, i.e. the industrialized nations of north America, Europe, Australia, New Zealand, japan and china, They are collectively Known as the *North**.

Developing Countries or underdeveloped countries is a euphemism for the poor and backward countries of Asia, Africa and Latin America in relation to the developed and rich countries belonging to the OECD*., OPEC*, and the CIS*. Developing countries are categorized as the *newly* industrializing countries (NIC's), like India, China, Taiwan, South Korea, Brazil and Mexico; the *developing countries* (DC's), i.e. most of the bigger and medium countries of Asia, Africa and Latin America; and the *least developed* countries (LDC's), i.e. the resourceless minstates or island states like Bangladesh, Burma, Maldives, Madgascar and Bolivia.

Devolution is used to describe the process of delegation or transfer of power from the centre of a unitary state or union to its local units.

Dialectical Materialism (materialism of enlightened dialectics of idealism) is a philosophical method formulated by Karl Marx to explain the process of social development. Social change occurs not from the interplay of ideas but from dialectical interplay of material forces.

Diaspora (Greek *dia* = through + *speirein* = to scatter) means both the scattering of the Jews in different countries as well as the communities thus scattered; the Jewish communities living outside the present-day Israel; in general members of any nation scattered abroad.

Dictatorship is opposite of constitutionalism and democracy. It covers all non-democratic forms of government. Alternative terms are autocracy, authoritarianism, despotism and patrimonialism.

Diego Garcia is a coral island in the Indian Ocean discovered in 1832 by a Portugese seafarer of that name. It is the largest among the 52 islands of the Chagos archipelago. It came under British control during the Napoleonic Wars and was governed from Mauritius. It now forms part of the British

Indian Territory. In December 1966 the USA and the UK concluded a 50-year treaty to build and jointly operate a strategic communications base on this island which became functional in 1971. The strategic importance of the island lies in the fact that it can be used as a launching pad for military interventions in the nearby regions.

Diplomacy (from Greek diploma = folded writing or document), Narrowly conceived diplomacy is the art and science of conducting negotiations and concluding treaties with foreign countries. Foreign offices and diplomatic services are meant to maintain diplomatic relations with other countries and achieve the foreign policy objectives. Broadly conceived diplomacy covers the whole gamut of the formulation and operationalization of foreign policy of a country. Thus we speak of American, European, Russian or British diplomacy.

Diplomatic Corps is the whole body of diplomatic representatives: ambassadors, ministers, papal nuncios and internuncios, and *charges d affaires* accredited to a given country. It is an informal conventional body and has no formal political organization or formal legal status. The corps assembles usually on ceremonial occasions. It is headed in Christian countries by the papal nuncio and in the non-Christian countries by the senior-most diplomat. He is called the doyen of the diplomatic corps.

Diplomatic Credentials or a *letter of credence* is signed by the head of state of a country accrediting the ambassador or minister plenipotentiary or envoy extraordinary of his country to another country. Th credentials are formally presented to the head of state of the host country in an official ceremony.

Diplomatic Privileges and Immunities are derived from the customary international law to enable the diplomatic personnel to perform their functions freely and fearlessly. They have been codified in the Vienna Convention on Diplomatic Relations, 1961. They include: inviolability of the premises of a diplomatic mission; immunity from local criminal jurisdiction; inviolability of diplomatic correspondence and records; immunity from local taxation; freedom of communication with home government and other diplomatic missions of the home country and freedom to hoist the national flage of the home country on the buildings of the diplomatic mission and display it on diplomatic vehicles, etc.

Diplomatic Protocol sums up the rules, customs, usages, conventions, and ceremonials which are observed voluntarily by all states in the conduct of diplomatic and inter-state relations. For instance manner of receiving visiting heads of states and order of precedence of the diplomatic envoys or proper words to address the different ranks.

Diplomatic Ranks. Under the Vienna Convention on Relations the heads of diplomatic missions have been placed into three categories:

1. ambassadors, nuncios and other heads of equivalent rank accredited to the head of state of the host country;
2. envoys, ministers and inter-nuncios accredited to the heads or state of the host country; and
3. *charges d' affaires* accredited to the foreign offices of the host country.

Except in matter of order of precedence and diplomatic etiquette no differential treatment is given to the heads of mission by virtue of their category.

An ambassador or a high commissioner or a papal nuncio is the highest ranging diplomatic functionary. Ministers rank below the ambassadors and are exchanged between countries whose relations are strained or who do not give much importance to their relations. A minister is officially either an envoy *extraordinary* or a minister plenipotentiary. The official residence of an ambassador is called an embassy, that of a high commissioner as a *high commission* while that of a minister is called a *legation,* A charge d' affaires is accredited to the foreign office rather than the head of the host country.

However in the absence of an ambassador or minister a *charge d' affaires* may perform his duties temporarily.

Diplomatics is a science of scrutiny of diplomatic papers and records while diplomatic history chronicles past happenings in interstate relations.

Direct Action is opposite of constitutional, legal or parliamentary action. In worker-owner disputes when normal methods of conciliation, mediation, arbitration and collective bargaining fail to resolve disputes workers resort to direct *action* which is synonymous with pressure or agitational politics. For instance, workers go on strike or sit in or demonstrate or siege the management to press their demands, similarly, in national politics direct action is justified when constitutional means for redressal of grievance prove ineffective. Direct action may be either violent or non-violent for instance, passive resistance, non-cooperation and civil disobedience, etc.. Gandhian satyagrah, is a form of direct action.

Dirigisme is a French term denoting a policy of state initiative, and state undertaking of developmental activities to ensure the health and stability of the national economy.

Disturbed Areas (Special Courts) Act, 1976 (India) was passed by Indian Parliament to enable the state governments to declare By a notification in the official gazette any area/ areas within that state where there was or there is extensive disturbance of public peace and tranquility by reason of differences or disputes between members of different religious, racial, linguistic or regional groups or castes or communities as *disturbed areas* for a period specified in that notification and may constitute any number of special courts for the speedy trial of persons prosecuted for committing offences/ in that area/areas. The special court would consist of a single judge appointed by the High Court upon the request of the state government.

Dollar Diplomacy is a term used to describe the American policy of seeking economic and political hegemony over Latin

America and then in China during the early twentieth century through aid, trade credit and investments, Latin Americans called it "Yankee imperialism" (Yankee or *yanqui* being an inhabitant of North America).

Domestic Policy or public policy is the sum total of all public objectives and the instruments to achieve such objectives which a government formulates to protect and promote public interest in the domestic sphere.

Dominion/Dominion Status. A dominion is laterally a territory possessed by a sovereign ruler or state. More specifically, it is the designation of Australia, Canada and New Zealand which were colonized by the people of British descent and were parts of the former British Empire. The term was first used in the British North America Act, 1867, to designate the union of the British-governed provinces of Ontario, Quebec, Nova Scotia, and new Brunswick under a nominated governor-general, a nominated senate and an elected house of commons. The term dominion was preferred to *kingdom* as it could offend the sensibilities of the North Americans who were staunchly anti-monarchist. New Zealand was given this designation in 1307. Australia got the designation of a. Commonwealth under the Commonwealth of Australia Act, 1900, but it is also a Dominion de *facto.* Besides these white ex-colonies of the British Empire,, India and Pakistan were granted Independence in 1947 as dominions and Ceylon (now Sri Lanka) became a dominion in 1348. The dominion status implies that the concerned country acknowledge the British Crown as its constitutional head while enjoying full self-government in internal and external affairs. In 2005 some sixteen member-states of the Commonwealth of Nations* acknowledges the British Crown as their constitutional head and carried the designation of dominion.

Dominion of India. The designation of India and Pakistan as dominions in the Indian independence Act, 1947, was a parting gift of the British government to Indian nationalists. In both dominions provisional constitutional orders were passed to make necessary modifications in the Government of India Act, 1935, which remained in force in both the countries until the commencement of the republican constitution in India on 26 January 1950 and the commencement of the republican constitution in Pakistan in 1958. The British-nominated governors-general were then replaced by elected presidents.

Domino Effect (from dominoes, the docile birds which fall spontaneously if one of the flock is shot down) refers to the reasoning of American generals during the Indochina war that if one of the noncommunist countries in the region is allowed to fall to communism other countries will follow in.

Double Criminality is a legal principle requiring that nobody should be charged or tried twice for the same offence.

Double Jeopardy is a legal principle requiring that nobody should be.punished twice for the same offence.

Double Veto. Under Article 27 of the UN charter each member of the UN Security is entitled to cast one vote. Decisions on procedural matters require an affirmative vote of any name Members including the concurring votes of the five permanent Members. Decisions on substantive matters require an affirmative vote of nine members including those of the five permanent Members. That means no decision can be taken if a permanent Member casts a negative vote on a substantive matter. This negative vote is informally called a veto, although this word is not mentioned in the Charter. However, the exclusion of procedural matters from the operation of the veto is nullified by the practice of double veto, if the question arises whether any Motion put to vote is of procedural or substantive nature, a Permanent Member first casts a negative vote to prevent the security council from treating the matter as procedural and then it casts its negative vote a second time to defeat the substance of the motion. This is known as double veto.

Dravid Munitra Kazgham, All-India Anna -- AIADMK is a regional political party operating in the states of Tamil Nadu and Pondicherry. It was founded by M.G. Ramachandran, a disciple of C.N Annadurai, who after the death of could not coexist with his successors and so broke away from the DMK to form his own party by the name of AIADMK in 1972. It came to power in Tamil Nadu for the first time in 1977.

Dravida Munitra Kazgham -- DMK (Dravid Progressive Front) is a regional political party active in the states of Tamil Nadu and pondicherry. It was founded in 1949 by C. N. Annadurai after breaking away from the Dravid Kazgham (DK) which he had founded along with his mentor and colleague E.V. Ramaswamy "Periar" in 1944. The DK had replaced the Justice Party which was founded as the Indian Liberal Federation in 1917 in the erstwhile Madras Province.

Druze is the plural of durzi. Druze are a religious sect holding beliefs similar to the Ismaili sect. They inhabit the Jabal al-Druze (Druze Mountain) of the Lebanon and in parts of Syria. They believe in the Fatimid Khalifa al-Hakim (996-1020 AD) as the tenth and last incarnation of God on earth in his second coming.

Due Process of Law. It is a recognized principle of the common law that nobody can be deprived of his life, liberty and property except under due process of law. Duc proccss means that the law and the legal processes should be administered with due care and that the processes must conform with fundamental rules of fairness and justice. Due process entails certain procedural safeguards that protect the individuals from unreasonable searches and seizures, double criminality, double jeopardy, compulsive self-incrimination, cruel and unusual punishments and excessive bails ensure open, public and speedy trial; give the defendants an opportunity to be heard and to be represented by a lawyer; and guarantee fair compensation for property taken for purpose.

Dumbarton Oaks Conference refers to a meeting of the USA, USSR, UK and china held in 1944 in Dumbarton Oaks- (name of a building) in Washington, DC. It finalized the proposals for the creation of a new World organization it was followed up by the United Nations Conference held in 1945 in San Francisco which adopted the Charter of the UNO.

Durand Line is the international boundary between Pakistan and Afghanistan. It was demarcated pursuant to an agreement signed between Amir Abdur Rahman, the king of Afghanistan and Sir Mortimer Durand, an officer representing the Government of India on 12 November 1893. The line starts from the junction-point of the Himalayan and Hindukush ranges in Gilgit in the north and stretches to the Kohi-Mulk-i-Siah in the south where the boundaries of Afghanistan, Iran and Pakistan converge. It is divided into three distinct sectors. The northern sector from Gilgit to Bajour is 350 mile long and runs through impassable mountains, The middle sector extends from Bajour to Nashki 700 miles long and runs through mountains rising to a height of between 6000 and 1100 feet. The southern sector stretches from Nashki to Koh-i-Mulk-i-Siah and runs through deep sand desert and barren mountains. The strategic importance of the line lies in the fact that such strategic passes as the Khyber, Gomal and Bolan Khojak are located across it.

Duty Drawback is a sum paid back on reexportation of goods on which an import duty was paid or exportation of goods on which excise duties were paid. Drawbacks should not be confounded with subsidies* and bounties. They merely enable the exporters to sell their goods in foreign markets at competitive

Dyarchy (1919) as introduced in the Indian provinces by the Government of India Act, 1919, was defined as a system involving two different principles of government, that is, responsibility in a limited sphere of provincial government and complete irresponsibility in a larger sphere, As a result, certain departments were transferred to Indian ministers responsible to the Provincial legislative council while the rest were reserved for administration by the executive council of the governor, completely irresponsible to the legislature.

E

East African Community--EAC was founded on 30 November 1999 by a treaty signed between Kenya Tanzania and Uganda. The treaty visualizes the creation of a customs union, a common mark a monetary union and eventually a political union east African states. The customs union was realized in 2004. The headquarters is in Arusha, Tanzania.

East Asia Coprosperity Sphere was proposed by Japan in 1940 for economic integration of east Asia (Burma, China, Indochina, Indonesia, Malaya, Philippines, Thailand and parts of the east Asian territories of former USSR) for achieving common prosperity.

East India Company (British) was incorporated as a commercial company in 1600 by a charter granted by Queen Elizabeth I. Early in the seventeenth century it received permission from the Mughal Emperor Jahangir to establish a factory at Surat. Some years later they bought a piece of land in the south and this was the beginning of the city of Madras. In 1662 the king of portugal presented the island of Bombay as dowry to King Charles II of England who gave it to the East India Company. In 1690 the Company founded the city Calcutta. The battle of Plassey fought in 1757 between the army of the East India Company and the forces of the Mughal Viceroy in Bengal Nawab Sirajuddaula resulted in the defeat of the latter because of the treachery of his grand vizir, Mir Jafar. Mir Jafar was the installed as the puppet nawab of Bengal but was dismissed in 1760. His successor was Mir Qasim who was nawab of Bengal from 1760 to 1763 when he was also deposed by the Company. Mir Qasim assembled his own and his allies' forces and fought battle in 1764 against the Company at Buxar but was defeated. Thereafter the Company became the de *facto* ruler of Bengal. In 1765 the Company managed to obtain the grant of *Diwani* (revenue administration) of Bengal, Bihar from the Mughal Emperor in Delhi. This brought, the vast area of Bengal, Bihar, Orissa and the east coast under their control. By the beginning of the nineteenth century Company's influence had spread up to the gates of the imperial capital Delhi. In 1799 they defeated Tipu Sultan of Mysore State who was supported by the French East India Company. The war at Serangapatnam eliminated both the rivals of the Company from south India. The Company up to now considered itself and functioned as agents of the Mughal Emperor in Delhi who was still the legitimate sovereign in India and in whose name money was coined till 1835 The Marathas were finally defeated in 1818 and Punjab was annexed in 1850. By this time the Company had become the *de* facto sovereign power in most of India, in 1856 the State of Awadh was annexed. However the Indian revolt of 1857 shook the foundations of Company's rule. The rebellion was suppressed with the aid and support of the natives themselves and the Mughal dynasty was extinguished, at this time the Company handed over the estate and administration of India to the British Crown who declared India as a Crown colony and brought it under its direct rule.

Eastern Question during the nineteenth and early twentieth centuries referred to the Ottoman Empire. European power politics was directed towards weakening and dismembering the "sick man of Europe".

Economic and Social Council of the UN General Assembly-- ECOSOC is the topmost policymaking organ of the UN General Assembly in economic and social matters. It is composed of 27 members elected by the General Assembly for a term of three years and one-third of them being elected every year. It meets twice a year in New York and Geneva. The functions of the ECOSOC include examination of international economic, social, cultural, and humanitarian problems and making recommendations to the General Assembly; coordination of the work of the UN Specialized Agencies*; maintenance of liaison with governmental organizations operating within its sphere of activity; and coordination of the work of the UN regional economic commissions,

Economic Community of Central African States was founded in 1983 by eleven central African countries to promote regional economic cooperation and eventually to create a free-trade area in central Africa. The headquarters* is in Libreville, Gabon.

Economic Community of West African States-- ECOWAS was created by fifteen countries of West Africa in 1976 under a treaty signed in 1.975 to promote regional economic and political cooperation in West Africa. Its headquarters is in Asokora, Abuja, Nigeria.

Economic Cooperation Organization --ECO is a regional consultation and cooperation organization created in 1985 in place of the defunct Regional Cooperation for Development (RCD) which was founder by Iran, Pakistan and Turkey in 1964 . The participating states since 1992 are: Afghanistan, Azerbaijan, Iran, Kazakhastan, Kyrghyzystan, Pakistan, Tajikistan, Turkemintan, Turkey and Uzbekistan. The headquarters is in Tehran, Iran.

Economic Development in a country is measured in terms of economic growth and technological innovations; increase in per capita incomes and poverty reduction; increase in foreign trade; increase in life expectancy and literacy rate; and all these leading to democracy and equality.

Economic Growth roughly means rapid and sustained growth of per capita product in a country's economy. According to

W.W. Rostow (*The Stages of Economic Growth,* 1960), economic growth proceeds through four stages: (1) the preconditions of takeoff; (2) takeoff; (3) the drive to technological drive; and (4) sustained economic growth with mass production and high mass consumption. Some essential concomitants of economic growth are productivity; technological innovations; consumption; accumulation of wealth; growth of foreign trade and investment; and social and political transformation (mass democracy and social welfare state).

Economic Imperialism is a policy of controlling the economy of other countries and expoitation of their economic resources.

Economic Sanctions refer to restrictive, preventive, coercive or punitive measures of an economic or military nature taken by a country or group of countries or the international community for alleged breaches of international obligations or any other ground. Blockage of trade, arms embargo, closing of seaports, airports and land routes for vessels, aircraft and vehicles of a target country or freezing of its financial and other assets. Under the Charter of the UNO sanctions can be imposed against a country committing aggression against another country or for any breach of an international obligation or violation of international law.

Economic Warfare refers to employment of all possible economic measures to undercut the economic potential or an enemy state and to undermine its warmaking ability. Such measures include embargo on enemy's imports and exports; blockade of shipping and civil aviation; boycott of enemy' businesses; preemptive purchase of strategic raw materials in the foreign markets; and counter-measures against enemy's economic warfare.

Eighth Schedule of the Indian Constitution. In the context of declaration of Hindi and Devanagari script as the official language of the Indian Union the Eight Schedule was included in the Indian constitution for the purposes of Article 344

(1.) and Article 351. Article 344 (1) mandates that five years from the commencement of the Indian constitution, the of India snail constitute an official language commission to recommend for the progressive use of Hindi as the official language of the Indian Union, and as a link language between the Union and the States and for restricting the use of the English language in the central administration. Such a commission was to consist, of a chairman and such other members as the President of India may appoint representing the different regional languages as specified in the Eight schedule, Accordingly, an Official Language Commission was appointed in 1955 which recommended that Hindi in Devanagari script should replace the English language as the official language of the Union from 1 January 1965 as stipulated in the constitution, its recommendations were examined by a joint parliamentary committee on the official language and on the basis of its report the Official Language Act, 1963 (as amended in 1967) was passed to give effect to the language policy. Article 351 mandates that the official language of the Union (Hindi) shall be developed *Primarily* by drawing its terminology from the Sanskrit language and *secondarily* from other languages of India as listed in the Eighth Schedule of the Constitution. The languages listed in the Eighth Schedule (as in 2005) are: Assamese, Bengali, Gujarati, Hindi, Kannada, Kashmiri, Malayalam, Marathi, Uriya, Panjabi, Sanskrit, Sindhi, Tamil, Telugu, Urdu, Nepali, Manipuri, Maithili, Bodo, Dogri and Santhali.

Eisenhower Doctrine (1957) was pronounced by President Dwight D. Eisenhower of the USA in the wake of the Suez War of 1956 to contain the influence of the Soviet Union and Arab nationalist forces backed by it in the Arab Middle East. The doctrine was an extension of the Truman Doctrine* of 1947 to contain communism.

Election Commission (India) is an independent constitutional authority under Article 324 of the Indian Constitution. It is composed of on Chief Election Commissioner and two other Election Commissioners (from 1 October 1993), all of equal rank and pay, for a term of five years. They are responsible for conducting free and fair elections to national parliament and state legislative assemblies in accordance with the constitution, the Representation of the People Act, 195 and the Rules framed under it, and other relevant laws and regulations. They act unanimously or by a vote of majority.

Electoral College in the USA is the body of presidential electors, chosen by the people in a general election, who the elect the President and the Vice-President of the USA. In India and the Federal Republic of Germany the electoral college (composed of elected members of the national parliament and state legislative assemblies) serves as a device for indirect election of the constitutional head of state.

Electoral Malpractices refer to use of unfair and corrupt means to win election. Most democracies, including India, have enacted preventive and punitive measures to curb electoral malpractices. Use of illicit money and exercise of unfair influence as well use of force and fraud in elections are cognizable offences under Sections A-E and A-F of the Indian Penal Code. Electoral malpractices have been defined under Sections 135 and 136 (10) (A) of the Indian Representation of People Act, 1951. A candidate found guilty of committing an electoral malpractice by an Election Tribunal is disqualified from contesting elections for a period of six years from the date of the judgement.

Electoral Swing in two-party electoral systems means that the diversion of a small percentage of voters of one major party to the other major party decisively tilts the balance in favour of the latter.

Electoral Systems may be divided into democratic and non-democratic. Democratic electoral systems may broadly be divided into (1) single-vote simple-majority systems where one candidate is elected from a single territorial constituency on the Principle of plurality (the winning candidate is declared elected if he gets more votes than any other individual candidate). It is not necessary to get a clear majority of the total votes cast. This is also known as *first-past-the-pole* system; (2) a clear-majority, two-ballot system. In the first round of polling those candidates who obtain a clear majority of votes (more than 50 per cent of the total votes cast) are declared elected. The unfilled seats are filled by a second round of polling in which two or three candidates who obtained most numerous votes in the first round compete for election. The candidate who gets a simple majority of votes cast is declared elected; (3) an electoral system based on proportional representation (PR) which takes one of the two forms: (a) the so-called Hare System or the quota system or proportional representation by single transerable vote (STV). This is the method of dividing the total number of voters by the total number of candidates contesting in a multi-member constituency or a regional constituency. The quotient thus obtained.is regarded as a requisite quota of votes to get elected. In this system all groups and communities get represented in the representative assembly in proportion to their strength in the constituency* or (b) proportional representation by means of a party list. In this system the whole country is made a single constituency. In general elections political parties present their list of candidates. The voters cast their votes in favour of party lists rather than individual candidates. The seats are apportioned among the parties in proportion to the percentage of votes cast in their favour.

Elite means a person or class possessing a high or special status in the society. The ruling elite is same as the ruling class. *Power elite* refers to those classes in the society who wield economic and political power e.g. the business and industry, finance capital and professional politicians

Elitism is opposite of populism or plebianism. The tendency to regard the rule by the high or the privileged class as preferable to popular or representative rule.

Elysee is the official residence of the President of the French Republic in Paris.

Embargo is an act of a government to arrest the ships of an enemy country and preventing them from leaving the ports, hence a trade embargo or arms embargo means prohibition of supply of goods or arms to an enemy country.

Emergency, 1975 (India) refers to the imposition of a constitutional dictatorship in India by the Prime Minister Indira Gandhi under a Proclamation of Emergency issued by the President of India on her advice on 25 June 1975. This Proclamation under Article 352 of the Indian Constitution was issued in spite of the fact that an earlier Proclamation issued under the same Article in 1971 was still in force. This measure was taken to round up her political opponents who were demanding her resignation as prime minister following a judgment delivered by the Allahabad High Court on an electoral petition against her which held her guilty of committing an electoral malpractice and, therefore, nullified her election to the Lok Sabha. The State of Emergency was terminated in February 1977 and fresh parliamentary elections were held in March

Emergency Powers in a constitutional state refer to special or extraordinary powers granted to the constitutional authorities under constitutional provisions or emergency-power legislations to deal with crisis situations. In democracies emergency or special powers can be used for a limited period or till the passing over of a crisis.

Emergency Regime is that authoritarian regime which came to power by declaring a state of emergency and remained in power by the exercise of emergency powers on a permanent footing making an excuse of the continuing emergency or crisis.

Emigré is French for a migrant.

Emigration/Immigration. To emigrate means to migrate out of the country and to *immigrate* means to migrate in to a country.

Eminent Domain in the inherent constitutional power of a sovereign state to acquire private property for public purpose on payment of just compensation.

Emissary is a special representative of a state or international organization sent to another state on a non-official, secret or open mission.

Emissary is an informal messenger or an ad hoc representative sent by one government or organization to another on some specific mission.

Empiricism or positivism is the opposite of apriorism; means deriving knowledge from experimentation or observation and analysis of facts: testing abstract theories about social events against empiric facts.

Enclave is part of the territory of a state enclosed by the territory of another state or states such as the German enclave of Busingen in Switzerland. A *diplomatic enclave* is the locality earmarked for the diplomatic missions of foreign countries.

End-of-History Thesis. Just as Karl Marx had claimed that the establishment of a classless and stateless communist society shall be an end of the dialectical process so does Francis Fukuyama in his *End of History and the Last Man* (1992) make liberal democracy the terminus of human history. As a result of cultural, economic and political globalization divergent civilizations of the world shall converge upon A single liberal democratic model leading to a free and affluent world society.

End-of-Ideology Thesis asserts the primacy of the materialistic orientations over the ideological orientation. An affluent industrial society tends to be free from ideological cleavages and class conflicts.

End-of-Sovereignty Thesis refers to the claim of the advocates of globalization that with the establishment of globalized world economy the sovereign state will be divested of many of its sovereign functions and thus immobilized by the global forces,

Enemy Alien is a foreign national living for the time-being in the territory of a country which is at war with his native country, for instance the Japanese living in the USA and the Germans living in the USSR during World War II.

Enforcement Measures are collective measures, including sanctions and deployment of armed forces, as decided by the UN Security Council in accordance with the Charter of the UNO to deal with a threat to international peace and security, or a breach of peace or an act of aggression.

English Channel is an arm of the Atlantic Ocean between England and France about 500 kilometers long. The Channel is connected with the North Sea by the Strait of Dover.

Enlightenment refers to an intellectual and cultural movement in Europe that gained momentum during the period from 1680 to 1780's. The century is also known as the ''age of reason''. It stood for the liberation of human mind from the bondage of traditionalism, obscurantism and authoritarianism. Its central beliefs were reliance on human reason and the idea of progress.

Enlistment is employment of persons as private soldiers for a limited or unlimited period, on a voluntary basis. It differs from *enrolment* for militia service or *conscription* which are compulsory.

Entente (French for understanding) is usually an informal and vague commitment and should not be Confounded with an *alliance* which signifies formal and definite commitments. For instance, the **Entente Cordiale** was signed between Britain and Russia on 21 March 1905 for joint defence against Russia and cooperation in foreign affairs which continued until World War I. (The centenary of the Entente Cordiale was celebrated simultaneously in Britain and France in November 2004) Similarly, the **Triple Entente** was an understanding arrived at between Britain, France and Russia during World War I for joint defence against imperial Germany and the Central Powers*.

Environmentalism is a movement directed at the preservation of the global environment which is threatened by such problems as global warming, environmental degradation, increasing air and water pollution and impending scarcities and depleting resources. The environmentalists induce governments and international bodies to initiate necessary policies and programmes to ensure environmental safety, sustainable development and maximise human security and well-being. This led to adoption of certain important steps such as the launching of the UN Environmental Programme* (UNEP) in 1975, the signing of the Montreal Protocol* in 1987 and the signing of the Kyoto Protocol* in 1997.

Envoy is a diplomat, minister or agent, inferior in status to a full ambassador and enjoying the same powers, for instance, *envoy* extraordinary or *minister plenipotentiary*.

Equilitarianism is opposite of elitism, aristocracy and meritocracy and synonymous with social levelling up, affirmative action and redistributive justice. It aims at bringing about socioeconomic and political equality in the society by removal of disparities, equalization of opportunities and redistribution of resources.

Equity (literally fairness and justice). In general it is equivalent to the principle of socioeconomic and political and legal justice. In international law it is the principle of "good faith" and what is "right and proper". In jurisprudence it is the principle of fairness and justice as being the spirit of all laws i.e.- equity means the fair and sound interpretation of the rules and recourse to general principles justice to correct; or supplement the provisions of the law. In English legal system equity is the distinctive name of a system of law existing side by side with common law and the statute law (together called the "law", and superseding these when they conflict with it. The rules of equity were developed by the Chancery during the 15th century to mitigate the difficulties of the common law and to provide relief to subjects when they failed to get the same from the common law courts. In due course, equity became a separate branch of the English law with separate courts of common law and equity coming into being and the lawyers divided between the practioners of the two branches. The double system of equity and common law courts was abolished by the Judicature Acts of 1873-1875. Thereafter common law and equity courts were merged and the same lawyers practised both the branches.

Erastianism is derived from the name of Thomas Erasmus (1524-1583}, a Protestant clergyman who denied the jurisdiction of the Church authorities to punish the sinners since the power of punishment can be exercised only by the worldly authorities. Although Erasmus did not mean it, Erastianism came to mean the primacy of the temporal over the spiritual power and the subordination of the church to the political state. For instance, Thomas Hobbes in his *Leviathan* (1651·) advocated that the sovereign must have absolute contro! over the religious establishment.

Eretz Israel (Hebrew for the "land of Israel") means the whole of biblical Israel (Judea and Samaria) and by implication a "greater Israel" comprising the whole of modern Palestine and the adjoining Arab lands.

Establishment is synonymous with an established order or a hierarchy of individuals and institutions that exercises power in a given political system.

Estate Duty is a direct tax levied on the estate (property) of a person on his death before the same passes into the possession of his successors. In India this duty is levied and collected by the Union of India but transferred to the states under the Estate Duty Act, 1953.

Estoppel (Latin for "preclusion") is a principle of jurisprudence resting on the principle of good faith and consistency, that precludes or stops a person from denying the truth of a representation or statement made by him or denying the validity of an action which has already been established as a matter of law. The principle applies equally to judicial proceedings, commercial transactions and inter-ste dealings. In accordancc with Article 45 of the Vienna Convention on the Law of Treaties (1969) no state has a right to question the validity of or revoke or suspend the operation of a treaty or withdraw from it after having concluded it willingly and acquiesced into its coming in force.

Estrada Doctrine (named after Estrada who was a foreign minister in the dictatorial government of the Institutional Revolutionary Party in Mexico) was A declaration of detachment from and non-intervention in the internal affairs of other countries in the expectation that other countries will desist from interfering with Mexican affairs.

Ethnic Culture refers to a particular way of life displayed by an ethnic group.

Ethnic Group refers to (1) non-English-speaking migrants from Northeastern Europe settled in the USA, or (2) any group identified on the basis of.its ethnicity (caste, tribe, language, region or religion within a nation-state.

Ethnic Nationalism refers to the quest of an ethnic group to preserve its particular ethnic identity or to attain its cultural, social, economic and political rights.

Ethnicity (from *Greek ethnos* and *etnia* = people) refers to peculiar cultural characteristics that impart a distinctive identity to a group. A cultural group that acquires a distinct ethnic identity in relation other cultural groups is defined as an ethnic group. An ethnic group differs from both race and nation. While race is a broader concept distinguishing a people on the basis of colour or certain physical features like the Aryan or Semitic or Mongoloid races an ethnic group may be part of a nation which is a form of all-inclusive ethnicity. There are many states which are *multinational* and there are many nations which are multiethnic (i.e. composed of different communities identifying themselves with different cultures, regions, religions, languages, tribes and castes, etc.). A distinction is made between ethnic nationalism and integral nationalism. While integral nationalism institutionalizes national identity by attaching it to a territorial state ethnic nationalism is but a particularistic form of nationalism which aspires only for self-assertion within a nation-state in cultural terms, rather than for self-determination within a territorial state. For instance, Welsh or Scottish or Sikh nationalism.

Ethnocentrism an opposite of cultural pluralism, is a parochial view of seeing one's own culture as superior to other cultures. According to W.G. Sumner in his *Folkways* (1906), ethnocentrism is a view of things in which one's own group is the centre of everything, and all others are scaled and rated with reference to it''

Eurocommunism as distinguished from the Soviets-type communism based on the orthodox Leninist notion of the dictatorship of the communist party, abolition of private property and collective ownership of all means of production, distribution and exchange, it represents the transformed ideology of the French, Italian, German and other Western European communist parties which shed away the orthodox notions of class struggle and totalitarian socialism in favour of individual liberty, democratic government and parliamentary or democratic socialism.

European Bank for Reconstruction and Development -- EBRD was founded in May 1990 with its seat in London and commenced operations in April 1991. Its sole purpose is to provide aid and investment for reconstruction and liberalization of the economies of the decommunized countries in central and eastern Europe and central Asia. Besides the 27 beneficiary countries the Bank is joined by all member-states of the European Union, the European Free Trade Area, and other countries including the USA, Australia, Canada, New Zealand, Japan, South Korea, and the European Community and the European Investment Bank.

European Central Bank-- ECB was founded on 1 June 1998 with its headquarters in Frankfurt, Germany, to issue the Euro, the single currency of the European Union, which replaced the European Currency Unit (ECU) on 1 January 1999 in accordance with the Treaty on European Union (the Maastricht Treaty*). The European Central Bank aims at maintaining price stability in the Euro area by controlling money supply, monitoring prices and limiting national budgetary deficits. It operates in conjunction with the national central banks of the twelve member-states of the European Union who joined the European Monetary Union* (EMU) on its inception.

European Community-- EC is a supranational regional community of 25 European states. The process of European integration started with the signing of a treaty in 1951 to create a European Coal and Steel Community (ECSC) which started functioning from 1952. TWO other communities namely the European Economic Community (EEC) or the common market and the European Atomic Energy Community (Euratom) were created under a treaty signed in Rome in 1956 which started functioning in 1958. The three communities were merged in 1967 and renamed as the European Community (EC) with common organs. On expiry of the term of the ECSC treaty in 2002 it was incorporated into the Treaty of Rome. Under the Single European Act, 1985, a single integrated European market came into being in 1992. The Treaty on the European Union signed in 1991 in Maastricht, Netherlands, provided for the creation of a European Union (EU) with single citizenship and a prospective single constitution. The EU was inaugurated on 1 November 1993. The EC is an integral part of the EU. While the EC has achieved functional integration of Europe the EU aims at its political integration. The central organs of the EC/EM are a European Council (European summit); a European Parliament; a Council of the European Union (formerly European Council of Ministers); a European Commission; and a European Court of Justice. The memberships in the

EC is coterminous with membership of the EU. In 2005 there were 25 members. Two more states signed accession treaties in 2005 and are expected to join the EU by 2007. The seat of the European Commission is in Brussels, Belgium, and that of the European Parliament and the European Court is in Luxembourg.

European Court of Human Rights was created on 1 November 1998 with its seat in Strasbourg, France, under the European Human Rights Convention of 1950, and superseded the European Commission on Human Rights. The Court is composed of a number of judges equal to the number of the signatory states. It hears complaints of individuals and the signatory states against violations of EHRC rights and freedoms by the signatory states.

European Economic Area--EEA is a free-trade zone between the European Union and the European Free Trade Area (EFTA) created in 1994. The three members of the EFTA which joined the EEA are: Iceland, Liechtenstein and Norway.

European Free Trade Area--EFTA was created in 1960 by Iceland, Norway and Switzerland with its seat in Geneva. It signed a Treaty of Association with the European Community in 1984.

European Integration refers to the process of economic integration in Western Europe achieved by means of creating supranational communities in particular functional areas under intergovernmental treaties.* The aim was to derive economic benefit from removal of customs and other non-tariff barriers, a single market with freedom of movement of capital, labour, and of free trade and investment, growth of business and evolving common foreign and economic policies towards the external world. The process started with the formation of the Organization for European Economic Cooperation (OEEC) in 1947 to implement, the American-sponsored Marshall Plan* for European economic recovery; the ECSC was formed in 1951 then the EEC and EURATOM in 1958; the three separate communities were amalgamated into one in 1967; and the European Union and the European Monetary Union were inaugurated respectively in 1993 and 1999.

European Investment Bank-- EIB was founded in 1958 under the Treaty of Rome (1956) with its seat in Luxembourg. It is joined by all the member-states of the European Union. It finances capital investment projects with a view to promoting balanced economic development within the EU. It provides also development assistance to non-EU countries which have signed agreements of association/cooperation with the EU.

European Monetary Union--EMU came into being on 1 January 1999 with Euro as the single currency of the EU area, issued by a European Central Bank*. The Euro became the single currency throughout the EU area (except Britain) on 1 January 2002.* The process of monetary integration was set in motion by the launching of the European Monetary System (EMS) in March 1979 with the European Currency Unit (ECU) as a single medium of exchange with a view to bring about monetary stability in Europe and create a monetary union in the long run. The Treaty on the European Union (Maastricht Treaty) was a landmark as it led to the inauguration of the EU on 1 November 1993 and the EMU on 1 January 1999.

European System of Central Banks -- ESCB was create in 1998 with its headquarters in Frankfurt, Germany, as a coordinating mechanism between the European Central Bank* (ECB) and the 25 national central banks of the member-states of the EU(12 states which participate in the EMU and 13 non-participants i.e. non-Euro countries). The 13 non-Euro banks have been accorded a special status. The objective of the ESCB is to coordinate monetary policies, limit budgetary deficits and maintain price stability in the area.

European Union -- EU came into being on 1 November 1993 one month after the ratification of the Treaty on the European Union signed by the European Council* in December 1991 in Maastricht, Netherlands. The three pillars of the European Union as envisaged in the Maastricht Treaty are: (1) the European Community (EC) with its established institutions, processes and procedures; (2) a common foreign and security policy with the Western European Union* (WEU) visualized as the potential defence wing of the European Union; and (3) cooperation in justice and home affairs* Besides, the treaty created a common European citizenship. The European Council signed Union a treaty on the Constitution of the European on 29 October 2004 in Rome. The constitution (which consolidates the treaties of Rome and the resulting community law into & single document) was to come into force after ratification by the national parliaments or by national referendums in all the 25 member-states of the EU within three years. However, referendums held in France and Netherlands in June 2005 resulted in the rejection of the constitutional treaty. After that the treaty was expected to be renegotiated and revised for resubmission for ratification.

The member-states of the EC/Eu are:

1951 Belgium, France, Germany, Italy, Luxembourg and Netherlands

1973 Britain, Denmark, Ireland

1981 Greece

1986 Spain, Portugal

1995 Sweden, Austria, Finland.

2004 Cyprus, Czech Republic, Estonia, Hungary, Latvia, Lithuania, Malta, Poland, Slovakia, Slovenia.

2005 Bulgaria and Rumania signed treaties of accession in April and are expected to join the EU in 2007. Talks were on for the accession of Turkey, Croatia, Serbia Montenegro, Bulgaria and Bosnia Herzegovina.

The principal institutions of the EU are:

(1) **The European Commission** with its seat in Brussels, Belgium. It is the executive organ of the EU. It is composed of 25 commissioners one from each of the member-states. After the ratification of the proposed European Constitution only fifteen will have the voting right drawn from varying states by rotation. The president of the commission is appointed by the European Council. He is required to seek the confidence of the European Parliament in favour of his commission as a whole and the parliament is empowered to force the resignation of the commission as a whole. The parliament can also pass a motion of no-confidence in individual commissioners but cannot force their resignation. The functions of the Commission include: to propose legislation to European Parliament and to the Council of the EU; to implement EU policies and programmes as approved by European Parliament; to execute the European budget; to enforce the Community Law in conjunction with the Court of Justice of the EU in all member-states; and to represent the EU in international affairs and negotiate agreements between the EU on one hand and the other countries, group of countries or international organizations on the other.

(2) **The Council of the European Union** (formerly the council of ministers) is the EU's principal decision-making organ but acts only on proposals submitted by the European Commission. One minister is drawn from each member-state. Its functions include legislation, in some matters independently and in many others in conjunction with European Parliament; coordination of policy between and among the member-states; conclusion of agreements with foreign states and international organizations; approval of the EU budget in conjunction with European Parliament; formulation and implementation of EU's common

foreign and security policy in accordance with the directions issued by the European Council; and coordination between national courts and police forces in criminal matters.

(3) **The European Council** or the European summit is the topmost policy-making organ of the EU. The Council acts through summit meetings of the heads of state or government of the member-states, their foreign ministers, and senior officials of the European Commission. It meets twice a year in the country currently holding the presidency of the Council of the EU or in Brussels. (This Council should not be confounded with the Council of Europe* which is a separate intergovernmental political organization.

(4) **The European Parliament** which meets at Luxembourg is composed of 732 members directly elected by the citizens of the member-states for a term of five years. (From 1967 to 1978 it was elected indirect by national parliaments; direct election started in 1979). Members of parliament are not grouped into national delegations but are divided on party lines. Its main functions are to legislate in conjunction with the Council of the EU; to scrutinize and approve the budget of the EU in conjunction with the Council of the EU; to supervise the executive organs of the European Community, and the Commission and Council of the EU; and to dismiss the Commission as a whole by a vote of no-confidence passed by a two-third majority. And

(5) **The Court of Justice of the European Community** which sits at Luxembourg, is responsible for protecting the treaties, laws and regulations of the Community by the subordinate officials and organs as well as by the governments of the member-states. It has jurisdiction over all cases arising under the Community Law and over the EU institutions. Governments of the Member-

states of the EU and the EU citizens in respect of matters falling under the jurisdiction of the EU. The court is compose of 25 judges, and eight advocates-general. One judge from each member-state is nominated by its government and appointed with the approval of the Council of the EU.

European Convention on Human Rights (1950) was signed by the member-states of the Council of Europe* to safeguard fundamental human rights and freedoms throughout the territory of the signatory states. It is enforced by the domestic courts of the signatories and individuals as well as governments of the signatory states can lodge complaints against violation of the rights guaranteed under ECHR with the European Court of Human Rights in Strasbourg, France, whose rulings are binding upon the member-states.

Ex Parte (Latin for ''without a party'') means after (l) Judicial proceedings instituted by individuals on their own behalf or for one party without having an adverse party or defendent: or (2) deciding the case in the presence of the plaintiff if the defendent fails to appear before the court on an appointed day.

***Ex Post Facto* Laws** are laws enacted to declare an event or fact as an offence after its occurrence: laws dealing retrospectively with an act committed in the past when it was not considered an offence. The American Constitution expressly forbids passing of such laws as they are inimical to individual liberty.

Excise Duties are indirect taxes levied upon articles of mass consumption and manufacture like textiles, medicines, liquors, tobacco, salt, and petrol etc. The excise duties are paid by the manufacturers into the public exchequer, then included in the retail price and passed on to the consumer.

Exclusive Economic Zone was defined under Articles 55-75 of the UN Convention on the Law of the Sea* (UNCLS) as an area beyond; and adjacent to the territorial sea, not extending beyond 200 nautical miles from the baselines from which the breadth of the territorial sea is measured* The adjacent coastal state does not have territorial sovereignty over this EEZ but has merely a sovereign right to explore, exploit, conserve and manage the resources of the EEZ with due regard to the legal rights of other states.

Executive Agreements (US) are the agreements concluded by the executive (i.e., the President of the USA) with foreign governments without seeking the approval of the US Senate. Such agreements can be made either under authority delegated by Congress and within limitations set by it or by the Pressient in his own right acting as the chief diplomat or commander-in-chief of the Union. But under the Case Act of 1972 the executive is bound to report the substance of each executive agreement to Congress. An executive agreement under the us differs from a treaty in this that under the US constitution a treaty may be negotiated and signed by the executive but cannot be enforced unless approved by a two-third majority of the Senate.

Executive Power as distinct from legislative or judicial power is the power of execution and enforcement of public laws; implementation of public policy and programmes; maintenance of internal law and order; defence of the country; maintenance and conduct of foreign relations; regulatory and rule-making power; police power; emergency power; provision of social security and relief and rehabilitation measures; and maintenance of sustained growth and full employment, etc.

Executive Branch is the counterpart of the legislative and judicial branches. The executive branch is concerned with the formulation and execution of public policy. It is composed of two layers: political executive (ministry) which formulates public policy and directs the permanent executive; and the permanent executive (bureaucracy or administration) which is responsible for running the day-to-administration under the direction, supervision and control of the political executive.

Executive Office of the President (US) is a complex of advisory and staff agencies meant to provide the President policy advice to enable him to meet his obligations as the chief executive. The EOP includes the following bodies: The white House Office; the Central Intelligence Agency; the Council of Economic Advisers; the Council on Environmental Quality; the National Security Council; the Office of Administration; the Office of Management and Budget; the Office of National Aids Policy; the Office of National Drug Policy; the Office of Policy Development; the Office of Science and Technology; the US Trade Representative; and the US Mission to the United Nations.

Executive Orders (US) are orders, having the force of law, issued by the President of the USA or executive agencies subordinate to him under rule-making authority delegated to him by the statutes of the US Congress.

Executive Privilege in the USA is similar to the Crown privilege in the UK. The President of the USA, and by extension his subordinates, have claimed the discretion to refuse to appear or to produce required documents before Congressional committee on the plea of protecting national interest.

Existentialism is a philosophy which denies the existence of God, of predestination or transcendental human norms. It believes in the contingent nature of human existence as well as of human values. Man in this world is alone and helpless. He has to fend for himself by compromising with the contingencies of his existence, The philosophy flourished in the pessimistic conditions following World War II but with the improvement of human condition subsequently it lost its appeal.

Exquatur, Consular is a permit issued by the foreign minister of a host country to the consular mission of foreign country enabling him to take up his consular duties. A consular mission may also be permitted to carry on its duties temporarily till an exquatur is granted.

Exterritoriality/Extraterritoriality means exercise of domestic jurisdiction on the territory of a foreign country. For instance international law exempts the diplomatic missions from the jurisdiction of the host country to facilitate their unhindered functioning.

Extradition in international law is the delivery of an accused or a convicted individual to the state where he is accused of, or has been convicted of a crime, by the state on whose territory he happens for the time being to be (Oppenheim). Extradition is not a legal duty. It is governed by intergovernmental treaties or national laws for instance, the Extradition Act of 1989 of Great Britain. Extradition of one's own nationals to foreign countries is controversial. Extraditable crimes and conditions of extradition must be laid down in the relevant treaties or extradition laws. Finally, refugees, political offenders and persecuted persons are not subject to extradition.

F

Fabian Socialism/Fabianism refers to the political ideas of the Fabian Society founded in England in 1888. Fabianism rejects the edeas of class struggle and violent revolution as a means of bring about socialism. On the contrary, it believes in the possibility of socialism through gradual and constructive reforms. Fabianism is synonymous with democratic evolutionary or parliamentary socialism. The term *Fabian* is derived from the name of Fabius Cunctator [delayer], a Roman general who became famous for his policy of moving against his enemy in slow steps and striking him with full force when he appeared to be worn out.

Fabian Society was founded in 1883-84 in London by Sidney and Beatrice Webb, George Bernard Shaw, Graham Wallace, Anne Besant and others to counteract Marx's advocacy of bringing social justice through class struggle and proletarian revolution. They preached, through their writings and speeches, inter-class harmony and cooperation and attaining socialism through gradual reforms and peaceful democratic action. Since 1906 the Fabian Society is affiliated with the British Labour Party which adopted the programmes and methods of the former.

Fair Deal (US) was the policy package proposed by President Harry S. Truman, in continuation of President F.D. Roosevelt's "New Deal" programme, to deal with social, economic and humanitarian problems of post- World War II era. The package was proposed to the Congress in 1949 but the Republican majority defeated it.

Falklands War (1982) was fought between Great Britain and Argentina over the British controlled Falkland Islands (called Melvinas by Argentina) which Argentina claimed as its territory. Britain defeated Argentina militarily and maintained its sovereignty over the islands.

Fascism (from Latin *fascis* = a buch of sticks or Italian *fascio* = a bunch of grapes) is an anti-democratic*, anti-liberal*, totalitarian political philosophy that preaches subordination of the individuals to the national collective (state) and submission of the people to the authority of a national leader as the personification of the national state and working for the revival of national glory. Some of the salient features of fascism are: authoritarianism, i.e. it is anti-liberal and anti-democratic; irrationalism and anti-intellectualism; opportunism, i.e. exploitation of social tensions and popular sentiments; reliance on force and fraud; militarism, regimentation, aggressive nationalism and territorial aggrandisement; cult of leadership; belief in the will of the leaders as the moving force in history; and totalitarian dictatorship, i.e. ''Every-thing of the state, nothing outside the state, and everything for the state''.

Fascist Grand Council (Italy) was a body composed of Fascist heavyweights created in 1928. Free elections and universal adult franchise were banned. The Council made an organ of the state, was empowcred to select and nominate the candidates for election to the Chamber of Deputies. Besides controlling elections the Council was responsible for overseing and coordinating government activities.

Federal Bureau of Investigation---Fight face (US) was created in 1908 as an agency of the Department of Justice to investigate , detect: and prosecute foreign espionage, criminal and terrorist activities and violations of federal laws which pose a threat to the internal security of the USA. Its Director is appointed by the President with the confirmation of the Senate.

Federal Court of India was the only organ of the All-India Federation as provided for in Part I of the Government of India Act, 1935, which was inaugurated in 1936 with its seat in New Delhi. On 8 January 1950 it was automatically converted into the Supreme Court of India, as provided for under Article 374 of the Indian Constitution.

Federal Union/Federation is a form of political union in which the federal constitution divides governmental powers and functions between two levels of government---the centre and the constituent units--so that each level functions autonomously within its own jurisdiction.

Federalism is the principle of division so powers between two or more levels of government. The principle ensures unity in diversity, devolution of authority and decentralization of administration.

----, Dual was a particular conception of American federalism upheld by Chief Justice Roger B. Taney of the American supreme Court that under the American Constitution the two levels of government were coewual in status and coodinate in function and that the powers delegated to the Union were limited by the powers reserved for the states under the Tenth Amendment. By the beginning of the nineteenth century dual federalism began to be replaced by cooperative federalism.

----, Cooperative is the current characterization of American federalism. As a result of the growth of intergovernmental cooperation and sharing of powers and functions the constitutional division of powers is merely a legal fact. The different levels of government do not operate in watertight compartments but cooperate with each other as interdependent parts of the same government.

----, Dual Fiscal means the distribution of fiscal resources or revenues between and among the different levels of government in a federal union. Because of disparities in size and resources no unit: can be financially self-sufficient.

A scheme of union-state fiscal relations is, therefore, indispensable.

Feedback as a concept derived from cybernetics means Information received back in reaction or response to or in consequence of an action or policy initiative. The feedback becomes an input into the policy-making process and leads to modification of the policy.

Fellow Traveller a pejorative term that was applied during the cold-war era by the anti-communists for the leftists who were, neither associated with the communists nor openly supporting communism. They were nevertheless held guilty of secret sympathy for the communists.

Felony refers to all species of grave crimes that are so declared in a statute (e.g. the Treason and Felony Act, 1848, of the UK) or were so recognized under English Common Law, which occasion forfeiture of property or goods or both or death penalty and other punishment according to degree of guilt. A felony differs from *misdemeanor* in that the latter comprises lesser offences entailing milder punishment.

Feminism as a philosophy and social movement arose in reaction to gender hierarchy and inequality and the subjection of women in the society. A consequence of male domination is that women in general suffer from illiteracy, poverty, ill - health, violence, lack of employment and income, poor working conditions, lack of legal protection, and general antipathy and bias. The feminists aim at generating an awareness of gender with a view to liberating the women from male domination and chauvinism and empowering them in all walks of life, economic, social, political, and cultural.

Fertile Crescent is the fertile land situated between the Mediterranean Sea and the Persian Gulf. It is the land of Palestine, Trans-Jordan, Syria and Iraq.

Feudalism (from *feud* = piece of land) refers to a particular state of social, economic, political and military relations associated with the ownership of land that prevailed in western and central Europe from the tenth century until the sixteenth century Feudal economy replaced the ancient serf. It: created a static custom-bound, graded society. The king on the top was the owner of all land on behalf of God. Then he granted his lands to his nobles and chiefs in return of their loyalty, tributes and military service in time of war. Such lands were called *fiefs.* The fief-giver was called the lord and the fief-holders as his vassals. The vassals in turn granted their lands to their own vassals and became their lords. Thus every lord became the ruler of his fief. On the basis of land-ownership society became divided into three permanent classes of nobility, clergy and peasantry* The peasants worked on the land of the landlords in return for a fixed share in the produce. The lords and vassals were bound by a code of feudal loyalties and every lord enjoyed immunity from the interference of his overlord in the governance of his fief. Feudal society was replaced by the modern capitalist society based on cash wages, freedom of contract and freedom of exchange.

Fidayeen (Arabic for ''self-sacrificers'') are guerilla fighters struggling against foreign occupation or oppressive domestic regimes. Singular is *fidayee.*

Field Marshal is the highest military rank in the army of the UK and other Commonwealth countries.

Fifth Column is a term used to describe a group of potential traitors and betrayer, the term originated from a statement made by the rebels against the democratic government of Spain in 1936 that they had four-columns advancing towards Madrid and a fifth column (of in side sympathizers ready to strike at government forces.

Fifth Republic of France came into being under the (Gaullist) constitution prepared by a constitutional drafting committee and adopted in a national referendum in 1958. The I republic existed from 1792 to 1799; II republic 1848-1851; III republic 1870-1940; and IV republic 1946-1958.

Final Act of the CSCE (1975). The signing of the Final Act or Declaration of the Conference on Security and Cooperation in Europe (the Helsinki Conference) on 1 August 1975 was the fruit of the deepening process of east-west *detente*. The CSCE represented the most important international conference convened in postwar Europe for the express purpose of legitimization of the post-war territorial status quo and creating a system of collective security between the NATO and the Warsaw Treaty Organization (WTO). The proposal for creating a system of collective security in Europe was made by the USSR in 1968 and the western powers became receptive of this idea as they desired to curtail the arms race, reduce military expenditure and increase cooperation with the USSR and eastern Europe. To prepare the ground for a collective security conference preliminary negotiations among 34 European states were started in November 1972 in Helsinki, Finland. They were resumed on 15 January 1973 and an agenda was finalized on 7 June 1973. It was decided to hold the conference in three stages--at the level of the foreign ministers in July in Helsinki; at the level of the Coordinating Committee in September in Geneva and a full-dress session of the heads of state/ government in 1974 in Helsinki. The agenda of the CSCE was organized under four major heads: problems relating to peace and security in Europe: cooperation in the fields of science, technology and natural environment; cooperation in humanitarian and other social fields and the followup action after the conclusion of the conference. The final session of the CSCE was attended by 35 states including Canada and the USA. The Prolonged and intractable negotiations were concluded by the signing of a on 1 August 1975 by the heads of state or high representatives of governments of 30 countries. They were: Austria, Belgium, Czechoslovakia, Denmark, Federal Republic of Germany, Finland, France, German Democratic Republic, Greece, Hungary, Iceland, Ireland, Italy, Luxembourg, Malta, Monaco, Norway, Netherlands, Poland, Rumania, San Marino, Sweden,

Switzerland, Turkey, the UK, the USA, the USSR and Yugoslavia. The Final Act is divided into three Parts. Part A declare the basic principles that shall govern the mutual relations of the participating countries. Part B dealt with the implementation of certain specied principles; and Part C concerned the followup action after the conclusion of the conference. The following principles were affirmed for the maintenance of peace and security in Europe: (1) Respect for sovereign equality and national sovereignty of all states; (2) renunciation of the use or threat of use of force in international relations; (3) the inviolability of the existing international borders in Europe; (4) a guarantee of the territorial integrity of all states; (5) pacific settlement of all international disputes; (6) non-intervention in the domestic affairs of each other; (7) respect for human rights and freedoms including the freedom of thought, conscience and religious faith and belief; (8) self-determination and equal rights for all nations of the world; (9) cooperation among nations; and (10) fulfilment by all states of their obligations under international law in good faith. Finally, the signatories undertook to abide by the principles of the Final Act and to endeavour to implement them unilaterlly, bilaterally, and multilaterally. A number of followup sessions were held in subsequent years, the first in 1977 in Belgrade. The Charter of Paris signed on 21 November 1990 committed the signatories to hold regular meetings of the heads of state/ government, minister and officials. The first summit held in Helsinki in December 1992 declared the CSCE to be a regional organization. The summit held in December 1994 decided to rename the CSCE as the Organization for Security and Cooperation in Europe (OSCE) and created its institutional infrastructure.

Final Act of the Uruguay Round (1994). The Uruguay Round of multilateral trade negotiations under the GATT* for the creation of a new international trading regime were started in 1978 and were concluded by the signing of a Final Act in

April 1994 in Marrakesh, Morocco. At he same time a separate agreement (the Marrakesh Declaration) was signed by the states which parties to the GATT to create a new international trade regulatory agency by the name of the World Trade Organization (WTO) which was inaugurated in Geneva on 1 January 1995. The GATT, 1995, along with an amended version of GATT, 1947, became an integral part of the WTO Agreement which contains some 29 legal texts and more than 25 ministerial declarations and decisions which cover the obligations of the member-states under the Agreement.

Finance Commission (India) is constituted by the President of India under Article 280 of the Indian Constitution every five years to make recommendations for determining the share of the states in the central pool of revenues and the principles governing the central grants-in-aid to states in need of assistance and any other matter referred to it by the President. The report of the commission is laid before the two houses of parliament and the government implements its recommendations through budgetary transfers to the states during the following stipulated period of five years. The Twelf Finance Commission constituted for the period 2005-2010 recommended the states share in the central pool of revenues at 30.5 per cent.

Fiscal Policy of governments relates to the control of their total revenues and total expenditures to achieve certain economic objectives. Fiscal policy deals with the question ask to how far gross revenues, gross expenditure and gross surpluses or gross deficits are likely to affect the national income, employment and the price level. Sometimes public expenditures are increased and taxes reduced to encourage investment and employment generation. Conversely, public expenditures are reduced and tax incentives withdrawn to control inflation and rising prices. Fiscal policy is implemented in conjunction with monetary policy* or monetary controls or both or without them.

Fiscal Responsibility and Budget Management Act, 2003 (India) provides for an institutional framework for pursuing a prudent fiscal policy aimed at sustained growth. It called for total elimination of revenue deficits by March 2008.

Flangc/Flangism. *Flange* was the name of the official party floated by the Spanish dictator General Franco in 1933. It was renamed as Flange Spanola Traditionalists in 1937. It resembled closely with the Italian Fascist Party. Hence *flangism* is synonymous with fascism. *Flanges** on the other hand, is the name of the Maronite Christian militia operating in the Lebanon.

Floor-Crossing is same as defection; crossing over the floor of a legislative house from one political party or group to another party or group, either on principle or for sheer expediency.

Food-for-Peace Programme (US) was an important component of American foreign-aid programme for the developing countries during the cold-war era. It was launched under the Public Law 48 (PL-48) passed by the US Congress to distribute surplus American foodgrains at subsidized rates to poor and needy countries of Asia, Africa and Latin America which suffered from droughts, floods, or famines. The recipients paid for American foodgrains in local currency rather than American dollars. The funds thus generated were kept in special deposit accounts with the central banks of the recipient countries to the credit of the American government. These monies were later lent back to the recipient governments and educational and research institutions to finance scientific, technological and economic development projects in those countries. These transactions constituted grants, subsidies, and loans at the same time. India was one of the beneficiaries of this programme during the 1960's which enabled her to tide over the food crisis caused by successive failures of the monsoons and shortfall in agricultural production. How-ever, with the success of the green revolution and increasing prosperity India dispensed with the American food-aid and during the 1980's paid back the accumulated balances to the American government.

Foreign Policy refers to the sum of principles guiding the conduct of a state in the external sphere to secure and protect its national interest. It is similar to domestic policy which is designed to secure and promote the public interest in the domestic sphere.

Forward Bloc, All-India was founded by Subhash Chandra Bose (1897-1945) in 1939 after he was forced to resign as Congress Presidential to secure the objective of Indian independence by implant struggle against the British. It was received after 1947 and is new recognized as a regional party in West Bengal and Bihar and is a constituent of the United Left Front in West Bengal.

Forward Policy designates any assertive and proactive policy as against passivity and going slow. Historically* the term is used to describe British policy towards the northwestern frontiers of India which was inhabited by the tribals. From 1840, onward the British government has followed a policy of 'closed frontiers' but during the 1890's tribal incursions into the settled areas became intolerable. A 'forward policy, was adopted to subdue the tribes by sending military expeditions.

Four Freedoms were proclaimed by President Franklin D. Roosevelt (1882-1945) in his State of the Union address to the US Congress in 1941 as the American objectives in entering World War II. They were: freedom of speech and expression; freedom of belief and worship; freedom from want; and freedom from fear. This declaration was followed up by the Atlantic Charter, issued in August 1941 and the Charter of the UNO, adopted in 1945.

Four Modernizations (China) ref to basic objectives of China's national reconstruction policy formulated in 1979 by the post - Mao reformist regime led by Deng Xiao Ping. The "four modernizations" Were modernization of agriculture;

modernization of industry; modernization of science and technology establishment; and modernization of national defence establishment. These objectives were to be achieved by scrapping of agricultural communes and restoration of private farming; economic liberalization and opening up of China for foreign trade and investment.

Fourth Estate refers to the press and the mass media of communications in democratic countries.

Franc Zone refers to a group of African countries (which were formerly colonies of France), besides the French Overseas Territories which pegged their national currencies to the French Franc. With effect from 1 January 2002 the Franc Zone countries pegged their currencies to the Euro. These countries are: Benin, Burkina Fasu, Cameroon, Central African Republic, Chad, Comoros, Republic of Congo, Ivory Coast, Equatorial Guinea, French Overseas Territories, Gabon, Guinea-Bissau, Mali, Niger, Senegal, and Togo.

Franchise is the right to vote; universal adult franchise or the principle of ''one man, one vote'' is the means by which people exercise their political sovereignty in/general election to elect their legislative and executive authorities.

Free Legal Aid Scheme (India) was formulated under the Legal Services Authorities (Amendment) Act 2002, to provide free legal assistance to the members of the Scheduled Castes* and scheduled Tribes*; victims of human trafficking; sufferers from natural calamities and industrial disasters; victims of caste and communal violence; destitutes; bonded labourers; women; children; disabled persons; and persons whose income is less than that prescribed by a state government for eligibility to receive free legal aid. Eligible persons can claim such benefits as the free service of a lawyer, payment of court fees and other incidental expenses from the designated legal services authorities appointed by the government at the district, state and national levels.

Free Trade Area of the Americas -- FTAA was first conceived as the hemispheric extension of the NAFTA* at the first summit of 34 American states held in 1994. If realized the FTAA would create a single hemispheric free trade zone (excluding Cuba) that would run from Alaska to Terra del Fuego. Its inauguration was blocked in 2005.

Free Trade is an opposite of protectionism which means an international trade regime broadly free from unfair tariffs and restrictions but does not mean total abolition of all trade taxes. The prominent of free trade regard the world as a single economic entity where unhindered exchange of goods and services and free movement of capital leads to comparative advantage, brings about collective prosperity and promotes peace and harmony among nations. The World Trade Organization* has been created to establish a regime of international free trade by means of international agreements arrived at voluntarily among the member-states.

Freemasonary. The freemasons' movement originated during the latter half of the nineteenth century as a secular alternative to the Roman Catholic Church. They belonged to the middle and lower-middle class in French society. They preached human unity and humanitarian and liberal values and practised philanthropy. In 1896 there were some 364 freemason lodges and about 24,000 freemasons. By 1926 the numbers had risen to 583 and 52,000. Thereafter the movement spread to Europe, America, Asia and Africa.

French Community was provided for under the Constitution of the Fifth Republic of France* as a successor of the former **French Union** (1946-1958) which comprised the French Republic and its colonies in Asia and Africa. The former French Union during Fourth Republic of France was like the former British Commonwealth and the French Community of the Fifth Republic was a voluntary association of former French colonies, like the Commonwealth of Nations, as it offered the French colonies either self-government within the Community or complete independence. The chapter of the 1958 Constitution of France dealing with the French Community was deleted in 1996 marking a final break with the French colonial past.

French Revolution (1789) refers to the totality of violent and revolutionary developments taking place in France during 1789-1799 that resulted in the overthrow of the ancient regime of absolute monarchy and hereditary nobility. It marked the supremacy of the middle class and rise of constitutional and democratic government.

Führer (German for leader) was title used by Adolf Hitler as leader of the Nazi Party in 1921 and thereafter as the Chancellor-cum-president of Germany in 1933.

Full Employment is a condition when the maximum number of workers are gainfully employed at any given time. Attainment and maintenance of full employment is one of the basic objectives of public in almost all developed countries. The meaning of the term can best be understood in comparison with the related terms--employment, unemployment, underemployment and over full-employment. Broadly speaking employment means employment or exploitation of any factor of production (land, raw material, capital and labour). Narrowly conceived it is the employment of workers in the economy.. Unemployment means that the factors of production are present but they are not put: to use, that is the workers are unemployed or jobless. Underemployment is a condition when it is not possible to employ all the workers. Some are employed while others remain unemployed. Even those who are employed get inadequate wages. Conversely full employment is a condition when maximum number of workers are employed at any given time. The number of vacant jobs is invariably greater than the number of the jobless. This phenomenon is associated with the developed economies of the North. However, there is no such thing as absolute full employment as even in the developed countries not less than three per cent workers are out of job at any given time. Similarly, over full employment is a condition when full employment exceeds 97 per cent and the demand for workers is not met.

"Full Faith and Credit." Article TV, Section 1 of the Constitution of the USA requires that full faith and credit shall be given in each state of the union to the public acts, records and judicial proceedings of every other state. Accordingly nobody can evade the execution of judgment made against him by a court in one state by transfering hits residence to another state.. The decree, of the first state shall be enforced through the legal machinery of the other state.

Fundamentalism (from *fundaments* = basic principles) means belief in and adherence to the orthodox or fundamental beliefs of religion and ethics. Fundamentalism or the Evangelical movement arose in the USA during the 1920's to counteract the relativization and marginalization of the Christian religion by secularism, atheism, natural science, ethically neutral social science and liberal theology. Hence fundamentalist is one who uphold the absolute validity of the orthodox religious and moral code against the onslaughts of atheism, materialism, sexual anarchy and libertarianism.

Fusion of Powers means the fusion of legislative and executive powers as against their separation. In the British-style parliamentary system of government the legislative and executive branches are fused together by the mechanism in of the cabinet while in an American-style tripolar system of and judicial government the legislative, executive and judicial branches are organically separate from each other and operate in a system of constitutional check and balances.

G

Gadgil Formula of allocation of development assistance from the Centre to the States for their development plans was approved by the National Development Council* in 1968 and was applied to the fourth five-year development plan and succeeding plans. The criteria for distribution of funds among the states were: 60 per cent on the basis of population; 10 per cent for economic backwardness; 10 per cent for continuing major and medium irrigation and power projects; 10 per cent on the basis of tax effort; and 10 per cent for special problems. The Gadgil Formula was modified by the NDC in 1980 and 1991 and by the Twelfth Finance Commission in 2005.

Gandhi-Irwin Pact (1931) was signed between M. K. Gandhi, the leader of the Indian National Congress and Lord Irwin, the Viceroy and Governor-General of India on 5 March 1931, It was: agreed that (1) the Congress shall discontinue civil disobedience and the British authorities shall take reciprocal measures; (2) in the constitutional scheme outlined at the first session of the Round Table Conference* "an all-Indian federation, responsible government, protection of Indian national interests* safeguards for minorities, and the financial credit of India; shall be regarded as basic points and adhered to; and (3) steps will be take for the participation of the representative of the Indian National Congress in the future sessions of the Round Table Conference.

Gandhism refers to a set of social and political ideas propounded and preached by M. K. Gandhi (1869-1948) which he derived from ancient and modern philosophical traditions, e.g. in the sphere of personal conduct adherence to non-violence, truth, purity, piety, continence and self-sacrifice; in the social sphere human equality, opposition to untouchability and caste oppression, upliftment of the poor and socially relevant basic education; and in the political sphere political and economic independence to be attained by ahinsa* and *satyagraha* religious toleration and communal harmony, a decentralized panchayat-based democracy, and a deregulated free economy.

"Gang of Four" (China) refers to four leading personalities in China who were the architects of the cultural Revolution* (1966-1977). They succeeded Chairman Mao Ze Dong in 1976. They were ousted by the rival faction of the Chinese Communist Party led by Deng Xiao Piang in 1977, tried in 1980 and expelled from the Party. They were: Mao's widow Jiang Quig, Zhang Chunqiao, Wang Hongwen, and Yao Wenyuan.

Gaullism refers to political ideas and preferences of General Charles de Gaulle (1890-1970), the leader of the Free French forces during World War II and the founder and first president of the fifth republic of France. They stress national unity and solidarity* restoration of national honour and prestige, presidential leadership in the state, a strong technocratic executive system, accountability of government, rationalized parliamentarism, political stability and economic progress.

Gaza Strip of occupied Palestine is a strip of land of 365 sqms in area and a population of 1.5 million situated on the easternmost coast of the Mediterranean, and bounded by Israel in the north and east and Egypt in the south. The strip was occupied by Egypt during the Arab-Israeli war of 1948 and remained under Egyptian control until 6 June 1967 when it was captured by Israel along with the Sinai Peninsula. Egypt ceded the area to Israel under the Egyptian-Israeli Peace Treaty of 1979. The area was placed under the interim rule of the Palestinian Authority in 1995. Israel withdrew its military from it in September 2005 and dismantled the Jewish settlements built there since 1967.

Gendarmerie (men-at-arms) is a corps of cavalry meant for routine patrolling, apprehending criminals, maintaining public order or safeguarding the frontiers. The singular is *gendarme* .

Gender Empowerment Index (GEI) was evolved by the UN Development Programme as part of its Human Development Index (HDI) to measure the level of empowerment of the women in the member-states The index is made of three indicators—the proportion of seats held by women in the national parliament; the proportion of female managers in the managerial force of the country; and the proportion of female professionals and technical workers in force. On the GEI the developed countries have fared better than the underdeveloped countries of Asia, Africa and Latin America, though variations are found among the developed countries.

General Agreement on Trade and Tariffs—GATT was signed in Geneva on 30 October 1947 by 28 member-states of the UN. It was conceived as a temporary multilateral trade regulatory agency to promote the ideal of international free trade by mutually agreed tariff reductions until such time as the proposed International Trade Organization* (ITO) came into being. Initially two-third of trade items between contracting parties were covered by concessional tariffs. The last round of trade negotiations under the GATT (the Uruguay Round) ended with the signing of a charter of the World Trade Organization (WTO) which replaced the GATT with effect from 1 January 1995.

General Agreement on Trade in Services—GATS was concluded by the member-states of the GATT in 1995. It considered foreign investment in services as one of the four modes of supply of services. In other words it declared an open door for foreign service providers. Twelve services including education were globalized and textile quotas abolished with effect from 1 January 2005.

General Revenue Sharing— GRS (US) was adopted as a via media between the conditional federal grants and block grants as a method of fiscal transfers from the Union to the States. It was first enacted by the US Congress by the State and Local Fiscal Assistance Act, 1972 which has since been renewed for five-year terms. The GRS is managed by the Office of Revenue Sharing in the Treasury Department of the US Government

General Will is neither will of all nor the public opinion. While the public opinion reflects the contemporary preoccupations of the public the general will represents the basic desires of all the people. It is synonymous with the public interest.

Generalized System of Preferences—GSP was proposed at the UN Conference on Trade and Development* (UNCTAD I) held in 1964 and accepted as a whole by the developed countries at the Multilateral Trade Negotiations held in 1979 in Geneva. Under the GSP regime the commodities of the developing had access to the markets of the developed countries with little or no duties. The GSP regime came to an end with the coming into being of the World Trade Organization* (WTO) on 1 January 1995. The European Union continues to follow a GSP to grant the developing countries access to the EU market at either zero duty or reduced rates.

Geneva Conventions refer to four international conventions signed in 1949 in Geneval and two additional protocols signed in 1977 to regulate the conduct of war. The conventions relate to the treatment of the wounded and sick soldiers on the battlefield; (2) the treatment of wounded, sick and shipwrecked soldiers at sea; (3) the treatment of the prisoners of wary and (4) the treatment of the civilian population in the war zone.

Gent1eman's Agreement is an informal understanding or agreement, whether written or unwritten, which though not legally binding, is nevertheless observed by the parties as a matter of courtesy. An instance is the gentleman's agreement arrived at between countries exporting nuclear technology in 1975 in London and the same was confirmed through exchange of letters among the parties in 1976.

Geopolitics is the English version of the German term **Geopolitik** which became a vogue in Nazi Germany. It is applied political geography. Its core assumption is that geography is the main determinant of the domestic and foreign policy of a country. Its objective is utilization of geographical information for strategic: planning and territorial expansion.

German Reunification Treaty (1990). The Treaty on the Final Settlement with respect to Germany was signed on 12 September 1990 in Moscow following the conclusion of talks between the Federal Republic of Germany (West Germany), the German Democratic Republic (East Germany), and the four allies of World war II— the USA, the USSR, Britain and France which paved the way under international law for reunification of Germany with Berlin as its capital which took place on 3 October 1990.

Gerrymander is the malpractice of tampering with the boundaries of electoral constituencies to give unfair advantage to a particular party. The pejorative term came in vogue after Massachusetts Governor Elbridge Gerry who in 1811 redistributed the electoral districts in his state in a way to suit his partisan interests that the state resembled a salamander. Certain groups are included or excluded to give unfair advantage to a particular party. *Affirmative Gerrymander* is resorted to in the us, under the impact of the philosophy of affirmative action, to enable certain minority groups to return their candidates.

Gestapo was the abbreviation of the *Gaeheimes Staats Polizeiamt* (Secret State Police) established in 1933 as the intelligence and surveillance force of the Nazi regime in Germany. It became a symbol of Nazi repression and terror.

Gibraltar Problem (from Arabic *Jabal el Tariq*-mountain of

Tariq, an Arab general) is a mountainous region ceded by Spain to Great Britain in 1713 and has since then been a British Crown colony. The recent Spanish claim for sovereignty over Gibraltar is pending before the UN General Assembly. In a referendum held in 2002, 99 per cent of the inhabitants of Gibraltar voted against the proposal for joint Spanish-British sovereignty. The strait of Gibraltar links the Mediterranean Sea with the Atlantic Ocean and is of great strategic importance.

Glasnost (Russian for "openness") refers to a policy of operated openness in the Soviet Society instituted by Mikhail Gorbachev, the General Secretary of the former Communist Party of the Soviet Union from 1985 to 1991.

Globalism is the highest stage of internationalism, while internationalism was a philosophy that modified the harshness of nationalism by stressing the need to address the common concerns of the nation states globalism stands for elimination of all national Barriers from the may of a muted gable community pursuing uniforms good and gable scale policies.

Globalization (to make global) is a process considered as inevitable and irreversible stage of international inter-dependence, particularly in the economic sphere. It is a process of creating a global economy transcending national boundaries and free from national and international regulation. It will override and regulate local economies. A globalized economy simply means a global free market (propped by the IMF*, IBRD* and the WTO*) which allows unfettered play to the finance capital and the multinational corporations of the developed countries. One school of thought view globalization as a triumph of liberalism on the world-scale while an opposite school looks at it as a recrudescence of nineteenth century imperialism and colonialis.

Glorious Revolution (1688-89) refers to the bloodless constitutional revolution in England that occurred in England during 1688-89. The basis of conflict between the Crown and Parliament was that the king asserted royal prerogative while parliament claimed the privilege of controlling the servants of the Crown. The struggle for supremacy ended in the victory of parliament and flight of reigning King James II to France. Thereupon parliament passed the Bill of Rights and installed William and Mary of Orange as the monarchs of England on their acceptance of the terms and conditions laid down in this instrument. The Glorious Revolution ushered in an era of constitutional limited monarchy and parliamentary sovereignty.

Gold Standard was the institutionalization of gold as the standard of value and medium international monetary exchange. The G.S was first adapted by Britain in 1821 and by the US in 1873. It prevailed up to 1933 when it collapsed. Even then value of a currency entitled to be determined in relation to gold and most countries accepted American dollars and British pond as the reserve currencies. The US in 1971 abaudued the convertibility of the dollar in gold and adopted a floating exchange rate. Most countries followed suit in 1973. Since then value of National currencies is determined not by gold but by market forces i.e. demand and supply.

Good-Friday Agreement (1998) was signed in April 1998 in Belfast, Northern Ireland, among the governments of the UK and Ireland, Sinn Fein and Northern Irish political parties whereby the Irish Republic renounced its claim to Northern Ireland and the UK agreed for introduce an executive system composed of both the protestant and Catholic parties. (See Northern Ireland Problem).

Good-Neighbour Policy (US) was adopted, in place of the "big stick policy", by President Franklin D. Roosevelt's administration. It implied an attitude of non-intervention in Latin America and development of friendly and good neighbourly relations with the countries of this region. The change of policy had taken place against the anticipated possibility of spread of communism in this region.

Good Offices and Mediation. Good offices refer to efforts by a third party to bring the parties to a dispute to the negotiating table. Once the negotiations start the third party withdraws. Mediation, however, involves a more active role. The mediator not only formulates the principles to form the basis of negotiations between the disputants but also oversees the discussions and facilitates a settlement. Conversely, arbitration requires prior agreement between the parties to refer their dispute to an arbitrator and to abide by his decision.

GOSPLAN was the State Planning Commission of the former USSR responsible for preparing a unified national economic plan for the whole country from the union level at the top to the village level

Government of the Assembly (France) was the institutionalization of the Jacobin (revolutionary) doctrine of national sovereignty. Sovereignty of the nation could only mean the sovereignty of its national assembly representing all sections and groups of the people (i.e. elected on the basis of proportional representation). This sovereignty could not be delegated to any person or body. So the assembly was to govern through a council of ministers subordinate to it. The doctrine resulted in the supremacy of parliament and subordination and emasculation of the government during the Third and Fourth Republics.

Grand Coalition means a coalition of almost all or most of the parties represented in parliament supporting the government. As a result there is either no opposition or a few minor parties are left to oppose the government. Such a phenomenon occurs occasionally in parliamentary democracies of continental Europe, as in the Federal Republic of Germany in October 2005.

Grant-in-Aid is the financial assistance given by one (higher) level of government to a (lower) level of government for a variety of purposes. Grants-in-aid maybe conditional or block or combination of both.

Great Depression refers to the great cyclycal crisis that resulted from the artificial economic boom in the USA during 1922-29. The crisis was caused by unprecedented speculation in the securities markets. The sudden crash of American stock prices triggered depression in America that soon engulfed the whole world. By 1932 American stock losses had reached the level of $ 75 billion. Factories and businesses were closed down and millions of workers were rendered jobless. The ill-effects of the depression were overcome by a series of economic revival and social rehabilitation measures implemented by the Roosevelt administration during 1933-39.

Great Powers occupy the top rank in the hierarchy of nation-states. Although sovereign equality of all states has been formally acknowledged since the Treaty of Westphalia till this day an inherent inequality of status exists because of disparities of size and population and uneven distribution of natural resources and potential among the nation-states. In international politics states are designated as "powers* because they are the embodiment of power—both as an end as well as a means, thus states are ranked as *great,* middle, and *small* powers. Because of their power potential the great powers are prime actors in international politics. However, the great-power status is by no means permanent and fixed. It is variable because of loss of power or extinction. A lot of reshuffling has taken place in the ranks of the great powers since the nineteenth century. Thus at the Congress of Vienna held in 1815 there were eight great powers—Britain, Austria, France, Portugal, Prussia, Spain, Sweden and Russia. With the decline of Portugal, Spain and Sweden their number was reduced to five. With the rise of Italy one more power was added to the list. When the thirteen north American colonies declared their Independence of Great Britain in 1776 the USA emerged as a great power in its own right. Then in consequence of the Sino-Japanese war of 1865 Japan attained the status of a great power. At the outbreak of world War I eight countries were recognized, as great powers—Britain, Austria-Hungary; France, Germany, Italy, Russia, USA and Japan. After World War I Austria-Hungary was dismembered and ceased to be a great power. Russia was out of the great-power club because of the Bolsehevik Revolution* in 1917. The Treaty of Versailles* of 1919 and the Covenant of the League of Nations for the first time formally recognized the great-power status of five countries which were made permanent members of the Council of the League of Nations—Britain, France, Italy, Japan and the USA. The USA did not join the League because the US Senate failed to ratify the Covenant. Russia was admitted to the League in 1937. After World War II the Charter of the UNO recognized the USA, USSR, Britain, France and China as great powers and made them permanent members of the UN Security council, since then India, Germany, Japan and Brazil emerged as regional big powers and have claimed a right to hold permanent seats in the UN Security Council. The term "superpower" (or global power) became a vogue in the wake of World War II to designate the new power-status of the USA and the USSR because of their preponderant military power and global strategic reach. The USSR vanished in 1991 and the USA remained the sole global power.

Greater Arab Free Trade Area—GAFTA was created on 1 January 2005 in pursuance of an Agreement to Facilitate and Develop Trade among the Arab Countries signed by the member-states of the Arab League* in 1981. In 2004 fifteen Arab states had agreed to join the GAFTA.

Group of Eight—G-8 is an informal grouping of world's richest eight countries founded in 1975 for consultations on adopting a common policy over macro issues of global development. The members are: Canada, France, Germany, Italy, Japan Russia, the UK and the USA.

Group-77—G-77 refers to the group of representatives of Asian, African and Latin American states in the UN General

Assembly whose number during the 1960's was 77. Although their number has increased to 133 in 2005 the original designation survives. Their membership of the G-77 is coterminous with their membership in the Non-Aligned Movement* (NAM) with the difference that while the G—77 deals mainly with economic and humanitarian issues, the NAM concentrates on political and strategic issues. The term G-77 came into vogue with their success in 1962 in securing the endorsement of the UN General Assembly of their proposal for convening a UN conference on Trade and Development*. Subsequently UNCTAD I was convened in 1964 in Geneva which approved a Generalized System of Preferences* (GSP) to benefit the developing countries. The G-77 was also instrumental in getting a Declaration on the Establishment of a New International Economic Order and an accompanying Programme of Action passed by the UN General Assembly in 1974. At the North-South summit of 22 countries held on 23-24 October 1981 in Cancun, Mexico, the developed countries refused to make any substantial concessions to the developing countries. Thereupon the G-77 called for *South-South cooperation* for achieving collective self-reliance. The first South summit of the G-77 was held on 12-14 April 2000 in Havana, Cuba, which issued a declaration ("Havana Declaration") emphasizing the need for a "new global humanitarian order aimed at reversing the growing disparities between the rich and poor".

Guerilla Warfare (from Spanish *guerilla* = minor war) was first used to describe the armed resistance of the Spanish people against the occupying French forces during the war of 1808-1814. Nowadays guerilla warfare refers to sporadic: and wanton attacks by irregular armed bands against their target during an insurrectionor a civil war or foreign invasion or foreign occupation. Now regular armies also raise guerilla units to combat the irregular guerilla forces.

Gulf Cooperation Council—GCC is an intergovernmental organization founded in 1981 by Bahrain, Kuwait, Oman,

Qatar, Saudi Arabia and the United Arab Emirates to promote regional cooperation in the Arabian peninsula and the Arabian Gulf region. Its headquarters is in Riadh, Saudi Arabia.

Gulf of Aqaba is the northeaster extension of the Red Sea. Its length is 100 miles and the width varies from 12 to 17 miles at different points. On its northwest lies Saudi Arabia and on its northeast is the Sina Peninsula. Its entrance is made narrow and hazardous by the location of the two islands of Tiran and Sanafar. Towards it end the Gulf is about five miles wide and this is the junction of Egyptian-Israeli, Jordanian-Israeli and Jordanian-Saudi-Arabian boundaries. On the Jordanian side is located the port of Aqaba, the lone sea-outlet for Jordan, which was constructed during World War I. On the Israeli side is locate the Port of Ailath which was constructed by the Israelis over an Arab village called Umm Rashrash captured by the Israelis after their signing of the Armistice Agreement with the Arabs in 1949.

Gulf War (1991) refers to the American military intervention with political backing from the regional allies against the Iraqi occupation of Kuwait in 1990. Iraqi forces were defeated and Kuwait's sovereignty restored. The second-gulf war was launched by the USA and its allies against Iraq alleging it possessed weapons of mass destruction (WMD's) which threatened the existence of the western world. As a result, Iraqi dictator Saddam Hussain's regime was toppled and Iraq placed under American military occupation which was still in force till the end of 2005.

H

Habeas Corpus Writ of (Latin *habeas corpus* = have the body) is a judicial remedy against arbitrary arrest and illegal detention available to the citizens of countries having a common-law tradition, including India. Any detained person, or somebody else on his behalf has a right to submit a petition before the court of law for the issue of a writ of habeas corpus. Acting on the petition the court orders the detaining authority to produce before it the reasons for: his arrest or detention. If the court is not convinced of the validity of the reasons shown it will order the immediate release of the detainee.

Hague International Conferences were convened in 1899 and 1907 and are regarded as precursors of modern international organization The first international conference was convened in Hague at the behest of Czar Nicholas II of Russia to consider the ways of establishing real and durable peace, promote disarmament and limit production of arms. The conference did a remarkable job by adopting a number of conventions relating to regulation of land and naval warfare, the pacific settlement of international disputes, and provision for the establishment of a Permanent Court if International Arbitration in the Hague. The second conference adopted a number of conventions codifying the rules of customary international law. A third conference was proposed to be held in 1915 but could not take place because of the outbreak of World War I in 1914. After the war the League of Nations was created as a permanent international organization to deal with questions of war and peace.

Hallstein Doctrine was declared in 1955 by Walter Hallstein, the foreign minister of the Federal Republic of Germany (West Germany) to the effect that the Federal Republic will break diplomatic relations with any country that recognized the German A Democratic Republic (the communist regime in East Germany). The only exception was the former USSR with which Federal Republic established diplomatic relations in 1948 to negotiate for the return of the German prisoners-of-war. The Hallstein Doctrine was superseded by *Ostpolitik* (eastern policy) pursued by the Federal Republic during the 1970's leading to normalization of relations with communist countries.

Hansard is the official report of the debates of the House of Lords and House of Commons of British Parliament published dally from London. The title is derived from the name of T.C. Hansard who was the first man to start publication of parliamentary debates in 1803.

Hare System. See Proportional Representation".

Head of Government. The office of the head of government, variously called the prime minister, first minister or chancellor, in parliamentary democracies is separate from the office of the constitutional head of state. In a parliamentary democracy The prime minister as the head of the cabinet, head of government and the leader of the parliamentary majority is the real chief executive.

Head of State whether he is an absolute monarch or a constitutional monarch or a directly elected president or an indirectly elected president or a nominated governor-general, a head of state presides over a state and is distinguished from the head of government who represents the parliamentary majority for the time-being. The head of state symbolizes the unity and continuity of the state and its stability. While the President of the USA (called solitary executive) is both a constitutional head of state and the real chief executive, the constitutional heads in parliamentary democracies reign but do not govern. They are bound to act only on ministerial advice. The only exception is the mixed presidential-parliamentary system of the Fifth Republic of France where the President of the Republic is directly elected by the people and is vested with certain independent powers and functions but the day-to-day administration is carried on by a non-parliamentary cabinet headed by a prime minister which is collective responsible before the National Assembly. The French style executive is also known as "bicephalous" (double-headed) executive.

Hegemony/Hegemonism. Hegemony implies the exercise of preponderant influence by a powerful state over a given region. It differs from *domination* in that while domination involves use of coercion to compel obedience from the dominated people *hegemony* implies voluntary compliance on the part of the people under hegemony with the will of the hegemon.. The examples are the hegemony of the USA over the Western hemisphere and of the former USSR over eastern Europe. *Hegemonism* in international politics is a policy of seeking hegemony over neighbouring countries or regions or the entire world; of claiming exclusive spheres of influence and of the right to intervention at will. Hegemonism is an antithesis of the principle of national sovereignty and sovereign equality of states enshrined in the Charter of the UNO. The UN General Assembly in its 34th session passed a Resolution on the Inadmissibility of the Policy of Hegemonism in international Relations.

Helsinki Conference. See "Conference on security and cooperation in Europe" (CSCE).

"Henry VIII Clause" (Britain). King Henry VIII of England (1509-1547) used to ask his Parliament to insert a clause in statutes passed by it empowering the King to make rules necessary and proper to carry out the aims and objectives of the statutes. The result was what came to be known as delegated legislation.

Heuristic Models are analytical constructs or abstract frameworks like Max Weber's ideal types or structural-functionalism or the systems theory that help a researcher in ordering and explaining the phenomena of the real world.

Hierarchy also called the pyramidal principle or the scalar process, is an ordering principle of all big organizations. All bureaucratic organizations are structured into graded levels or steps. At the top of the pyramid is the chief executive or the top management, below is the middle management: playing a supervisory role and the bottom is the operating level. There obtains a unity of command from the top to the bottom and all levels are linked in a chain of command. A single line of authority runs from the top to the bottom and a single line of responsibility moves fro the bottom to the top. Thus the organization operates as an integrated whole.

High Commissioner is a term used in different contexts (1) the chief diplomatic representative one member of the Commonwealth of Nations accredited to another member is called a *high commissioner* enjoying the status of a full ambassador; his chancery is called a *high commission* ; (2) the term is also used to designate the highest official vested with administrative or diplomatic functions deputed by a suzerain power to a dependent state or territory; and (3) the term is also used to designate high officials of international organizations vested with some special functions, e.g. the UN High commissioner for the Refugees or the UN High Commissioner for Human Rights*.

High Seas also called open seas are oceans, seas, gulfs and straits (excluding the territorial waters and inland seas and lakes) which are regarded as international seas belonging to the whole of humanity and open for navigation and exploitation by all nations. Customary international law has guaranteed freedom of navigation through the high seas and exploitation of its resources by all nations whether littoral or noon littoral or landlocked. No state is allowed to control any part of the high seas or claim sovereignty over any part of the high seas or deny freedom of navigation or exploitation to other states.

Hind Swaraj is the title of apolitical treatise written by M. K. Gandhi in 1908 during his stay in South Africa wherein he analysed the causes of India's social and cultural degradation, poverty and backwardness and political subjection. He attributed all evils in India's national life to British imperialism. No improvement could be expected without attainment of *swaraj* (self-government).

Hind/Hindu. *Hind* is the ancient Arabic name (anglicized as India) for Hindustan or the country which lies to the east of the river Indus. Arabic *Hindi,* Hindustani and Hindu are applied to the inhabitants of India. However, in modern times the term Hindu became reserved for Indians following the indigenous religions of Sanatan Dharma, Jainism and Buddhism to the exclusion of Indians following Christianity, Islam or Zorostrianism.

Hindi/Hindustani. Hindi, or High Hindi or *Sanskrit-nishtha* Hindi, or Hindi written in the Devanagari script, was made the official language of the Indian Union and of the north-central states of Uttar Pradesh, Bihar, Madhya Pradesh, Jharkhand, Chhattisgarh, Delhi, Haryana and Rajasthan. *Hindustani* was a term devised during the inter was period to designate the mixed language incorporating both Hindu and Urdu or the *lingua franca* of northern India written in both the Persian and Devanagari scripts. It was visualized by M.K. Gandhi, Jawaharlal Nehru and other Indian leaders as the national language of an independent India. Hindustani was conceived as an ideal solution for the language problem in India but partition of the country in 1947 removed the need to accommodate the Urdu language written in the Persian script so Hindustani was abandoned altogether and Hindi in Devanagari was declared to be the official language of the Indian Union.

Hindi-Urdu Conflict. In India before 1947 was an offshoot of the political rivalry between the Indian National Congress and the All India Muslim League, which eventually developed into the communal conflict between the Hindu and Muslim communities. The Urdu language, written in the Persian script, evolved during the seventeenth century and onwards from the *khari boli* dialect spoken in and around Delhi. The new dialect, variously designated as *Hindawi, Rekhta* (mixed dialect) or *zaban-i-Urdu-i-Mualla* (the language of the royal camp), had by the nineteenth century become the *lingua franca* of north India and was understood in the rest of the country. As the name suggests, Urdu was the product of commingling of native Indians and immigrant communities which assimilated its vocabulary from native dialects as well as the Arabic, Persian and Turkish languages. The differentiation of Hindi from Urdu was started by the East India Company* which established the Fort William College in 1750 in Calcutta for the training of the officials of the Company. Here was laid the distinction between Hindi and Urdu. Under instruction from the British some Indian writers were employed to write language textbooks in the Devanagari script (hitherto reserved for scribing the Sanskrit texts) with the admixture of Sanskrit, words. This new medium came to be associated with, the Hindu community. At the same time, some other writers were employed to write textbooks in Urdu in the Persian script with the admixture of Persian and Arabic words and this medium came to be associated with the Muslim community. /Hindi-Urdu conflict started during the latter half of the nineteenth century when Hindu nationalists demanded that the British authorities replace Urdu by Hindi in the lower courts and educational institutions. The government of the United Provinces was the first provincial government in British India to make the use of Hindi compulsory in the courts of law in 1900 creating much consternation among the Urdu-speaking community. The question of language became acute with the introduction of provincial autonomy under the Government of India Act, 1935. However, a *modus vivendi* was found by adopting both Hindi and Urdu in the northern Provinces as the languages of the courts and for teaching in schools and colleges. Thereafter a consensus emerged for making the Hindustani (a composite language made of both Hindi and Urdu and written in both the Persian and Devanagari scripts) as the future national language of an independent India. However, with the partition of the country in 1947 the need for accommodating the demand of the Urdu-speakers was removed. The Constituent Assembly of India, therefore, declared Hindi in the Devanagari script as the official language of the Indian Union. After independence the use of Urdu in the official administration, in the courts of law and as the medium of instruction in schools was discontinued.

Hindu Mahasabha, All-India had its origins in a series of local *Hindu sabhas* (associations) formed in the provinces of Panjab and Bengal during 1905-06. The provincial-level Hindu Sabha formed in 1913 resolved to convene an all-India conference of the Hindus in Haridwar (UP, India) on the occasion of *kumbh* (grand religious congregation of the Hindus held ever twelfth year on the banks of river Ganges) of 1915. Thus was born the All-India Hindu Sabha which was renamed as the All-India Hindu Mahasabha in 1921. It enjoyed mass following during the interwar period and worked in close cooperation with the Indian National Congress. Its objectives included the promotion of the unity and strength of the Hindu nation through *shuddhi* (conversion of non-Hindus to Hinduism) and *sanghatan* (organizing the Hindus on a single platform); ensuring the supremacy of the Hindu race, Hindu nation and Hindu culture; establishment of *Hindu Raj* (Hindu state) in India; and popularization of Sanskritized Hindi written in Devanagari script. The military wing of the AIHM was called the Hindustan National Guards. The AIHM was totally opposed to giving of any concessions to the Indian Muslim minority and counteracted the All-India Muslim League demands for separate electorate, weightage, a federal constitution, provincial autonomy or later the demand for Pakistan. After attainment of independence in 1947 the Mahasabha in 1948 resolved to suspend its political activities on the ground that most of its objectives had been achieved under Congress Raj but vowed to continue the struggle for the attainment of the ideal of *Akhand Bharat* (restoration of the political unity of India through the undoing of Pakistan and Bangladesh). The AIHM soon faded from the political scene of India. It still exists in name and maintains a party office in New Delhi but its place was taken first by the RSS, and Bharatiya Jana Sangh, then by the Bharatiya Janata Party, and the Vishwa Hindu Parishad.

Hindu-Muslim Conflict in India was unknown before 1857. The Indian Revolt of 1857 was a turning-point in inter-community relations in India. Although both Hindus and Muslims had participated equally in the revolt against misrule of the British East: India Company the British singled out the Muslims for retribution and vindictive action. British anti-Muslim policy continued until 1870's when the British became aware of the rise of nationalism among the majority Hindu community. To counteract the influence of the Indian National Congress they turned to Muslims favourably and helped in the organization of the All India Muslim League in 1906, introduced separate electorate for the Muslims in 1909 and gave them weightage in public services The British were successful in implementing their imperialist policy of divide and rule by keeping away the Muslim upper classes from the Indian National Congress. However, the Congress-League Lucknow Pact of 1916 and the alliance between the All India Khilafat Committee and the Indian National Congress in 1920 for a joint fight against the British were turning points in Hindu-Muslim relations. But relations were soured in the wake of the publication of the Motilal Nehru Committee Report in 1928 which denied the right of the Muslims to elect their representatives to legislative bodies through separate electorates. This led to the formulation of Jinnah's Fourteen Points in 1929 which were unacceptable to the Congress. The Congress-League political struggle over the shape of the future constitution of India and provincial autonomy deepened after the first general elections to principal legislative association held under the Government of India Act, 1935*. Disappointed with the Congress attitude the League passed its Lahore Resolution in 1940. Meanwhile the failure of the Cripps' mission in 1942 and the Cabinet Mission Plan of 1946 created a political deadlock in India which was broken by the acceptance by all major Indian political parties of the British-sponsored Partition Plan in 1947 which became the basis of partition of India into the two dominions of India and Pakistan under the Indian Independence Act, 1947. The Hindu-Muslim political conflict during 1937-1947 was an offshoots of the Congress-League conflict. Only the people of Muslim majority provinces favoured the demand of Pakistan. The Muslims of the rest of provinces where they were in a minority had nothing to do with Muslim League politics. Although partition of the country in 1947 resolved the Congress-League conflict it exacerbated the anti-Muslim feelings in India since 1947.

Hindutva (Sanskrit for "Hinduness") refers to the particularity of the Indian race, religion and culture which is claimed by some parties to be the basis of the Indian nation and state. The idea, of *Hindutva* or Hindu nationalism had its pedigree in the Arya Samaj movement of the nineteenth century and the All India Hindu Mahasabha formed in 1915. The ideology of Hindu nationalism was systematically formulated by the Hindu Mahasabha leader V.D. Savarkar in his *Hindutva* (1923; reprinted in 2003) and the second Supreme Leader of the Rashtriya Suwyam Sewak Sangh (RSS) M. S. Gowalkar in his *We. Or Our Nationhood* Defined (1939). On the basis of this ideology a militant Hindu nationalist movement was launched after 1984 by the Vishwa, Hindu Parishad which culumuted in the demolition of a mosque in Ayodhya in 1992 and coming to power of the Hindu Nationalist Party Bhartiya Janta Party at the Centre in 1998.

Historical Materialism is the materialistic interpretation of history. It is the Marxist approach to the analysis of human history and social development. All human history is a history of class struggle. Class relations change with the change in the economic system of an era. From primitive communism human society has progressed to serf economy then to feudal economy and from feudal to the modern capitalist economy. These stages are marked by the struggle of serfs and slave-owners, landlords and the vassals and the bourgevoisie and proletariat. Through the dialectical process of history the present bourgevois society is bound to give way a socialist society and is destined to come to an end with the coming into being of a stateless and classless communist society.

Hitlerism refers to dictatorial policies and tyrannical methods similar to those adopted by Adolf Hitler (1889-1945), the founder of the Nazi Party and the head of the Nazi state from 1933 to 1945.

Holism is the opposite of atomism that is the wholes are more than the sums of their parts and cannot be explained in terms of the properties of their parts and their interrelationships. The systems approach, structural-functionalism and functional Marxism are instances of an holistic approach.

Holy Alliance was an alliance of Russia, Austria and Prussia created by a treaty signed on 26 September 1815 in Paris. The moving force of the alliance was Czar Alexander I of Russia. Its stated objective was to uphold and promote Christian values in their national and international dealings but the real purpose was to combat and suppress revolutionary nationalism in the wake of the Napoleonic Wars. It was a sort of mutual security system of European monarchies joined later by other monarchs except those of Britain and Turkey. The Holy Alliance became defunct by the 1870's,

Holy Roman Empire existed from 962 AD to 1802 AD as a political grouping of Europe's Catholic principalities and regions. It was headed by the holy Roman Emperor and sanctified by the holy Pope of the Roman Catholic Church.

The Emperor exercised suzerainty over the local units. The holy Roman Empire claimed to/be the successor of the original Roman Empire which had ceased to exist by 476 AD. Until the emergence of the modern national states in Europe from the sixteenth century onwards the Holy Roman Empire functioned as a Christian commonwealth but had lost its effective power and prestige as a result of the Thirty Years' War* (1618-1648), and was finally dissolved in 1806.

Home Guards (India) was a voluntary force firsts raised in November 1946 to assist the regular police in dealing with civil disturbances. After 1962 Home Guards of the states and union territories were integrated into a unified force for deployment as am auxiliary force. They also perform civil defence duties. The expenditure on the home guards is jointly met by the Union and the States.

Home Rule refers to the phenomenon of internal self-government in a colony or an overseas province of an empire or a, regional unit of a unitary state.

Home Rule League was the movement launched by Congressmen during 1914-16 to press the British Government to grant India internal self-government. Two parallel home rule leagues were launched by two leaders of the Indian National Congress—Mrs. Anne Besant and Bal Gangadhar Tilak. They attracted not only the extremist youth who were kept out of the Congress since 1907 but also large numbers from the middle classes. But the movement did not touch the masses. The movement was one factor leading to the Montagu Declaration in 1917.

Hormuz, Strait of is a passage, about 65 to 95 kms wide, connecting the Arabian Gulf with the Gulf of Oman. In the north it is bounded by Iran and in the south by the Arabian peninsula. The strait is of great strategic and economic importance as much of the oil of the Arabian Gulf area is hipped through this passage. Within this strait are located the Iranian-controlled islands of Hormuz, Qeshm, Abu Musa, and Little Tumb and Great Tumb.

Human Development Index (HDI) was evolved by the UN Development Programme to measure human development in the member-states in terms of three basic criteria: (1) longevity as measured by life expectancy at birth; (2) knowledge as measured by adult literacy rate and gross enrolment in primary, secondary and tertiary education; and (3) standard of living as measured by gross domestic product (GDP) per capita. The index value lies between zero and one. The UNDP publishes an annual **Human Development Report.** Member-states are ranked according to their score on this index.

Human Rights or natural or fundamental rights of man are those essential rights and freedoms without which human beings cannot live a decent and civilized life. They have been the most important issue of human society from about: 2000 years before Christ till our own times. The Greek, Roman and Christian philosophers have grappled with this problem. With the rise, of constitutionalism these rights came to be guaranteed through written legal instruments. The Magna Carta* (1512), the Petition of Rights (1628), the English Bill of Rights (1689), the French Declaration on the Rights of Man and Citizen (1789), and the first ten amendments to the US Constitution (1791) are some examples. Respect for human rights is one of the universally recognized principles of international law. States are duty-bound to respect and protect these rights and freedoms within their jurisdiction. Respect of and protection of human rights throughout the world was included among the basic objectives of the world body in its Charter passed in 1945. To promote this objective the UN General Assembly on 10 December 1948 adopted the Universal Declaration of Human Rights and supplemented it by two Covenants adopted in 1966. One is the Covenant on the Civil and Political Rights which came into force from 23 March 1976 and the other is the Covenant on the

Economic, Social and Cultural Rights which came into force from 3 January 1976. Other international instruments in this regard include the Convention on Freedom of Association and Assembly (1948), the Anti-Genocide Convention (1948), the Convention on Women's Rights (1952), The Convention on the Rights of Children, the Convention on Refugees (1951), the Convention on the Status of Stateless Persons (1954), the Convention on Prevention of Forced Labour (1957), the Convention on Prohibition of Discrimination in Employment and Profession (1958), the Convention on Prohibition of Discrimination in the Educational Field (1960), the Convention on Prohibition of all forms of Racial Discrimination (1965), the UN Declaration on the Rights of Persons belonging to National or Ethnic, Religious and Linguistic Minorities (1992). Two most important regional conventions are the European Convention on Human Rights (1950) and the Final Act of the Conference on Security and Cooperation in Europe (1975). The European Convention was incorporated into the British law as the Human Rights Act, 1998, which came into force in October 2000.

Human Rights Commission, UN was founded in 1946 with its headquarters in Geneva to monitor the protection of human rights throughout the world. It consists of 53 members elected for a three-year term by the Economic and Social Council of the UN General Assembly giving adequate representation to the various geographical regions of the world. Besides, a Sub-Commission on the Minorities was created whose 26 members are elected by the UN Human Rights Commission from among candidates nominated by the member states. In conjunction with the UN High Commissioner for Human Rights the UN Sub-Commission reviews the practical application of the UN Declaration on Minorities and monitors the condition of minorities exposed to violence. Both report to the UN General Assembly through the ECOSOC.

Human Rights Committee, UN was created in accordance with the UN Covenant on the Civil and Political Rights (1966) to monitor its observance by the signatories. Its 18 members are elected by the signatory states for a four-year term. The Committee reports periodically to the UN General Assembly through the ECOSOC.

Humanism refers to all philosophies or tendencies which are centered on humanity or the human individual as an end in himself. All humanists preach humanistic values like respect for human life; the dignity of the human person; equality of human beings; right to self-determination and self-realization, etc. Humanism has its origins in the Judaic-Christian-Islamic religions, stoicism, modern liberalism and early Marxism.

Humanitarianism means concern with the sustenance and well-being of the humanity by means of philanthropy, charity, relief and rehabilitation and welfare services.

I

Icarianism is synonymous with utopianism; from *Voyage to Icarie* (1840), a work written by Utopian socialist philosopher Etienne Cabet (1788-1856) who depicted am imaginary socialist paradidise on earth. Icaria is an island southeast of Greece.

Idealism. As an opposite of materialism, idealism takes one of the two forms: *subjective* or epistemological idealism as represented by Berkeley, Hume and Mill. It is summed up in the phrase: "to be is to be perceived". Berkeley, for instance, perceived an independent cause of human perception---God. The other is the absolute or *metaphysical* idealism as represented by Hegel, Fichte and Schelling. All matter is merely a reflection of the ultimate idea. The real is the rational. For instance, Hegel holds the state to be a personification of God upon earth. Conversely, the idealism of Green, Bradley and Bosanquet represents a moralistic conception of the nature and function of the state the state is an ideal institution providing for the development of human personality. In this sense idealism is opposite of utilitarianism. Finally, as an opposite of philistinism idealism implies espousal of virtuous, noble ends in life.

Ideologue is an orthodox exponent of an ideology.

Ideology is a set of interrelated ideas and beliefs explaining the past and present of human society and prescribing a programme of action for a better future.

Ijtihad (Arabic for an inquiry with due diligence in matters of jurisprudence) is the exercise of his independent judgment by an Islamic scholar and deduction by logical reasoning of subsidiary rules from the primary rules of the *shariat* to deal with emerging situations and newer problems. Hence a *Mujtahid* is a theologian-jurist among the Twelver Shiite sect who after graduating from one of the Shiite seminaries located in Iran and Iraq becomes competent to guide the laity in matters of religion and law.

Illegal Migrants (Determination by Tribunal) Act, 1983 was passed by Indian Parliament to detect the illegal Bangladeshi migrants who settled in the State of Assam on or after 25 March 1971 and provided for their deportation from India. Sub-section (1) of Section 8 of the Act laid down that any original native of Assam could make an application before the IMDTA tribunal against any suspected illegal migrant residing within three kms from the place of residence of the applicant. The applicant had to provide the proof of the illegal migrant status of the suspect. The Act was declared unconstitutional by a bench of the Indian Supreme Court in June 2005 on the ground that facilitated "foreign aggression" against Assam.

Impeachment is the judicial proceeding of indicting high officials of state for sedition, subversion of the constitution, high crimes or grave misconduct, etc. by a parliament and dismissing them from office.

Imperial Preferences referred to British policy of allowing duty-free imports from the countries of the Commonwealth into the British market. The policy was pursued during the interwar period and thereafter and received international section with the signing of the GATT* in 1948. However, when the UK joined the European Community in 1973 imperial preferences were replace by special trading agreements between the EC and many countries of the Commonwealth.

Imperialism (from *empera* = rule) is a policy of seeking domination over foreign peoples and countries. Imperialism may take many forms— political, military, economic or cultural.

Imperialism, Leninist Theory of, was made of the following elements: (1) Imperialism is the highest stage of capitalism; (2) the capitalists-imperialists are out to subjugate peoples and nationalities in search of markets and investment avenues; (3) inter-impearialist competition is bound to lead to imperialist and colonialist wars; (4) hence the revolutionary task of the proletariat is to wage class struggle within the capitalist countries and to wage war against imperialism in the colonies.

Implied Powers are powers implied in the powers expressly delegated to the Congress of the United States under Article 1 of the US Constitution; the powers that are "necessary and proper" to carry into effect the expressly granted powers.

Impoundment in the USA means refusal by the President of the USA to spend moneys appropriated by the Congress for reasons stated by him.

Incrementalism is a policy of allowing only marginal increments at a given time and not sweeping changes. An incremental budget is one which treats the ongoing programmes as givens and accommodates only minor or marginal increments (increases) within available resources.

Indemnity, Act of (indemnity = immunity) is an act passed by a parliament to immunize the armed forces against judicial proceedings for acts committed by them under martial law.

Independent MP is a member of parliament who does not became a member of any parliamentary party and votes on his own conscience. He is free to support either the ruling party or the opposition or join either.

Independent Regulatory Commissions (US) are quasi-legislative, quasi-judicial regulatory agencies outside the Departments of American federal government The Interstate Commerce Commission was the first independent federal regulatory agency created under the Interstate Commerce Act, 1887.

The Board of the Governors of the Federal Reserve System was established in 1913 to supervise the national banking and credit systems, The Federal Trade Commission was created in 1914 to prevent unfair trade practices in interstate commerce. Similarly, the Federal Power Commission was formed in 1920; the Radio Commission in 1926; the Securities and Exchange Commission in 1934; the Federal Communications Commission in 1934; and the National Labour Relations Board in 1936. Among the recent additions are the Federal Election Commission and the Nuclear Regulatory Commission, They are created by an act of the US Congress which defines their jurisdiction and makes monetary allocations for their functioning. Their members are nominated by the President of the USA and confirmed by the Senate and in some cases the president also appoints their chairmen. The President cannot remove them except in some specific cases as authorized by the statute. Their decisions are subject to judicial review. They are called "independent" in the sense that the term of their members is longer than the term of the President for the time-being and the individual members retire one at a time. The President, therefore, has no control over the composition of these commissions. Secondly, the President cannot remove them at will; the causes of their removal are defined by the Congress in the relevant statute. Thirdly their decisions are final and binding, and cannot be subjected to presidential review or veto or suspension. Finally, these commissions operate independently of the President as there are no established channels of communication between them and the President.

India-Bangladesh Agreement of Friendship, Cooperation and Peace was signed between the Indian prime minister Indira Gandhi and the Bangladesh prime minister Sheikh Mujeebur Rahman on 19 March 1972 in Dacca, capital of Bangladesh, for a term of 25 years. It laid down the principles governing bilateral relations of the two countries, after the expiry of its term in 1997 the agreement was renewed for another term of 25 years.

India-Bangladesh Treaty on Sharing of Ganges Waters. The problem of sharing of waters of river Ganges arose with the opening of the Farakka Barrage built on the river on the Indian side of the Indo-Bangladesh border in 1974. The first water-sharing agreement was signed between the two governments in 1977 which guaranteed Bangladesh a minimum of 34,500 cubic feet of water per second (cusecs) between months of October and June every year. The second agreement which dropped this guarantee was signed in 1982 and expired in 1988. The third agreement was signed in 1996 for a term of 30 years and to be reviewed every five years. It provided for sharing of the Ganges waters evenly between the two countries when the flow of waters was below 70,000 cusecs. Bangladesh would receive 35,000 cusecs when the flow was between 70,000 and 75,000 cusecs and India to receive 40,000 cusecs when the flow exceeded 75,000 cusecs.

India-Bhutan Treaty (1949) confirmed the status of Bhutan as an Indian protectorate and continued its special relationship with India. Bhutan is sovereign Himalayan kingdom ruled by an hereditary king (called *Druk Gayalmo*, i.e. Dragon King). To ensure its security and safety against its bigger neighbours Tibet and China, Bhutan signed a treaty with British India in 1910 and became an Indian protectorate. The Government of India assumed the responsibility of Bhutan's defence and foreign affairs and guaranteed non-interference in its internal affairs. The same relationship was renewed with independent India and the Bhutanese subjects continue enjoy freedom of movement, doing business and entering employment of government throughout India. In 1971 Bhutan was admitted to the United Nations with India's support and was also allowed to raise and maintain a Bhutanese national army.

India-China War (1962) was fought in October 1962 over the question of India-China border which was disputed by China. The origins of the India-China border conflict lay in the post-1949 shift in Chinese foreign policy. The Chinese government declared that whatever territory belonged to China in the past must be regained and integrated with China. With this objective the Chinese army occupied Sinkiang in 1949 and Tibet in 1950, the two countries which were nominally under the suzerainty of the Chinese emperor during the nineteenth century but were independent since the Chinese republican revolution of 1911. Tibet being a buffer between British India and china, the British Indian authorities had secured trade and other extraterritorial rights in Tibet. They had also signed an agreement with the government of Tibet in 1914 demarcating the Indo-Tibet border, which is known as the "MacMahon Line" After the Communist revolution in China in 1949, the Chinese quickly occupied Sinkiang and Tibet. In 1954 they persuaded the Government of India to conclude an India-China Agreement on Trade in Tibet (the so-called panchsheel agreement) by which they made India to relinquish her extraterritorial rights in Tibet and thus implicitly recognize Chinese sovereignty over Tibet. Soon afterwards the Chinese started publishing maps which showed large chunks of Indian territory across the MacMahon Line as part of China. Chinese military incursions into the Indian territory in the northeast and Ladakh started in 1958 and by 1962 they had established their military presence there. The Chinese claimed these areas as their own and repudiated the MacMahon Line on the ground that the British imperialists had imposed it upon China. The Government of India launched military action to dislodge the Chinese troops from its territory but the Chinese troops taking advantage of their higher positions and skill in mountain warfare defeated the Indian troops. When India turned to the west for military assistance against China, the Chinese declared ceasefire unilaterally and retired behind a self-demarcated Line of Actual Control in the northeast. Diplomatic and trade relations between the two were ruptured. Relations were gradually normalized since 1980's and a Joint working group was established to resolve the longstanding border dispute. Talks were continuing till the end of 2005 with no final settlement in sight.

Indian Military Academy was founded in 1932 in Dehradoon to prepare the cadets for commission into the Indian Army.

Indian National Army (INA) was formed during World War II in Burma and Malaya to fight the war of national independence against the British by Subhash Chandra Bose who had escaped from British capacity in India to Singapore in 1943 where he proclaimed a provisional national government of India with himself as its president. In 1944 the INA fought a pitched battle with the British Indian troops on the outskirts of Imphal, Manipur, but were hampered by heavy rains from further advance, After the Japanese surrender in 1945 the INA personnel were

Indian National Congress was founded in 1885 in Bombay as an annual conclave of pro-British educated Indians but soon developed into a nationalist organization. In 1906 it launched the *swadeshi* and boycott movement/ in 1908 it adopted the goal of attaining colonial self-government for India; and in 1916 it made a common cause with the All-India Muslim League* to struggle for constitutional advancement of India. After World War I it became a mass revolutionary movement under the leadership of M.K. Gandhi seeking national independence by means of non-cooperation and civil disobedience. However, it contested provincial elections held in 1937 under the Government of India Act, 1935 and formed its ministries in nine of eleven British Indian provinces. It resigned office in 1939 and launched the "Quit India" movement against the British in 1942. After World War II led the Interim Government, and after transfer of power in 1947 became the ruling party in both the centra and the provinces. In 1969 the party split into INC (Organization) and INC (Requisitionists). The INC (R) led by Indira Gandhi was further split in 1979 into the INC (Indira) and INC (Jagjivan Ram). While the Jagjivan. Ram faction soon faded into obscurity, the Indira faction survived. Those opposed to Sonia Gandhi's becoming the president of the Congress (I) broke way from it in 2000 to form ship the Congress Nationalist Party under the leadership of Sharad Pawar.

Indian Ocean is that expanse of waters enclosed in the north by India, Pakistan and Iran; in the west by the Arabian Peninsula and Africa; in the east by the Malayan peninsula, Indonesia and Australia; and in the south by the Antarctica. It is separated from the Atlantic Ocean at the longitude of Cape Iglehas and from the Pacific Ocean at the longitude of Tasmania. The width of the Indian Ocean between Africa and Australia is 6,200 sqr. miles but towards the north it is narrowed as India and Sri Lanka divide it into the Gulf of Bengal and the Arabian Sea. The Arabian Sea is connected with the Red Sea through the Bab al-Mandab and with the Arabian Gulf through the Straits of Hormuzh. The total area of the Indian Ocean is 28, 400,000 sqr. miles and it constitutes 20 per cent of the water bodies of the globe.

Indian Ocean Area covers the Asian and African countries located around the Indian Ocean— India, Pakistan and Iran in the north; the Arabian peninsula and Africa in the west; and the Malaysian peninsula, the Indonesian archipelago and Australia in the east.

Indian Penal Code (IPC) was first enacted by the British Indian government on 1 January 1862; it has since then been amended from time to time. The Government of India announced in 2005 to enact- a revised and updated version soon.

Indian Revolt (1857) or the "Sepoy Mutiny" according to the British, against misrule of the East India Company started in May 1857 with the mutiny of the Indian soldiers of the Company in Meerut which soon assumed the character of a popular rebellion which spread to Delhi, Northwest Province, parts of central India and Bihar. The revolt was spearheaded by the Indian chiefs and landlords dispossessed by the British. The rebels were united only by an anti-British feeling and lacked any national feeling or unity of purpose or a unified leadership or organization. The company forces with their superior strategy, military organization and the support of the Sikhs, Gurkhas and the loyal native princes crushed the rebellion. The Mughal dynasty was extinguished and India became a crown colony under the Government of India Act, 1858.

Indian Union is the successor of the Dominion of India (15 August 1947-25 January 1950). Article 1 of the Indian Constitution declares India that is Bharat shell be Union of States. The term is derived from the proposed "All-India Union" of the Cabinet Mission Plan* of 1946 and is also reminiscent of the American Union (the term union implies political unity and territorial indivisibility). The Indian Union is composed of 28 States and six Union Territories (centrally administered areas) The States with their capitals in the bracket are: Andhra Pradesh (Hyderabad); Arunachal Pradesh (Itanagar); Assam (Dispur); Bihar (Patna); Chhattisgarh (Raipur); Goa (Panji); Gujarat (Gandhinagar); Haryana (Chandigarh); Himachal Pradesh (Shimla); Jummu & Kashmir (Srinagar); Jharkhand (Ranchi); Karnataka (Bangalore); Kerala. (Thiruvanthapuram); Madhya Pradesh (Bhopal); Maharashtra (Mumbai); Manipur (Imphal); Meghalaya (Shillong); Mizoram (Aizwal); Nagaland (Kohima); Orissa (Bhubaneshwar); Panjab (Chandigarh); Rajasthan (Jaipur) Sikkim (Gangtok); Tamilnadu (Chennai); Tripura (Agartala); Uttar Pradesh (Lucknow); Uttaranchal (Dehradon); and West Bengal (Kolkata). The Union Territories are: Andaman & Nicobar; Dadra & Nagar Haveli; Daman & Diu; Lakshdweep; and Pondicherry. The territory of the States and the union Territories has been specified in the First Schedule of the Indian Constitution.

Indictment (from Latin *indicare* = to indicate or exhibit) is defined by Blackstone as "a written accusation of one or more persons, of a crime or a misdemeanor, preferred to and presented upon oath by a grand jury".

Individualism accords supreme importance to the human individual and regards his freedom as an absolute. Man is the centre of the universe and determiner of all social, political, economic norms, structures and relationships. Society is merely a collection of individuals and is neither apart from them nor prior to them nor above them. The philosophy of individualism can be summed up in three basic points: (3) the individual is the source of all social norms and values: they are created, practised and upheld by them; (2) the individual is an end in himself rather then a means to some other end; and (3) Morally all individuals are equal in worth so no individual should be made entirely an instrument for the well-being of other individuals. Individualism during the 18th and 19th centuries gave birth to liberalism which along with the advocacy of individual liberty recognized the necessity of social regulation of liberty and state intervention in social, economic and political affairs* Extreme individualism is now a sterile concept and has no adherents.

Indochina or French Indochina referred to the former federation of states comprising the French colony of Cochin China and the French protectorates of Tonkin, Annam, Laos and Cambodia. Later Cochin China, Tonkin and Annam were merged to form a new state of Vietnam with its capital at Hanoi. During World War II the French withdrew from the area but after the defeat of Japan tried to regain their colonial control over Vietnam. The French army faced the resistance of the Vietminh (the national liberation front) which in 1946 declared the independence of Vietnam in 1946. The first Indochina war between the Vietnamese nationalist and French colonial forces ended with the defeat of the French army. The Geneva Conference held in 1954 led to signing of agreements dividing Vietnam into North (communist-controlled) and south (American-backed non-communist) and recognizing Laos and Cambodia as independent and neutral states. The second Indochina war started with the formation of the Viet Cong an start of guerilla activity against the American-installed government in South Vietnam which eventually led to American military intervention in South Vietnam and the resulting war (1959-1973) ended with the signing of Paris Peace Accords between North and South Vietnam in 1973. The agreement led to withdrawal of American forces from South Vietnam and eventually to merger of the North and South into a new Socialist Republic of Vietnam in 1975.

Indo-Tibetan Border Police Force—ITBPF was originally formed on 24 October 1962 to patrol along the Indo-Tibetan border. It was reconstituted as an armed force of the Indian Union under the Into-Tibetan Border Police Force Act, 1992. It guards not only the Indo-Tibetan border but may also be assigned other duties.

Indus Waters Treaty (1960) was signed by the representative of the governments of India and Pakistan and the International Bank for Reconstruction and Development (IBRD) on 19 September 1960 for equitable sharing of the waters of the Indus river system. The treaty allotted the three easter rivers of Ravi, Beas and Satluj to India and the three wester rivers of Indus, Jhelum and Chenab to Pakistan. The treaty also created a permanent Indus Commission composed of technical experts of the two countries to hold annual meetings to monitor and review the implementation of the treaty. Before 1947 these rivers which originate from the Himalayas and flowing through the subcontinent fall into the Arabian Sea, fed the irrigation canals of the undivided Province of Punjab. After 1947 Indian attempt at damming and diverting the rivers to block flow of waters to Pakistan territory led to friction between the two countries. The dispute was resolved through mediation by the World Bank.

India-Nepal Treaty (1950) continued and reaffirmed Nepal's special relationship with India inherited from British Indian regime. By this treaty India is committed to defend the national independence and territorial integrity of Nepal and Nepal has undertaken not to allow third parties to use its soil for activities inimical to India. Nepal is also bound to procure its weapons only from India. In accordance with this treaty Nepal enjoys trade and transit rights which are governed by trade and transit treaties signed between the two countries periodically. The Nepalese (and Bhutanese) subjects enjoy the freedom of movement, doing business and entering government services throughout India. Nepal's special relationship with India is rooted in the geographical and historical fact that it is the only Princely State of India which maintained its independence of the British Empire. The Nepali Gurkha bands used to raid Indian planes for loot and plunder. This provoked the East India Company to launch a was against Nepal in 1814. The Nepalese were defeated in 1816 and forced to sign the Treaty of Sugauli with the British under which the British annexed the Kumaun Hills to India and Nepal accepted the East India Company as its lord paramount. By 1860's the Nepalese had formed a *de facto* alliance with the British. Nepal accepted British supervision of its foreign relations and permitted recruitment of Gurkhas to the British Indian army. In return, the British guaranteed Nepal's external security non-interference in its internal affairs.

India-Pakistan Agreement on Bilateral Relations (1972), also known as the Simla Pact, was signed between the Indian prime minister Indira Gandhi and the Pakistani President Zulficar Ali Bhutto in the midnight of 2/3 July 1972 at the end of their summit meeting held in Simla from 28 June to 2 July 1972 to deal with the consequences of the India-Pakistan war in 1971 over east Bengal. The agreement laid down the principles governing bilateral relations. The crux of the agreement was the conversion of the ceasefire line in Jummu and Kashmir resulting from the India-Pakistan war in 1948 into a Line of Control which was made inviolable till a final settlement of the dispute was reached.

India-Sri Lanka Agreement (1987) committed India to ensure the national independence and territorial integrity of Sri Lanka. India agreed to deploy an Indian peacekeeping force in Sri Lanka to disarm and immobilize the Tamil insurgents and Sri Lanka agreed to grant provincial autonomy to Tamil-dominated northern and eastern provinces of Sri Lanka. Before the Indian peacekeeping force could accomplish its mission Sri Lanka demanded the withdrawal of Indian troops. The Tamil problem remained unresolved. However, Sri Lanka in 2004 signed a free-trade agreement with India.

India-USSR Treaty of Peace, Friendship and Cooperation (1971) was signed for a term of 20 years between India and the former USSR on 9 August 1971 in New Delhi against the backdrop of the deepening crisis in east Bengal. It was conceived as a diplomatic shield for India's contemplated intervention in east Bengal. A new Indo-Russian Treaty of Friendship and Cooperation was signed in 1993 during Russian President Boris Yeltsin's state visit to New Delhi.

Inflation and Deflation. Inflation means expansion of the money supply and deflation means its contraction. When expansion of money is coupled with decline in production of goods the result is an imbalance between demand and supply* Inflation occurs when too much money chases too few goods. Conversely, deflation occurs when money supply contracts and the purchasing power of money rises so too little money purchases too many goods.

Infrastructure means the underlying structure or the foundation. The economic infrastructure refers to a set of physical assets and facilities which serve the economy and the society as a whole, e.g. the networks of railways, roads, airports, seaports, bridges, canals, power houses, public transport, warehouses, cold storages and a system of public education, healthcare and medical services, etc. A sound infrastructure is regarded as one of the prerequisits of economic development of a country.

Inherent Powers are those proses neither expressly delegated to the US Congress nor implied by them but claimed by the Union government as ingrained in its position as the supreme national government.

Injunction is an order or decree issued by a court of law in a judicial proceeding to an individual or government agent compelling him a to perform or restraining him from performing a certain act. Violation of an injuction constitutes contempt of court and is punishable. Injunctions may be *restrictive* or mandatory; may be *interim* (interlocutory) or *permanent.* An interim injunction is granted after the issue of a writ to maintain the status quo till the disposal of a case. A permanent injunction can be granted only when a plaintiff has established his legal right or the actual or threatened infringement of his legal right by a defendent.

Inner Party Democracy was one of the working principles of the former Communist Party of the Soviet Union (CPSU, along with democratic centralism , which allowed free discussion at all levels of the party structure so long as a final decision was not taken. Once a matter was decided finally all party members were bound by the party line and no dissent and opposition was allowed. Inner party democracy operated so long as Vladimir Lenin lived. It was nullified under Stalinist dictatorship.

Innocent Status. Innocent is the opposite of wicked or fraudulent i.e. free from guilt or sin or blameless. The innocent status implies that the person is harmless and innocuous and does not transgress the law.

Inquisition (from Latin *inquirer* = to find out) originally referred to a body of inquisitors or prosecutors appointed by the Roman Catholic Church during the Middle Ages to hunt down the heretics and dissenters and either exile them or confiscate their property or burn them alive. Hence used for any arbitrary or vindictive inquiries.

Institutionalism is the opposite of behaviouralism. Its basic idea is that institution have a life and momentum of their own and can play a deceive role in bringing about social change.

Institutionalization is the process by which social changes, movements and innovations endure in time in the form of permanent operating institutions. For instance, if a political movement is not institutionalized in the shape of a political party or regime it soon dies out.

Instrumentalism refers to a philosophical approach advocated by John Dewey *in his Logic: the Theory of Inquiry* (1938). He asserted that methodology and theory assume meaning and legitimacy if they are helpful in solving problems. Whether a socio-economic paradigm is relevant and useful depends on the consequences it leads to during the course of its application to concrete socio-economic problems.

Intelligence Bureau (India) is an attached office of the home ministry of the Government of India responsible for collecting, coordinating and communicating to all ministries, either on its own initiative or on call, information relating to the security of India. The IB is headed by a director. It maintains the Central Finger Print Bureau in Kolkata, the Central Detective Training Schools in Kolkata and Hyderabad, the offices of the Government Examiner of Questioned Documents in Kolkata, Hyderabad and shimla and the Central Forensic Laboratories in Kolkata, and Hyderabad.

Intergovernmentalism is synonymous with federalism i.e. networking between the different levels of government — national, state and local.

Intergovernmental Relations, Advisory Commission on (US) was created in 1959 by the American federal government as a research and policy-advisory body to recommend measures of improvement in federal-state relations. It published numerours reports and studies.

Interim Government (1946) was envisaged by the Cabinet Mission Plan* of 16 May 1946 as an interim executive composed of the representatives of major Indian political parties to replace the Governor-General's Executive Council as a first step towards transfer of power from the British to Indian hands and to remain in office till such time as the prospective Constituent Assembly of India framed a constitution for the proposed Union of India. The Interim Government was constituted by the Governor-General on 24 August 1946 with the leader of the Congress Party Jawaharlal Nehru as Vice-chairman and other Indian leaders. The Muslim League raised objections regarding the number of its nominees and kept away from it but later agreed to join it. So it was reconstituted on 25 October to accommodate four members of the Muslim League. The Interim Government remained in office till the transfer of power on 15 August 1947. .

Intermediate Nuclear Forces Treaty (1987) was signed between the USA and the former USSR to eliminate intermediate-range nuclear missiles from Europe, It was the first disarmament measure between the east and west made possible by the process of detents.

International Adjudication means legal settlement of inter-state disputes through the international arbitration tribunals or the International Court of Justice, in accordance with the Convention on the Pacific Settlement of Disputes and the Charter of the UNO.

International Bank for Reconstruction and Development—IBRD (popularly known as the World Bank) was established in 1945 as a specialized agency of the UN to provide long-term financial assistance at concessional rates for postwar reconstruction and development in the member-states. The World Bank has two affiliates the International Development Association (IDA) which provides soft loans to the developing countries and the International Finance Corporation (IFC) which was created in 1956 to provide loans to private entrepreneurs in the developing countries. The IBRD had 151 states as its members in 2005. Every member has a weighted vote in proportion to the number of shares held by it in the Bank. The headquarters is in Washington, D.C.

International Confederation of Free Trade Unions—IFCTU was founded in 1949 with its headquarters in Brussels, Belgium, by non-communist trade-union federations after seceding from the communist-dominated world Federation of Trade Unions* (founded in 1945 with headquarters in Paris; shifte to Prague, Czechoslovakia in 1949). In 2005 the IFTU had 232 organizations in 153 countries as its affiliates.

International Court of Justice—ICJ was established in 1945 as the principal judicial organ of the UNO. All members of the UN are signatories to its statute. It is composed of 15 judges and has its seat at the Hague. It has jurisdiction over cases referred to it by the contending parties with mutual consent. It also delivers advisory opinions on legal questions referred to it by the UN General Assembly or the UN Security Council or other organs of the UN.

International Criminal Court — ICC was established under a Statute signed by 120 states in July 1998 in Rome, Italy. The USA was among the original signatories but in May 2002 withdrew its signature from the Statute and declared its immunity from the jurisdiction of the prospective ICC. The Statute came into force on 1 July 2002 and the ICC was inaugurated on 11 March 2003 in the Hague, Netherlands. It is a permanent international judicial authority, having a special relationship with the UN. Its objective is to uphold rule of law throughout the world and to try and punish individuals and groups found guilty of committing the crimes against humanity, war crimes, and crimes of ethnic cleansing and genocide. In 2005 the number of states which were parties to the Statute of Rome was 139. The ICC us composed of a president, two vice-presidents, three chambers with 18 permanent judges (elected by the assembly of the representatives of the signatory states for varying terms of three or six or nine years), a chief prosecutor, two deputy prosecutors, and a registrar.

International Labour Organization— ILO was established in 1919 and became a specialized agency of the UN in 1946.

In 2005 it had 171 states as members. Its headquarters is in Geneva. The ILO has been responsible for conclusion of a number of international conventions for Improvement of labour standards and for monitoring labour conditions and protecting labour rights throughout the world.

International Law or the law of nations is the body of customary principles, rules, practices, usages and maxims that regulate the conduct of nation-states in relation to each other. Although there is no world government to enforce them yet the states voluntary adopt them and regard; them as binding. Their sanction lies in their practical necessity, the force of tradition, and the sanction of the community of states. The main sources of international law are customs and usages, treaties and conventions, equity and the works of jurists.

International Law Commission was established by the UN General Assembly in 1947 to promote the progressive development and codification of customary international law as well as drafting international conventions to deal with contemporary problems and issues. The ILC is composed of 35 experts in international law who are elected by the UN General Assembly for a term of five years. Their seat is in Geneva. The preliminary drafts of the Commission are circulated among the member-states through the UN Secretariat to elicit their opinions. Once their opinions are received a final draft is prepared and reported to the UN General Assembly for adoption.

International Monetary Fund--IMF was established along with the world bank in 1945 as a specialized agency of the UN to facilitate international trade and economic cooperation by stabilizing exchange rates and help the states facing difficulties of balance of payment through the Special Drawing Rights, and advances. The IMF has 151 members. Its headquarters is in Washington D.C.

International Organization is a product of the application of the idea of the welfare state to the international community. A host of international intergovernmental organizations have been created by means of international agreements to regulate international relations and to promote cooperation in multifarious functional areas for maximizing common benefit, international organization is also a subfield of international relations dealing with international institutional

International Politics refers to the sum of inter-state relations and interactions which involve in some measure conflict of interest. As a subject of study it deals with the dynamics of the state system, national power, foreign policy and diplomacy, war and peace and mechanisms limiting the power-play among nation-states e.g. international law, international organization and diplomacy.

International Red Cross and Red Crescent is a global humanitarian organization founded with the specific purpose of providing relief to the sick and wounded in times of crisis. The Red Cross movement is compose of two bodies. The International Committee of the Red Cross (founded in 1863 in Geneva) is meant to operate during war times and the League of Red Cross and Red Crescent Societies (founded in 1919 in Geneva) operates during peacetime to help the victims of natural calamities, man-made disasters and other emergencies. It affiliates the national Red Cross and Red Crescent Societies.

International Relations refers to the sum of international relations both intergovernmental and transnational, of both political and non-political type. As a subject of study it is an interdisciplinary and multi-disciplinary field covering inter-national politics, foreign policy, diplomacy, international organization, international strategy, international economics, international education, etc.

International Seabed Authority is an international intergovernmental organization created in 1994 in pursuance of the UN Convention on the Law of Sea* (1982) and the Agreement Relating to Implementation of Part XI of the UN Convention on the Law of Sea (1994). Its headquarters is in Kingston, Jamaica.

International Trade Organization—ITO was the proposed third pillar of the Bretton Woods system besides the IMF* and IBRD* to usher in a new international economic world order. An international trade conference was convened in 1947 in Geneva in which the 23 participating states adopted the General Agreement on Trade and Tariffs* (GATT) as an interim measure to regulate international trade and tariffs till such time as the proposed ITO came into being. The conference also adopted a draft, charter of the organization. The Charter was adopted at a second conference held in 1948 in Havana, Cuba, and came to be known as the "Havana Charter" The ITO was scheduled to be inaugurated in 1951 after the ratification of the Charter by the requisite number of states. Since the Charter was boycotted by the socialist block and the requisite number of state could not ratify it the organization did not come into being. In its absence the GATT remained the working mechanism of regulating international trade and tariffs till the World Trade Organization* (WTO) was launched on 1 January 1995.

International Trade Union Movement refers to mechanisms of cooperation and coordination among the national trade union organizations at the international level. At the present the international trade union movement operates through three major international confederations of labour organizations: (l) the International Confederation of Free Trade Unions* (2) the world Federation of Trade Unions; and (3) the World Confederation of Labour*.

International Usage refers to informal rules of courtesy and ceremonials which though not being like the customary rules of international are nevertheless observed by the sovereign states in their mutual dealings. They may have legal force if made part of legal or contractual obligations.

Internationalism is a term first used by Jeremy Bentham to designate a spirit of amity and cooperation between nations. It is closely associated with nationalism because no individual state can live in isolation from the rest of the world,

Internationslism is rooted in international interdependence, international division of labour and calls for maintenance of international peace and security and cooperation in furtherance of common interests. Internationalism is not an antithesis of nationalism but its supplement and complement as it is an antidote for the common, evils of exclusive nationalism. True internationalism is, therefore, opposed to all extreme and aggressive forms of nationalism—racism, imperialism,, colonialism. Nazism, fascism, chauvinism and isolationsim. At the same time, internationalism implies a certain measure of voluntary surrender of national sovereignty in the interest of harmonious international relations, and acceptance of the limitations of international, law, international organizations, international morality and the world public opinion. Internationalism got a fillip with the convening of the Hague Conferences*, the foundation of the League of Nations* in 1919, and the of the UNO in 1945.

Inter-Parliamentary Union —IPU was founded in 1889 in Geneva to promote contacts and exchanges of views among the members of national parliaments with the aim of developing representative institutions and promoting international understanding and cooperation. It is joined by 138 states and five international parliamentary unions as association members. In 2003 the Inter-Parliamentary Conference was renamed as Inter-Parliamentary Assembly which meets twice a year in different countries.

Interpellation is a parliamentary motion that originated in the Third Republic of France for seeking an explanation from the ministry on a given question. The ministry had to resign if it could not tender a satisfactory explanation.

Interpol is the acronym of the International Crime Police Organization which was founded in 1923 in Paris as an intergovernmental agency to coordinate between the police departments of member-states to track down individuals and groups engaged in transnational criminal activities It deals particularly with counterfeiting of currency, forgery and fraud, smuggling and narcotics traffic. In 2005 the Interpol had 184 states and twelve dependent territories as its members. Its headquarters in Lyon, France.

Inter-State Council (India). As provided for under 363 of the Indian Constitution the Inter-State Council constituted for the first time by a Presidential notification issued in June 1990. It is composed the Prime Minister of India as chairman, six Union Cabinet ministers (home, finance, agriculture, railways, road transport and law), and all the chief ministers of the stated union territories.. The Council is meant to be a forum for inter—state consultation, coordination of policies, developmental cooperation and resolution of inter-state conflicts. The Council was last reconstituted on 25 June 2004.

Inter-State Water Disputes Act, 1956 (as amended in 1986) provides for adjudication of disputes relating to waters of inter—state rivers and river valleys in India.

Iranian Constitutional Revolution (1906) was the outcome of the spread of European ideas of political freedom and constitutional government among the Iranians during the latter part of the nineteenth century. Discontent with misrule of the reigning Qajar dynasty led to a coalition of the three classes of the Iranian society—the intellectuals, the clergy and the merchants who formed secret societies throughout Iran to preach the ideas of a constitutional government and a representative assembly. In 1906 about 12000 constitutionalists assembled in Tehran and began agitating for promulgation of a constitution and convening of a national assembly. To avoid trouble the ailing King Muzaffaruddin Shah agreed to their demand. The king promulgated a constitution, as drafted by the functionaries of the state, guaranteeing popular sovereignty, constitutional monarchy, rule of law, civil liberties and representative and responsible government. The first national assembly elected 1907 drafted and enacted a supplementary constitution in 1907.

Constitutional government operated till 1911 after which because of the inherent weaknesses of the Iranians and machinations of the foreign powers, constitutional rule was replaced by despotic rule. Constitutional government existed in name till the revolution of 1979 but actual power was wielded by the king and his courtiers.

Iranian Revolution (1979) was the outcome of the uprising of the Iranian masses under the leadership of the democratic forces the shiite clergy and the anti-royal guerilla forces during 1978-79 which led to the overthrow of absolute monarchy in Iran and its replacement by the Islamic Republic of Iran.

Iran-Iraq War (1980-88) was started by Iraqi dictator Saddam Hussain against Iran after repudiating the Iran-Iraq agreement signed in 1975 defining the Iran-Iraq border in the middle of the river Shatt al-Arab. Taking advantage of Iran's internal chaos in the aftermath of the revolution in 1979, Iraq invaded Iranian territory claiming its sovereignty over the whole of Shatt al-Arab and the Iranian province of Khuzestan which is inhabited by the Arabs. The war ended in a stalemate and a ceasefire was agreed to in 1988.

Iron Curtain refers to the USSR policy of blocking movement of people and goods across the border between east and west Europe that resulted from World war II with a view to insulate communists-controlled eastern Europe from the influence of western Europe. The term was first used by Sir Winston Churchill in 1946 and soon became the symbol of the East-West cold war. The iron curtain was finally lifted by the signing of the Charter of Paris in 1990 by the member-states of the Conference on Security and Cooperation in Europe (CSCE)

Iron Law of Oligarchy was presented by Robert Michels in his *Political Parties* (1911) to point out that political organizations in democracies are controlled by an core of elites. Hence he was pessimistic about the prospects of democratic accountability.

Irredentism (from *italia irredenta* = unredeemed Italy) refers to the Italian resurgence movement during the nineteenth century to unit unite the outlying Italian states with Italy. Hence the term is applied to any movement which seeks annexation or integration of a territory inhabited by an ethnic, linguistic or cultural group having affinity with the irredentists, e.g. Nazi Germany's claim over Czechoslovakia and Afghanistan's claim over pushtu-speaking Northwest Frontier Province of Pakistan.

Islamic Development Bank--IDB was established by the 55-nation Organization of Islamic Conference (OIC) in 1973 with its headquarters in Jeddah, Saudi Arabia, to provide loans and grants to the poor countries of the Islamic world.

Isolationism refers to American foreign policy pursued during the period 1789 to 1941 of keeping away from foreign military alliances and international conflicts and of concentrating on national development within the American continent. Isolationism meant isolation from military alliances and international wars and did not preclude diplomatic, commercial, cultural and other contacts with foreign countries.

It may be general or partial or local. It may be for a specified or unspecified term. However, it does not mean either temporary or permanent peace. It may be followed by resumption of hostilities or conclusion of peace. It is different from a *cease-fire* which is ordered by an international organization, e.g. the Security Council of the United Nations.

Ittehadul Muslimeen, Majlis-i- (the Association for Muslim Solidarity) was a social service organization floated by Salahuddin Owaisi in 1937 in the erstwhile State of Hyderabad. The organization was banned after Indian military takeover of the Nizam's state in 1948. It was revived in 1957. It is recognized as a regional political party in Andhra Pradesh and takes part in parliamentary, state and local elections.

J

Jamaat-i-Islami Hind (the Islamic Association of India) was founded by Abul A'la Maududi (1903-1979), a theologian, in 1941 in the city of Hyderabad for propagating Islamic ideology. From there he migrated to Pathankote city in east Panjab in 1945 where he founded a *Darul Islam* (Islamic Mission). Maududi advocated the establishment of an Islamic system of government in a united India and therefore vehemently opposed M. A. Jinnah's two-nation theory and the demand of Pakistan as injurious to the political cause of Islam. However, finding his movement's prospects as bleak after the Partition of 1947 he shrewdly migrated to the newly created Pakistan and established there the Jamaati-Islami Pakistan as a political party campaigning for the objective of creating a theocratic state in Pakistan. The Jamaat left behind in India changed its objective from the establishment of an Islamic state to that of establishment of a religiously-oriented society in India. The Jamaat operates in India, Pakistan, Bangladesh and the Indian-occupied State of Jammu and Kasmir as organically separate units. The Indian unit does not take part in electoral politics but the units in Pakistan and Bangladesh participate in electoral politics.

Jamiat-i-Ulama-i-Hind (the League of Theologians of India). The anti-British Muslim theologians founded a *Darul Uloom* (theological seminary) in 1867 in Deoband Town of Saharanpur district of the United Provinces in India as the base of their religious and political activity. These theologians formed in 1920 the *Jamiat-i-Ulama-i-Hind* as an all-India forum of the Muslim theologians. The *Jamiat* found a natural ally in the Indian National Congress. They joined the non-cooperation and civil disobedience programme of the INC and later counteracted the All-India Muslim League's demand for a separate homeland for Muslims. After independence in 1947 it ensured the support and loyalty of the Indian Muslim minority to the INC. By 1970's its influence among Muslims had declined because of internal factionalism and splits.

Jana Gana Mana is the opening stanza of a patriotic poem written in Bengali by the Poet Rabindra Nath Tagore. It was first sung at the annual session of the Indian National Congress held in 1911 in Calcutta. As proposed by Pandit Jawaharlal Nehru, the leader of the house, the Constituent Assembly of India on 24 January 1950 adopted it as the first national anthem of the Indian Republic. *Vande Mataram**, a song written in Sanskrit, occurring in Bankim Chandra Chatterji's Bengali novel *Anand Math* was adopted as the second national anthem.

Janata Dal was a national level political party formed by V.P. Singh in 1988 in Bangalore by the merger of his Jan Morcha (formed by ex-Congressmen who deserted the Indira Congress in the late 1980's) with the remnants of the Janata Party* and the Lok Dal* (Bahuguna). The Janata Dal then formed the National Front* with the Telegu Desam Party*. In parliamentary elections held in November 1989 Congress (I) won only 192 out of 545 seats while the Janata: Dal got 141 seats. Although a minority the Janata Dal succeeded in forging a coalition government with the National Front which elected V.P. Singh as its leader. He was then appointed as prime minister with the support attended from outside by the Bharatiya Janata Party* and some left parties. Singh resigned as Prime minister after failing to win a vote of confidence in the Lok Sabha and was replaced by Chandrashekhar, also of the Janata Dal, in November 1990. The Janata Dal was defeated by the Congress (I) in parliamentary elections held in May-June 1991. The greatest achievement of the Janata Dal government was the resurrection of the 1980 report of the Backward Classes Commission headed by the late Bindeshwari Prasad Mandal (the Mandal Commission) which had identified 3, 743 castes as backward and declared them eligible to get a 27 per cent reserved quota of jobs in central government. The implementation of the Mandal formula was accompanied by much civil strife. The JD later split into JD (United), JD (secular) and the Rashtriya Janata Dal.

Janata Party was formally launched on 1 May 1977 with the merger of five erstwhile non-communist parties—the Bharatiya Lok Dal*, Congress (Organization), Bharatiya Jana Sangh*, the Samykt Socialist Party and the Swatantara Party. The process of concerting of the non-communist anti-Congress opposition parties Started in January 1977 when the emergency regime of Indira Gandhi announced holding of parliamentary elections in March 1977 and released her political opponents kept in prison since the declaration of internal emergency on 25 June 1975. Guided by Jayaprakash Narayan (1902-1979) the five non-communist parties decided to form an electoral alliance christened as the Janata Party to field common candidates to give straight fight to the candidates of the ruling Congress (I). The alliance was also joined by the Congress for Democracy led by Jagjivan Ram and Hemvati Nandan Bahuguna who had recently deserted the Indira Congress. The alliance contested the parliamentary elections held in March 1977 on the BLD' election symbol of *haldhar* (bearer of ploughshare) and secured more than two-third of seats in the Lok Sabha and formed its government under the leadership of Morarji Desai (1896-1995) As provided for in the charter of the Janata Party the five constituent units met separately to decide their liquidation as separate entities and merger with the Janata Party. The formal inauguration of a single Janata Party with the merger of the five former political parties was announced in its first convention held on 1 May 1977 in New Delhi.. The convention also adopted a party constitution, formed state party units and elected Chandrashekhar as its first party president. The Janata Party now an absolute majority of seats in the Lok Sabha and forward its government with Morarji Desai as subsequently it also won state assembly elections in most of the states and formed its ministries. The Morarji government was toppled in 1979 by the desertion of a faction of Janta Party led by Charan Singh who formed the so-called Janata Party (Secular) and was appointed prime minister with Congress (I) supporting it from outside. The withdrawal of Congress (I) support to Charan Singh government by the Congress (I) necessitated his resignation and fresh parliamentary elections in January 1980. The Janata Party lost heavily and then disintegrated. The former Jana Sanghis left the Janta Party formed the Bhartiya Janta Party (BJP) in April 1980, the former BLD elements reorganized themselves as the Lok Dal and the rump Janata Party merged in the Janata Dal in 1988.

Jeopardy means danger. In law it refers to the condition of a person charged with an offence and thus put in danger of being punished. Double jeopardy is prohibited in constitutional democracies, that is, nobody can be exposed to jeopardy for the same offence twice.

Jharkhand Mukti Morcha was started as a movement for the creation of a separate state of Jharkhand in the northern part of the existing state of Bihar, inhabited by tribal people. Jharkhand State was created in 2002. The Jharkhand Mukti Morcha is recognized as a regional political party in the state of Jharkhand.

Jihad (Arabic jihad fi sabilillah = striving in the way of God) has like go many other social concepts no single meaning or definite content. It is enjoined by the Quran as the most important religious obligation of the believers after the four pillars of the Islamic faith: prayers to God five times daily; fasting for self-purification during the month of Ramadhan;

pilgrimage to Mecca once in a lifetime subject to capacity; and paying *zakat* or purification tax at one-fortieth of the value of one's assets of a specified quality held over a period of one year, as charity to the disabled, poor and needy. *Jihad* variously means defence of the faith against its enemies; struggle against oppression and tyranny, struggle against social evils, or striving for the betterment of the people. The concept is more akin to Gandhian *satyagraha* than to Christian crusades which had imperialistic implications.

Jinnah's Fourteen Points were formulated in 1929 summing up the political demands of the Indian Muslim minority in response to the proposals of the Nehru Committee report published in 1928. The Nehru Committee had repudiated separate electorate for Muslims and recommended for joint electorate of all communities An All-Parties Muslim Conference was convened in February 1929 to consider the Nehru proposals. Drawing upon the proposals adopted at this conference, M. A. Jinnah (1876-1948), the leader of the Muslim League, formulated a draft 14-point resolution for adoption by a meeting of the League held on 28 March 1929 in New Delhi. The League could not adopt this resolution as it became split between those favouring joint electorate and those sticking to separate electorate. However, these points formed the agenda of the Muslim League till 1940. Jinnah's fourteen points were: (1) India should be a federation with a centre vested with enumerated powers and residual powers to be vested in the provinces; (2) a uniform measure of autonomy to be introduced in all provinces; (3) adequate and effective representation of minorities should be ensured in every province without reducing the majority in any province to a minority or even to equality; (4) in the Central Legislative Assembly the Muslim: representation should be not less than one-third of total seats; representation of different communities by means of separate electorates should continue as at the present, provided that it shall be open for any community at any time to give up its separate representation in favour of joint electorate; (6) any territorial redistribution that might become necessary at any time shall not in any way affect the Muslim majority in the Punjab, Bengal and the Northwest Frontier Province; (7) full religious freedom should be guaranteed to all communities; (8) no bill or resolution or any part thereof should be introduced in any legislative or elective body if three-fourth of the members of that community in that particular body oppose such a measure on the ground that it will be injurious to the interests of that community; or, alternatively, such other method be devised as may be found feasible and practicable to deal with such cases; (9) Sind should be separated from the Bombay Presidency; (10) constitutional reforms should be introduced in the Northwest Frontier Province and Baluchistan on the same scale as in other provinces; (11) adequate share should be ensured for the Muslims in the public services of the country; (12) adequate constitutional safeguards for the protection of the culture, language, religion, personal laws and charitable institutions of the Muslims be provided; (13) Muslims should be given a reserved quota of at least one-third seats in central and provincial ministries; and (14) the constitution of India should not be changed without the concurrence of the constituent provinces of the Indian federation.

Joint Consultative Machinery (India). On the pattern of the Whitley Councils in Great Britain the Government of India launched a Scheme for the Joint Consultative Machinery and Compulsory Arbitration for Central Government Employees on 8 September 1971, to redress employee grievances and to settle employee claims in joint consultation between the representatives of the government and the employees.

Joint Resolution in the US Congress may originate as a joint resolution of the House of Representatives or the joint resolution of the Senate and must be approved by both houses and signed by the President of the USA. There is no practical difference between a joint resolution and a legislative bill but a joint resolution deals with a particular matter such as a single appropriation. Constitutional amendments are also proposed by joint resolutions but they do not require presidential signature..

Judgment and Decree. A judgment is a sentence of a court of law, a judicial decision or an order in court in consequence of a suit or legal action. A decree is a command or order following a judgment to put the substance of the judgment into force.

Judicial Activism and Judicial Restraint. The primary function of the judiciary in a constitutional democracy is to interpret the constitution and laws, to settle the disputes brought before it in accordance with the law and to set aside the *ultra vires* acts of the executive. Judicial activism refers to judicial intervention in matters of administrative, political, social and economic policy, which properly belong to the legislative and executive branches, and issuing directives to the public authorities as a result of the so-called "public interest litigation". The controversy over the role of the judiciary as a passive interpreter and an impartial adjudicator and its role as a policy-making organ parallel to the legislative and executive organs, is far from settled. Those who want to keep away the judiciary from the arena of social and economic controversy advocate judicial restraint, i.e. the courts should entertain only strictly legal and judicial questions and avoid questions pertaining to the sphere of the legislative and executive authorities.

Judicial Precedents. It is a principle of English common law that previous decisions or methods of proceeding must serve as authoritative rule or pattern in similar cases. The body of judicial precedents is called the *case law* i.e. the law settled by decided cases.

Judicial Question as district from a political and administrative question is one that requires judicial interpretation, application or adjudication.

Judicial Review or constitutional review is the power of a constitutional or supreme court to review the constitutional validity of the acts of the legislative and executive branches and to declare them as unconstitution and null and void if found contrary to or violative of the constitution. This doctrine prevails in constitutional systems where the constitution is regarded as the supreme law. A supreme court must exercise the power of judicial review to maintain the supremacy of the constitution by nullifying the unconstitutional act of the subordinate branches.

Jurisdiction (from Latin *jurisdictio* = declaration of *jus* or law) is the authority which a court of law has to decide certain matters that are litigated before it or questions that are tried before it; The court having original jurisdiction is the court that is legally competent to hear a case first. It is called a court of first instance or the trial court. Bureaucratic organizations similarly operate according to the principle of functional jurisdiction. Where there is bureaucracy there is hierarchy; and where there is hierarchy the question of jurisdiction arises. Jurisdiction means that a particular operating level or a particular functionary is competent under the rules to perform a particular function or set of functions and that alone. Jurisdiction defines the obligation of an employee to do certain things and not to attempt others. It is a part of an internal division of labour within an organization, T*erritorial* jurisdiction under national and international law means the competence of the national state or its territorial subdivisions to exercise jurisdiction over property and persons or acts or events occurring within its territory.

Jurisprudence is the science of law or study of the principles of law; a jurist is a scholar of law or one who specializes in the science of law.

Jury. The institution of jury is a survival from the middle ages. It is associated with the judicial systems of England and other countries of Anglo-Saxon origin which follow the English common law. Under common law the citizens are guaranteed the right of trial by peers (equals) to ensure impartial and fair trial. A jury is thus a body of persons sworn to decide matters involving legal facts. In jury trials the jury is independent of the judge. The judge decides the questions of law, sums up the evidence for the jury and discharges the accused or passes the sentence. Nobody can be tried unless found guilty by the jury. Juries of different categories: grand, petite, coroner's or advisory. A grand jury (composed of 12 to 30 persons) is formed to hear evidence of accusations in criminal cases and if evidence is admissible decide to indict and put the accused on trial. Petite juries are composed of between six and 12 imperial persons. The juries give their verdict either unanimously or by an absolute majority. The jury system was abolished in India under the Criminal Procedure Act, 1973.

Jus Cogens means the basic principles of customary international law. Article 53 of the Convention on the Law of Treaties (1968) declared that a treaty shall be void "if, at the time of its conclusion, it conflicts with a peremptory norm of general international law". Such norms must be accepted and recognized by the community of states as a whole. *Jus Cogens* norms are nonderogable and peremptory, enjoy the highest status within customary international law, are binding upon all states and cannot be preempted by a treaty.

Just War. The concept of a just war in traditional international law has two aspects: (a) *jus ad bello* (right to go to way) and (b) *jus in bello* (right in war). The former implies certain general principles, namely, that the war should be waged only for a just cause like self-defence or enforcement of claims; that relative justice of the claims of the belligerents should be considered; that war should be instrumental in achieving a just outcome; that war should be a proportional response to the wrong committed by an adversary; that war could only be declared by the constitutional authorities of the states; and that a war should be waged only as a last resort when all available remedies have been exhausted. The principles of *jus* in *bello* were more or less incorporated in the Geneva Convention of 1864 regarding the conduct of war. This Convention was superseded by the Geneva Conventions of 1906, 1929 and 1949 which laid down detailed humanitarian legal obligations upon the combatants in respect of just and humane treatment to the sick and wounded in the war and the medical staff attending them and the safe custody and repatriation of the prisoners of war. Other norms relating to an international war are that civilians and non-military sites should not be attacked and if an attack on a military target becomes necessary civilian casualties should be kept to the minimum similarly, a war should be terminated as soon as the limited objective for which it was waged is achieved without demanding unconditional surrender or seeking total victory.

Justice literally means adjustment of contending claims; it is akin to equality. *Platonic* justice means an adjustment which gives each of the three social classes representing reason, courage and appetite, its right and proper place in the state. Justice of the state is the due performance of its functions by each class. Similarly the justice of the individual is the due performance of functions by each part of the individual mind. *Numerical* justice means equal distribution of public offices or deserts among the individuals according to predetermined criteria. *Redistributive* justice is taking of resources from the rich and redistributing them among the deprived to bring about social equality. *Social* justice is attainment of social equality; *Political* justice is attainment of political and civil rights and equality. *Economic* justice is attainment of equality of opportunity. *Legal* justice is attainment of natural justice through the due process of law.

Justice of Peace is the lowest-ranking local magistrate in Great Britain. The office originated in 1327. As the name indicates, the function of a JOP is to keep king's peace in a local area placed under his jurisdiction. He can also try certain minor criminal and civil cases. He may also perform certain ministerial functions as servant of the Crown. The justices of peace in England are appointed and can be dismissed by the Lord Chancellor*.

Justiciable/unjusticiable. A matter or claim is justiciable when it can legally be raised before a court of law for enforcement. If it is not amenable to judicial action it is non-justiciable.

K

Kamraj Plan was believed to have been conceived by Prime Minister Jawaharlal Nehru as a tactic to ease out certain people opposed to him from their ministerial posts. At his behest a resolution was drafted by some chief ministers led by K. Kamraj, the chief minister of Madras State and a Nehru loyalist,, in August 1963 asking senior Congressmen to resign their ministerial posts and devote themselves to the revitalization of the Congress Party organization. The plan was formally endorsed by Nehru and adopted by the Congress Working Committee on 8 August and approved by the All-India Congress Committee on 10 August. As a follow-up Nehru offered his resignation first which was rejected. Then followed the resignation letters from all chief ministers and central cabinet ministers. On 24 August Nehru accepted the resignations of six central ministers and six state chief ministers. Hence the usage *Kamrajization* i.e. getting rid of opponents by subtle means.

Kargil War (1999) was believed to have been started by the Pakistan army over the head of the civilian government to sabotage a possible deal over the disputed territory of Jummu and Kashmir to be struck between the Indian Prime Minister Atal Behari Vajpayi and the Pakistani Prime Minister Nawaz Sharif (See "Lahore Declaration"). The Pakistani army captured the heights of the Kargil sector of the Ladakh region of the Indian-held Kashmir. The Pakistani forces had to in withdraw in the face of stiff Indian military resistance and intense diplomatic pressure exerted by the west.

Kashmir Dispute. The Princely State of Jammu and Kashmir was one of the 550 and odd Indian states which enjoyed internal autonomy subject to paramountcy of the British Crown. The Indian Independence Act, 1947, provided that on 15 August 1947 the paramountcy of the British Crown over the Indian states shall lapse and the British government shall be absolved of all contractual obligations towards them. They were therefore given the option of acceding either to the Dominion of India or the Dominion of Pakistan whichever was contiguous to them or remain midepoudent They were entitled to sign a stand-still agreement, with the contiguous dominion to get some breathing space before taking a final decision. One such agreement was signed by Maharaja Hari Singh, the ruler of Jammu and Kashmir, with the Dominion of Pakistan. The procrastination on the part of the Maharaja led to invasion of the state by the tribal bands from the Northwest Frontier Province statedly with the purpose of liberating the state from autocratic rule. Tribal invasion in 1948 was followed by military intervention of Pakistan. The ruler called for military assistance from India which was granted on the condition that the Maharaja first sign the Instrument of Accession to the Indian Union which he did. Thereupon India lodged a complaint with the UN Security Council against Pakistan's invasion. The UN Security Council ordered a cease-fire in Kashmir which left one-fifth of the Kashmir territory under Pakistan's occupation (designated as "Azad Kashmir"). Thereafter the UN Security Council passed a resolution asking both countries to withdraw their troops from the territory of Jammu and Kashmir and hold a plebescite to ascertain the wishes of the people of the state regarding the status of the state. Both parties agreed to hold the plebiscite as ordained by the UN Security Council. However, the signing of US-Pakistan Mutual Defence Agreement in 1954 provided the Indian government with an excuse for backing out of its commitment on holding a plebiscite. Basing its claim over the state on the instrument of accession signed by the Maharaja India annexed the whole of the state to the Indian Union and declared it to be an integral part of India. Pakistan, on the other hand, controverted Indian control insisting on the implementation of the UN Security council resolutions as a means of final resolution of the dispute.

Kavery Waters Dispute (India), In India 16 out of 18 major river basins cover two or more states of the Indian Union. The sharing of the waters of such rivers has often become a matter of conflict between reparian states and may be such conflicts have been settled amicably in accordance with the constitution and laws. However, the sharing of the waters of the Kavery river between the upper reparian state of Karnataka and the lower reparian state of Tamil Nadu has been a matter of dispute between the two over decades. An agreement in this regard arrived at between the erstwhile Princely state of Mysore and the erstwhile Madras Presidency in 1925 expired in 1975. The sharing arrangements continued for some time but later Karnataka's reluctance to release waters due to Tamil Nadu revived the dispute. Meanwhile, Indian Parliament passed the Inter-State Matters Disputes Act, 1956; to settle such disputes in accordance with the constitution. Accordingly, the Government of India constituted the Kavery River Water Dispute Tribunal in 1991. On 25 June 1991 the Tribunal passed an Interim Order (IO) fixing provisional quotas of both the states till a final award was made. However, Karnataka refused to accept thc IO. On an appeal by the Tamil Nadu government the Supreme Court upheld the validity of the IO and directed Karnataka to abide by the award. Karnataka again refused to carry out the Supreme Court directive. During 1995-96 Tamil Nadu government again went in appeal to the Supreme Court which now directed the Government of India to find a paramount solution either by consensus among the parties or by making a unilateral central award. The Government of India thereupon persuaded the Karnataka government to discharge its obligation under the IO and simultaneously constituted a political body by the name of the Kavery Waters Authority to supervise the implementation of the IO and to arrange negotiations between the two parties to find out an amicable permanent solution of the problem.

Kellog-Briand Pact (1928) refers to the General Agreement on Renunciation of War which was signed in Paris on 27 August 1928 between the USA, Britain, France, Germany, Japan and other countries to usher an era of peace after World War I. The signatories renounced the right to resort to war as an instrument of national policy and opted resolve their mutual disputes by peaceful means in accordance with international law. The treaty was first drafted by the French foreign minister M. Briand and then improved upon by the American Secretary of State Frank B. Kellogg. However, power politics soon triumphed over idealism and in consequence the Kellogg-Briand pact, became a mere scrap like its predecessor the Locarno pact of paper.

Keynesianism or keynesian economics refers to anti-cyclical measures advocated by John Maynard Keynes (1883-1946): Revive the economy by deficit financing* or pumppriming; increase investment; lower real wages; give subsidies and credits to producers; regulate interest rates on loans; expand non-productive consumption; and increase military expenditures, etc..

KGB is the acronym of the Russian *Komitet Gosudrastvene Bezopasnosti* (State Security Committee) which was the Soviet counterpart of the American CIA during the cold-war era. The KGB was the last in the series of Soviet central intelligence agencies created in 1954 for democratic espionage and surveillance as well as intelligence operations throughout the world.

Khaksar Movement (from Persian *khaksar* = humble) was launched in 1931 by one Inayatullah Khan Mashriqi (1885-1963), a former civil servant who appeared to have been inspired by the Fascist movements in contemporary Europe. His eccentricity as well as eclecticism is evident in his multi-volume *Tazkirah (*reminiscenses) written in the Urdu language.. The *Khaksars* were a band of fanatic Muslims who wore khaki uniform, adopted *belcha* (crowl) as their emblem, and indulged in routine military drills. They had no definite political or social programme except that they believed in human liberty, equality and justice and dedicated themselves to social service. They suffered heavily for their opposition to British imperialism. At the same time, they were opposed to both the Indian National Congress and the All-India Muslim League. The movement had petered out by the outbreak of World war II.

Khalistan Movement (Khalistan = Sikh homeland) is rooted in both the *Khalsa Panth* (the Sikh religion) founded by Guru Govind Singh in 1399 as well as the *Khalsa* (the Sikh state) founded by Maharaja, Ranjit Singh (died 1839) which was annexed by the British in 1850. Since then the Sikh community has aspired for a national homeland of their own. The Singh Sabha during the nineteenth century demanded a Sikh homeland; the Akali Dal demanded a "Sikhistan" during the 1940's; the Dal Khalsa launched armed struggle for the attainment of "Khalistan" in 1981 (the term is believed to have been coined by a Sikh soldier in 1947); and the Sikh expatriats formed the so-called "National Council of Khalistan" abroad. The Sikh militancy in Panjab was suppressed by the Indian military during the 1980's beginning with the so-called "Operation Blue Star" launched in 1984.

Khilafat (anglicized as Caliphate) literally means succession and vicegerency. *Khilafat* is the exercise of spiritual and temporal authority over the community of the faithful after the demise of the Prophet Muhammad. The *Khalifa* (Caliph) was both the successor of the Prophet in religious matters and the commander of the faithful in their temporal affairs. A distinction is made between the true and elective *khilafat* resting on the consent of the people; and the hereditary autocratic *khilafat* which followed the reign of the first four rightly guided successors of the Prophet—Abu Bakr, Omar, Usman and Ali. The hereditary *khilafat* soon degenerated into despotism and un-Islamic conduct which led to bifucation of the religious and temporal authority of the *khalifa.* While temporal authority belonged to the Amir religious authority was assumed by the Islamic scholars and jurists The rule of the first four true *Khalifas* was followed by the hereditary Umayyad dynasty which in turn was succeeded by the hereditary Abbasid dynasty. After the destruction of the Abbasid empire one member of the Abbasid family migrated to Egypt where he was anointed as a ceremonial *khalifa.* When the Ottomans occupied Egypt they took this man to Istambul.. Upon his death the Turkish Sultan transferred the title of the *khalifa* to his own person. In this capacity he pretended to be the spiritual head of the world community of the faithful. The institution of *khilafat* was abolished by the Grand National Assembly of the Turkish Republic in 1924. Thereafter some sporadic attempts were made to revive the institution but without a success since it became obsolete in the changed circumstances of the twentieth century.

Khilafat Movement was spearheaded by the jamiat-i-Ulama-i-Hind* and other orthodox religious organizations with the Ali brother's (Mohamed Ali and Shaukat Ali) in the forefront during the period 1919-1924 demanding from the British government the protection of the person of the Sultan-Caliph of the Ottoman Empire who became a captive of the foreign occupying forces after the defeat of Turkey in World War I and disintegration of its overseas empire. The Muslims were agitated because of their sentimental attachment with the Turkish Sultan being supposedly the religious head of the World Islamic community. Since the British government gave no assurance whatever anti-British agitation was intensified. The government retaliated by arresting the Ali Brothers, the leaders of the movement. Sensing the intensity of Muslim feeling about the question M.K. Gandhi declared the support of the Indian National Congress for the cause of khilafat. Thereafter a Central Khilafat Committee was formed in Bombay which elected Gandhi as one of its members. In return for Congress support to the khilafat movement the Muslims joined the Congress-led non-cooperation movement against the British. The cause of khilafat was completely undermined when the Turkish Grand -National Assembly first separated the office of the *khalifa* from the government of the Turkish state in November 1922 and then abolished the khilafat altogether in March 1924. However, the Central Khilafat Committee still maintains its office in Mumbai city.

Khudai Khidmatgar (Urdu for "servants of God"), also known as the frontier red shirts, was a social service organization raised by the frontier Gandhi Khan Abdul Ghaffar Khan in the Northwest Frontier Province in 1920. In 1931 this organization became an affiliate unit of the Indian National Congress and represented it in the Northwest Frontier Province, The organization was banned by the British in the wake of the civil disobedience movement, (mainly composed of American troops) under American command to halt the aggressor. The combined US-South Korean forces succeeded in repulsing the communist forces beyond the 38th parallel, the dividing line between South and North Korea. However, tempted by their success the American forces penetrated deep into North Korean territory and approached the Manchuraian border of China. Sensing a threat to the national security of China the Chinese communist army intervened on behalf of the North Korean forces and after fierce battles succeeded in pushing back the American forces to the 38th parallel. The conflict ended with the restoration of the status quo. An armistice agreement was signed in July 1953 and the Korean peninsula remains divided across the 38 parallel since then.

Know-How means the aggregate of non-patented scientific and technological knowledge, professional expertise, industrial and trade secrets, management techniques, etc. in the possession of the corporations or governments of the developed countries.

Korean War (1950-53) was started by the pro-Soviet communist regime of North Korea by invading the pro-American South Korea in June 1950. Towards the end of World War II the Korean penisula was jointly occupied by the American and Soviet forces, the Americans occupying the south and the Soviets occupying the north, They created separate governments in the two regions. Under the wartime agreement both forces withdrew from the Korean peninsula after the war The north Korean regime seeing a military vacuum in south Korea, after withdrawal of American forces capture it. In response to communist aggressive the American government raised the question before the UN Security Council which declared a breach of peace in the Korean peninsula and authorized the despatch of a UN Expeditionary Force

Kosovo Problem. Kosovo is the largest province of Serbia with an area of 10,887 sqrkms and a population (1991) of 1, 956,196 of which 90 per cent belong to the Albanian ethnic minority. Its capital is Prestina. Before 1990 Kosovo was an autonomous province of Yugoslavia with an elected provincial assembly and a provincial government. But an amendment of the Yugoslavia constitution in 1990 scrapped provincial autonomy and dissolved the provincial assembly. The Albanian minority rebelled against this and in the resulting civil war more than 200,000 Albanians were uprooted from their homeland. The Albanian leaders formed a Kosovo government-in-exile in Zaghreb, Croatia, and proclaimed a sovereign Kosovan republic. However, the UN Interim Administration Mission granted provincial autonomy to Kosovo in May 2001 with an elected provincial assembly and an elected president. A NATO-led multinational peacekeeping force has been stationed in Kosovo since then to keep peace in the region.

Ku Klux Klan is an underground terrorist organization of the white racists in the USA founded in 1915 to launch violent attacks against ethnic and minority groups like the blacks, Hispanics, Jews and foreign immigrants. It is opposed to pacificism, international cooperation, birth control and immigration of foreigners into America.

Kulak is a Russian word for the rich landlords in the countryside.

Kuomintang (mandarin *Guomindang*) was the Chinese Nationalist Party formed in 1910 by Sun Yat Sen which in 1911 overthrew the Manchu dynasty and proclaimed the Republic of China. The Kuomintang ruled China up to 1949. Meanwhile the Chinese Communist Party (formed in 1920) emerged as a major political and military force during the interwar period. The nationalists and the communists joined hands to fight against Japanese aggression in Manchura in 1930 and against Japanese occupation of China during World War II. However, after the end of the war intense struggle for supremacy developed between the two and their civil war ended with the victory of the communists and proclamation of the People's Republic of China on 1 October 1949. The nationalist regime under Chiang Kai Shek fled to the island of Taiwan which is continuing to survive as the "Republic of China" despite intense pressure from the People's Republic for its integration with the mainland.

Kyoto Protocol (1997). The Kyoto Protocol to the UN Framework Convention on Climate Change (UNFCCC) was signed in December 1997 in Kyoto, Japan, mandating specified reductions in the emission of greenhouse (carbon based) gases that contribute to global warming. By 2003 some 183 countries had acceded to it. Russia ratified the protocol in October 2004. It became UN law and came into force with effect from 16 February 2005. The USA which has only four per cent of the world population but limits 24 per cent of quantity of carbon dioxide reneged from the protocol in 2001 on the plea that the interest of the American workers cannot be sacrificed for the sake of climate protection and reiterated its opposition in October 2004.

L

Lahore Declaration (1999) along with a memorandum of understanding was signed by Atal Behari Vajpayi, the prime minister of India, and Nawaz Sharif, the prime minister of Pakistan, on 20 February 1999 in Lahore, Pakistan. The two leaders committed their countries to preventing the outbreak of a nuclear war between them by accident, putting a moratorium on further nuclear testing and intensifying efforts to resolve bilateral disputes including the dispute over the State of Jammu and Kashmir.

Lahore Resolution (1940) was passed by the All-India Muslim League in its Lahore session held on 23 March 1940. I reads: "Resolved that it is the considered view of this session of the All-India Muslim League that no constitutional plan would be workable in this country or acceptable to the Muslims unless it is designed on the following principles, viz. that geographically contiguous units are demarcated into regions which should be so constituted, with such territorial adjustments as may necessary, that the areas in which the Muslims are numerically in a majority, as in the Northwestern and eastern zones of India, should be grouped to constitute independent states in which the constituent units shall be autonomous and sovereign".

Laissez Faire (French for let alone). Against feudal limitations on freedom of economic activity early liberals raised the slogan: *Laissez Faire et Laissez Passer* (let alone and let pass). They wanted unlimited freedom of economic activity and opposed all sorts of state intervention in the social and economic spheres as contrary to individual liberty.

Lal Bahadur Shastri National Academy of Administration. A National Academy of Administration was founded in Mussoorie (Uttaranchal Pradesh) in 1959 as a subordinate office of Ministry of Home Affairs, Government of India,, by the merger of the Indian Administrative Service Training School established in 1947 in New Delhi) and the Staff College (set up in 1957 in Simla, Himachal Pradesh) to provide integrated training to the recruits of the All-India and Class I Central Services. The Academy was renamed as the Lal Bahadur Shastri Academy of National Administration in 1967. At the present it is a subordinate office of the Department of Personnel, Ministry of Personnel, Public Grievances and Pensions, Government of India.

Latin America refers to non-English speaking countries of North America, South America, Central America and West Indies. The inhabitants of twenty republics of this part of the western hemisphere variously speak the Spanish, Portugese and French languages,, belong to non-Anglosaxon stock and follow the Catholic religion. It is named Latin because of its association with Latinic stock, religion and languages to distinguish it from North America (USA and Canada), the majority of whose inhabitants are English-speaking Anglo-Saxon Protestants.

Latin American Free Trade Area—LAFTA was established in 1960 and was superseded by the Latin American Integration Association founded in 1980.

Latin American Integration Association—LAIA was established in 1980 with its headquarters in Montvideo,, Uruguay to achieve economic integration in Latin America. The member-states are: Argentina, Bolivia, Brazil, Chile, Colombia, Cuba, Ecuador, Mexico, Paraguay, Peru, Uruguay, and Venezuela.

Law (from Latin *lex* = to lay). The term is used in three distinct senses: (1) as the command of the political sovereign or the state (positive law) which must be obeyed compulsorily by the subjects; (2) as ethical norms or moral obligations (natural law/ which must be followed voluntarily by their adherents; and (3) as logical or deductive necessities or regularities in nature (scientific law) which remains valid unless falsified. Positive law is called *positive* because they exist by *positio* (state sovereignty). The law of the western world is divided into two streams: the British common law and the Roman civil law, each being distinguished by its peculiar usages and precedents. Laws are categorized into specialized braches of civil, criminal, administrative and constitutional laws. *Statute* is a body of laws enacted by a legislative authority (e.g. a parliament) as distinguished from customary laws and the common law. *Case* law refers to the body of judicial precedents or past rulings and judgments which are regarded as binding upon the courts.

Law Commission of India. After Indian independence the British practice of appointing a law commission from time to time to look into and suggest necessary reforms in the legal and judicial system of India on a continuous basis was resumed in 1955. The forest Law Commission of India was constituted in 1955 as a subordinate office of the Indian Law Ministry, the seventeenth commission was reconstituted on 1 September 2003 for a period of three years. The Law Commission is composed of four members: two retired judges of the Supreme court, a member-secretary and a senior advocate. So far it has submitted 189 reports.

Law of the Sea. The UN Convention on the Law of the Sea (UNCLOS) was adopted by the third UN Conference on the Law of the Sea in 1982. The first conference was convened in 1950, the second in 1960 and the third in 1973.

Law of Treaties. The Vienna Convention on the Law of Treaties (1969) codifies the norms of customary international law regarding procedure of conclusion, ratification, enforcement, interpretation, amendments, invalidation, abrogation or suspension of treaties and the consequences thereof. The Convention also prescribes the manner of their ratification and registration with the depositaries. Pursuant to the UNCLOS and the agreement signed in 1984 to implement Part XI of the UNCLOS an International Seabed Authority representation of was constituted in 1994 with representation of 138 member-states and its seat in Kensington, Jamaica. In 1996 an, International Tribunal for the Law of the Sea was created at Hamburg, Germany, to interpret and apply the UNCLOS and adjudicate disputes arising under it.

League of Nations was the first ever international organization created under a Covenant of the League of Nations agreed to by the Allied Powers in the Peace Conference on 28 April 1919 in Paris and appended to the Treaty of Versailles*. The League came into being January 1920 with its seat in Geneva. It was composed of a Council representing the five great powers and four others chosen by the General Assembly. The General Assembly was composed of all member-states, each having one vote. Its main objective was to maintain international peace by enforcing a system of collective security in the place of hitherto prevailing power politics which was held responsible for recurrence of international conflicts and wars. The League became dysfunctional with the outbreak of World War II in 1939, was replaced in 1945 by the UNO* and was formally dissolved in April 1946.

League of the Arab States or the **Arab League** is a regional organization of 22 Arab states with its headquarters in Cairo, Egypt, which was created under a Charter signed on 22 March 1945 in the Preliminary Conference on Arab Unity held in Alexandria, Egypt. Its objectives include consolidation of Arab unity and solidarity, promotion of cooperation in political, economic, social and cultural affairs, and resolution of intra-Arab conflicts.

League of the Islamic World *(Raabitah al-Aalam al-Islami)* is a Saudi-financed religious foundation based in Mecca, Saudi Arabia, which was founded by King Faisal ibn Saud in 1962 to promote contacts among the religious institutions throughout the Islamic world; to promote Islamic theological studies; to grant scholarships for religious studies and to hold international conferences and seminars on religious themes. This quasi-governmental body should not be confounded with the Organization of the Islamic Conference. **(Mo'tamar al-Aalam al-Islami)** which is an intergovernmental organization of 57 Muslim states meant as a consultative forum and a cooperative mechanism to solve the common problems of the Muslim countries.

Lebanese Civil War (1975-89). The Republic of Lebanon is situated in Western Asia with Beirut as its capital. It is bordered by Syria to the north and east and by Palestine/Israel to the south with a 220 kms coastline on the eastern shore of the Mediterranean Sea. Lebanon was a part of the Syrian province of the Ottoman Empire from the sixteenth century till its defeat in the first World War in 1918. In 1919 the League of Nations granted France the mandate to administer Syria. France in 1920 separated the Lebanon from Syria with a view to developing it as a Christian-dominated state. France administered the Lebanon (along with Syria) as a mandated territory until it declared its independence 26 November 1941. It proclaimed itself as a republic in 1943 and its sovereignty was recognized by France in 1944. Lebanon's population is divided into ethnic, religious and denominational sects-- Maronite Christians and other Christian sects; the Sunnite Muslims; the Shiite Muslims; and the Druze. An unwritten "national pact" arrived at among the communities formed the basis of the Lebanese political system under which executive and legislative offices were distributed in the ratio of six Christians to five Muslims. Similarly, the seats in the Chamber of Deputies (renamed as the National Assembly in 1979) were distributed among various denominational communities in varying ratios, accordingly, a convention developed that the office of the President of the Republic shall be reserved for a Maronite; that of the Prime Minister for a Sunnite Muslim; and that of the Speaker of the National Assembly for a Shiite Muslim. TO preserve the notional majority of the Christian community no official census was ever taken. This political settlement came under heavy pressure with the outbreak of the civil war in 1975 first between the Maronite Christian militia and the Palestinian refugees and then between the Christian and Muslim militias. Each side tried to establish its political supremacy in the Lebanon. The civil war was halted by the acceptance by all sides of a peace plan proposed by the Arab League in September 1989. According the Lebanese National Assembly (elected in 1972) met in Taif, Saudi Arabia, in October 1989 to adopt a new national charter which provided for transfer of executive authority from an independent President to a parliamentary cabinet composed of equal number of Christian and Muslim ministers; election of a new national assembly with seats distributed equally between the Christian and Muslim communities; and disbanding of all denominational militias and stationing of a Syrian peacekeeping force which was withdrawn in 2005.

Lebensraum is German word meaning living space. It refers to the argument of the Nazi regime in Germany (1933-1945) that since the German homeland was no longer sufficient to accommodate the growing German population the German nation was entitled to acquire the living space abroad.

Left and Right. The terms *left* and *right* originated during the French Revolution of 1789-1799 to mark the division of the pro-monarchy and anti-monarcy forces. In the revolutionary national assembly those who were against monarchy were seated on the left hand of the speaker and those who supported monarcy were seated on his right. Hence the terms came to be applied respectively to progressive and conservative forces. The *centre* designates the forces of moderation, those who tread the middle path between the extremes of the left and right.

Legal Services Authority, National was established in India under the NALSA Act, 1987 (as amended in 2002). It is responsible for overseeing the administration of the free legal service scheme throughout the country. The Act accorded the L*ok Adalats** the status of regular civil courts and made their awards final and binding upon the parties and non-appealable.

Legation. The right of legation, under international law means the right of a sovereign state to accredit its diplomatic envoys to other sovereign states and to receive their diplomatic representatives in return. The *legation* is the diplomatic premises housing an envoy extraordinary or minister plenipotentiary. A legation ranks below an embassy.

Legislative Veto (US) was a device used by the US Congress to block executive action not-liked by it. Generally, congress inserted a provision in legislative bills to the effect that it shall be entitled to veto any executive regulation or act it did not agreed to The legislative veto was declared as unconstitutional by the US Supreme Court on the ground that it violated the separation of powers inherent in the Constitution. Thereafter Congress takes recourse to Joint Resolutions* to block executive measures.

Legitimacy. In democratic theory and practice the concept of legitimacy is irrevocably bound with the concepts of sovereignty, law, authority, governance and political obligation. Every government must seek and maintain its legitimacy. A government may be considered as possessing legitimacy when its authority and policy is voluntarily accepted by the general public. Legitimacy is derived from legality, accountability, popular consent and government's efficiency and performance. On the reverse, *delegitimation* occurs when crucial support groups of a regime defect and search for alternative political arrangements.

Leninism refers to the contribution of Vladimir Lenin to classical Marxism, particularly his theory of the party and state and his interpretation of imperialism as the highest stage of capitalism. He asserted that the workers by their own effort are capable of only trade-unionism and cannot wage a revolution. They must be guided by professional revolutionary vanguard. The vanguard party must operate according to principles of strict unity and disciple, primacy of the central leadership and subordination of the majority to the minority. After the revolution the vanguard party shall form the leading and guiding force of the society and the nucleus of its political system. All state and public organizations shall be directed by an inner core of communists. Communism was defined as collective ownership of all means of ownership, distribution and exchange and centralized planning and management of the economy. He summed up the revolutionary struggle in an age of imperialism in three points: anti-colonialism, anti-imperialism and aid to national liberation movements.

Leviathan means a great ship and, figuratively, the ship of state, the artificial corporation that exercises sovereignty over its members' after Thomas Hobbes' political treatise *Leviathan* (1651).

Libel and Slander. Libel is defamation by written words while *slander* is defamation by word of mouth. Both are considered as offences under the law. The written libellous material as well as its writer both are called *libellous.* The defamatory speech is called *slanderous* and the speaker is slanderer.

Liberal International was founded in 1947 in London as the union of 90 liberal parties in 58 countries. It aims at coordination of efforts to spread democracy, promote human rights and advocate liberal economics throughout the world. It has been accorded the status of a consultative body with the Economic and Social Council of the UN General Assembly and with the Council of Europe

Liberal refers to a political system which ensures individual liberty, representative and responsible government, civil liberties and rule of law, e.g. UK and France.

Liberalism was the philosophy of the rising middle class of entrepreneurs during the eighteenth century in Europe who demanded abolition of all feudal restraints and fetters on the freedom of movement and economic activity of the individuals. The fundamental tenets of liberalism are: (1) a belief in human liberty and equality; (1) a belief in human rationality; (2) a belief in the inevitability of human progress. L.T. Hobhouse enumerated the articles of liberal faith as: (1) civil liberty; (2) fiscal liberty; (3) personal liberty; (4) social liberty; (5) economic liberty; (6) domestic liberty; (7) local, racial and national liberty; (8) international liberty; and (9) political liberty or popular sovereignty and self-government.

Libertarianism is a philosophical approach that emphasizes the absolute value and worth of individual liberty and opposes the ever-increasing authority of a coercive and regulatory. It advocates that individuals should pursue their own good rather than sacrifice themselves for the good of a party or the society or the state. It combines the natural rights of life, liberty, property and pursuit of happiness with an advocacy of free market as a-remedy for all social evils.

Limited War or regional war is the opposite of a general or world war. A limited war is limited in both its nature and scope. While a general or total war is fought for achieving total victory over an enemy a limited war is fought for a limited objective and within a limited geographical area.

Line and Staff. The line function or authority in an organization means the function or authority of those in the chain of command to direct and control their subordinates; a line agency is, therefore, an agency which commands and governs. The staff function or authority, on the other hand, means the function or authority of assisting, supporting and advising those in the chain of command in the performance of their line function; a staff agency is, therefore, one which renders professional or policy advice or provides technical assistance or performs any other supportive functions for the line agencies.

Lobby. A lobby is a corridor of a building but in the USA it became a symbol of pressure group activity. Lobbies are professional groups of individuals who are hired by interest groups to protect or promote their interests by contacing and influencing the legislators and government officials. Pressure group activity is so much ubiquitous in US politics that the lobbies have come to be describes as "the third house" of the US Congress. They are active not only at the national level but at state and local levels as well.

Locarno Pact (1925) was signed in Locarno on 1 December 1925 between Belgium, Britain, France, Germany and Italy to guarantee peace and non-aggression in Western Europe. Germany undertook to resolve her territorial disputes with Belgium, Czechoslovakia and France through arbitration rather than use of force. For the first time in human history the great powers renounced war and committed themselves to maintaining collective security. The five signatory powers declared their readiness to come to the aid of any one of the signatories if attacked by a non-signatory power. In consequence of the signing of this treaty Germany was admitted to the League of Nations and France vacated the German territory of Rhineland much before the time stipulated in the Treaty of Versailles. However, with Nazi dictatorship firmly entrenched in Germany Hitlar repudiated the Locarno pact in March 1936 and militarized Rhineland heavily. Soon afterwards Belgium, sensing a threat to its security from the German renuciation of the treaty, withdrew itself from the obligations of the treaty. Later developments demonstrated the primacy of power politics over collective security and international morality.

Lok Adalats were first floated in India as informal conciliation forums to enable the litigants to settle their disputes outside the regular courts by mutual agreement. By the Legal Service Authorities Act, 1987 (as amended in 2002) regular civil courts Lok Adalats have been given the status of for pre-litigation conciliation and settlement of disputes concerning public utility services. The awards of the Lok Adalats are now enforceable like the decrees of civil courts, are binding upon the parties, and final and non-appealable. Their jurisdiction covers all legal disputes pending in the civil, criminal and revenue courts or tribunals except non-compoundable criminal cases.

Lok Pal/Lok Ayukt. Lok Pal in India has the same meaning as the Scandinavian ombudsman (pronounces as omboozman). When appointed this official will be competent to probe into charges of corruption and misconduct of the high officials and ministers of the Government of India. Lok Ayukt is the designation of an official whose appointment is provided for in the respective state legislations and this official has already been appointed in many states. The proposal for appointing a national-level ombudsman (Lok Pal) was first made by the Administrative Reforms Commission of India* in 1967. The Commission was so much overwhelmed by the prevalence of corruption in the Indian administration that it recommended for immediate appointment of a *Lok* Pal. A Lok *Pal* bill was introduced in Indian parliament in 1968 which lapsed in due course. Fresh bills were introduced in 1971, 1977 and 1985 and allowed to lapse. A private-member's bill was introduced in 2002 which was also not acted upon. Finally, an official bill was introduced in 2004 which is still under consideration of a parliamentary standing committee.

Lomé Conventions refer to a series of conventions signed between the European Community (EC) /European Union (EU) and the least developed countries of Africa, the Caribbean and the Pacific (the ACP countries) which were formerly colonies of European powers. The Lomé Conventions established an overall trade and aid relationship between the EC/EU and the ACP countries. They represent an intersection of two approaches to trade between of the developed and developing countries: one of reciprocal concessions and the other of non-reciprocal. the former was represented by agreements of association between the EC and former European colonies.

They were replaced by the two Youndé Conventions*. Youndé Conventions were succeeded by the Generalized System of Preferences* (GSP) negotiated under the General Agreement on Trade and Tariffs *(GATT) and the Lome Convention allowing duty-free entry of goods and commodities of the ACP countries in the European market on a non-reciprocal basis.

Lomé I was signed on 28 February 1975 in Lome, capital of Togo, for a period of five years between the EC and 46 ACP countries. It allowed duty-free access to all industrial products and 96 per cent of agricultural commodities of the ACP countries to the EC on a non-reciprocal basis and increased development aid to them from the EC sources.

Lomé II was signed between the EC and 58 ACP countries for the period 1981-85 which continued the provisions of the previous Convention and made additional concessions in the form of the STABEX system (to stabilize the prices of commodities exported by the ACP countries) and the MINEX (a regime for maintaining the prices of the minerals exported by these countries).

Lomé III was signed between the EC and 64 ACP countries for the period 1985-90 and Lome IV was signed between the EC and the ACP countries for a period of ten years which continued the existing arrangements till its expiry in February 2000.

Lomé IV was signed between the EU and 71 ACP countries in May 2000 in Fiji for a period of twenty years. In due course non-reciprocal trade preference for all except 38 poorest ACP countries are planned to be replace by regional free-trade agreements. In 2003 it was announced that ACP countries which received preferential prices for their sugar in the EU were to lose this benefit in the near future.

M

Maastricht Treaty (1991). See "European Union.

Machiavellianism refers to an amoral approach to politics; brutal pursuit of power for the sake of power; reliance on force fraud and thuggery in the achievement of one's objectives; power politics as advocated by Niccolo Machiavelli (1469-1527).

MacMahon Line refers to the international boundary between India and China as demarcated by an agreement signed between the representatives of India, China and Tibet in 1941 in Simla (Himachal Pradesh, India). The Line is named after the official of the British Indian government who led the Indian delegations for the talks.. The Chinese occupied Tibet in 1950. In 1954 an Indian-China agreement on Tibet ("the panchsheel agreement") was signed under which India relinquished its rights and assets in Tibet in favour of China and recognized China's sovereignty over Tibet. Thereafter, China repudiated the MacMahon Line by depicting large chunks of Indian territory in Ladakh and the northeast frontier region as its own. China's recurrent incursions into Indian territory started in 1958 and eventually led to a full-scale border war with China in 1962. India suffered a military defeat and China occupied Indian territory which it claimed as its own..

Macropolitics deals like macroeconomics with broad issues of public policy affecting the general masses or broad interests like business, industry, labour or agriculture. Macropolitical decisions are taken at the highest level of government by the legislative and executive authorities acting together.

Mafia is in Italian the "black hand" i.e. a loose criminal organization. The *Mafiosi* (plural) are individuals, bands or cliques who indulge in underhand, illegal, unethical and anti-social dealings and transactions for the sake of self-aggrandizement.

Maghreb is the Arabic for the Arab West i.e. the North African countries of Algeria, Libiya, Morocco and Tunis. The *Mashreq* (Arab East) comprises the countries of the Arabian peninsula, the Fertile Crescent and the Arabian Gulf.

Maghreb Agreement was signed between the European Community (EC) and some developing countries of the southern Mediterranean littoral in 1976. The agreement extended the trade and aid benefits to these countries similar to those given under the Lome Conventions.

Maginot Line (pronounced as "Majino") was a line of defence with heavy fortifications built all along France's eastern frontier with Germany after World War I to guard against a possible land invasion of France by Germany. The line was named after André Maginot, the French minister of war (1922-24; 1929-31), who conceived it and got it in place. The line, considered almost impregnable at the time, was rendered redundant when the Nazi forces broke through in 1940 at Sedan and occupied France.

Magna Carta (1215) or the Great Charter was a royal charter signed by King John of England in 1215 in the face of his rebellious nobles granting them their rights and privileges. It: declared that nobody shall be deprived of his life, liberty and property except under due process of law* and everybody shall have the right to be judged by his peers (trial by jury). Magna Carta is regarded as the keystone of the liberties of the English people. Together with the Petition of Right* of 1628 and the Bill of Rights* of 1689 it constitutes the "Bible of the English Constitution".

Maintenance of Internal Security Act --MISA was enacted by Indian Parliament in 1971 to confer powers of preventive detention upon the government to deal effectively with threats to internal security of India, especially from external sources and foreign-inspired espionage activities. It was amended by the emergency regime of Indira Gandhi in 1975 and 1976 to provide for preventive detention of political opponents on the ground of creating internal disturbance. The Act was repealed by an act of 1978.

Malacca, Strait of is a strategic passage between Malasia and Indonesia connecting the Indian Ocean with the Pacific Ocean.

Malthusianism refers to theory of population control presented by Thomas Robert Malthus (1766-1834). His theory is based on two assumptions: (1) food is an essential need of life; and (2) the mutual attraction of the male and female sexes is a permanent natural phenomenon. Since population tends to increase by geometrical proportions while food production can at best increase at arithmetical rates the prospects of human well-being are bleak. He therefore recommended birth control to check population growth and overcome mass poverty. *Neo-Malthusians* are those Who advocate contraceptive methods to check population growth.

Managerial Revolution. James Burnham in his *The Managerial Revolution* (1941) predicted that the growth of industrial society will lead to the transfer of actual management of enterprises from their owners to the managerial class who will later manage the rest of the society as well.

Manchukuo was the name given by the Japanese to Manchuria after their occupation and colonization of it in 1930. The region was restored to China after Japanese defeat in 1945.

Mandal Commission. See "Backward Classes Commission".

***Mandamus*, Writ of** (Latin *mandamus* = we command) is issued by a superior court on a petition by an individual or association of individuals directing a lower court or a government official or agency to perform certain duties required of it by law, the performance of which is not optional or discretionary,

Mandarins were the high-level civil servants of imperial China. Now this term is applied to top-level bureaucrats in parliamentary democracies who tender expert advice to the political executive. *Mandarin* is also a dialect of the Chinese language spoken by the majority Han community.

Mandate (authority/command). A government in a democracy is expected to carry out the policy and programme it offered to the public at the last general election and was elected on that basis. Therefore the fulfilment of promises made and the measures proposed to the electorate becomes mandatory or obligatory. This is the vague notion of *mandate* which seems to have emerged during the latter part of the nineteenth century. However, under certain circumstances, governments have sometimes reneged on their promises or even acted against their mandates.

Mandates *(1919)*. After the defeat of the Central Powers (Germany, Turkey, Austria-Hungary and Italy) at the hands of the Allied Powers (Britain, France and others) in world War I the question arose how to dispose of the colonial possessions of the defeated German and Ottoman empires. Therefore, a system of *mandates* was created under Article 22 of the Covenant of the League of Nations whereby these colonies were entrusted to the victorious powers who were mandated to prepare them for self-government For instance, Palestine became a mandate of Great Britain which became the mandatory power enjoined to create a Jewish "national home" in that country. Syria and the Lebanon became French mandates. Namibia was placed under the administration of South Africa. In fact, mandates were a legal cover for division of the spoils of World War I the victors. The Mandated countries became independent after World War II and the system of mandates was replaced by the UN Trusteeship Council entrusted with the task of decolonization.

Manifest Destiny refers to the hegemonistic doctrine of the American statesmen during the early part of the nineteenth century asserting that the Divine Providence had made it a "manifest destiny" of the inhabitants of north America to colonize the continent for the Atlantic coast to the pacific coast and to expand beyond its natural bounds to provide for free development of its fastly growing population. The result was the expansion of the USA from the Atlantic coast to the Pacific coast and towards the end of the century conquest of Hawai, Guam, Puerto Rico and the Philippines.

Maoism refers to the theoretical contribution of Mao Ze Dong (1893-1976) to Marxism-Leninism. Just as Lenin had adapted Marx's ideas to the particular conditions of Russia similarly Mao adapted them to the particular conditions of China. In fact, Maoism is the Chinese brand of Marxism. His main contributions' are the recognition of the peasantry as a revolutionary class; struggle through guerilla warfare; first revolution in the countryside then encirclement of cities; impossibility of peaceful coexistence with the imperialist camp; democratic participation under party guidance; transformation of individuals into social beings through reform of thought processes; and continuous cultural revolution,

March on Rome (1922) was organized by the Fascist Party led by Benito Mussolini on 28 October 1922 to topple the democratic government of Italy which they held responsible for all the deprivations of Italy after World War I. While the Fascist bands were still outside Rome, the king, anxious to avoid trouble and bloodshed, appointed Mussolini as the prime minister and invited him to form a new government. The Fascists thus were able to establish their dictatorship by a mere show of strength and without firing a single shot.

Marginal Utility means that the value of anything is deduced from the utility of its last unit that satisfies the least important requirement of the subject.

Marshall Plan (1947) refers to the European recovery plan proposed by US Secretary of State George B. Marshall in 1947. The US offered massive assistance for industrial recovery of the war-ravaged economies of Western Europe including Western Germany. The condition was that Europeans implement this plan on a multilateral basis aiming at the economic rehabilitation of Western Europe as a whole. As a follow-up a European Economic Cooperation Conference was convened in Paris in July 1947 which created the Organization for European Economic Cooperation (OEEC) to implement the Marshall Plan. The programme was implemented during 1948-51. US Congress appropriated $ 13.5 billion (more than 100 billion in today's value). Within a brief period the beneficiary countries were able to restore their pre-war production level and repaid the American aid. The success of the Marshall Plan gave an impetus to the process of European integration.

Martial Law / Military Law. In old times martial law and military law were synonymous but in modern times they are entirely different phenomena, while military law is that part of national law which deals with maintenance of order and discipline in the ranks of the armed forces and provides for punitive measures against incidence of indiscipline, insubordination and desertion,, etc. martial law is an intermediate stage between normal order and a state of lawlessness. When law and order breaks down entirely in a part of the country or in the whole of the country because of any reason and the civil authority is unable to cope with the situation martial law is declared to restore normalcy by summary measures. It is an extraordinary preemptive measure. The military officer incharge of martial law administration is called the martial law administrator. Martial law authorities and the armed forces are exempted from judicial proceedings against acts done during martial law by an act of indemnity passed by parliament. Declaration of martial law is a prerogative of the executive branch of government.

Marxism-Leninism refers to the body of philosophical thought of Karl Marx as reinterpreted and adapted by Vladimir Lenin.

Maslow's Theory of Motivation was propounded by Abraham H. Maslow (1908-1970) in his *Motivation and Personality* (1954). He pointed out that in every human person there exists a hierarchy of human needs: physiology, safety, social esteem and self-actualization (in an ascending order). As a lower need is satisfied the next higher needs becomes pressing and dominant. As one need is satisfied it no longer acts as a motivation. To motivate him his higher needs must be addressed and satisfied.

Mass Media of communication refer to both print and electronic media such as newspapers, magazines, radio, television and the internet which transmit massive quantity of information to the large masses of the public both at home and abroad. They are distinguished from personal communications such as letters, telegrams and telephonic talks. Mass media are an indispensable part of the democratic process and are called "the fourth estate".,

Mediterranean Area. The Mediterranean Sea is an inland sea enclosed by three continents of Europe, Asia and Africa. It is connected with the Atlantic Ocean by the Strait of Gibralter. The Mediterranean area includes the littoral countries of the Mediterranean—Albania, Greece and Italy in the west and Cyprus, Egypt, Lebanon, Palestine/Israel, Libya, Algeria, Morocco and Tunis in the east..

Melting Pot or the American melting pot refers to the strong assimilative tendency of the American society; the immigrants get *Americanized* automatically, i.e. absorbed into American culture.

Mercantilism was an economic approach prevalent in Europe during the sixteenth and seventeenth centuries. It called for state for state regulation of foreign trade with a view to maximize exports which fetched precious metal (the medium of exchange) and minimize imports which implied outflow of precious metals. In those times the reserves of gold and silver were regarded as the foundation of a nation's wealth and power. Such emphasis on acquisition of precious metals was a characteristic of the Middle Ages when gold and silver were regarded as the mainstay during natural calamities and wars.

McCarthyism is synonymous with ideological witch-hunting and political persecution. After Senator Joseph McCarthy who was staunchly anti-communist and obsessed with the imaginary threat of communist subversion in the USA. He is reported to have raised an alarm on 9 February 1950 by pointing out the existence of allegedly communist officers in the US Department of State. His decade-long anti-communist campaign spoiled the careers of many innocent people.

Mercosur. See ''Southern Common Market''.

Merit System of recruitment to public was introduced by Napoleon I in France. The merit system replaced the patronage or spoils system. In the merit system the selection is made on the basis of a candidate's merit as determined through competitive examinations open to all individuals and classes. Meritocracy (rule by merit) has the same It is the opposite of both hereditary aristocracy as well mediocrity.

Meritocracy is rule of merit, opposite of patronage as well as mediocrity

Messiah (Hebrew *mashiah* or Arabic *masiha* = the anointed/holy figure) is used either (l) for Jesus Christ as the redeemer of the mankind; or (2) an expected king who will be sent by God to liberate the Jews and recover the kingdom of Israel; or (3) anybody who is believed to be the redeemer of his people. Hence *messianism* is the belief in the mission of an expected *messiah* who will uproot evil and establish justice.

Micropolitics deals with political behaviour of groups and communities at the micro or local level. Like microeconomics micropolitics assumes that people's attitudes towards public policy are primarily determined by self-interest.

Middle East/North Africa. The term Middle East, originated in Great Britain during the nineteenth century, designated a vast lying between Singapore and the Arabian Gulf (called middle because it was situated between the Far East and the Near East Turkey). It was due to the exigencies of world War II that: Britain made Egypt the centre of its war operations and term Middle East came to be applied to Egypt and the adjoining areas. It was in this restricted sense that the that the term became a vogue in the postwar period and even the people of the Arabland adopted it. The Middle East now includes Turkey and Iran, the Nile Valley (Egypt and Sudan), the Fertile Crescent (Syria, Lebanon, Iraq, Palestine and Israel), the Arabian peninsula and the Arabian Gulf. The American usage "the Near and Middle East" has the same meaning. In India and China the term "West Asia" is preferred because the region lies in the west of these countries. "North Africa" includes the Arabic-speaking countries of Algeria, Libiya, Morocco and Tunis. Because of its close.ethnic, linguistic, religious and cultural affinity with the Arab world the region is also known as *Maghreb* (the Arab West) the *Mashreq* in contradistinction of the *Mashreg* (the Arab East) which refers to the Arab countries of the Middle East.

Middle Kingdom (*Zhong Quo* in Chinese) is the ancient name of China dating from c. 1000 B.C. The Chinese people regarded themselves as the centre of civilization surrounded from all sides by barbarian people. The Chinese character for China is which is indicative of the centrality of the country. The great wall of China was built to defend the Middle Kingdom against invasion by the barbarians.

Middle Powers are those state which because of their medium area, population and military potential are not expected to play a major role in world politic but nevertheless can exert some influence in alliance with the great powers or independently within their own regions like Turkey, Iran, Pakistan, South Africa, Nigeria, Argentina and Brazil.

Militarism is the policy of pursuit, enhancement and glorification of military power for the sake of raising national prestige. It accords the military class a supreme status within the national society and the state. It tends to use force and coercion in dealing with domestic and foreign opponents. Warmongering is considered a divine function and military training is imparted to all citizens to inculcate the virtues of manliness and courage, patriotism, heroism honour and dignity and unity and discipline.

Military Government refers to the takeover of the civil administration by the military authorities in a territory or country occupied by a foreign military force. It should not be confounded with martial law*.

Military Law is that part of the national law which deals with the recruitment, organization, compensation, conduct and discipline, etc. of the armed forces. It should not be confounded with martial law*.

Militia is an armed force made of volunteers raised by a government to maintain internal security; armed forces maintained by the States of the American Union which make up the National Guard; armed bands raised and deployed by totalitarian parties to control the population.

Ministerial Act is an executive act in the performance of which the concerned personnel has no personal discretion.

Ministerial Responsibility in parliamentary democracy means the responsibility (moral, political and legal) of the body of ministers as a whole before the elected chamber of parliament. The cabinet or the council of ministers is a collective parliamentary executive meant to exercise executive authority collectively and own the responsibility for all the policies and actions of the government collectively.

Ministerial Staff is the subordinate clerical staff working in an executive department; the non-officer class of employees.

Minorities Commission. See "National Commission on Minorities"*

Minorities Treaties were concluded after World War I which bound most of the Central and East European States to protect the ethnic minorities within their territories, to ensure them freedom religious faith and belief and practice, and to preserve their language and culture and to provide for the education of their children in their mother-tongue.

Minorities. In the realm of politics the terms "majority" and relative and "minority" are relative and (shifting concepts. There can be no permanent political majority or minority. However, in the social and cultural realm minorities are those minor groups which differ from the major group among whom they live in terms of their race, nationality, ethnic origin, religion, culture language or place of birth. They do not become salient as minorities unless they are subjected to deprivation, oppression or discrimination by the majority community.

Misdemeanor in law means a minor offence in contrast to felony*, punishable by fines or imprisonment for short terms.

Missile Technology Control Regime—MTCR was informally agreed to in 1987 by the Group of Seven or G-7 (Canada, France, Germany, Italy, Japan, the UK and the USA) in an attempt to prevent proliferation of weapons of mass destruction by restricting the international sales of ballistic and cruise missiles as well as their components and technology. In spite of this regime India, Iran, Israel, North Korea and Pakistan developed indigenous missiles.

Modern Liberalism refers to that stream of liberal thought that departed from the old stream of liberalism which arose in the second half of the nineteenth century and twentieth century and is represented by T.H. Green, L.T. Hobhouse, Frederick Hayek, Alfred Nozick and John Rawls. Modern liberalism is also characterized as democratic collectivism or democratic welfarism. It realized the necessity of state regulation of or intervention in the social and economic spheres to remove social evils and imbalances created by *laissez faire* economics and unbirdled capitalism, to ameliorate the condition of the poor and needy by redistribution of resources, and to provide for the basic needs of the citizens by creating a network of social and welfare services.

Modernity as opposed to traditional or feudal way of life began in Europe with the beginning of an industrial age from about 1760 AD onwards and later became a universal phenomenon. It; has been defined as a particular historical period, a body of philosophical thought and a cluster of institutions at the same time. The institutional manifestations of modernity are: in *politics* the consolidation of secular political power in the shape of centralized and bureaucratic nation-state; centralized control of military power; technicalization of warfare; concepts of sovereignty and legitimacy; and emergence of an international system of nation-states. In *economic* emergence of a capitalist industrial economy; monetaized exchange; reliance on science and technology; a free market operating on the principles of freedom of enterprise, freedom of exchange and free competition. In *society* withering away of traditional feudal values and hierarchies and their replacement by modern values and modern social stratification. Finally, in the cultural realm the feudal culture was replaced by a secular materialistic culture and its associated philosophy of individualism, rationalism, secularism and liberalism.

Modernity and Tradition. Talcott Parsons in his *The Social System* (1951) has elaborated Alfred Toennies' distinction between *gemeinschaft* (community) and *geselschaft* (society) into five major dilemmas or patterns of orientation that confront an actor in a given social situation. These pattern variables represent the dichotomy of tradition and modernity. They are: affectivity versus affective neutrality; self-orientation versus collective orientation; particularism versus universalism; ascription versus achievement; and role diffuseness versus role specificity. The first of these pairs represents the traditional while the second represents the modernist orientation. According to Parsons, social change accompanying industrialization involves a movement from affectivity to affective neutrality; from particularism to universalism; from ascription to achievement; and from role diffuseness to role specificity.

Modernization means making modern. It is the process of adaptation by which traditional societies of the east may become modern by adopting the goals of technicalization, industrial development, economic growth, full employment, democratization and rule of law.

Modus Vivendi (mode of understanding) is an instrument recording an international agreement of a temporary or transient nature, intended to be replaced by an arrangement of a more permanent or detailed character later on. A *modus vivendi* does not require ratification.

Monetary Policy refers to sum total of measures taken by a government or its central bank to expand or contract the money supply and the bank credit to achieve specific objectives. This is done either by raising or lowering the interest rate. The common objectives of monetary policy are: to maintain a high level of employment and production; to maintain the existing price level; and to stabilize the value of the national currency and to conserve its foreign currency reserves. Monetary policy is sometimes implemented in conjunction with fiscal policy.

Monroe Doctrine (1823) refers to American policy towards the western hemisphere declared by President James Monroe in his annual message to the US Congress on 2 December 1823. The background of this policy was that during the Napoleonic wars in Europe the Spanish and other European colonies in Latin America had declared their independence and became republics. After the defeat of Napoleon however the Holy Alliance* was planning to intervene militarily to restore these former colonies to Spain. At this juncture, the USA declared its opposition to reimposition of colonial rule in Latin America, took the whole of the western hemisphere under its protection; and closed it for ever for European colonization and intervention. Monroe declared:" The American continents, by the free and independent condition which they nave assumed and maintained, are henceforth not to be considered as subjects for future colonization by any European powers, and that European intervention in this hemisphere could not be viewed in any other light than as the manifestation of an unfriendly disposition towards the United States. He also disclaimed any intention of the USA to take any part in the wars of the European powers or "in matters relating to themselves". The **Theodore Corollary** to the Monroe Doctrine was enunciated by President Theodore Roosevelt on 2 December 1904. It was occasioned by the indebtedness of the Dominican Republic and mounting pressures of the European lenders for repayment of their loans. Roosevelt declared that chronic misconduct on the part of any state in south-central America may compel the USA to exercise an international police power as the only means of enforcing international obligation in this area. He thus forbade European interventions in the internal affairs of Latin America.

Montagu Declaration (1917) was made by the secretary of State of India Edwin Montagu in the house of continues stating the goal of future British policy in India as that of gradual development of self governing institutions with a view to progressive realization of responsible government in India as an integral part of the British Empire.

Montagu-Chelmsford Reforms (1919) refer to Indian constitutional reforms which were formulated by Edwin Montagu, the Secretary of state for India, and Lord Minto, the Governor-General of India, and embodied in the Government of India Act, 1919. The crux of the reforms was the introduction of a system of dyarchy (responsibility is a partial area and irresponsibility in the larger of administration in the British Indian provinces. This was done in pursuance of the Montagu Declaration on 20 August 1917 that the goal of British policy in India in the future is that of increasing association of Indians in every branch of the administration and the gradual development of self- governing institutions with a view to the progressive realization of responsible government in India as an integral part of the British Empire Dyarchy was conceived as the first step in the British plan of gradualism. The main features of the Government of India Act, 1919 were: complete local self-government at the grassroots; partial responsibility in the provinces; and complete irresponsibility at the centre.

Montreal Protocol (1987) to the Vienna Convention for the Protection of the Ozone Layer was signed by the industrialized countries of the world committing themselves to terminate manufacture of ozone depleting chemicals especially chloroflurocarbons (CFC) by 1 January 2005. However, an intergovernmental conference of the parties to the Protocol held in Montreal in March 2004 granted more time to 11 of the industrialized countries to meet their obligation under the Protocol. (Ozone gas covering the earth's upper atmosphere absorbs the ultraviolet rays emitted by the sun which is considered a major cause of skin cancer and eye cataract). The Executive Committee of the Montreal Protocol under the UN Development Programme assists the parties to eliminate the use of ozone-depleting substances.

Montreaux Convention (1936) was signed on 20 July 1936 in Montreaux, Switzerland. The Convention regulates international shipping through the Bosporus and Dardennells* and superseded a protocol attached to the Treaty of Lausanne (1923) which had undermined Turkish sovereignty over the straits. The Montreaux Convention restored Turkish sovereignty over the straits and permitted Turkey to remilitarize them.

Morley-Minto Reforms (1909) refer to constitutional reforms jointly formulated by Lord Morley* the secretary of State for India, and Lord Minto the Viceroy and Governor-General in India, which were embodied in the Indian Councils Act, 1909.

The main features of this Act were enlargement of the legislative councils to provide more avenue for the association of Indians with the work of legislation; the provision of a non-official majority in legislatures but real power war still vested in the officials and introduction of separate electorate for the Muslim feudal class and special electorate for the landlord class. The British government declared that these reforms were not intended to introduce responsible government in India. The British, however, succeeded by these reforms to win over the moderate section of the Indian National Congress and isolate the extremists; the loyalty of the Muslim feudal class was bought by giving them separate electorate and that of the landlord class by giving them special electorate; and the Anglo-Indian bureaucracy was assured beyond any doubt that there was no question of introducing responsible government in India.

Mosca's Theory of the Ruling Class. Gaetano Mosca in his *The Ruling Class* (1939) gave an empirical evidence of his view that the ruling class or the elites is formed on the basis of resources and opportunities possessed or particular functions monopolized by certain groups such as military skill, industrial and business management or religious functions, etc. This rule by the people is a fiction.

Most-Favoured-Nation Clause is usually included in the bilateral trade agreements which commits both the signatories to extend to each other all such facilities and concessions which they provide to any other country.

Mujahideen (plural of Arabic *mujahid* = one who struggles in the way of God) are according to the text of the Quran those believers who struggle in the path of God by way of defending the faith against its enemies or confronting the evil or combating tyranny and oppression. However, beyond the religious realm the term has also been applied for guerillas fighting for national liberation or against foreign occupation or against unjust rule.

Multilateral Investment Guarantee Agency—MIGA was established in April 1988 with its headquarters at Washington, D.C., as an autonomous member of the World Bank Group*, for providing global insurance to private investors against political risks and to encourage private investment in the member-countries;

Munich Agreement was signed on 29 September 1938 by British Prime Minister Nevil Chamberlain, the French Prime Minister M. Daladier on the one side and the Nazi dictator Adolf Hitler and the Italian Fascist dictator Benito Mussolini on the other side, Under this agreement Britain and France allowed Hitler to occupy that part of Czechoslovakia that was inhabited by German-speaking Students and that was claimed by Hitler as part of Germany. Soon after the signing of the agreement Hitler occupied the whole of Czechoslovakia. In the conclusion of this agreement neither the affected country (Czechoslovakia) nor Russia which was a co-gurantor of the independence of Czechoslovakia along with Britain and France was consulted. The Munich agreement became infamous for shameless appeasement of aggressors. The territorial demand of Hitler was accepted to avoid the threat of a war in Europe.

Muruwwat (Arabic for manliness) refers to the Arab-Islamic code of honour emphasizing personal honesty and integrity; a sense of personal honour and dignity; piety and filial loyalty and generosity towards the kinsfolk and friends, etc.

Muslim Brotherhood or properly the Society of the Muslim Brothers *(Jamiat al-Ikhwan al-Muslimeen)* was founded in 1929 in Egypt by Hasan al Banna (1906-1948), who became its supreme guide. Its objective was the reformation and reconstruction of the Egyptian society and state according to Islamic principles. The movement was banned by the Egyptian government in 1948 because of its rising popularity among the masses and its leader was assassinated in mysterious conditions. The movement went underground and resurfaced in 1952 after the army revolt of that year which it had supported. Perceiving it as a political threat the military regime also banned it in 1954. Then it shifted to Damascus, Syria. But merger of Egypt and Syria as the United Arab Republic in 1958 again led to its outlawing, Although persecuted by the Arab governments the Muslim Brothers are still active in the political life of Egypt and Jordan. The present Supreme Guide is Muhammad Mahdi Akif.

Muslim League, All-India was established on 30 December 1906 in Dacca by prominent leaders of the Muslim feudal class who had assembled there for the annual session of the All-India Muslim educational Conference. Its founding resolution mentioned three objectives of this body: to promote feelings of loyalty towards the British government; to protect the political and other interests of the Muslim community; and to prevent hatred between Muslims and other communities of India; The League adopted its constitution 1908 and in 1913 amended its constitution to include the attainment of self-government for India as one of its basic objectives. In 1916 the League signed a pact (Lucknow Pact*) with the Indian National Congress to work together for the implementation of a joint scheme of constitutional reforms after the first world War. In the postwar period the Congress bypassed the League and did not agreed to its demands for continuation of separate electorate for the Muslims, a federal constitution guaranteeing provincial autonomy to the provinces and other Muslim demands. The failure of the Congress after the 1937 provincial elections to accommodate the League in its ministry in the United Provinces in accordance with a pre-election understanding between the two, was the starting-point of Congress-League misunderstanding and political conflict. The conflict of the two parties reached its utmost height during the years of the second world War and thereafter till a settlement was reached between the two over the partition of India into the dominion of India and the dominion of Pakistan as a prelude to transfer of power under the Indian Independence Act, 1947. After Independence the AIML migrated to Pakistan where it formed the government of the new state.

Muslim League, Indian Union. After the migration of the leaders of the former All-India Muslim League to Pakistan in and after 1947 the body became defunct in north-central and eastern India. However, the Madras State unit of the party was reconstituted by its leader the late Muhammad Ismail in 1947 as the Indian Union Muslim with an amended constitution professing allegiance to the Indian Union. Soon another unit was organized in the Travancore-Cochin State (later Kerala). Both units have since then taken part in local, state and national elections on a secular platform. It is recognised as a regional political party in Tamil Nadu and Kerala by the Election Commission of India.

Muslim Majlis- i-Mushawarat, All-India (Muslim Consultative Council) was founded in 1964 in Lucknow, Uttar Pradesh, in the wake of devastating anti-Muslim riots that occurred in recent years in different parts of India. It was a consultative forum of various Muslim organizations and groups to consider the common problems facing Indian Muslims and to find their solutions. With this aim it undertook to send delegations to different parts of India to remove the misunderstanding of the non-Muslims about the Muslims. The Mushawarat opposed the termination of the minority character of the Aligarh Muslim University by an emergency ordinance imposed by the Government of India in 1965. On the eve of the fourth General Election in India due in 1967, the Mushawarat formulated a strategy of extending support to such candidates of secular political parties who pledgee themselves to work for the furtherance of Mushawarat's objectives after getting elected. One consequence was that the Muslims voted overwhelmingly in favour of non-Congress candidates denting Congress' strength. After 1967 the forum eclipsed because its President, Syed Mahmud, a Congress leader, deserted it accusing it of being anti-Congress and the secular candidates elected with its support paid no heed to its objectives. The forum still exists in the form of splintered groups but with no tangible policy or programme and hardly any influence among the Muslim masses.

N

Naga Insurgency (India). Nagas are tribal people belonging to the Indo-Mongoloid group inhabiting areas contiguous to the northeastern hills of India. The area was brought under British control during the nineteenth century. The British isolated this area from the people of the adjoining Assam province and encouraged their Christianization through the foreign missionaries as a result of which the Naga tribes became Christian. After 1947 the area was centrally administered as the Naga Hills Tuensang Area. Insurgency started during 1950's against Indian rule and for national independence. To pacify the rebels the area was renamed as Nagaland in 1961. It was granted the status of a State of the Indian Union enjoying certain special privileges on 1 December 1964.

Nagorno Karabakh Problem. *Nagorno* in Russian means "mountain" and *Karabakh* is the Russian form of Azeri *Qara Bagh* which is a province of the Republic of Azerbaijan. The conflict between Armenia and Azerbaijan over the Armenian-majority province of Karabakh was rooted in the fact that the irredentist Armenian inhabitants of the province claimed the right to national self-determination and merger with neighbouring Armenia, in the wake of the dissolution of he USSR and independence of both Armenia and Azerbaijan. In 1992 Armenian forces invaded Karabakh and occupied it and created a corridor between Armenia and the occupied territory. The counterattack by Azerbaijan forces were repulsed by the Armenians. A ceasefire between arranged by the Commonwealth of Independent States (CIS) but international mediation failed to resolve the conflict till 2006.

Nation (from Italian *nasci* = to be born) is a territorial community which living in a common homeland, develops a feeling of unity with a common identity and common destiny based on their race, religion, culture, language or history, any one of them alone or in combination. As a result of historical-political developments taking place since 1500 AD nation has become the basic unit of human community. When a nation (cultural community) organizes itself into a state (legal community) it is called a *nation-state.*

National Capital Region (India) was created under the Government of National Capital Territory Act, 1991, which came into force in 1993. The NCR is composed of the former Union Territory of Delhi and some adjoining areas. Delhi was renamed as National Capital Territory and given a status short of full statehood. The Act provided for the election of an NCT legislative assembly and a responsible council of ministers with a chief minister at the head. The old office of the Lt. Governor was retained.

National Character refers to those relatively persistent personality characteristics, behavioural attributes, cultural traits and institutional structures of a nation that distinguish it from other nations. The term was superseded by political *culture.*

National Commission for Backward Classes (India) was established under the National Commission for Backward Classes Act, 1993, passed by Indian Parliament in pursuance of a directive issued by the Supreme Court, for entertaining, examining and advising the government on requests received from the members of the public for inclusion in of certain castes or their exclusion from the lists of the Other Backward Classes (OBC's), as notified by the government, or complaints regarding overinclusion or under inclusion in the said lists, under the NCBC Act, the advice tendered by the Commission shall be binding upon the Government.

National Commission for Minorities (India). In accordance with a policy decision taken by the Janata Party government at the centre a *Minorities Commission* was established as an advisory body by a Resolution of the central home ministry dated 12 January 1978. It was given a statutory status by the National Commission for Minorities Act, 1992. The NCM is composed of a chairperson, a vice-chairperson, and five other members representing the different religious minorities of India. They are appointed by the Government of India for a term of five years. The Commission looks into complaints of discrimination against minorities (Muslims, Christians, Sikhs, Buddhists, Parsis and Jainis) and makes recommendations to the government for their redressal. The Commission is nearly belong under the home ministry and has enforcement process The NCM is sought to be made an independent constitutional body by the Constitution (103 Amendment) Bill, 2004 and the National Commission for Minorities (Repeal) Bill, 2004. Both were referred to the parliamentary Standing Committee of Social Justice and Empowerment in June 2005.

National Commission for Scheduled Castes and Scheduled Tribes was established by the Constitution (65th Amendment) Act, 1990. It replaced the Special Officer for the welfare of the scheduled castes and scheduled tribes provided for under the original 228 of the Indian Constitution. The Commission is composed of a chairman, a vice-chairman and five other members appointed by the government for a term of five years. It is responsible for overseeing the implementation of the constitutional safeguards for the scheduled castes and scheduled tribes. It also inquires into specific complaints of discrimination against these communities and advises the government on matters referred to it. Its reports are laid before Indian Parliament and state legislative assemblies.

National Commission for Women (India) was created under the National Commission for Women Act, 1990 as an advisory body under the central home ministry meant to review constitutional and legal safeguards relating to women, inquire into cases of atrocities against women, and hear petitions from women and advise the government for the redressal of their grievances.

National Conference, All Jammu and Kashmir was a representative organization of the Kashmiri people originally founded by the Kashmiri leader Sheikh Muhammad Abdullah (1905-1982) as the **All-Jammu and Kashmir Muslim Conference** in 1930 to protects the rights of the Kashmiris against autocratic Dogra rule. It assumed the name of the National Conference in 1938 to accommodate the Kashmiri Pandit community of the Kashmir valley. The NC ran the government of the Jammu and Kashmir with its leader SM Abdullah as the prime minister from 1947 to 1953. In 1953 Abdullah was dismissed from premiership and imprisoned for alleged treason. Thereafter, the National Conference was merged with the Indian National Congress which became the ruling party in Jammu and Kashmir. The National Conference was revived in 1966 after Bakhshi Ghulam Muhammad was dismissed as chief minister on corruption charges. It was reorganized in 1975 by Abdullah in consequence of his agreement with Prime Minister Indira Gandhi signed in 1974 which allowed him to become the chief minister of the State after disbanding the Plebiscite Front*. The NC ruled in Jammu and Kashmir from 1975 to 2003 when it was dislodged from power by the People's Democratic Party-Indian National Congress combine.

National Democratic Alliance—NDA (India) is an electoral alliance between the major political party the Bharatiya Janata Party* and minor regional political parties namely the Telugu Desam Party,* the Janata Dal* (United), the Jammu and Kashmir National Conference,* the All-India Anna D.M.K.,* the Assam Gano Parishad and others. The NDA formed the government in 2000 and was defeated in the general elections of 2004 and was succeeded by the coalition government formed by the United Progressive Alliance* (UPA) led by the Indian National Congress (Sonia).

National Development Council NDC (India) was created by a Resolution of the Government of India in 1952. It is composed of the Prime Minister at the head, all chief ministers of states and union territories, and a number of central cabinet ministers. The functions of the NDC, as recast according to the recommendations of the Administrative Reforms Commission* (1966-70) are: (1) to prescribe guidless for the formulation of the national development plans including the assessment of resources for same; (2) to consider the national development plan as formulated the Planning Commission; (3) to consider important questions of social and economic policy affecting national development; and (4) to review the working of the national plan from time to time and to recommend such measures as are necessary for achieving the aims and targets set out in the national development plan.

National Economy is the sum of all economic activities in agriculture, industry, extraction and services.

National Front (India) was formed in 1988 as a coalition of four national parties—the Janata Party, the Lok Dal, the Communist Party of India and the Communist Party (Marxist) — and three regional parties — the Telegu Desam of Andhra Pradesh, the DMK of Tamil Nadu and the Assam Gano Parishad. After the parliamentary elections held in October 1989 V.P. Singh, the leader of the Janata Dal, the largest constituent of the National Front, was elected as the leader of the National Front and sworn in as prime minister of India on 2 December 1989. His government was supported by the Bharatiya Janata Party from outside.

National Human Rights Commission—NHRC (India) was created under the Protection of Human Rights Act, 1993 (as amended in 2000) to protect human rights as guaranteed under the UN Covenant of Civil, and Political Rights and the UN Covenant of Economic, Social and Cultural Rights of 1966. Since India is a signatory to both the international covenants the Protection of Human Rights Act, 1993, was passed to give effect to their provisions as an international obligation. The is a fact-finding body empowered to conduct inquiry into specific complaints of violations of human rights and to take remedial measures. It is composed of five members appointed by the Government of India for five years with a chairman who should have been a chief justice of India. The chairperson of the Commission for Minorities; the chairperson of the National Commission for Women, and the chairperson of the National Commission for the Scheduled Castes and Scheduled Tribes are deemed members of the NHRC for discharging certain functions as provided for under the Act. All individuals and groups are entitled to petition the NHRC directly on their address at Faridkot House, Copernicus Marg, New Delhi 110001.

National Identity is a way of differentiating one national community from other communities. National identity may be based on race, ethnicity, culture, religion or language.

National Integration is the process of integrating diverse, disparate, hetereogeneous, and often mutually conflicting elements in the body bolitic into one homogeneous national community working for common national goals. National Integration may be achieved either by assimilation from the above or by accommodating and cultivating pluralism from below. Fissiparous tendencies arise along a vertical axis in the society, namely the centre-periphey axis where the problem of the localities and regions under one central government arises and a horizontal axis where caste, communal cultural, linguistic and religious diversities pose a challenge to national unity. Integrationist policies are formulated just to cope with these problems. Promotion of national unity and integrity for instance has been made one of the objects of the Indian states in the preamble and Article 51-A of the Indian Constitution.

National Integration Council (India) was formed by the Government of India in 1958 in the wake of the linguistic reorganization of states in India to ckeck fissiparous tendencies and promote national unity and integration. The major contribution of the early NIC was the adoption of the three-language formula* and its implementation throughout India to bring about emotional integration of the north and south. The NIC became dormant for a long time after the Chinese aggression against India in 1962 as it created an unprecedented feeling of national unity. When the Janata Party came to power in the centre in 1977, the Government of India created a Minorities Commission* in 1978 to protect the minorities against discrimination and oppression and promote communal harmony. It was decided to observe 19 November 1981 as the National Integration Day and thereafter every year. The practice was discontinued after the demise of the Janata government in 1979. The Minorities Commission also recommended the setting up of a National Integration Commission to advise the National Integration Council but that recommendation was never implemented. The last meeting of the NIC was convened in 1991 to deal with the crisis created by the movement for the construction of a temple over the site of a 15th century mosque in Ayodhya which could not stem the tide of extremism. The NIC became defunct after the demolition of the Ayodhya mosque on 6 December 1992. The NIC was reconstituted by the Government of India with the prime minister of India as its chairman and 143 other members including all chief ministers of states and union territories a number of central cabinet ministers, the leaders of opposition political parties, representatives of non-governmental organizations, and some eminent public figures. Its first meeting was held on 31 August 2005 in New Delhi.

National Interest or national good of a country is the sum of those values and interests considered as vital for the survival, well-being and progress of a nation. Just as public interest or good is the guiding principle of domestic policy similarly national interest is the guiding principle of foreign policy of a state as well as the criterion for its evaluation.

National Judicial Academy was established by the Government of India in 1993 with its seat in Bhopal, Madhya Pradesh, as a society registered under the Registration of Societies Act, 1860.

National Legal Services Authority—NALSA (India) was created under the Legal Services Authorities Act, 1987 (as amended in 2002) to oversee the setting up and functioning of Lok Adalats in all districts of India as statutory conciliation forums. These are to be provided in all government departments, public sector undertakings and statutory corporations. Their jurisdiction covers all civil cases and comoundable offences and have been accorded the status of civil courts so that their awards are final, binding upon the parties and non-appealable. Besides NALSA provides legal awareness and literacy and organizes legal aid clinics and counselling and conciliation centres in the districts. The Legal Services Act designates the following as legal committees/authorities to dispense free legal aid to persons eligible under the Act to receive free legal aid. The Supreme Court Legal Services Committee, if the matter is pending before the Supreme Court; the High Court Legal Services Committee in every High Court if the matter is before the High Court; the State Legal Services Authority with its seat in the state capital; the District Legal Services Authority in every district (the District Judge being the ex-office chairman of the District Authority); and the Taluka Legal Services Committee at the taluka level.

National Police Academy (India) was originally set up as the Central Police Training College on 15 September 1948 in Mount Abu, Rajasthan, to impart training to the probationers of the Indian Police Service (IPS). It was renamed as Sardar Patel National Police Academy. It is headed by a director with the rank of an inspector-general of police.

National Security Act, 1980 (India) was enacted by the Indira government on 27 December 1980 as a replacement of the Maintenance of Internal Security Act* (MISA) repealed by the Janata government in 1978. The NSA provides for preventive detention of anti-social, anti-national, disruptive and secessionist elements. It was amended in 1984, 1985, 1987 and 1988. The Act is till in force.

National Security Council (India) was first constituted by the Government of India on 19 November 1998 to consider and give policy advice on matters connected with the national security of India. It is headed by the Prime Minister of India, a National Security Advisor appointed by the Prime Minister, and the Home Defence and Finance Ministers of the Central Cabinet, the Deputy Chairman of the Planning Commission and the Chiefs of Army, Navy and the Air Force. The NSC was reconstituted in 2005.

National Security Guard (India) was formed in 1984 as an elite anti-terrorist force of the Indian Union to provide extrasophisticated security cover to high-ranking members of government, officials and politicians. Besides its also deployed to carry out special anti-terrorist missions.

National Tax Tribunal (India). A legislative bill contemplating the constitution of a national tax tribunal was reported to have been approved by the Council of Ministers on 3 September 2004.

Nationalism is a psychological condition in which the nation-state becomes the centre of the supreme loyalty of its members. It amounts to worshipping the idol of the nation or nation-state. It implies assertion of national identity, an aspiration for national self-determination, and if national independence has been achieved, an urge to enhance national honour and prestige.

Nationalist Congress Party is a breakaway faction of the Indian National Congress (I) formed by Sharad Pawar and his associates on 27 May 1999 opposing the election of Sonia Gandhi (an Italian by origin) as president of the Indian National Congress The NCP and the INC have formed a coalition government in Maharashtra State and the NCP is a constituent of the INC-led United Progressive Alliance government at the centre.

Nationality is both a legal and a cultural concept. In a legal sense nationality is synonomous with citizenship, the legal status of being the national or citizen of a state. As a cultural concept it refers to minority ethnic groups living in a nation-state who are distinguished from the majority group by their particular race or ethnicity or culture. It is in this sense that the Scots and Welsh in the UK and the Sindhis Blochs and Pathans in Pakistan and the Pushtuns, Tajiks and Uzbeks in Afghanistan are regarded as different nationalities.

Nationalization is the taking over of private property or enterprise into national i.e. state ownership.

Nationalization is the process of making national, that is, taking private property into public ownership by the state.

Nationalized Banks (India). The Government of India on 19 July 1969 nationalized 14 major banking companies in India having deposits of not less than Rs. 50 crore by an Ordinance. The Ordinance was converted into an Act of Parliament in August 1969 but was declared as unconstitutional by the Supreme Court of India on 10 February 1970 on the ground that the compensation paid to the owners was not fair and adequate. To overcome the Supreme Court judgment the government amended Article 30 of the Constitution to provide that private property can be acquired for public purpose for an amount determined by the government. Thereafter the government issued a fresh Ordinance on 14 February 1970 resuming the control of the 14 nationalized banks with retrospective effect from 19 July 1969. The Ordinance was replaced by an act of parliament passed in March as the Banking Companies (Acquisition and Transfer of Under-takings) Act 1970. Each of the nationalized bank then became a statutory corporate body. The banks nationalized in 1969 were: Central Bank of India; Bank of India; Panjab National Rank; Bank of Baroda; United

Commercial Bank, Canara Bank; United Bank of India; Dena Bank; Syndicate Bank; Union Rank of India; Allahabad Bank; Indian Bank; and Bank of Maharashtra. In 1978 six more private banks whose deposits had exceeded Rs 50 crore were acquired: Panjab and Sind Bank, Vijiya Bank; Corporation Bank; Andhra Bank; New Bank of India and Oriental Bank of Commerce. The State Bank of India and its seven subsidiaries (State Bank of Bikaner & Jaipur, State Bank of Hyderabad, State Bank of Mysore, State Bank of Patiala, State Bank of Surashtra, State Bank of Indore and the State Bank of Travancore) were already owned and managed by the government. The group of government owned and nationalized banks is known as public sector banks and their policy is determined by the Indian Public Sector Banks Association.

Natural Justice is called natural because it is required by human nature or reason. Justice the end of all legal process. The principle enjoins open, impartial and fair trial of a case before a court of law or a legal authority The end of natural justice can be meet by observing the following rule: (1) act fairly, in good faith, without bias, and in a judicial temper; (2) give each party an opportunity to present his case personally or through a counsel and not to hear one side behind the back of the other side; (3) nobody should be made a judge in his own case; (4) a man must, be given an advance notice of the charges levelled against him;- (5) all relevant documents submitted to the court should be made available for inspection by both the parties; (6) the accused must be given an opportunity for self-defence and to be represented by a lawyer and (7) the opportunity for appeal to higher courts should not be denied. Justice should not only be done but also seen to be done.

Naturalization is the legal procedure of granting nationality or citizenship to a foreigner. A naturalized citizen has the same rights and duties as a native citizen but in the USA only a citizen born in the country is eligible to become a candidate for the office of the President of the USA. A *naturalized* citizen is a counterpart of the *native* citizen and enjoys the same legal status and rights and assumes the same legal obligations as the natural born citizen.

Nawwab/Nawab (Arabic for deputy; viceroy; vicegerent) was originally the title of the provincial governors appointed by the Mughal Emperor in Delhi to administer the provinces and regions of the Indian empire. With the decline of the Mughal Empire after 1707 these rulers proclaimed their autonomy in their areas and then became feudatories of the British East India Company while retaining the title of "nawab".

Naxalbari Movement (1967) refers to the armed rebellion of the landless tribals, peasants and members of the Scheduled Castes against the landlords in the Naxalbari Subdivision of the Darjeeling District of West Bengal State in India, during June-August 1967. The agricultural economy of the area was dominated by the large tea-estates owned by the big landlords who were exempt from land-ceiling laws. The landless captured the surplus land of these estate-holders. The rebellion was suppressed by the armed forces of the state.

Naxalism (from Naxalbari Movement of 1967) refers to an extreme left-wing ideology of effecting redistribution of land in the Indian countryside by means of armed strugglc The term *Naxalites* is used for radical left-wing revolutionaries, influenced by Mad) Ze Dong's political ideas, who want to overthrow the existing order of land-owner-ship in the Indian countryside by armed class struggle, e.g. the Communist Party of India (Marxist-Leninists), the Communist Party of India (Maoist) and the People's War Group (PWG).

Nazism/Natzism (from *Natzi* the abbreviation of *Natzional Sozialist* or the National Socialist German Workers Party) was the totalitarian, racialist, fascist ideology of the German Natzi Party under its leader Adolf Hitler which ruled Germany from 1933 to 1945. The Natzi philosophy consisted of five elements; (1) the doctrine of blood-and-soil" or cultural nationalism; (2) the doctrine of the supremacy of the Aryan race of Which the Germans are the most excellent and talented branch; (3) anti-Semitism i.e. elimination of the Jews as the main cause of the woes of the German people; (4) repudiation of liberal democracy in favour of totalitarian dictatorship; and (5) militarism and expansionism.

Nehru Committee Report (1928) was the positive side of the boycott of the all-white Indian Statutory Commission (the Simon Commission*) whose formation was announced by the British government in 1927. Lord Birkenhead, the Secretary of State for India, brushed aside the Indian objection with this remark that the Indians were not capable of framing a constitution for themselves. To meet this challenge the Indian National Congress convened an All-Party Conference in February 1928 to consider the question of a future constitution of India so that the same could be presented to the British government for enactment. The conference therefore appointed a committee of eminent jurists with Pandit Motilal Nehru as its chairman to prepare a constitutional draft. The Nehru Committee on 10 August 1928 submitted a report entitled A Constitution for the Future Commonwealth of India. The crux of the report was the demand that the British government should immediately confer upon India the status of a dominion of the British Empire, (implying complete internal self-government). The Indian National Congress adopted this report in its annual session held in December 1928 in Calcutta and asked the British government to enact it within a year. The British rejected the report outrightly. Then the Indian National Congress in its annual session held in December 1929 in Lahore amended Article 1 of its Constitution to declare that the objective of the Indian National Congress shall be the attainment of *Purna Swaraj** (national independence) and withdrew the scheme outlined in the Nehru report. The Congress decided to observe 26 January 1930 as "Independence Day" when every member of the Indian National Congress was asked to sign a pledge to dedicate himself for attaining independence for the country. It was followed up by the second civil disobedience movement start with the Dandi March.

Nehru- Liaquat Agreement (1950) was signed between India's Prime Minister Jawaharlal Nehru and Pakistan's Prime Minister Liaquat Ali Khan on 8 April 1950 and ratified by parliaments of India and Pakistan on 10 April by which the signatories committed themselves to protect the life, liberty and property of religious minorities left in each other's territory after partition of India in 1947.. Since the agreement was never abrogated it is still in force technically.

Neocolonialism refers to indirect economic, political, military and other forms of domination exercised by former colonial powers of Europe over the newly independent former colonies in Asia and Africa.

Neo-Corporatism refers to functional representation of corporate (organized) interests like agriculture, industry, business, etc. in public policy-making. Major policy decisions are arrived at between public bureaucrats and the representatives of the organized interests and announced bypassing the parliament. Neo-Corporatism is the opposite of pluralism which enjoins that all policies must have the approval of elected parliaments. It favours state over voter sovereignty and public over private power in policy-making.

Neo-Liberalism represents a resurgence of the classical *laissez faire* and a return to the free market as a guarantor of personal freedom and social and economic growth. Neoliberals (the new right) stand for liberalization and privatization and oppose all forms of state intervention in the economic sphere.

Neo-Malthusianism is revival of the Malthusian argument that food production will always lag behind population growth. To save mankind, from starvation population planning through birth control measures is indispensable.

Neopatriarchy is a term applied to the traditional Arab societies which are marked by the persistence of patriarchical authority, feudal relations and dictatorial rule by single individuals or clans who deny their people political rights, stifle freedom of expression and monopolise economic benefits for their familites and clans.

Netizen is a person who spends most of his time surfing the internet.

Neutrality and Neutralization. Neutrality is a voluntary policy assumed by a state for the time-being in relation to a state of war affecting the states located around the war zone A neutral state assumes a passive stance of non-involvement on any side and action in return for assurances of its safety and security. Neutrality can be terminated any ' time. An example is the American declarations of neutrality in 1793, 1838, 1914 and 1939. *Neutralization* is conferment of a permanent neutral status upon a country by the collective agreement of the great powers and on a contractual basis. Thus no state can be neutralized without is consent nor can it renounce its neutrality unilaterally. The great powers guarantee the national independence and territorial integrity of a neutralized state on the condition that it will not on a military alliance or enter a war except in self-defence. The UNO and other non-military organizations are an exception. The examples are Switzerland (1815) and Austria (1955). The concept of *non-alignment* on the other hand was evolved after World Mar II by some newly independent countries of Asia and Africa to keep away from the military blocs of the superpowers in an era of East-West cold war to preserve their independence and freedom of judging each international issue on its merit. A non-aligned country could even join a military alliance if it national interest so required.

New Deal. The phrase "New Deal" was first used by Franklin D. Roosevelt (1882-1945) in his acceptance speech in 1932 and later came to be applied to the package of his reformist, regulatory and economic recovery legislations and the accompanied administrative agencies, that was implemented during the period of his presidency from 1933 to 1945. Most important legislations were the National Industrial Recovery Act Agricultural adjustment Act; National Labour Relations Act; and the Social security Act. The New Deal agencies were: the National Recovery Administration; Agricultural Adjustment Ad-ministration; Public Works Administration; work Projects Administration; Security and Exchange Commission; Deposit Insurance Corporation ;Tennessee Valley Authority, Rural Electrification administration and Social Security Administrator The New Deal was a socialistic programme undertaken to overcome the devastation caused by the Great Depression* (1929-33).

New International Economic Order (NIEO) was an ideal formulation meant to usher a new international economic order that was fair and just for the developing world. The formulation was contained in two historic declarations sponsored by the Group of &&* and adopted by the UN General Assembly in 1974. The first was Declaration on the Establishment of a New International Economic Order and the accompanied Programme of Action; and the second was the Charter of Economic Rights and Duties of States, Some of the salient features of the NIEO were: (l) doubling the official development assistance (ODA) from the developed countries to the developing countries; (2) reduction of tariffs on the exports of the developing countries to the developed world and enhancement of their export quotas; (3) a role for the Group of 77 in the decision-making process of the international financial institutions; (4) less intervention by the IMF and IBRD in the financial affairs of the developing countries; and (7) international regulation of the activities of the multinational corporations operating in the developing countries. Since the subsequent North-South negotiation failed to commit the developed countries to make any substantial concessions on this score the NIEO became a pipe-dream.

New Right in the western world, represented for instance, by late Ronald Reagan of the USA and Margaret Thatcher in the UK, are the ultraconservatives who apply the *laissez* faire to the problems of contemporary society, state, market and the individuals and call for elimination of all forms of state intervention in economic affairs. They are committed to preservation of traditional values associated with family and community and call for freedom with responsibility.

Nihilism is cult of nullification. A nihilist is one who having lost all faith in the existing social and political order finds meaning only in the destruction of the objects of hatred. The term is supposed to have originated in Czarist Russia.

Nine-Power Treaty (1922) was signed between the USA, UK, Japan and six other countries in their conference held in Washington, D.C. by which they undertook to respect the national sovereignty and territorial integrity of China and upheld the American principle of "Open Door" in China (i.e. non-monopolization of the Chinese market by the European powers). However, this treaty proved a mere scrap of paper when Japan invaded and occupied Manchuria in 1930 and none of the signatories came to the rescue of China.

Ninth Schedule was added to the Constitution of India in terms of Article 31-B (inserted by the Constitution (first) Amendment Act, 1950, which proclaims that Parliament in exercise of its legislative sovereignty may, by a constitutional amendment, insert any national, or state land reform or zamindari abolition laws or any other measure taken by any authority at any level, in the Ninth Schedule and thereby make them immune from judicial review and nullification on the ground for their being violative of the fundamental rights guaranteed under Part III of the Constitution.

Nobel Prizes were instituted in 1900 by the Nobel Foundation of Sweden out of money bequeathed by the Swedish scientist Alfred Nobel in accordance with his will. Six prizes are given every year to persons selected for making extraordinary contributions in the fields of physics, chemistry, physiology or medicine, promotion of international peace, literature and economics. The peace prize is awarded by the Nobel Committee and the rest by the Nobel foundation. The economics prize was instituted in 1968 by the Bank of Sweden which undertook to donate an annual sum to the Nobel Foundation for this purpose.

Nomenclatura (Russian for persons of name or distinction) referred to the office-holders and functionaries of the former Communist Party of the Soviet Union (CPSU) who became a privileged class in the Soviet socialist society.

Non-Aligned Movement— NAM is a political grouping of the non-aligned countries of Asia, Africa and Latin America which originated with the holding of the first summit conference of heads of state or government of 25 non-aligned countries in 1960 in Belgrade, former Yugoslavia. It has no permanent secretariat or headquarters, 13th NAM summit conference was held on 24-25 February 2003 in Kualalumpur, Malaysia, attended by 116 countries.

Non-Alignment, also called positive neutrality, neutralism or independent foreign policy was the foreign policy approach or outlook of the newly independent countries of Asia and Africa, in the context of bloc-politics of the East-West cold war from 1947 onwards, of avoiding military alliances of the great powers and retaining their freedom of action in the international field by judging each international issue on its merits. Early exponents of this approach were Jawaharlal Nehru of India, Josip Bronz Tito of former Yugoslavia, Jamal Abdun Nasir of Egypt, and Kwame Nkrumah of Ghana. With more and more countries adopting this approach they took the shape of the Non-Aligned movement*.

Non-Cooperation Movement (India) was first launched by the Indian National Congress under the leadership of M.K. Gandhi in 1920 to protest against the Rowlatt Act, 1919, (which supposed civil liberties} and to press the demand for introduction of fully responsible government *(swaraj)* in India. The movement was suspended in 1922 after the occurrence of a violent incident in Chaurichaura of Gorakhpur District in the United Produces. The non-cooperation and civil disobedience movement was resumed on 26 January 1930 to press the demand for *Puma* Swaraj* (complete national independence) for India. The movement was suspended after the signing of the Gandhi-Irwin agreement* on 5 March 1931 which enabled the INC to take part in the British-sponsored Round Table Conference* convened in London to consider the Indian constitutional problem.

Non-Departmental Public Bodies—NDB's, also called quasi-governmental organizations (QUAGO's), are public agencies of administrative, regulatory or service-providing character which are created outside the government departments but working under the supervision of ministers, to deal with the public directly free from the red tape and interference of the departmental hierarchy.

Nordic Council was founded in 1952 with its seat in Copenhagen, Denmark, as a consultative forum of Denmark, Finland, Iceland, Norway and Sweden. Under a treaty of cooperation signed between these countries in 1962 these countries cooperate through a Nordic Council of ministers. The Council of Ministers reports every year on progress made in the designated areas of cooperation.

North Africa is a geographical region including the Arabic-speaking countries of Algeria, Libiya, Morocco and Tunis. The region is known as the Arab Maghreb (Arab West) in contradistinction with the Arab Mashrq (the Arab East) which includes the countries of the Nile Valley, the Green Crescent, the Arabian Gulf and the Arabian peninsula.

North America is one of the two continents (the other being South America)* in the western hemisphere which comprises the United States, Canada and Mexico.

North American Free Trade Area — NAFTA came into existence on 1 January 1994 in pursuance of an agreement signed between the USA, Canada and Mexico on 17 December 1992.

North Atlantic Treaty Organization — NATO is a collective self-defence organization of 26 countries of the North Atlantic region (North America + Europe) formed in 1949 with its headquarters in Brussels, Belgium, under the North Atlantic Treaty signed by 12 countries on 4 April 1949 in Washington, D.C. Its objective was to create an integrated military command of the area for collective self-defence against the perceived threat of aggression by the USSR and the Communist Bloc. The NATO operates under the guidance of its political organ — the **North Atlantic Council** which is the highest authority of the NATO composes of one representative from each member-state. NATO partners are represented in Brussels by their ambassadors/ liaison officers. Militarily, the NATO armed forces are integrated into three regional commands— the **European Command,** headed by the Supreme Commander, Europe; the **Atlantic Command**, headed by the Supreme Allied Commander, Atlantic; and the **Channel Command,** headed by the Allied Commandeer-in-Chief, Channel. Besides, there is a **Strategic Air Command** (SAC) under American command. Member-States in 2005: Belgium, Bulgaria, Canada, Czech Republic, Denmark, Estonia, France, Germany, Greece, Hungary, Iceland, Italy, Latvia, Lithuania, Luxembourg, Netherlands, Norway, Poland, Portugal, Rumania, Slovakia, Slovenia, Spain, Turkey, the UK, and the USA.

North/South. North designated the developed countries of North America, Europe and Japan; and the South refers to the developing countries of Asia, Africa and Latin America.

North-Eastern Council (India) is a zonal council* created in August 1972 with its headquarters in Shillong, Meghalaya, under the North-Eastern Council Act, 1971. It objective is to accelerate the development of the North-Eastern region of India by formulating, financing, and coordinating the implementation of regional development projects in conjunction with the state governments in the region.

Northern Ireland Problem Ireland was an independent country till its merger with the United Kingdom under the Act of Union, 1800. The Irish Parliament was extinguished in 1801, and Ireland was given representation in the two houses of British Parliament. However, Irish nationalists were not satisfied with this. Therefore, the Liberal government in Britain passed the Irish Home Rule Act in 1886 to create a new parliament for Ireland and grant internal autonomy to Ireland. But foreign affairs and defence were in British hands. This did not satisfy the Irish who staged a revolt in 1916 against British rule which was crushed by the British army. Two years later the Irish nationalist party Sinn Fein won most of the Irish seats in the British House of Commons in the general election. But they kept away from the House of Commons and established their own assembly in Dublin. Soon the Irish National Army was constituted which started guerilla warfare against British rule in 1919. Thereafter, Britain passed the Government of Northern Ireland Act, 1920 which created separate parliaments for northern and southern parts of Ireland to operate under the authority of the central parliament. This Act came into force in 1921 when a separate parliament was elected for six out of nine counties of the Ulster province of Ireland and vested it with the authority to oversee the internal administration of this area. This was the area which was settled by the Scottish immigrants under British rule who were Protestants and in due course they formed their majority in the northern part. The Irish minority in Northern Ireland and in South Ireland were Catholics. However, this settlement was not acceptable to South Ireland. Negotiations between the British government and Sinn Fein led to the signing of Anglo-Irish Treaty in 1921 which came into force in 1922. Under this treaty 26 counties of South Ireland seceded from the United Kingdom and formed the Irish Free State (later renamed as Republic of Ireland).

From 1921 till 1972 Northern Ireland had its own parliament which was dominated by the Protestant Unionist parties who segregated the Irish Catholic minority from government and politics, The Catholics resented the Protestant supremacy and their exclusion from public life. First they started a civil rights movement, then started the series of riots between the Catholic and Protestant communities. Meanwhile the Irish National Army started its terroristic activities to force the merger of Northern Ireland with south Ireland. In 1969 the British Army was deployed in Northern Ireland to assist the local police. When the law-and-order situation deteriorated in Northern Ireland the British government took over its administration in its own hands. Protesting against the Unionist government of the region resigned. The central government then terminated the regional government and appointed a Secretary of State for Northern Ireland with membership of the British cabinet to administer the affairs of Northern Ireland. Britain opened negotiations with southern Ireland to secure the rights and interests of both the communities in Northern Ireland and to crush the terrorist movement. The negotiations led to the signing of an Anglo-Irish Agreement on 15 November 1985, in Hillsborough, Northern Ireland Under this agreement both governments recognized that no political settlement of the Northern Irish problem will be imposed without the consent of the majority in Northern Ireland. As a follow up an Intergovernmental conference was initiated to protect the interests of both the Protestant and Catholic communities in Northern Ireland The newly installed Labour government in Britain in 1997 announced that it shall find out a solution to the Northern Irish problem which is acceptable to both the communities. Subsequent negotiations between British, Irish Republican and Northern Irish representatives led to the signing of the so-called Good Friday Agreement on 10

April 1998 in Belfast. Under this agreement the Irish Republic renounced its claim over Northern Ireland, the British government announced to hold a referendum on its proposal for election of a Northern Irish Assembly and regional devolution, and the Protestant and Catholic parties in Northern Ireland agreed to a scheme of power-sharing in a new executive. The Good Friday Agreement was approved by an overwhelming majority in referendums held in both parts of Ireland, Accordingly the Northern Irish Assembly was elected on 25 June 1998. The Assembly in its first session held on 29 November 1999 elected a ten-member Executive Committee including both the Protestant and Catholic ministers. Thereafter the Westminster Parliament passed on 1 December the Government of Northern Ireland Act, 1999, and transferred power over a member of regional matters to the Northern Irish Assembly and the Executive Committee elected by it. Thus Northern Ireland got a sort of home rule. On the same day the parliament of the Irish Republic met to delete from the Irish constitution the article that proclaimed Northern Ireland as part of the Irish Republic.

Nuclear Non-Proliferation Act, 1978 (USA) was passed by the US Congress to prevent the proliferation of nuclear-weapons capability while preserving the peaceful use of nuclear energy as well as to establish a comprehensive set of controls, including application of the safeguards under the supervision of the International Atomic Energy Agency (IAEA) and creation of a stable framework for international nuclear cooperation and exchange of nuclear material and technology. The main provisions of the American Act are: (l) American nuclear exports to a country which did not itself already possess nuclear weapons capability would cease if that country exploded a nuclear device or terminated a safeguards agreement with the IAEA (sanctions were imposed against India and Pakistan in the wake of their detonations of nuclear devices in 1998); (2) Similarly American supplies would be discontinued in case of a country which assisted a non-nuclear state to achieve direct capability to manufacture or otherwise acquire nuclear weapons, and also in case of any country which exported a nuclear reprocessing facility to the sovereign control of a non-nuclear weapons state; (3) the US government would facilitate the establishment of an International Nuclear Fuel agency to make nuclear fuel available to countries adhering to non-proliferation norms in the event of their supplies from the normal sources were cut off; and (4) Prior US approval would continue to be compulsory before US-supplied nuclear fuel was reprocessed and such approval would be given on condition that such reprocessing will not increase the risk of nuclear proliferation.

Nuclear Non-Proliferation Treaty--NPT. The draft of the NPT was approved by an 18-nation Committee on Disarmament in March 1968. It was to come into force after ratification by the three depository states (USA, USSR, and UK) and 40 other states. The draft was approved by the UN General Assembly and the Security Council in June 1968 and opened for signatures on 1 July 1968 on which date it was signed by the three depositories -- the USA, the USSR and the UK and 58 other states. It came into force on 5 March 1970 for a period of 25 years and was extended indefinitely in 1995 as provided under Article X of the NPT. Adherence to the treaty is required of both the nuclear and non-nuclear states.

Under Article I of the NPT each party to the treaty undertakes not to transfer to any recipient whatsoever nuclear weapons or explosive devices or control over such weapons or explosive devices directly or indirectly; and not in any way to assist, encourage or induce any non-nuclear-weapon state to manufacture or otherwise acquire nuclear weapons or other nuclear explosive devices.

Under Article II each party undertakes not to receive the transfer from any transferor whatsoever of nuclear weapons or other nuclear explosive devices or of control over such weapons or explosive devices directly or indirectly;

and not to manufacture or otherwise acquire nuclear weapons or other nuclear explosive devices; and not to seek or receive any assistance in manufacture of nuclear weapons or other nuclear devices.

Under article III each party undertakes to accept safeguards, as set for in an agreement to be negotiated and concluded with International atomic Energy Agency (IAEA) in accordance with the Statute of the IAEA and the Agency's safeguards system for verification of the fulfilment of its obligations assumed under the NPT with a view to preventing diversion of nuclear energy from peaceful uses to nuclear weapons or other nuclear explosive devices. Also each party undertakes not to provide: (a) source or special fissionable material, or (b) equipment or material especially designed, or prepared for the processing, use or production of special fissionable material, to any non-nuclear-weapon state for peaceful purposes, unless the source or special fissionable material shall be subject to safeguards required by Article II of the NPT. Non-nuclear-weapon, states party to the NPT shall conclude agreements with the IAEA it meet the requirements of Article II either individually or together with other states in accordance with the Statute of the IAEA.

Article IV of the NPT declares that nothing in this Treaty shall be interpreter as affecting the inalienable right of all the parties to the Treaty to development research, production and use of nuclear energy for peaceful purposes without discrimination and in conformity with Articles I and II of the NPT.

By 2005 IAEA safeguards agreements were in force with 142 countries. Of these 71 countries had declared nuclear capability and were put under safeguards. Of the nuclear states Israel, India and Pakistan refused to sign the NPT.

Article X of the NPT provided that 25 years after entry

into force of the treaty a conference shall be convened to decide whether the treaty shall continue in force indefinitely or extended for a fixed period or periods. Accordingly a review conference was held in 1995 which extended the NPT for an indefinite term but provided for convening a conference every five years to review the implementation of the provisions of the treaty. The first review conference was held in 2000 and the second conference convened on 2 May 2005 in New York was attended by 190 states.

Nuisance (from French *nuire* = to hurt) means either (1) some obnoxious act or thing or condition that hurts public sentiments, or (2) a person, thing or condition that causes annoyance or inconvenience to the public.

Null and Void (from Latin *nullus* = nothing; zero + *void* = empty) is something declared as invalid and having no legal effect; something that is devoid of significance and value.

Nuncio (Italian for messenger). Nuncios are the representatives of the Pope as the head of the Roman Catholic Church accredited by the Vatican to foreign countries, occupying the rank, privileges and immunities of ambassadors. If Pope's representative is a cardinal his designation is *legate.* The objectives of Vatican's diplomatic representation in foreign countries as defined in Canon Law 267 are: (1) to cultivate good relations between the Holy See and the host country; (2) to act as watchdog of the interests of the Roman Catholic Church in the host country and to keep the Pope informed of the conditions and developments in the host countries; and (3) in addition to these, to exercise such other functions as are assigned to papal representatives.

Nuremberg Trials refer to the trial of Nazi war criminals by an International War Crimes Tribunal which met in Nuremberg, Germany, during 1945-46. It sentenced 12 Nazi military officers to death and seven to long-term imprisonments. The tribunal was set up by a Charter approved by the UN General Assembly defining crimes against peace, war crimes and crimes against humanity.

O

Obiter Dictum is Latin for an interposed opinion or statement which though not having a direct relation with the issue at hand may nevertheless be helpful in explaining the facts of the case.

Oceania (South Sea Islands) refers to groups of islands in the central and southern Pacific Ocean. These islands are loosely grouped into Melanesia, Micronesia and Polynesia.

Office of Profit is an employment with salaries, allowances and fees attached to it. In the United Kingdom the House of Commons Disqualification Act, 1957, contains a list of disqualifying offices which excludes the holders of political and ministerial offices by virtue of ministerial responsibility but includes, inter alia, civil servants of the Crown, holders of certain judicial offices, members of regular armed forces, members of police forces, and members of certain committees, commissions and boards. The list may be amended by an order-in-council. Article 101 (a) of the Indian Constitution declares: "A person shall be disqualified for being chosen as, and for being, a member of either House of Parliament if he holds any office of profit under the Government of India or the government of any state other than an office declared by Parliament by law not to disqualify its holder from becoming a member of Parliament". A similar provision has been made in respect of the state legislative assemblies under Article 119 (1) (a) of the Constitution.

Official Language Act, 1963 (India). Article 343 (1) of the Indian Constitution declared that Hindi in Devanagari script shall be the official language of the Indian Union. However, since Hindi was not developed enough to replace the existing official language English Clause (2) of the same Article provided for continued use of English as the official language of the Union for an initial period of fifteen years. It also provided that the Government of India shall appoint an official language commission to recommend ways and means of introducing Hindi as the official language of the Union from 26 January 1965. An Official Language Commission was appointed in 1955 which made recommendations for the introduction Hindi as the official language. The report of the OLC was considered by a Committee of Parliament on the Official Language which reported in 1963. The Official Language Act, 1963, was passed to give effect to the recommendations of the OLC and CPOL. It provided that as from 26 January 1965 Hindi shall replace English as the official language of the Union. However, the people of non-Hindi southern states were opposed to the introduction of Hindi as the sole official language of the Union as it would put the candidates from the south at a disadvantage in matters of public employment as compared with the candidates from the Hindi-speaking north. To pacify the non-Hindi states Prime Minister Jawaharlal Nehru gave an assurance that English will continue to be used for official purposes for as long as the non-Hindi states desired. But as the date for the introduction of Hindi neared the people in the south became restive and a violent agitation was launched against the alleged imposition of Hindi over the non-Hindi-speaking people. The government then declared that the official language act will be amended to retain English as the second official language and as the medium of communication between the centre and non-Hindi states for so long as the non-Hindi states did not agree to sole use of Hindi as an official language. Accordingly, the Official Language (Amendment) Act, 1967, was passed to give a statutory shape to Mr. Nehru's assurance by making English an associate official language of the Union along with

Hindi for an indefinite period. Present language practice in the central government is governed by the Official Languages Rules, 1976, and the official language policy is implemented through the Official Language Department in the Home Ministry aided by eight regional implementation offices.

Official Secrets Act (India) was enacted in 1932 on the pattern of the British official secrets act to maintain secrecy and confidentiality in the transaction of official business. However, the Right to Information Act, 2005, has been enacted to ensure greater transparency in the transaction of government business and greater accountability of the administration.

Oligarchy (from Greek *oligoi* = few + *arkhein* = to rule) is government by a few, as opposed to democracy. It refers both to a coterie of powerful individuals or an elite or a class or a party controlling an organization or institution or state, as well as a system of government based on rule by a few. It should be distinguished from both *aristocracy* (government by the best, whether an hereditary nobility or a meritocracy) and *plutocracy* (government by the rich class) although both are government by the few.

Oligopoly (from Greek *oligos* = few + *pollein* = to sell) is in the realm of business and economics a situation or arrangement in which a limited number of producers of certain goods or providers of certain services exclusively regulate the supplies and determine the prices. Like monopoly it is contrary to the principle of free competition in a liberal market.

Ombudsman (pronounced as *omboozman)* is the designation of an independent and impartial investigating officer first appointed in Sweden then in other Scandinavian countries, to look into public grievances and get them redressed. Following this example, a **Parliamentary Commissioner for Administration** was appointed in Britain in 1967; a ***Mediateur*** in France in 1973; ***Lok Ayukts*** (people's commissioners) were appointed in some Indian states during the 1970's; and a legislation for the creation of a ***Lok Pal*** (people's grand commissioner) at the national level is pending before the Indian parliament.

Ombudsman, European. The office of the European Ombudsman was created by the Treaty on European Union and the first ombudsman was appointed in July 1995. He is appointed by the European Parliament from among its own members for a renewable term of five years. He receives, investigates and makes recommendations to the European Parliament on complaints lodged by the European citizens and governments. He also submits an annual report to the European Parliament on the work done by him.

Open-Door Policy (US) refers to American policy towards China first declared by the US Secretary of State John Hay in 1899 by sending identical diplomatic notes to the European great powers calling upon them to keep the door of China open for trade and commerce for all countries. By implication this amounted to an American declaration against European monopoly over trade in China, and in favour of equal rights for America for trade and commerce in China. Thus by a single stroke of pen the Americans acquired for themselves all commercial rights and privileges in China which the Europeans had obtained by force and fraud. The open door policy was further fortified by issuing a similar diplomatic note in 1900 declaring the commitment of the USA to uphold the national independence and territorial integrity of China. By implication this placed an American bar on a possible colonization of China by the Europeans. The same policy was embodied in the Nine-Power Treaty* of 1922.

Open Seas or high seas are seas and oceans which are not under the sovereignty of any state but belong to the mankind as a whole. The customary international law guarantees freedom of navigation to all nations through international seas and waterways and exploitation of their resources. However, open seas are differentiated from territorial seas, maritime bays, territorial straits, gulfs and bays. Though connected to the high seas these are under the national jurisdiction of the concerned states.

Opinion Polls refer to gathering of the opinions of a cross-section of the population on any given issue by random sampling and applying the statistical measuring techniques, such as the Gallup Poll or the Harris Poll.

Order-in-Council is an executive made rule having the force of law. In the UK an order-in-Council can be made by the Sovereign in the Privy Council in the presence of at least three ministers of the Crown. Orders-in-Council are made either in exercise of royal prerogative* or under acts of parliament granting rule-making power to the executive.

Organization of the Black Sea Economic Cooperation -- OBSEC was originally formed as Black Sea Economic Cooperation (BSEC) in 1992. The name was changed to OBSEC under a charter adopted in 1998. It is meant to promote economic cooperation in the Black Sea region. Its headquarters is in Istambul, Turkey. Members are: Albania, Armenia, Azerbaijan, Bulgaria, Georgia, Greece, Moldova, Rumania, Russia, Turkey and Ukraine Egypt, France, Germany, Israel, Italy, Poland, Slovakia and Tunis have been accorded the status of observers. Iran and Uzbekistan are candidates for membership.

Organization for Economic Cooperation and Development-- OECD was created on 30 September 1961 pursuant to a convention signed in 1960 in London by the members of the Organization for European Economic Cooperation (OEEC) which was a mechanism for coordinating the implementation of the Marshall Plan* for European recovery. It is a forum for harmonization and coordination of the economic policies of the developed world. Its headquarters is in Paris, France. Members are: Australia, Austria, Belgium, Canada, Czech Republic, Denmark, Finland, France, Germany, Greece, Hungary, Iceland, Ireland, Italy, Japan, Republic of Korea, Luxembourg, Mexico, Netherlands, New

Zealand, Norway, Poland, Portugal, Slovakia, Spain, Sweden, Switzerland, Turkey, UK, and USA. The European Commission also takes part in the deliberations of the OECD.

Organization of American States -- OAS is a regional organization of the western hemisphere meant for regional collective security and economic cooperation. It was created by a Charter adopted by the International Conference of American States held in 1948 in Bogota, Colombia. The immediate impetus to the Bogota Charter was the signing of the Inter-American Treaty of Reciprocal Assistance signed in 1947 in Rio de Janeiro. The OAS is the successor of the International Union of the American Republics founded in 1890. The OAS joins together 35 countries from north, south and central America, which meet in an annual General Assembly or in extraordinary sessions. A number of countries from outside Americas have been given the status of observers. The headquarters is in Washington, D.C.

Organization of Arab Petroleum Exporting Countries OAPEC is a cartel of Arab petroleum producing countries established in 1968 to coordinate the production and pricing policies. Members are: Algeria, Bahrain, Egypt, Saudi Arabia, Syria, Iraq, Kuwait, Qatar, Libya and the UAE. Its headquarters is in Kuwait.

Organization of Islamic Conference--OIC is an intergovernmental consultative forum of 57 Muslim states from Asia and Africa. The Organization took shape at a conference of the heads of state or government of Islamic states convened by King Faisal Ibne Saud of Saudi Arabia in September 1969 in Rabat, Morocco, to protest against the burning of the Al-Aqsa mosque in Jerusalem (the holiest place for Muslims after Ka'aba in Mecca) by the Jewish extremists. The OIC holds periodic meetings at the level of foreign ministers and the heads of state/government. Its headquarters is in Jeddah, Saudi Arabia.

Organization of Petroleum Exporting Countries--OPEC is a cartel of petroleum producing countries created in 1960 in Vienna, to coordinate the policies of member-states regarding production levels and pricing of oil. Members are: Algeria, Gabon, Indonesia, Iran, Iraq, Kuwait, Libya, Nigeria, Qatar, Saudi Arabia, United Arab Emirates and Venezuela.

Organization of Security and Cooperation in Europe--OSCE was created by the Charter of Paris for a New Europe* signed by the 55 member-states of the Conference on Security and Cooperation in Europe* (CSCE) on 21 November 1990. The Charter converted the CSCE into the OSCE and made it a permanent European arrangement with the objectives of maintaining regional security, promoting regional cooperation and managing crises in Europe and the CIS region. The Charter of the OSCE reiterates and reaffirms the principles, purposes and objectives of the Final Act of the CSCE* adopted in 1975 in Helsinki, Finland. The headquarters of the OSCE is in Vienna, Austria.

Outer Space Test Ban Treaty was signed between the USA, USSR and the UK in July 1963 in Moscow. The treaty prohibits nuclear tests in the outer space, seabed and the open seas. It was also agreed that in the due course underground testing will also be prohibited. The Partial Test Ban Treaty was followed up by the signing of the Nuclear Non-Proliferation Treaty* (NPT) and the Comprehensive Test Ban Treaty* (CTBT).

P

Pacific Islands Forum-- PIF is the new name of the South Pacific Forum (founded in 1971) since 2000. It is a consultative forum of heads of government of sixteen self-governing island-states of the South Pacific plus Australia and New Zealand. Its headquarters is in Suva, Fiji.

Pacific Settlement of International Disputes means resolution of international disputes by means of conciliation, negotiations, mediation, arbitration or international adjudication. The pacific settlement of international disputes has been enjoined by the twin Hague Conventions on the Pacific Settlement of International Disputes adopted in 1899 and 1907; by the Covenant of the League of Nations in 1919; by the Charter of the UNO in 1945; and by the OSCE Convention on Conciliation and Arbitration adopted in 1992. The Hague Conventions created a Permanent Court of Arbitration (which was neither permanent nor a court) consisting of a panel of some 120 judges nominated by the states signatory to the Conventions. From this panel the parties to a dispute could select members of an arbitration tribunal to be appointed to arbitrate between them. The Covenant of the League of Nations provided for a Permanent Court of International Justice which was established in the Hague in 1920. The Permanent Court was succeeded by the International Court of Justice (ICJ) created in Hague in 1945, which is one of the main organs of the UNO. The OSCE Convention established, a Court of Conciliation and Arbitration in 1994. Parties to a dispute may submit it to the Court for settlement by the Arbitration Tribunal or the Conciliation Commission.

Pacifism is the general philosophy of peace and amity among the mankind through amicable settlement of disputes and peaceful coexistence. The pacificist pursuits range from popular education and propaganda to research and publication. The influence of peace movements international relations has been enormous. They take a cosmopolitan view of world affairs, uphold the ideals of human brotherhood and equality and look forward to the savation of the mankind through moral regeneration. Peace, moreover, has been an implicit objective of international law, international organizations and globalization and even the policies of nationalism, internationalism, imperialism (e.g. *Pax Brittanica*) and balance of power.

Pacta Sunt Servanda is a principle of customary international law which requires that a pact once concluded is binding upon the parties to it no party to an agreement can free itself unilaterally from the obligations assumed under a treaty. The opposite principle is that of *rebus sic stantibus* which means that with the change of circumstances a treaty may lose its relevance.

Pakhtunistan/Pashtunistan (from *Pakhtun* = people) was the name given by Afghan irredentists led by Khan Abdul Ghaffar Khan (1890-1996) to the North-West Frontier Province of Pakistan, who demanded its integration with the neighbouring Afghanistan on the ground of its ethnic affinity with Afghans. The Soviet occupation of Afghanistan in December 1979 spelled the end of the Pakhtunistan movement as millions of Afghan refugees were fed and sheltered in Pakistan from 1979 till the withdrawal of Soviet forces in 1988.

Pakhtunwali (the way of Pakhtun or pathans) is the code of honour of the pathan people of Afghanistan. It is marked by a strong sense of personal honour and dignity, courageousness, manliness, generosity, keeping of word, and support to kinsfolk, allies and friends, etc.

Palestine Liberation Organization---PLO was formed under

Palestinian National Charter adopted in May 1964. Article I of the Charter declared that Palestine is the homeland of Arab Palestinian people and that it is an indivisible part of the Arab homeland and the Palestinian people are an integral part of the Arab nation. Article II declared that Palestine, with the boundaries it had during British mandate* is an indivisible territorial unit. Article IX declared that armed struggle is the only way to liberate Palestine from Israeli occupation. The PLO was composed of a Chairman, an executive committee, a central council and a Palestine National Council (parliament). The first session of the PNC was held in Jerusalem in May-June 1964. Yasir Arafat (1929-2004), the leader of the dominant Guerilla group Fateh *(Harakat Tahrir* al-Filastin), was elected as the chairman of its executive committee in 1964 and occupied this pot until his death in 2004. In November 1988 the PNC declared independence of Palestine in accordance with Resolution 181 (partition plan) of the UN General Assembly of 1947, with East Jerusalem as its capital. Under Oslo accords signed between PLO and Israel both parties mutually recognized each other. In return of PLO's renunciation of armed struggle against Israel, PLO was promised limited home rule in part of the occupied territories. An interim agreement signed between PLO and Israel on 28 September 1995 in Washington, DC, provided for the creation of a Palestinian Authority with legislative and executive organs to take over municipal administration over 17.2 of the occupied territories, pending a final settlement of the Palestine problem.

Palestine Problem. Palestine was an Arab country for centuries till it was conquered by the Turks in 1517 and governed as a province of the Ottoman Empire until their defeat in World War I. During the war Turkish forces were expelled and Palestine was occupied by British forces. After the war, instead of being given the right of self-government in accordance with Woodrow Wilson's "Fourteen Points" Palestine was detached from the Ottoman Empire under the

Treaty of Severs of 1920 and allotted to Great Britain as a mandate of the League of Nations which incorporated the Balfour Declaration* of 1917 promising the creation of a Jewish national home in Palestine. Palestine was under British mandatory rule during 1919-1948. Under their rule the British created a semi-official Jewish Agency to arrange for the immigration of European Jewry into Palestine and Jewish colonization of the country. In view of mounting Arab-Jewish conflict after World War II Britain referred the question of Palestine to the UN Security Council in 1947 and announced its withdrawal from Palestine by 14 May 1948. The UN General Assembly passed a resolution in November 1947 partitioning Palestine into an Arab and a Jewish state. On withdrawal of British forces from Palestine on 14 May 1948 the Jewish Agency proclaimed the State of Israel over the territory allotted to the Jewish state under the UN partition plan. The armies of the neighbouring countries invaded Palestine to forestall the establishment of Israel. Arab armies were defeated with large chunks of territory allotted to the Arab state lost to Jews. Jordan which had occupied the West Bank during the war annexed it in 1950. Israeli boundaries emerging out of the armistice agreements signed with the Arab states in 1949 were guaranteed by the Tripartite Declaration*, 1950. During the six-day war against the Arabs in 1967 Israel took the Sinai peninsula and Gaza Strip from Egypt, the West Bank from Jordan and the Golan Heights from Syria. The Sinai was returned to Egypt under the Egyptian-Israeli Peace Treaty of 1979. Jordan relinquished its sovereignty over the West Bank on 31 July 1988. Until 2006 Palestine remained under Israel's military occupation.

Palestinian Authority is an interim municipal authority created to exercise municipal rule over a limited area of the occupied Palestine in respect of certain specified subjects. The Authority was created under the Interim Agreement between PLO and Israel on the West Bank and the Gaza Strip signed on

28 September 1995 with an elected president, an elected national assembly and a responsible council of ministers headed by a prime minister. This arrangement is to continue till a final peace agreement is signed between Israel and Palestine.

Pan Movements (pan =all) are movements of unity and solidarity based on race, region or religion e.g. pan-Slavism, pan-Arabism, pan-Americanism, pan-Asianism, pan-Africanism or pan-Islamism.

Panama Canal was dug to connect the Atlantic Ocean with the Pacific Ocean across the territory of Panama state. A treaty signed in 1903 between the USA and Panama allowed the USA to build and operate the canal in perpetuity in lieu of an annual payment to Panama. The canal was opened for traffic on 15 August 1914. Panamian pressures on the USA led to signing of a new treaty between the USA and Panama which recognized Panamian sovereignty over the canal zone. The administration of the canal was placed under the joint control of the USA and Panama till the end of 1999. In 2000 the US forces withdrew from the canal zone and the administration of the canal was vested in the Panama government.

Pan-American Union is the old name of the General Secretariat of the Organization of the American States located in Washington, DC. The first International Conference of the American States held in 1889-90 had created the Commercial Bureau of the American Republics in Washington, DC. The fourth conference held in 1910 changed the name of the Bureau to the Pan American Union The ninth conference held in 1948 in Bogota adopted a charter to create the Organization of the American States* (OAS) and made the Pan-American Union its general secretariat.

Panchayati Raj (India) is a system of democratic local self-government for rural India introduced in 1958. Democratic institutions are created at the village, block/taluqa, and district levels.

The three levels of government are organically linked together. These institutions are responsible for providing civic services to the local people, and overseeing the implementation of local development projects.

Panchsheel or the "Five Principles" of peaceful coexistence were adopted as the guiding principles of independent India's foreign policy in 1947. They are: Mutual respect for each other's territorial integrity and national sovereignty; mutual non-interference in each other's affairs; mutual non-aggression; equality and mutual benefit; and peaceful coexistence.

Panipat, Battle of (1761) was fought between the Maratha forces and the invading army of the Afghan chieftain Ahmad Shah Durrani which ended with the defeat of the Maratha forces and decline of Maratha power in India. The Marathas had in the wake of the decline of the Mughal Empire after the death of Aurangzeb in 1707 established a number of dominions in Poona, Baroda, Gwalior and Indore and were aspiring to gain political supremacy over India. In 1739 Nadir Shah's invasion and plundering of Delhi had further weakened the Mughal Empire and strengthened the Marathas. Then the Battle of Panipat broke their backbone.

Panjab Accord (1985) was signed between Rajiv Gandhi, the prime minister of India, and Harchand Longowal, the president of the Akali Dal* in Panjab, under which the government undertook to pay compensation to the kin of Sikhs killed during the anti-Sikh riots of 1984; institution of judicial inquiry into the anti-Sikh riots of 1984; and rehabilitation of Sikh soldiers discharged from the Indian army, etc.

Panjabi Suba Movement was launched by Master Tara Singh (1885-1967), the leader of the Akali Dal in Panjab in 1961 for the creation of a Panjabi Suba out of the Indian State of Panjab (under the States Reorganization Act, 1956). Tara Singh went on a fast-unto-death for 43 days in support of this demand but failed to influence the government. The movement was revived by Sant Fateh Singh in 1965 who succeeded in forcing the Government of India to effect the division of existing Panjab into a Panjabi-speaking State of Panjab and an Hindi speaking State of Haryana under the Reorganization of States (Panjab and Haryana) Act, 1966.

Paradigm is a set of fundamental beliefs or a conceptual framework that guides a researcher in selecting, organizing and interpreting his data.

Paramountcy (suzerainty) refers to the constitutional relationship between the British Crown as the suzerain power and the semi-autonomous Princely States in India as dependent entities. The doctrine of paramountcy was declared by the Government of India in 1877. British paramountcy was established partly by conquest, partly by treaty and partly by usage. Paramountcy implied British control over external affairs and defence of the native states and the right to guide their internal administration through a political agent or resident appointed by the British government. This constitutional relationship between the British Crown and the native princes lapsed on 15 August 1947. Clause 7 (1) (b) of the Indian Independence Act, 1947, provided that as from 15 August 1947 The suzerainty of His Majesty over the Indian States lapses, and with it, all treaties and agreements in force at the date of the passing of this Act between His Majesty and the rulers of Indian States, all functions exercisable by His Majesty at that date with respect to Indian States, all obligations of His Majesty existing at that date towards Indian States or rulers thereof, and all powers, rights, authority or jurisdiction exercisable by His Majesty at that date in or in relation to Indian States by treaty, grant, usage, sufferance or otherwise.

Parkinson's Law refers to the inherent tendency of bureaucracy to inbreed and multiply, as caricatured by C. Northcote Parkinson in his *Parkinson's Law or the Pursuit of Progress* (1968).

Partial Test Ban Treaty. See "Outer Space Test Ban Treaty."

Partition of Bengal (1905) refers to the division of the composite Province of Bengal in 1905 into the provinces of East and West Bengal for stated reason of administrative convenience. However, the Bengali nationalists took it as a British attempt to divide the people of Bengal on communal lines and launched an incessant agitation against it till the British government was forced to annul the partition of Bengal in 1910.

Partition Plan (1947) or the Mountbatten Plan refers to the British scheme to partition the Indian subcontinent into two separate dominions of India and Pakistan as a solution of the Indian constitutional problem in the wake of the collapse of the Cabinet Mission Plan* of 1946. The scheme was agreed to by the Indian National Congress, the All-India Muslim League and the Akali Dal and was embodied in the Indian Independence Act, 1947 which provided for transfer of power to the Dominions of India and Pakistan on 15 August 1947.

Party Line is the policy or decision declared by the top leadership of dictatorial parties (e.g. communist or fascist) which is absolutely binding upon the rank and file.

Paternalism (from Latin *pater* = father) stands for an attitude of patriarchical or protective benevolence towards the dependents or subjects; overbearing guardianship; authoritarian rule.

Pax Brittanica (British peace) refers to peace and stability that prevailed on the European continent by means of British policy of maintaining a balance of power effected through the preponderance of British naval power.

Peace is the opposite of disturbance or disorder. It implies existence of amity between individuals or groups. In international relations peace means either of the three phenomena: the cessation of a state of war e.g. the Peace of Westphalia or the Paris Peace Conference; or absence of conflict and existence of normal relations between and among nations; or prevalence of tranquility and stability by virtue of the hegemony of a power e.g. *Pax Romana, Pax Brittanica* or *Pax Americana.*

Peace of Westphalia (1648) refers to the peace settlement in Europe at the end of the 30-year war. It marked the end of the Holy Roman Empire as an effective political force and laid the foundation of the modern nation-state system based on principles of national sovereignty, territorial integrity and sovereign equality of nation-states.

Peace Treaty is concluded by the belligerents to end the state of war and usher in a state of peace marked by resumption of diplomatic relations and normal cooperation, e.g. the Paris Peace Treaty of 1919.

Peaceful Coexistence denotes absence of conflict and tension and prevalence of normal relations between and among nations. The UN General Assembly adopted in 1970 a Declaration of Principles of International Law Concerning Friendly Relations and Cooperation among States in accordance with the Charter of the UN'' laid down seven principles already enshrined in the Charter of the UN: To refrain from threat or use of force against territorial integrity and political independence of any state; to seek pacific settlement of international disputes; to refrain from interference in the domestic jurisdiction of other states; to perform the duty of cooperation with other states in accordance with the Charter of the UN; to respect equal rights and self-determination of peoples; and to recognize sovereign equality of all states; and to fulfil in good faith the obligations assumed under the UN Charter;

Peerage (from peer = equal/noble) is the status of being a peer or noble. It is a survival from England's feudal past. Under Common Law the Crown has a prerogative of creating any one from the commoners a peer of the realm. Up to 1958 peerage was hereditary, i.e. the feudal titles, granted by the crown were transferred from the title-holder on his death to his eldest son or daughter. But the Life Peearage Act, 1958, enabled the Crown to create life peers, i.e. peers whose title was not hereditary but lapsed with their death. The Renunciation of Peerage Act, 1963, authorized a hereditary peer to renounce his peerage for his life and become a commoner. On his death the title is inherited by his successor.

Peers of the Realm (UK) are the lords or noblemen who had a seat in the British House of Lords by virtue of their hereditary right. Hereditary lords carried the different titles of the duke, marquess, earl, viscount, and baron/ baroness. In 1999 all but 91 elected hereditary peers were excluded from the House of Lords.

Pentagon (US) is the pentagonal building in Washington, D.C., which houses the US Department of Defence. It symbolizes the American military establishment.

Penumbra Theory of Rights refers to the Ninth Amendment of the American Constitution which declares that "The enumeration in the Constitution of certain rights shall not be construed to deny or disparage others retained by the people." The American Constitution adheres to the tradition of natural rights. The enumeration of rights in the first ten amendments (collectively called the Bill of Rights) is neither exhaustive nor final. As declared by the American Supreme Court, other rights and freedoms may exist in the penumbra (shadow) of the specifically mentioned rights and must also be recognized and protected.

Perjury (from Latin *perjurium*=offence) is under English common law an offence of falsely swearing to facts in a judicial proceeding. To constitute this offence the party must have been lawfully sworn to speak the truth by some court, judge or officer having competent authority to administer an oath; and under the oath so administered, he must wilfully assert a falsehood in a judicial proceeding respecting some fact which is material to the subject of enquiry in that proceeding.

Permanent Court of Arbitration was created in 1900 in the Hague in pursuance of the Hague Convention on the Pacific

Settlement of International Disputes (1899). It was merely an arbitration forum.

Permanent Court of International Justice was created in 1919 in the Hague under a statute to settle disputes arising out of bilateral or international treaties. It was replaced in 1945 by the International Court of Justice. However, the decisions of the PCIJ continue to serve as precedents for the ICJ.

Persian Gulf (called the **Arabian Gulf** by the Arab countries) is an extension of the Arabian Sea between the Arabian peninsula and Iran. Its length from the estuary of the Shatt al-Arab river to the Strait of Hormuz is about 805 kms. The Strait of Hormuz connects the Persian Gulf with the Arabian Sea through the Gulf of Oman. The Persian Gulf includes both the Strait of Hormuz and the Gulf of Oman. **The Persian Gulf area** refers to the littoral countries of Iran, Iraq, Kuawait, Bahrain, Qatar, Oman, Saudi Arabia and the United Arab Emirates (UAE). The UAE was formed in 1971 as a federation of seven Arab sheikhdoms which were formerly British protectorates and became independent in 1971 after British withdrawal from the Persian Gulf area.

Persona Non Grata (Latin for unwanted person). A diplomatic or consular agent may be declared *persona non grata* by the host government for indulging in activities incompatible with his diplomatic functions or for any other reason. Upon this declaration the sending government is obliged to recall the person or persons named along with their families from the host country within the specified time-limit.

Personal Laws in India. Personal law in India means the customary religious codes of different religious communities governing their ''personal'' matters, i.e. marriage and divorce, succession, adoption, etc. A uniform civil code cannot be imposed because of the diversity of religions and sects. Personal laws were enacted by British Indian government to make them enforceable through the civil courts. The tradition has been followed in independent India. Some of the personal laws in operation are: the Hindu Widow Remarriage Act, 1856; the Converts' Marriage Dissolution Act, 1886; the Indian Divorce Act, 1869; the Indian Christian Marriage Act, 1872; the Qazis Act, 1880; the Anand Marriage Act, 1929; the Parsi Marriage and Divorce Act, 1939; the Dissolution of Muslim Marriage Act, 1939; the Special Marriage Act, 1954 (does not apply to Jammu and Kasmir); the Hindu Marriage Act, 1955; the Foreign Marriage Act, 1969; the Muslim Women (Protection of Rights on Divorce) Act, 1986; and the Central Waqf Act, 1995.

Personality Cult refers to the attribution of extraordinary qualities to and glorification of a leader by his followers.

Petite Bourgevoisie (petty middle class) is a class interposed between the bourgevoisie and the proletariat, e.g. the working peasants, small shopkeepers, urban artisans and craftsmen, etc.

Petition (request or submission). The Bill of Rights, 1689 guaranteed the right of the subjects to petition the Crown for the redressal of their grievances. Similarly Indian Constitution grants the citizen the right to petition the state authorities for the redressal of their grievances.

Petition of Right (1626). In the first parliament of King Charles I, which met in 1626, the commons refused to grant supplies to the Crown until certain rights and privileges of the subjects, according to them were being trampled upon by the servants of the Crown, were solemnly guaranteed by an act of parliament. With this aim they framed a petition to the king, in which after reciting various statutes by which their rights and privileges were recognized, they asserted four basic principles: no taxation without consent of parliament; no imprisonment without cause having been shown; no billeting (compulsory accommodation of soldiers in the homes of civilians}; no imposition of martial law in time of peace. The King was heartily in favour of royal prerogative and lukewarm towards parliamentary privilege. His evasive and unconvincing reply did not satisfy the Commons. The conflict between parliament and crown eventually led to the civil war, puritan revolution and beheading of Charles I in 1641.

Planning Commission (India) was created by a resolution of the Government of India in 1950 as a staff agency to prepare the drafts of the five-year national development plans. The Commission was made a Department of the Government of India in 1971. It is headed by the prime minister with a full-time deputy chairman nominated by him to look after its day-to-day functioning and composed of a number of official and non-official experts.

Plassey, Battle of (1757) was fought in Bengal between East India Company's forces led by Robert Clive and the army of Nawab Sirajuddaula, the ruler of Bengal. The British won the war by winning over his prime minister Mir Jafar to their side and by a host of other fraudulent means. Some people regard the year of 1757 as the beginning of the British empire in India. In 1761 the Company obtained the grant of *Diwani* (revenue administration) of Bengal, Bihar and Orissa from the Mughal emperor and in due course became the *de facto* sovereign ruler of these areas. The Company gradually extended its dominion to the heartland of India till most of India had come under their control by 1857.

Plebiscite is seeking people's opinion on a specific question submitted to them just as in a referendum. It differs from a referendum in that it is specifically used to ascertain the wishes of the people of a disputed territory to settle the question of sovereignty, e.g. the plebiscites held in Irian Jaya in 1969 and in Namibia in 1989.

Plebiscite Front. The Jammu and Kashmir Plebiscite Front was formed in 1955 by Mirza Muhammad Afzal Beg (1908-1982), an associate of Sheikh Muhammad Abdullah and a leader of the dissolved National Conference, against the backdrop of the dismissal of Abdullah as the prime minister of Jammu and Kashmir and his imprisonment on charges of treason in 1953. The Plebiscite Front was organized to press the demand for holding a plebiscite in Jammu and Kashmir to settle its status in accordance with the UN Security Council resolutions of 1948. The Front was declared an unlawful association. It was wound up in 1975 under an accord signed in 1974 between erstwhile prime minister Indira Gandhi and Sheikh Muhammad Abdullah (released from prison in 1968). Under this agreement Abdullah was appointed chief minister of Jammu and Kashmir with the Congress legislature party supporting him from outside. Abdullah then revived the National Conference, won the next assembly elections under its banner and formed the ministry.

Plural Society/Pluralist Society. A *plural* society, as defined by J.S. Furnival in his *Colonial Policy and Practice* (1948), is a society composed of disparate heterogeneous groups and communities which meet in the market-place to do business but otherwise keep to themselve and have no sense of community with other groups. A pluralist society, on the contrary, is a liberal society which joins diverse cultural, ethnic, regional, linguistic and religious groups in a democratic community.

Pluralism is the opposite of unitarism. It is a philosophy of peaceful competitive coexistence of diverse, classes,' communities and interests in the society to maintain peace and stability. In a pluralist democracy the state ensures liberty and free play to a plurality of competing groups and acts lime a rule-maker and neutral umpire between the competing interests.

Police Power in general is the power of a government to maintain peace and security in the country. In particular, police power means the general power of the public authorities to regulate affairs of the society during emergencies when normal legal arrangements prove inadequate to deal with the situation. It differs from emergency power in that emergency power is granted under the law while police power is implicit in the executive function.

Police State refers to a non-democratic authoritaran state which relies solely on coercion and repression of the people by means of secret police, intelligence networks and detention camps to secure people's obedience.

Policy Science is applied social science with a focus to deliver advisory inputs into the process of socioeconomic policy-making and planning.

Polisario is the abbreviation of the *Frente Popular para la Liberacion de Sagma el-Hamra y Rio de Oro* (the Popular Front for Liberation of Western Sahara) which proclaimed in 1976 the Sahrawi Arab Republic and established its government-in-exile in Algeria.

Political Action Committee (US). As provided in the Federal Election campaign Act 1971, interest groups are permitted to form political action committees to raise funds to finance the election campaigns of their favoured candidates in federal elections.

Political Alienation is isolation or withdrawal of a person or community from the political process. It differs from a path which suggests indifference or non-participation. Alienation results from an intense feeling towards the futility of political participation. Alienation may take any or all of the five forms: powerlessness, normlessness, marginalization, self-estrangement and isolation.

Political Culture is the sum of values, beliefs and attitudes within which a political system operates.

Political Development refers to the process of transition of a traditional society from a primitive or feudal political system to a modern democratic political system. Political development is associated with democratization. Lucien Pye in his Aspects of *Political Development* (1966) has singled out three major themes that characterize political development: (1) equality in political life; (2) political capacity and governmental performance; and (3) differentiation and specialization of structures.

Political Economy (from Greek *economica* = household management) is the public economy of a state. The discipline of political economy was founded by Adam Smith in late eighteenth century with his *Wealth of Nations.* It was an amalgam of economics and politics. But political structures and administrative problems and policies were excluded from its purview during the early nineteenth century. Towards the end of the nineteenth century the term political economy was replaced by economics, concentrating specifically on economic analysis. Political economy was revived during the second half of the twentieth century to study macro-economic policy and planning on both the national and international levels such as budgetary policies and management and their impact on the general public.

Political Identity means the distinction which a group nation assumes by considering its race, nation ethnicity, culture, religion, region or language or class as the source of its unity and solidarity.

Political Modernization (modernization=making or becoming modern). The process of political modernization entails, according to some comparativists, some major transformations e.g. (1) differentiation of political structures and specialization of roles; (2) secularization of political culture; (3) concern with equality, distribution, justice and participation; (4) capacity and adaptability; (5) decocratization; and (6) nation building and state-building.

Political Obligation (submission of the individuals to the authority of the state). In a constitutional democratic state individuals voluntarily obey the law of the state because they regard its authority as legitimate and just as it is based on popular consent and represent the general will.

Political Participation refers to the participation of the individuals and groups in the political process, to influence public decision-making in favour of their individual or group interests. Participation may be solitary or collective, organized or spontaneous, peaceful or violent, legal or illegal, or effective or ineffective. People may participate in politics by joining interest groups or political parties or electoral campaigns or contesting in elections or by holding public office.

Political Process refers to the continuous interaction between the political system and other sub-systems in a society by which the society makes demands on the political system and the Political system responds by making appropriate to meet them.

Political Question is any matter which falls within the regulatory or policy-making jurisdiction of the legislative and executive authorities of the state.

Political Realism or power politics is the opposite of political idealism. Political action should be guided not by moral principles but by the *real* (material) facts of political life, i.e. power and interest; also political pragmatism, i.e. politics ought to be an art of the possible or practicable; it is also a philosophical approach advocated by Hans J. Morgenthau in his *Politics among Nations* (1948) for the study of international politics.

Political Rights of Women, UN Covenant on was passed by the UN General Assembly in 1952 making it obligatory for all nations to accord their women the political right to vote and to become candidates for political office.

Political Socialization. Socialization is the process of transmitting a culture or value-system to an individual. *Political* socialization refers to the process through which the individual learns about politics, acquires political values and becomes faciliar with the political system.

Political Sociology is a branch of the wider field of sociology that deals with political phenomena in their social setting. Some major themes are: political stratification, political elites and leadership, authority and legitimacy, political parties and pressure groups, bureaucracy, voting and elections, etc.

Political Stability means not only absence of revolution or recurring crises in a political system but also its ability to absorb the occasional stresses and strains, to adjust to the changing conditions and to meet the new demands made by the society while maintaining its identity and continuity.

Political System is in general synonymous with state, government or political regime. But analytically it is a wider term than the state because it includes not only the formal and legal institutions of the state but also the informal groups and forces and the customs, conventions and political values that constitute the framework of its governance.

Politician/Statesman. A politician is a person who is either engaged in party politics as a full-time profession; or a person who seeks political office for personal gain through the electoral process; or a person holding political offices in government. The term Statesman, on the other hand is a dignified term reserved for public men of high stature, or holders of high constitutional and governmental offices, renowned for their role in national and international politics.

Politicization refers both to (a) making an occurrence or event or phenomenon assume a *political* i.e. conflictual character; or (b) to arouse a group or community politically i.e. to make them politically conscious, which is a precondition for political mobilization.

Polity is used for any of these: an amalgam of state and society; a political organization; a particular form of political organization of a state; or a particular form of political constitution.

Poll Tax was a capital tax levied on the citizens during the nineteenth century in lieu of voting rights. It was abolished in the USA very early. In the UK the Conservative government of Margaret Thatcher imposed a poll tax in 1990 but was withdrawn in face of opposition by the public.

Polyarchy is a term used by Robert Dahl to characterize mature and stable democracies in Western Europe and North America. A polyarchy is majority rule accompanied by rule of law, civil liberty* free and free elections, and competitive pluralism.

Polycentrism (existence of multiple centre or poles) refers to the phenomenon of disintegration of unitary ideological movements or power blocs.

Poona Pact (1932). Under the Communal Award* the British government had accorded special electorate to the Depressed Classes (untouchable castes). Considering it an attempt by the British government to divide the Hindu community, M.K. Gandhi, the leader of the Indian National Congress, went on a fast-unto-death against it. Thereupon B.R. Ambedkar, the leader of the untouchables, opened negotiations with Gandhi and signed with/an agreement by which he relinquished special electorate for the untouchables in favour of reserved seats for them in joint electorate with caste Hindus. The Poona pact as signed on 26 September 1932 was incorporated in the Communal Award and the untouchables were given representation accordingly in the general elections held in 1937.

POSDCORB is an acronym for Luther Gullick's summary of principles of administration. Each letter represents a particular principle: planning, organization, staffing, directing, coordinating, reporting and budgeting.

Post-Behaviouralism is an advocacy of employment of both empirical and normative approaches to social analysis with a bias *towards building a policy* science for social improvement

Post-Industrial Society is that which has surpassed the state of industrialization and entered the stage of high technology. It is characterized variously as ''information society'', ''knowledgeable society'' and ''scientific state'' etc. Affluence leads to reduced hours of work and abundance of leisure.

Positivism (From *positio* = sovereignty) in social science refers to empiricism or application of scientific approach to social analysis founded by august Comte (1798-1857) who aimed at a "positive philosophy" of society or scientific sociology. A positivist approach is the opposite of theological, metaphysical and normative approaches. Positive or scientific knowledge is what can be empirically tested and proved. Logical positivism is synonymous with scientific empiricism.

Post-Modern Society is a postindustrial society. If a modern (i.e. industrialized) society was marked by an emphasis on popular rights, autonomous egoism, the primacy of the economic factor, mass production and consumption, the technological drive and permanent revolution, a post-modern (i.e. post-industrial) society is characterized by an emphasis on collective obligation and social responsibility; interdependence of man, society and the natural environment; controlled growth; selective innovations to suit human needs; and maintenance of dynamic equilibrium in the society and economy.

Postmodernism refers to a set of ideas extending from literary criticism (where it started) to architecture, geography, social sciences and international relations. It is a general intellectual movement represented by such philosophers as Michel Foucault, Jacques Derrida and Jean Baudrillard. Postmodernists are critical of what they call "modernity", hence their name. Postmodernism suggests absolute disenchantment with and a radical departure from the theories of modernity. e.g. liberalism, Marxism, structuralism, functionalism, feminism, etc. There is no exact date of start, of this movement like that of renaissance nor there is an agreed set of post modernist ideas and beliefs. However, postmodernists, in general, are critical of the notion of "objective truth". According to them, modernity has made rationality an end in itself which far from being a progressive force has resulted in such outcomes as the Holocaust, environmental degredation and nuclear and other weapons of mass destruction, Modern social science also worships rationality and technicality and ignores the moral and political imperatives. This leads to moral amnesia. Similarly, postmodernists also doubt the possibility of generalization which is at the heart of positive or empirical social science. Generalizations form the bases of ''scientific'' laws meant to explain and predict social reality. However, for postmodernists, not generalizations and abstract models but historical contingency and, indeed, the contingency of the moment is central to human understanding of the social reality The search for generalizations is not only misguided and misleading but unwittingly serves to reinforce the legitimacy of the existing power structures and the social status quo as expressions of an ''objective'' reality. The postmodernists call for *deconstruction* or critique of dominant representations, which are implicated in the production of power, instead of a search for *generalization* to legitimate the social status quo.

Potsdam Agreement (1945) was signed between the three allies of the second World war --the USA, the USSR and the UK-- in Potsdam, Germany, to divide the territory of defeated Germany and the capital city of Berlin into four military occupation zones--American, British, French and Russian-- and to transfer German sovereignty to the occupation authorities of the respective occupation zones. The Agreement created a four- power Allied Control Council and laid down the terms of denazification, demilitarization and democratization of Germany. The onslought of the Cold War led the western allies to integrate their occupation zones and proclaim the Federal Republic of Germany (FRG) in 1949. In response, the USSR created the German Democratic Republic (GDR) in the eastern zone. Berlin remained divided into eastern and western zones. The divided Germany remained a hotbed of east-west cold war until its reunification in 1991.

Power Politics (from German *machtpolitik)* is synonymous with struggle for power. In power politics the end justifies the means. It entails reliance on the use of force, fraud, intrigue and whatever to achieve political ends. As an analytical approach power politics refers to the analysis of all political phenomena in terms of power and pursuit of power.

Power and Authority. Power and authority are interrelated and interdependent concepts. They are the two facets of the same coin. Power is capacity to compel obedience or force compliance. When power is exercised legitimately (constitutionally) it patakes a moral quality. Employment of force or coercion is no longer necessary to make people obey; people render voluntary obedience because they believe in the legitimacy of the wielders of power. Power gets converted into authority, the moral right to make and enforce rules. Power may exist without authority but there can be no authority without power. Authority is derived from and depends upon power and it is not otherwise. Authority is power plus consent, or power plus legitimacy or power plus institutionalization.

Praetorianism (from *praetorian* guards who defended the Roman emperors) refers to a political condition or regime under which civilian authorities operate under the overlordship of military authorities such as in Pakistan and Bangladesh.

Pragmatism is the opposite of dogmatism; a philosophical approach represented by such philosophers as William James, John Dewey and George Herbert Mead. Main tenets are: rejection of preconceived principles in favour of looking forward to the consequences of action; the fallibility of knowledge; the social nature of knowledge; an acceptance of an open universe subject to novelty and complexity; and belief in human ability to achieve self-realization and self-actualization.

Praxis (Greek for practice) is the counterpart of theory; doing versus thinking; also application of theory. In Marxist philosophy ''the unity of theory and practice'' means the obligation of the Marxists to translate the revolutionary theory into revolutionary action.

Preamble is the introductory or opening part of a constitution, or charter or legislative act or a convention or a treaty which declares the purposes and principles underlying that instrument.

Preemptive Strike is the massive first strike without limits and restraints that cripples an enemy's military capacity such as Japanese strike against the American naval headquarters at Pearl Harbour in 1944 or Israeli air strike against the airfields of the neighbouring Arab countries on 6 June 1967) in anticipation of a military strike by an adversary.

Prerogative (from Latin *prae* = before + *rogos* = right) means a right or power which is available to somebody excluding others. In the United Kingdom Royal Prerogative is the sum of those exclusive powers, rights and privileges (executive, legislative, financial, judicial and ecclesiastical) which the Common Law has vested in the Crown to the exclusion of Parliament. Some of these prerogatives are exercised by the Sovereign personally while most of the others are exercised by the servants of the Crown in the name of the Crown without seeking prior approval of Parliament. The courts of law are barred from looking into their validity or exercise. Examples are declaration of war; conclusion of peace; conduct of diplomatic relations; appointment and dismissal of the prime minister, etc.

Prescription. The doctrine of prescription under traditional international law implied that mere possession of a property or territory over a long period of time conferred upon the occupier the legal title of ownership. The principle is incompatible with basic principles of modern international law.

President of the Council is a member of the cabinet of the UK government and minister-in-charge of the affairs of the Privy Council.

President's Rule (India). Article 356 of the Indian Constitution provides that if the President of India (acting on the advice of the Council of Ministers) is satisfied on the report of the governor of a state or otherwise, that the constitutional machinery in a state has broken down he may by a Proclamation dismiss the provincial ministry and take over the administration of the state in his own hands through the medium of the provincial governor who is the representative of the central government.

Pressure Groups, also called political groups, are private interest groups, associations or movements which exert political pressure ("lobbying") upon policy-making authorities of the state to make them act in their favour. They differ from political parties in that their objective is confined to securing and promoting their group interests instead of contesting elections to form government.

Prestroika (Russian for restructuring) refers to a series of reform measures initiated by Mikhail Gorbachev, General Secretary of the Communist Party of the Soviet Union from 1985 to 1991, to restructure and rehabilitate the command economy of the USSR. Simultaneously he introduced reforms like *glasnost* (openness) and democratization to liberalize the Soviet society. However, the failure of Gorbachev reforms led to the breakup of the USSR in November 1991.

Prevention of Corruption Act, 1947 (India) was enacted for effective prevention of bribery and corruption in public services, The Act was amended in 1952 and again in 1964 to give effect to the recommendations of the Committee on Prevention of Corruption under the chairmanship of K. Santhanam appointed by the Government of India in 1964. The latest Prevention of Corruption (Amendment) Act, 1988, Consolidated and amended the existing law on prevention of corruption in public services. There were provisions in Chapter IX of the Indian Penal Code to deal with public servants and those who abet them by way of criminal misconduct. There were, besides, provisions in the Criminal Law Amendment Ordinance, 1944, to enable the attachment of illegally begotten wealth through corruption including transfers of such wealth. The Prevention of Corruption (Amendment) Act, 1988, incorporated all these provisions with modification to make the provisions more effective in corruption among public servants. Among other things, the Act widened the scope of the definition of the expression "public servant", incorporated the offences mentioned under Sections 161 to 165 A of the Indian Penal Code, enhanced penalties provided for these offences, and incorporated a new provision that the order of the trial court upholding the grant of sanction for prosecution would be final if it has not already been challenged and the trial has commenced. To expedite the proceedings provisions for day-to-day trial of cases and prohibitory provisions with regard to grant of stay and exercise of powers of revision on interlocutory orders were also included.

Prevention of Terrorist Activities Act--POTA was a draconian measure enacted in 2002 by the Bharatiya Janata Party-led National Democratic Alliance government at the centre to deal with terrorists and terroristic activities. In due course allegations: of its widespread misuse against religious minorities and political opponents were made. The POTA was amended in 2003 to modify some of its most objectionable provisions. The Congress-led United Progressive Alliance government at the centre, acting in fulfilment of an electoral promise made by the UPA, promulgated two ordinances on 21 September 2004. One to repeal the POTA (2002) and the other to provide for its alternative by amending the Unlawful Activities (Prevention) Act, 1967. The Ordinances were converted into Acts of Parliament on 9 December 2004. The POTA repeal act did not provide for automatic lapse of these cases registered under POTA and pending before the designated (POTA) courts. But constituted on 19 October 2004 three Review Committees, each headed by a retired High Court judge, to review the cases pending before the courts on a selective basis and report to the government within a year.

Preventive Detention Act, 1950 (India). In consequence of the commencement of the Constitution of India on 26 January

1950, all Public Safety Acts passed by the various provincial legislative assemblies before 1947 to provide for detention of persons without trial were declared as null and void by the respective High Courts on the ground that they violated Article 21 (which guaranteed the right to life and personal safety) of the Constitution. However, various state governments pressed the centre for enacting a national preventive detention law to curb the hard-core criminals. The Constitution of India (Article 22) authorizes the legislature to enact a law of preventive detention for certain specified reasons, such as defence, security and territorial integrity of India and the like. In exercise of this power the Parliament first enacted a Preventive Detention Act in 1950 as a temporary measure to lapse after one year. However, it was extended from time to time through continuation acts and was finally allowed to lapse in 1969. It was replaced by a permanent law MISA* in 1971 (repealed in 1978); then by the National Security Act (NSA) in 1980 (still in force) and the Unlawful Activities (Prevention) Act, 2004; besides, preventive detention was also provide for in the Essential Commodities Act. Conservation of Foreign Exchange and Prevention of Smuggling Act, 1974; Maintenance of Essential Services Act; TADA, 1985 (expired in 1995); and POTA, 2002 (repealed in 2004). Under a preventive detention law an individual may be detained without trial for a specified period/periods and constitutional safeguards mentioned in Part III of the Indian Constitution will not be applicable to the detenue. Preventive detention is an extraordinary exception to rule of law and can be justified only in extraordinary situations threatening the national security of India. However, there always exists a possibility of abuse or misuse of the power of preventive detention by executive authorities. The Indian Constitution has, therefore, laid safeguards to prevent the abuse of a preventive detention law. The firstly government is empowered to detain a person under a preventive detention law only for a period of three months. It the government wants to detain the person beyond three months it must obtain & report from an Advisory Board, who will examine the papers submitted by the government and the detenue to the effect that detention is justified. The members of the Advisory Board shall be qualified to be appointed as judges of the High Court. Secondly, the detenue shall be informed, as soon as possible, of the grounds of his detention but not facts which the detaining authority considers to be against public interest to disclose; Thirdly, the detenue must have an earliest opportunity of making a representation against the order of his detention. A law that violates any of the conditions imposed by Article 22 is liable to be declared as null and void and an order of detention which violates any of these will similarly be nullified by the court and the detenue set free.

Princely States. Under British rule the territory of India was divided between 11 Provinces directly administered by the British government and some 601 Princely states (also called Indian States or native States) which enjoyed a limited measure of internal self-government under the paramountcy* of the British Crown* They were unique of their kind in the world and varied greatly in their size and socio-political conditions, some of them were viceroyalties of the Mughal Emperor and were allowed by the British to continue as feudatory chiefs; some in Marwar and Rajputana predated the Mughal era; and some were defeated by British armies and turned into feudatories. Of them about fifteen were major states: Hyderabad, Jammu and Kashmir, Mysore, Tranvancore, Baroda, Gwalior, Indore, Cochin, Jaipur, Jodhpur, Bikaner, Bhopal, Patiala, Junagarh and Rampur. After them came a-number of medium--size principalities; and then there several hundreds of tinay estates mostly in Kathiawad, western India and Punjab. These states were ruled by hereditary and autocratic princes. At the beginning of the nineteenth century about 40 of them had entered into treaties with the British East India Company and the rest had engagements or *sanads*. When India became a Crown colony under the Government of India Act, 1858, these states were not integrated with British India but turned into a "subsidiary state system" under the paramountcy* (suzerainty) of the Government of India. They were placed under the supervision and control of the Political Department of the Government of India* The relationship of paramountcy-dependency implied that the native princes shall remain loyal and faithful servants of the British Crown and the British government shall protect them against internal disturbance and external threats. But their internal autonomy was nominal. Real power lay with the British government exercised through the residents or political agents deployed in these states. They guided the policy and administration of these princes. A British force was deployed to keep the rulers in power. The Crown Representative's Police (CRP) was created in 1937 to assist the rulers to curb internal political agitations. The Indian Independence Act, 1947, declared that as of 15 August 1947 the British paramountcy over the Princely States shall lapse and gave the states the option of acceding either to the Dominion of India or the Dominion of Pakistan depending on geographical contiguity or remain independent. After independence the Political Department was converted into the States' Department which arranged for the accession of the states situated within the Dominion of India to this Dominion which became the Union of India with effect from 26 January 1950.

Prisoners of War (POW's) Soldiers of one belligerent country taken into custody by another country during a war are called prisoners of war (POW's). The custody and treatment of the POW's is governed by the Fourth Convention adopted by the Hague Peace Conference of 1907, the Geneva Conventions* of 1949, and the Supplementary Protocols of 1977. These legal measures ensure the safe custody, humane and just treatment of the POW's and their safe repatriation to their home country.

Privatization is the opposite of collectivization or nationalization or socialization. It means transfer of assets owned by the state to private ownership. It differs from *liberalization* which means restructuring of the centrally planned or regulated socialistic economies into unregulated free market economies, or replacement of socialism by capitalism.

Privilege means a beneficial exemption from general rules of law. A privilege may be *real* i.e. belonging to some place like embassies, religious shrines or national monuments, etc. or *personal* i.e. attached to heads of state, ambassadors, judges, members of parliaments, or judicial witnesses, etc. The latter may superficially appear to be a departure from the tradition of rule of law but are in fact indispensable for the performance of the particular functions assigned to these persons.

Privy Council (the body of king's private advisors) arose in Britain during the twelfth century out of the Great Council (of nobles). It exercised, till the late seventeenth century, the legislative, executive, administrative, financial and ecclesiastical authority of the Crown in the name of the King. When during the late seventeenth century the strength of royal advisors exceeded 100 and it became impossible for the king to consult with all of them he started consulting with a select body of advisers. This inner committee of the Privy Council later came to be named as Cabinet Council or Cabinet and while the Privy Council exists till this day as a constitutional body its real authority has been transferred to the cabinet. All members of the British cabinet and the Speaker of the House of Commons are still administered the oath of office as Privy Councillors because the cabinet does not have a standing in law. In law, the prime minister and other ministers are still king's advisers, and they remain Privy Councillors for life even if they cease to be members of government. A Privy Councillor carries the title of "Right Honorable" (Rt. Hon.) before his name. The present strength of the Privy Council is about 300 members. Besides the cabinet ministers it includes prominent persons from the dominions* made Privy Councillors by the Queen. The main function of the Privy Council is the promulgation of Royal Proclamations and making of Orders-in-Council* on the advice of ministers concerned. The Council performs a host of other functions like granting of royal charters or registration of professional bodies through its committees. The most important of these is the Judicial Committee of the Privy Council (Lords-of -Appeal + the Lord Chancellor) which hears appeals against decisions of the high courts of the dominions and other British dependencies.

Procés-Verbal is a legal record of the terms of an agreement arrived at between parties or a minute of the proceedings of a diplomatic meeting or conference. The term is also applied to a treaty relating to a minor or technical matter or concerning a minor alteration in an existing convention. A *proces-verbal* comes into force from the date of its signing and does not require ratification, proces-verbal is also appended to a treaty or convention to explain or interpret its difficult or obscure terms.

Progressivism is the opposite of reactionism. A *progressive* is one who believes in progress while a reactionary is opposed to progress. The Marxists-Leninists, for example, call themselves progressivists because they believe in a dialectical end of history while their opponents are dubbed as bourgevois reactionaries because they are opposed to dialectical progression of history.

Proletarian Revolution refers to the overthrow of the bourgeoisie by armed uprising and its replacement by the dictatorship of the Proletariat.*

Proletariat was first used by Karl Marx to describe the class of industrial worker that came into being after the Industrial Revolution. It is derived from Latin *proles* i.e. the progeny of the destitutes or the *proletari* i.e. the harlots and menial workers in ancient Rome.

Propaganda (something which is propagated) is propagation of ideas and manipulation of information with a view to influence the minds and behaviour of the people.

Protection of Human Rights Act, 1993 (India) was passed by Indian parliament to implement the twin Covenants on the Civil and Political Rights and on the Economic, Social and Cultural Rights adopted by the UN General Assembly in 1966, and signed and ratified by India. The Act created the National Human Rights Commission* as a fact-finding and advisory body.

Protectionism is a policy of protecting domestic economy against foreign competition by imposing high tariffs on imports, subsidizing domestic industries and creating other barriers against free trade.

Protectorate is a country, usually small and weak, which comes under the protection of a big and strong country by voluntarily surrendering the responsibility of its foreign affairs and defence to the protecting state under a treaty signed between the protected and the protector. The examples are Bhutan and Puerto Rico.

Protocol is used in three different senses: (1) an official document attached to a treaty as a supplement or addendum; (2) an intergovernmental agreement dealing with routine or relatively less important matters than those requiring the conclusion of a formal treaty or convention and (3) the *diplomatic protocal* which is the sum of customs, conventions, rules, usages and ceremonials observed by the diplomats during diplomatic intercourse. The diplomatic protocol is entirely evolutionary and conventional. For instance, order of precedence; manner and method of paying state visits; reception of foreign dignitaries and diplomats; formalities of organizing international conferences and conducting diplomatic negotiations; and modes of address, etc.

Provincial Autonomy (1935) refers to establishment of fully responsible government in the provinces of British India under the Government of India Act, 1935, under which provincial elections were held in 1937. The Seventh Schedule of the Act divided governmental powers and functions into three lists-- central, provincial and concurrent. Provincial administrations were granted legislative, administrative and financial autonomy in respect of provincial and concurrent matters with certain limits and safeguards.

Public Accounts Committee (India) is a standing committee of Indian parliament constituted each financial year by selecting 15 members from the Lok Sabha and seven from the Rajya Sabha. Membership is distributed among the parliamentary parties roughly in proportion of their strength in the houses. The primary function of the PAC is to examine the appropriation and financial accounts of the Government of India and the report of the Comptroller and Auditor-General thereon. It brings the and wastage instances of misappropriation and misuse and wastage of public funds to the attention of the government. It is a crucial parliamentary mechanism to ensure the financial accountability of the administration.

Public Administration is the sum of all agencies and procedures meant to implement public policy. As a subject of study public administration deals with the public administrative system, policy and process at all levels of governance.

Public Interest is the sum of values that are considered as essential for the safety and well-being of the community. This is the objective of all public policy.

Public Opinion. By public is meant the body of citizens and opinion refers to the thinking and preferences of the citizens on a given issue of public life at a given time. Public opinion is neither unitary nor fixed. In a democracy public authorities seek to ascertain the wishes and preferences of the majority or given sections of the population to formulate policies which are acceptable to the people.

Public Policy is the sum of objectives and corresponding plans of action directed towards preserving, protecting and promoting public interest.

Public Sector of the national economy is composed of all enterprises and industries which are owned by the government but enjoy operational and financial autonomy under the respective legal instruments ceating them. Distinguished from the private sector which is sum of enterprises, businesses and industries owned by private individuals and corporations.

Public Undertakings (India) refer to all public enterprises and establishments of commercial and infrastructural nature directly owned and managed by the government or indirectly through public corporations, companies, authorities and trusts.

Public Utilities refer to all basic services and facilities which are indispensable for civic life, e.g. supply of water, electricity and gas, sewage disposal, telecommunications and public transport. Traditionally these utilities are kept as public monopolies to protect them from exploitation by the private interests for private profit. However, capitalist countries have privatized these utilities subject to regulation by public authorities.

Puritan Revolution or the republican revolution in England resulted from the civil war of 1642-1648 between the royal forces led by King Charles I, who stood for Royal Prerogative, and the parliamentary forces led by the Puritans, who stood for Parliamentary Privilege. The struggle ended with the defeat of the royalists, the beheading of Charles I, abolition of monarchy and the House of Lords, and declaration of England as a commonwealth (republic) and a protectorate (to be governed by the Lord Protector Oliver Cromwell, the leader of the parliamentary forces The monarchy and the House of Lords were restored in 1662.

Purna Swaraj (complete independence). When the British government rejected the demand of the Indian National Congress to accord India the status of a Dominion of the British Empire, as formulated under the Nehru Committee report* of 1928, the Indian National Congress adopted, on 31 December

1929 in its annual session held in Lahore, the attainment of *puma swaraj* as the goal of the Indian National Congress. It decided to observe the day of 26 January 1930 as Independence Day and thereafter every year and to launch civil disobedience movement for the attainment of national independence.

Putsch (push) is a sudden move by a junta to topple a civilian government and take over power.

Q

QUANGO is an acronym for quasi-non-governmental organization. QUANGO'S are also called quasi-governmental organization (QUAGO's) or non-departmental public bodies (NDPB's). These are regulatory or service-providing agencies created outside the departmental structure, though placed under the authority of a minister, to deal with the public directly and efficiently without the red-tape and interference of departmental bureaucracy.

Quisling is a pejorative term used for native collaborators of foreign occupying forces; after Vidkun Quisling who headed the puppet regime installed in Norway by the Nazi occupation authorities on 1 February 1942.

Quit-India Movement (1942) was launched by the Indian National Congress, in pursuance of a resolution passed by the All-India congress Committee on 8 August 1942 in its meeting held in Bombay, to force the British authorities to leave India immediately. This step was necessitated by the failure of the made earlier Cripps proposals/to satisfy the Indian National Congress.

***Quo Warranto*, Writ of** (Latin *Quo Warranto* = by what warrant). A writ of QW is issued by a court in cases of disputed elections or illegal appointments to public posts. The court decides the propriety of the A procedures followed or the adequacy of qualifications and propriety of procedures laid down for an appointment.

R

Raan of Kutch. *Raan* means desert and Kutch is a district of the Indian State of Gujarat. Formerly it was a princely state* merged in Gujarat in 1960. Raan of Kutch (area 23, 310 sqr. kms.) is a salt waste with a fertile string along the Gulf of Kutch in the north of the district. The Raan is situated between the Indian State of Gujarat and the Pakistani Province of Sind. The demarcation of the border between India and Pakistan in this area was left out of the Radcliff Award* in 1947. Pakistan later claimed about 3,500 sqr miles lying to the north of the 24th parallel (about half of the Raan) as its own while India claimed the whole area as belonging to it. This territorial dispute led to the outbreak of fighting between Pakistani and Indian forces on 9 April 1965. A bilateral ceasefire agreement was signed on 30 June which provided for reference of the dispute to an arbitration tribunal composed of three members none of whom was to be a national of either India or Pakistan. One member was to be nominated by the Government of India and one by the Government of Pakistan. The chairman was to be nominated jointly by the two governments but failing an agreement between the two by the Secretary-General of the UN. The tribunal with its chairman nominated by the UN Secretary-General was constituted on 22 December 1965. It held its meetings in Geneva from 15 February 1966 to 14 July 1967. The tribunal announced its final award on 19 February 1968. It awarded about 3, 200 sqr. miles of the disputed territory to India-and the remaining portion of about 350 sqr. miles to Pakistan. The award was accepted by both the parties and the boundaries were demarcated accordingly. Even after the settlement of the dispute over the Raan of Kutch the adjoining Sir Creek* area remained disputed and talks between India and Pakistan to resolve the dispute were continuing in 2005.

Racial Segregation refers to the policy of the white regimes in the USA and South Africa to forcibly prevent the blacks from commingling with the whites in public schools, buses, parks, residential areas and other public conveniences, and from marrying the whites. It was followed by a policy of *desegregation.*

Racism/Racialism. Race is an anthropological concept broader than the concepts of nation, tribe and ethnic group. Humankind is divided into various racial categories on the basis of their colour and physical features e.g. the Aryan. Semitic, African, Australoid, Mongoloid or Cinic races. Racism or racialism is a belief in the superiority and supremacy of one's own race over all other races and this ideology implies hatred of and discrimination against other races. The *varna** system, practice of untouchability, Nazism,* anti-Semitism , racial segregation and apartheid are different forms of racism. Racialism has been outlawed by the UN Declaration of the Elimination of all Forms of Racial Discrimination passed in 1963. Similarly, Resolution 3379 of the UN General Assembly passed on 10 November 1975 declared Zionism* as a form of racism and imperialism.

Radcliffe Award (1947). After the collapse of the Cabinet Mission Plan* of 1946 Lord Wavell was replaced by Lord Mountbatten as the Viceroy and Governor-General of India early in 1947 to expedite a political settlement in India. After securing the agreement of the principal Indian political parties he announced a plan for partition of the Indian subcontinent into two separate dominions of India and Pakistan on 3 June 1947. Accordingly, the Indian Independence Act, 1947 was passed to transfer power to the two Dominions of India and Pakistan on 15 August 1947. To implement the Partition Plan (Mountbatten Plan*), the Government of India announced on 30 June 1947 the appointment of three boundary commissions for partioning the three provinces of Panjab, Bengal and Assam on a communal basis. Each Boundary Commission was composed of two non-Muslim and two Muslim judges of the High Court of the concerned province. Four days later Sir Cyril Radcliffe, an English officer of the Indian Civil Service (ICS), was appointed as common chairman of the three boundary commissions. In each case the native members failed to draw the boundaries by mutual agreement. Eventually the Chairman had to exercise his individual judgment in drawing the final boundary lines in Panjab and Bengal, according to the terms of reference of the Commissions. The Muslim majority Sylhet district of Assam was asked to decide in a referendum either to join India or Pakistan (the majority voted in favour of Pakistan). The boundaries thus demarcated were announced on 18 August 1947, three days after the transfer of power under the Indian Independence Act causing unnecessary displacement of people and massacres. The delineation of boundaries between India and Pakistan came to be known as the **Radcliffe Award** and the boundary line as the **Radcliffe** *Line.*

Radical Humanism refers to political philosophy of M.N. Roy (1857-1954), an Indian Marxist who took part in the organization of the Communist International* (Comintern), then abandoned Marxism-Leninism and became a votary of liberal humanist democracy. His radical humanism is a synthesis of liberty, equality, justice, rationalism, secularism and non-violence. Roy had founded the Radical Democratic Party in 1940 which was dissolved in 1948. His followers in 1969 formed the Indian Radical Humanist association to propagate his ideals. Roy had also started a weekly entitled *Independent Indian* in 1937. It was restarted as a monthly entitled *Radical* Humanist in 1970.

Radicalism (from Latin *radis* = root) is advocacy of radical or root or basic change in the realm of thought or society or politics.

Raison d' Etat (reason of state) means that a statesman is free to act in the interest of the state as the situation requires. More specifically, the "reason of state" implies the obligation of the statesman to put the expediency of the state above accepted moral and legal principles.

Ramakrishna Mission was established in 1909 in Calcutta as a philanthropic and social service organization by the followers of swami Ramakrishna and Swami Vivekanand.

Rapallo Treaty (1922) was signed by Germany and the USSR in 1922 in Rapallo, Italy, whereby Germany recognized the USSR *de jure* and both the signatories cancelled each other's pre-war their debts and renounced/war claims. Rapallo enabled Germany to trade with the USSR and import Soviet weapons technology to overcome the arms embargo imposed by the Versailles Treaty*.

Rashtriya Swayam Sevak Sangh -- RSS [the National Volunteers' Union] was formed by Keshav Baliram Hedgewar (1889-1940) in 1925 in Nagpur (Maharashtra State, India) as a militant youth wing of the Hindu nationalist All-India Hindu Mahasabha. As adopted in 1949, its Constitution proclaims the necessity of "uniting the Hindus by eradicating the fissiparous tendencies arising from diversities of sect, faith, caste and creed and from political, economic, linguistic and provincial differences amongst Hindus, to make them realize the greatness of their past, to build up an organized and well-disciplined corporate life"; and to bring about an all-round regeneration of the Hindu society). Article 3 of the Constitution declared the objective of the RSS as to weld together the diverse groups within the Hindu society and to revitalize and rejuvenate the same on the basis of its *dharma* (religion) and *sanskriti* (culture) that it may achieve an all-sided development of the *Bharat Varsha* (the Aryan homeland). The RSS has a strength of about one million cadres organized through local *shakhas* (branches) spread throughout India. It is headed at the national level by a *Sarsanghchalak* (Supreme Leader) elected for life. The programme of the RSS includes indoctrination of the Hindu youth and imparting physical and military training to them.

Rational Choice Theory revolves around calculation of cost and benefit before action. The theory explains the engagement or non-engagement of the people in the political process. Its basic premise is that people in politics aspire to achieve their objectives by most efficient means, because they are rational, self-interested beings; For instance, Anthony Down in his *An Economic Theory of* Democracy (1957) argued that microeconomic models can best explain political behaviour in general and voting behaviour in particular.

Reaction/Reactionary. Reaction is revulsion from and opposition to a new ideology or system and sticking to some past ideology or order. For instance, feudal reaction against liberalism and democracy; the imperialist reaction against nationlism; and reaction of the capitalists against socialism and communism. The opposition is between progressives who believe in social progress and a new social order, and reactionaries who are opposed to social change and aspire to preserve the old static order.

Realpolitik (German for power politics) means amoral politics politics without morality. The interest and expediency of the state takes precedence over all moral, religious or humanistic considerations. *Realpolitik* is a method of statecraft which may include the use or threat of the use of force, use of fraud and treachery; opportunistic alliances and counter-alliances breach of trust and international obligations; and any other political or military means.

Rebus Sic Stantibus is a principle of international law which stipulates that with the change of circumstances treaties concluded between parties are no longer binding unless modified by the parties.

Recognition. A state becomes a member of the community of states with attendant rights and obligations under international law when it is recognized by other states. If there is an abnormal change of government in a state either by internal revolution or a coup d' etat or foreign intervention other governments recognize it de *facto* (as an existing political fact) but when the same government demonstrates its ability to discharge its international obligations it may be recognized *de* jure (as a legitimate authority) entitled to establish normal diplomatic relations with the recognizing states. The *Estrada* doctrine of recognition does not recognize the necessity of a formal act --signifying the recognition of a government. Mere continuation or restoration of diplomatic relations is an enough proof of recognition. The doctrine was propounded in 1930 by Genero Estrada, erstwhile foreign minister of Mexico. The *Tobar* doctrine of recognition was enunciated in 1907 by Carlos Tobar, erstwhile foreign minister of Equador, stipulating that a government coming to power as a result of a revolution or a *coup* d' *etat* should not be recognized unless a freely elected legislature of that country approves the change of government. .

Referendum is a democratic device of ascertaining people's opinion. In a referendum an issue is placed before the electorate who vote only in "yes" or "no". Referendum are widely held in Switzerland, some American states and the European Union.

Regional Arrangements is a vague term used in Article 52 of the UN Charter for regional collective security alliances/ organizations, like, OAS, NATO, the Arab League, or the OSCE. The Article allows the states to form regional collective security arrangements provided their terms and activities are not inconsistent with the principles and purposes enshrined in the UN Charter.

Regional Cooperation for Development--RCD. see "Economic Cooperation Organization."

Regional Integration means functional integration of a particular geographical region by means of supranational authorities or communities. Its basic premise is that peace, development and prosperity can better be achieved by economic integration. While preserving their separate national sovereignties and governmental structures the member-states of a regional community surrender part of their sovereignty in specified functional areas to supranational authorities for the sake of collective benefit. The classic example is the European Union/European Community.

Regionalism in national politics is a subnational tendency of asserting regional political identity at the cost of a national identity and according primacy to regional interest over national interest. In international relations regionalism is an approach of promoting regional security, regional cooperation or functional integration.

Relative Deprivation is a feeling of being deprived on the part of a deprived group in relation to the privileged groups in the society,

Rentier Class/State. A rentier class refers to those who live on unearned income derived from investments in the capital market and lead a life of leisure and profligacy. A *rentier* is one which derives its revenue from royalties on its natural resources e.g. oil, natural gas or minerals, let out to foreigners for exploitation.

Representation of People Act, 1951 (India) as supplemented by the Conduct of Election Rules, 1961, lays down the electoral procedure, defines electoral malpractices, and provides for disqualification of candidates for national and state elections. It was last amended in 2002 to incorporate a number of electoral reforms.

Reprieve (from French *repris* = withdraw) means withdrawal of a prisoner from the execution of a law for a certain time. Any court which is competent to award execution of the law is also empowered to grant a reprieve either before or after the judgment.

Republic (from French *republique* and Latin *res publica* = commonwealth or political community) means a democratic state; a democratic state not headed by a constitutional monarch but by an elected head of state; an opposite of monarchy in which power is lodged not in one absolute monarch but in more than one person like democracy, aristocracy or oligarchy.

Republican Party of India was founded by B.R. Ambedkar in 1950 to protect the political interests of the former untouchable castes. It is recognized as a regional political party in the state of Maharashtra. It is divided into two factions.

Republicanism is the opposite of monarchism and synonymous with espousal of democratic principles--popular sovereignty, representative government, rule of law and civil liberty, etc.

Res Communis means common property of the mankind which cannot be subjected to any state's sovereignty, like the open seas, outer space or the Antarctica.

Res Judicata (from Latin *res* = thing; matter + *judicata* = adjudicated) is a matter that has been adjudicated by a competent court, tribunal, arbitrator or any other judicial authority. A matter already decided judicially cannot be reopened for judicial proceeding again. Also, it is an absolute principle of international law that a judgment having the authority of *res judicata* is judicially binding upon the parties to a dispute.

Research And Analysis Wing--RAW (India) is an intelligence network created in 1971 as a wing of the Cabinet Secreatariat of the Government of India to gather information of political and strategic importance from India's neighbourhood.

Resolution of Remembrance (1931) was read out and passed at the behest of the Indian National Congress in thousands of pubic meetings organized throughout India on 26 January 1931, to observe the first anniversary of India's independence Day. (See also "Purna swaraj").

Revisionism in the religious and ideological realm is the opposite of orthodoxy; means revision or reinterpretation of received tenets according to changing needs and circumstances. In international politics, however, revisionism is the opposite of *status quoism* which means a policy of seeking a revision of the status quo which is regarded as unfair and unjust.

Revivalism refers to a movement for the revival or restoration of the pristine or pure religion e.g. Vedic, evangelical or Islamic revivalism. It should not be confounded with fundamentalism*.

Revolution literally means a revolutionary movement in space or time. In the intellectual and social realm a revolution is an overturning of an established ideological, political or social order and its replacement by a radically different order, e.g. the French, Bolshevik, Chinese and Iranian revolutions; or industrial revolution, information revolution or biotechnological revolution.

Rider is an amendment, usually not germaine, which its sponsor hopes to get passed by including it in a proposed legislation. Riders become law if bills incorporating them are enacted.

Right to Information Act, 2005 (India) which come into force on 12· October 2005 guarantees citizens' right to seek and obtain information from government and public agencies. The Act covers all agencies and personnel of the central and state governments, municipal bodies, panchayati raj institutions and all organizations receiving grants-in-aid from the government. It aims at ensuring a transparent, accountable, responsive and responsible administration. It provides for appointment of information commissioners/ officers in all government departments and agencies to hear appeals against denial of information to the citizens by public servants excluding matters connected with national security.

Riot (from French *riote* = quarrel) is a disturbance of public peace caused by a violent crowd fighting among themselves. A riot differs from an *affray* in that while the former involves violent groups the latter denotes a mere scuffle or fighting between two or more individuals in a public place. In Britain a Riot Act was passed in 1715 (repealed in 1967) to prevent breach of public peace. The Act declared the refusal of an assembly of 12 or more persons to disperse after a lawful authority had read but a portion of the Act to them and asked them to disperse, an act of felony. Article 147 of the Indian Penal Code* (IPC) recognizes rioting without the use of weapons as a bailable cognizible offence punishable by imprisonment for up to two years or fine or both. Similarly, rioting with the use of lethal weapons is recognized under Section 148 as a bailable cognizible offence punishable with imprisonment for up to three years or fine or both. The Disturbed Areas (Special Courts) Act, 1976, was passed to provide for speedy trial of persons accused of committing offences under the Indian Penal Code during caste and communal riots.

Round Table Conference (India) was held in London during 1929-32 to deliberate over a future constitution for India. The idea of convening an RTC was proposed in the report of the Simon Commission* (1929). Accordingly, Lord Irwin announced on 31 October 1929 that the government will invite the leaders of major Indian political parties and of the Princely states to meet in an RTC with British authorities in London to deliberate over the Indian constitutional problem. The first session of the RTC was held towards the end of 1929. It was attended by representatives of all Indian parties except the Indian National Congress. But Gandhi-Irwin Agreement* led to participation of M. K. Gandhi in the second session as the sole representative of the INC. The first session of the RTC deliberated over the constitution of the central government; the second over the constitution of the provincial government; and the third over the question of communal representation. Since the Indian leaders failed among themselves to evolve a scheme of communal representation the British government unilaterally announced the Communal Award* in 1932. At the end of the second session the British government issued a White Paper summarizing the deliberations of the RTC, which together with the Communal Award, became the basis of the Government of India Act, 1935.

Rule of Law or supremacy of law is the opposite of arbitrary rule and despotism. Here "Rule" means government but law itself cannot govern; government of law means that the rulers govern strictly in accordance with the laws and are themselves bound by these laws, further Law means the regular (statute) law, excluding all forms of non-positive laws like customs and conventions, moral principles, religious canons, etc. The Rule of Law is not a single rule. It is rather a collection of conventional rules evolved over time to bind the hands of the government. It includes the sovereignty of regular law; equality before the law; equal protection of and equality of opportunity under the law; the due process of law; and the independence and impartiality of the judiciary.

Russian Federation became on 25 December 1991 the successor to the former Russian Soviet Federated Socialist Republic (RSFSR) with its capital at Moscow, which was formed by the Bolsheviks in 1917 as the successor of the former Russian Empire. In 1922 the RSFSR became the nucleus of the Union of Soviet Socialist Republics (the USSR or the Soviet Union). The USSR was formally dissolved on 8 December 1991 when the governments of Belarus, Russia and Ukraine abrogated the Union Treaty of 1922. On 25 December 1991 Mikhail Gorbachev resigned as the president of the USSR and the Supreme Soviet (parliament) of the RSFSR voted to change the name of the RSFSR to that of the Russian Federation. The Russian Federation is a multiethnic, federal, democratic republic with an American-style presidential system of government. The Russian Federation is composed of 21 nominally autonomous constituent republics, one autonomous oblast (region), 49 administrative oblasts and six krais (provinces). There are also ten autonomous okrugs (districts), nine of which are placed under the jurisdiction of the oblast or krai within which they are located. The Russian Federation is believed to be the home of about 110 nations, nationalities and ethnic groups.

Ruwandan Cenocide (1994) refers to the massacre of about one million Ruwandans and displacement of two million because of political conflict between the majority Hutu tribe (85% of population) and the minorigy Tutsi tribe (14% of population) in Ruwanda during 1994.

S

Sabotage means subversion and destruction; from *sabots* the wooden shoes that peasants tossed into newly invented machines during early days of the industrial revolution in the vain hope that such action will save cottage industry and their manual jobs. Hence *saboteur* is one who indulges in sabotage.

Sahrawi Arab Democratic Republic (SADR) was proclaimed by the Polisario* in Western Sahara with a government-in-exile in Algeria formed on 27 February 1976. Western Sahara was a Spanish colony which was transferred in equal proportion to Morocco and Mauritania in February 1976. In 1979 Mauritania surrendered its portion in favour of the SADR but Morocco annexed this territory and refused to recognize the SADR. In 1982 the SADR was admitted to the Organization of African Unity (OAU) as a member without the right to attend its meetings. Morocco withdrew from a OAU in 1985 in protest. By 1992 the SADR was recognized by 75 countries and in 2000 it become the full member of the African Union (AU) after ratification of its Constitutive Act. In April 1991 the UN Security ''Council created the UN Mission for the Referendum in Western Sahara (MINURSO) which was made responsible for holding a referendum in Western Sahara in accordance with the plan of 1988. In April 2004 the UN Security Council extended the mandate of the MINURSO until. October of that year and passed a resolution calling upon both Morocco and polisario to accept the UN plan for granting immediate self-rule to Western Sahara. Morocco, however rejected it and offered local autonomy under Moroccan sovereignty.

Samajvadi Party (Hindi *samajvadi* = socialist) was founded by Mulayam Singh Yadav, after breaking away from the Janata Dal, on 5 November 1992 in Lucknow (Uttar Pradesh, India) to articulate the interests of the other backward classes (OBC's). It is recognized as a regional political party and its influence is confined to the state of Uttar Pradesh.

Samurai was the Japanese warrior class that ruled Japan from the seventeenth century up to the Meiji Restoration in the first half of the nineteenth century.

Sanctions in international relations refer to preventive or punitive measures, usually of a non-violent nature, taken by individual states or a group of states or a regional organization or the UN security Council against a state found guilty of violating its international obligations. Sanctions include prohibition of trade with the target country, an embargo on arms supply, or aerial and naval blockade, etc.

Shanghai Cooperation Organization--SCO was formed as an intergovernmental forum for economic and technical cooperation in the Central Asian region, in 2001. Members are: China, Kazakastan, Kyrghysia, Russia, Tajikistan and Uzbekistan. India, Iran, Mongolia and Pakistan have been given the status of observers. A secretariat of the SCO was established in Beijing, China, in 2003.

Sanghatan (Sanskrit for organization) was the principal objective of the All-India Hindu Mahasabha (founded in 1915). Hindus who are weak because they are divided on the basis of caste, creed, language and region must be united on a single political platform to enhance their political power and protect their interests against other communities.

Sanskritization refers to the process of upward mobility of individuals and groups in the caste-ridden Hindu society. An affluent individual or a group of individuals belonging to a lower caste can improve his their social status by emulating the customs, rituals, practices and life-style of the higher castes.

Sarkaria Commission. A Commission on Union-State Relations with Justice R.S. Sarkaria as chairman was appointed by the Government of India in 1983 to look into the existing pattern of union-state relations and recommend necessary reforms. The Commission, which reported in 1988, while upholding the general philosophy and the pattern of union-state relations implicit in the Constitution of India addressed a number of grievances of the states particularly as regards the distribution of revenues between the centre and states and the misuse of Article 356 of the Constitution. Many of its recommendations were acted upon by the government. Particularly, the states' share in the central pool of revenue was enhanced to 30.5 per cent and an Inter-State Council* was created in 1991 to promote horizontal cooperation among the states.

***Sarvodaya* Movement** (Sanskrit *sarvodaya*= welfare of all). *Sarvodaya* was the title M.K. Gandhi gave to his translation in Gujarati of John Ruskin's *Unto This* Last. Four Principles of Political Economic (1911). The concept was picked up by Acharya Vinoba (Vinayak) Bhave (1895-1994), a disciple of Gandhi. He believed that social change was not possible by legislation from above but by moral exhortation. He, therefore, started the *Sarvodaya* movement in 1948 with the formation of a central organ called *Sarva Seva Dal* (Public Service Group) at Maganwadi, Wardha, Maharashtra. This organ was to provide guidance and leadership to *sarvodaya* workers organized in a network of local *Sarva Seva Dals* spread throughout India. The essential features of the movement were: *bhoodan/gramdan; sampattidan* (donation of property); *buddhidan* (donation of knowledge); and *jivandan* (devoting one's life to social work). This moralistic movement soon fizzled out because of the indifferent attitude of a materialistic society.

Satyagraha (Sanskrit for truth-force) means search for truth; soul-force non-violent resistance to wrongs; insistence on truth without becoming uncompromising; avoidance of anger and hatred; insistence on full agreement on fundamentals before accepting a settlement; and winning the heart of the adversary. *Satyagraha* (non-violent non-cooperation and civil disobedience was conceived by M.K. Gandhi as a political weapon to fight for national independence against British imperialism.

Scheduled Castes refer to such castes, races, or tribes or parts of or groups within such castes, races or tribes as are deemed under Article 341 of the Constitution of the Indian Republic to be *Scheduled* (listed) castes for purposes of that Constitution i.e. reservation of seats for them in the House of People and state legislative assemblies, reservation of jobs for them in central and state public services, and provision of other social, economic and educational benefits. The present scheduled castes are the former untouchable castes which were designated as "depressed classes" under the Government of India Acts, 1919 and 1937 and given special benefits. Article 341 of the Indian Constitution provides that the President (of India) may with respect to any state or union territory, and where it is a state, after consultation with the Governor thereof, by public notification, specify the castes, races or tribes or parts of or groups within castes, races or tribes which shall for the purposes of this Constitution be deemed to be Scheduled Castes in relation that state or union territory. Parliament may by law, include or exclude from the list of scheduled castes any caste, race, or tribe or part thereof specified in a notification. A 17.5 per cent quota for them in the legislatures, public service jobs and educational institutions have been reserved for them. A National Commission for the Scheduled Castes was created to monitor the implementation of the constitutional and legal safeguards for them and report to the President

Scheduled Tribes refer to aboriginal communities living in the forest belts and hilly areas of India. After 1947 the Government of India continued the British practice of scheduling tribal areas and providing protection and welfare. Article 342 of the Indian Constitution declares that the President (of India) may with respect to any state or union territory, and where it is a state, after consulting with the Governor thereof, by public notification, specify the tribes or tribal communities or parts of or groups within tribes or tribal communities which shall for the purposes of this Constitution be deemed to be the Scheduled Tribes in relation to that state or union territory. Parliament may by law include or exclude from the list of scheduled tribes specified in a notification, any tribe or tribal community or part thereof or groups within any tribe or tribal community. Accordingly, a new list of these tribes drawn and notified by the Government of India in 1950 and has been revised from time to time. A quota of 2.5 per cent in legislatures, public service jobs and educational institutions has been reserved for them **The Scheduled Castes/Scheduled Tribes (Prevention of Atrocities) Act, 1989** was passed to prevent the occurrence of atrocities against the members of the SC's/ ST's since the provisions of the Indian Penal Code and the Protection of Civil Rights Act, 1955, were found to be ineffective in checking the atrocities against these communities. The Act defined atrocities against SC's/ST's and prescribed trial by special courts of such offenders and relief and rehabilitation to the victims of atrocities.

Schengen Accord (1995) was signed on 26 March 1995 at Schengen, Netherlands, by Austria, Belgium, Denmark, Finland, France, Germany, Greece, Iceland, Italy, Luxembourg, Netherlands, Norway, Portugal, Spain and Sweden. The agreement, open for accession to other European states, abolished internal border controls on movement of persons and goods between the signatory countries and the rest of the European Union. This was a first step towards a European Union without internal boundaries open for free movement of the citizens of the EU.

Schuman Plan (1950) as the forerunner of European integration was conceived by the French foreign minister Rober Schuman to pool together European coal and steal resources. The plan led to the signing of the European Coal and Steal Community Treaty in 1951. It was motivated by the French desire to overcome the military threat of a resurgent Germany by drawing her closer to Europe.

Secretary of State (from French *secretaire* = keeper of secrets). The office of the Secretary of State originated in England during the middle ages as the king's chief minister and private advisor. He was the keeper of the king's signet and the privy seal. In the performance of his official functions he was aided by four clerks. With the growth of the business of state departments of state were created and were manned by secretaries of state. Nowadays the secretaries of state and the ministers of the Crown have the same status. In the US, however, the office of the Secretary of State is the equivalent of the British foreign secretary or the Indian foreign minister.

Secular State is the opposite of theocracy. As embedded in the European and American constitutions the secular state rests on three essential principles: Separation between church and state; state neutrality towards religion and non-interference in religious affairs; and constitutional guarantee of religious freedom and non-discrimination on religious grounds.

Secularism (from Latin *saeculum* = present time) is the opposite of spiritualism and synonymous with laicism. It is a philosophical approach first advocated by Thomas Holyoke that personal conduct and morality, social relations, education and politics should be governed by rational, materialistic, this-worldly considerations rather then by irrational, supernatural, and other-worldly considerations. It should not be confounded with *atheism* which means denial of God and renunciation of religion.

Secularization is the evolutionary process whereby individuals and institutions give up the supernatural and irrational in favour of a rational and scientific approach to the organization of human thoughts and action. Secularization is considered as an essential prerequisite of modernization.

Sedition covers actions that incite disaffection towards or spread discontent or encourage rebellion against the legally constituted government of a country. Seditious activities are defined differently by the laws of different countries and may include espionage, Sabotage, subversion or any other acts aimed at overthrowing the government of one's own country. Nobody can be convicted of sedition except under due process of law. Sedition differs from treason.

Selbeschrankung (German for self-restriction) refers to the positivistic doctrine that international law acquires binding force because it consists of rules which the sovereign states accept by voluntary self-restriction. Thus international law is regarded as law by virtue of its being an extension of the municipal law or an external manifestation of the public law.

Senatorial Courtesy (US) is a convention observed by the members of the US Senate irrespective of their party affiliation. The President of the USA must consult with the Senators of his own party belonging to a state before making nominations for federal appointments in that state. In case of default the entire Senate unites to defeat Presidential nominations.

Separate Electorates for religious minorities in India was part of British imperialist policy of divide and rule. From the outset the British ruled out territorial representation as unsuitable for India and considered represention on the basis of community, class and interest as conducive to preservation of British supremacy. On this basis Indians were nominated for the first time to the legislative councils under the Indian Councils Acts of 1861 and 1892. It was at the behest of the British that the All-India Muslim League* was formed in 1906 which was encouraged to make a demand for introduction of separate electorate for the Muslims. Muslims were given separate electorate under the Indian Councils Act, 1909; the Christians, Sikhs and Parsis under the Government of India Act, 1919; and the number of communities, classes and interests given separate or special electorates increase to 18 under the Communal Award* of

1932. Separate electorate meant that to fill seats reserved for a particular religious community a separate constituency composed of voters of that community will be created in which only the members of that community could stand as candidates and only voters of that community could vote. A voter registered in a communal constituency was not eligible to vote in any other constituency.

Separation of Powers is a constitutional principle which is the opposite of fusion or union of powers. It was first advocated by the English philosopher John Lock as a safeguard against royal absolutism, taken up from him by the French thinker Montesquieu and embedded in the 1978 Constitution of the USA. The principle enjoins that to keep the government within its legal limits the three powers—legislative, executive and judicial—should be kept separate from each other and allowed to work together in a system of constitutional checks and balances. Separation of powers should not be confounded with *division of powers*. The former relates to interagovernment differentiation of powers at any level while the latter refers to distribution of powers between the levels of government such as in a federal state.

Seventh Schedule of the Indian Constitution contains three lists of powers and functions: the Union List; the State List; and the Concurrent List. The Union Parliament can make law in respect of matters listed in the Union List; the state legislative assemblies can make law in respect of matters listed in the State List; both the union and state legislatures can make law in respect of matters listed in the Concurrent List but in case of conflict between state and central laws made in respect of a matter listed in the Concurrent List the central law shall supersede the state laws. The residual power is vested in the Union.

Sheriff is the highest law-enforcing officer in a county. The office of sheriff originated in medieval Europe.

Shiv Sena was formed by Bal Thakray in 1966 as a militant group of the native Maratha youth in the State of Maharashtra to protect the rights and interests of the Maratha people and expulsion of non-locals from Maharashtra. It captured the Bombay Municipal Corporation in 1985. It takes part in state and national elections and is recognized as a regional political party.

Shiites (from Arabic *shia'* = party) refers originally to the partisans of Ali ibne Talib, the fourth khalifa or successor of the Prophet Muhammad in his struggle against Amir Mu'awiyya who had rebelled against central authority. Later shiism developed as a separate sect within the community of Muslims which denied the validity of the institution of *khilafat** and claimed that the Prophet had before his death nominated Ali as his successor and the *imam* (leader) of the Muslims, The Shiites themselves are divided into many sub - sects like those who believe only in the *imamat** of Ali, those who believe only in the *imamat* of two of his successors; those who believe in only seven *imams*; and those who believe in twelve *imams* in a direct line of succession from Ali. The latter are also called *ithna - ashari* (Twelvers) . They differ from the mainstream Muslims (the Sunnites) in their religious beliefs, rituals and institutions. The Twelvers deny the authenticity of the compilations of the traditions of the Prophet by Sunnite scholars and rely on the traditions of their own imams. In law they follow their own Jafari school.

Shraman (Sanskrit for common man) is the opposite of *Brahman;* the person belonging to the highest *varna* in the four-fold hierarchy of the *varnas* of the Vedic religion. A *shraman* is in practice a follower of the Budhist faith who believes in the essential brotherhood and equality of all human beings. It is Arabicized as *samani* (a Budhist).

Shuddhi (Sanskrit for purification) was one of the objectives of the All-India Hindu Mahasabha (formed in 1915). The Mahasabha was concerned with the decline of Hindu population and the growth of the population of minorities in India. It therefore adopted *shuddhi* (bringing back the members of the low castes who had converted to Islam and Christianity to the Vedic fold by purification i.e. reconversion) as a way for increasing the Hindu population.

Shudra (Sanskrit for menial castes) refers to the bottom category of low castes assigned menial occupations in the four-fold hierarchy of *varnas* (Brahmans, Kshatriyas, Vaish and Shudra). The castes and tribes outside this hierarchy were designated as *adi-shudra* (outcastes) and declared untouchable. The individuals and castes belonging to the three upper *varnas* are called *savarna* (people of *varna* or fair colour) The outcastes or untouchables are called *avarna* (people without the varna or fair colour). The *shudra* are also called the "middle Castes" occupying an intermediate position between the upper or *Savarna* castes and out castes (untouchable). Under the Constitution of India they are designated as the "other backward classes" (OBC's) a 27 per cent reserved quota in public services of the India and state governments.

Siachen is a Himalayan glacier, one the longest mountain glaciers in the world, situated at a height of 7470 meters from the sea level, in the Karakoram range north of Kashmir. It is about 76 kms long and its width varies from two to eight kms. The glacier is located on the northern tip of the Line of Control in Jammu and Kashmir between India and Pakistan demarcated in accordance with the Simla agreement* of 1972, which stretches from Samba in Jammu region to Point NJ 9842 in the Ladakh region. The 90 kms stretch from this point to the Chinese border could not be demarcated then. In 1984 Indian forces occupied occupied about two-third of the glacier claiming it as Indian territory. Pakistani forces then tried to dislodge the Indian forces and occupied about one-third of the glacier. In 2003 a ceasefire between the two forces was agreed to and talks were on during 2005 for withdrawal of the forces of both parties from Siachen.

Sikkim's Integration (1975). Sikkim was a tiny Himalayan principality situated between Tibet, Bhutan, Nepal and India.

Since the fourteenth century it was ruled by the Namgyal dynasty and its hereditary ruler carried the title of Chogyal (Maharaja) till 1975. Sikkim became a British Indian protectorate by virtue of the Treaty of Titalia signed between Sikkim and the Government of India in 1817. The same relationship was renewed and reaffirmed by the Indo-Sikkimese Treaty signed in 1950. Sikkim was later made an Associate State of the Indian Union by virtue of the Constitution (Thirty-Fifth) Amendment Act, 1974. In 1975, however, Sikkim was integrated with the Indian Union as its 22nd State by virtue of the Constitution (Thirty-Sixth) Amendment Act, 1975. The Chogyal was deposed and a responsible ministry was instituted under an India appointed Governor as the constitutional head.

Simla Conference (1945) refers to a conference of representatives of major Indian political parties and communities convened on 21-22 June 1945 by the Viceroy and Governor-General of India Lord wavell, to consider his plan for transfer of power in India and reconstitution of his Executive Council by including the representatives of different parties and communities as a first step. The conference ended in failure as the Indian National Congress and the All-India Muslim League differed on the number of seats to be shared between them. Thereafter the British government announced that fresh provincial elections in India will be held in 1946 and from the representatives so elected a Constituent Assembly will be formed to frame the future constitution of India.

Simla Deputation (1906) refers to a delegation composed of 30 representatives of the Muslim feudal class in British India led by Sir Sultan Muhammad Khan Aga Khan* which waited upon the Viceroy and Governor-General Lord Minto in Simla on 1 October 1906 and presented him an address containing the demands for separate representation of Muslims in the legislative councils and grant of weightage for them in the public services. The Viceroy promised to consider these demands sympathetically. It was believed that the address was drafted by the English principal of the Muhammedan Anglo-Oriental College (MAO College) W.A.J. Archbold, who acted as an intermediary between British authorities and the Muslim notables. As a follow up the All-India Muslim League was established on 30 December 1906 and the government introduced separate electorate for the Muslims under the Indian Councils Act, 1909.

Simla Pact (1972). See "India-Pakistan Agreement on Bilateral Relations".

Simon Commission (1929) refers to the Indian Statutory Commission under the chairmanship of Sir John Simon, appointed by the British government in terms of the Government of India Act, 1919, to examine the working of dyarchy* in India and to report on future constitutional reforms. The Commission was boycotted by both the Indian National Congress and the All-India Muslim League on the ground that Indians were not represented on it. The report of the Simon Commission was published on 27 May 1930. It recommended for abolition of dyarchy in the provinces, introduction of full responsibility in the provinces and retention of irresponsible executive at the centre. It also recognized the necessity of creating a federation but as a remote possibility. Till such time it recommended for the creation of an Advisory Council of Greater India to serve as a link between British India and the Princely States*. The Simon report became the basis of the deliberations of the Round Table Conference* (1929-32) and the Government of India Act, 1935.

Single European Market was created under the Single European Act signed by the member-states of the European Community (EC) in 1987. The SEA removed the non-tariff barriers and border controls that hindered the free movement of goods, commodities, services and labour and capital in the community. The single market came into being on 1 January 1993. The SEA also extended the competence of the EC into fields of technology, environment, regional policy, monetary policy and external policy

Sinkiang (in Chiness Xinjang pronounced ''Shin'jyang'' and meaning ''new frontier'') is officially the Xinjiang Yughur Autonomous Region of the People's Republic of China. It has an area of 1, 650,257 skms and a population of 18, 459, 511 (in 2000). Its capital is Ureumqi. It is the largest province of China in term of territory and rich in petroleum and other natural resources. The policy of Sinification pursued since 1949 has reduced the native Ughur Muslim population which belongs to the Turkic stock and speaks a Turkic dialect and constituted 74 per cent of the population in 1953, to parity with the Chinese settlers brought from the mainland. Xinjiang occupies the northwestern corner of China bordered by Mongolia to the northwest, central Asian republics of Kazakastan, Kyrghyzystan and Tajikistan to the northeast. Afghanistan and Pakistan-occupied Kashmir to the southwest, Tibet and India to the southeast, and the Chinese provinces of Qinghai and Gansu to the east. Sinkiang was an independent country in the past centuries. It was occupied by the Mancu dynasty and annexed as a Chinese province in 1881. It enjoyed a sort of an autonomous status from 1911 to 1949 as easter Turkestan. After the Communist Revolution the Chinese red army occupied it in 1949 and it was annexed to the PRC. It was given the status of an Autonomous Administrative Region in 1955.

Sir Creek is a 60-mile long strip of water lying between the Raan of Kutch* in India and the Sind Province of Pakistan, whose ownership became disputed between India and Pakistan because the Radcliff Commission* did not demarcate the inter-national border in this area in 1947. On side of the Creek is under Pakistan's control and the other under India's. Pakistan claims the ownership of all the 17 creeks lying along the Sind coast while India claims half of the area of the seventeenth creek (Sir Creek) as belonging to it. The survey teams of India and Pakistan completed joint survey of the area in January 2005 and were to submit a joint report which would form the basis of further talks between the experts of the two countries to resolve the dispute.

Social Contract is a political concept formulated by philosophers during the middle ages to defend the subjects against the despotism of absolute kings. The essence of this concept is that government is a result of contract arrived at between the rulers and the ruled.

Social Darwinism refers to the argument of Herbert Spencer and the like Darwinists in favour of natural selection and survival of the fittest in the social realm. They oppose all forms of state interference in the social and economic affairs of the society as it hinders free competition and the selection of the best and the fittest. Charles Darwin's theory of natural selection was expounded in his On *the* Origins of *Species* (1859).

Social Engineering is the opposite of spontaneous evolutionism. It refers to the moulding of social attitudes, behavioural patterns and developmental process according to a preconceived blueprint.

Socialism is a term first used by Jeremy Bentham as an opposite of individualism and capitalism. Socialistic ideas originated in reaction to the excesses of early *laissez faire* capitalism. Socialism is a diffuse concept. There is no consensus either on its ends or means. The idea of common good or social justice is the common denominator of all varieties of socialism. *Utopian* socialism is not a systematic body of ideas but refers to diverse formulations of piecemeal social reforms presented by Claude Henri Saint-Simon, Charles Fourier, and Robert Owen. Such concepts were dubbed as *utopia*n (imaginary) by Karl Marx to distinguish his brand of socialism which he characterized as *scientific* as he based it on a "science" of historical and dialectical materialism.* Marx's revolutionary socialism was opposed by *evolutionary* and democratic socialism of the Fabians. It is also called parliamentary socialism and social democracy. Marxian socialism gave birth to Marxism-Leninism*, Trotskyism and Maoism. Market socialism is the latest offshoot of Chinese communism which means competition between state enterprises along with a private sector of economy.

Socialist International was formed in 1951 in London as a consultative forum of 57 socialist parties of different countries. Its objective is the propagation of socialist ideals and promotion of cooperation and exchange among socialist parties and movements of the world. It holds its annual sessions in London. The origins of this body lie in the International Workingmen's Association (the First International) founded by Karl Marx and Frederick Engels in 1868 in London. It was dissolved in 1876. It was succeeded by the International Socialist Congress founded in 1889 in Paris (known as the Second International). At the outbreak of World War I it split into a nationalist and an internationalist factions and disintegrated. It was revived in 1919 as Labour and Socialist International; was renamed as the International Socialist Conference in 1946; and renamed again as the Socialist International in 1951.

Socialist Movement (India) started with the formation of the Congress Socialist Party in 1934 by Acharya Narendra Deva,· Ram Manohar Lohia and Jaya Prakash Narayan and other Congress socialists within the Indian National Congress. When the Congress banned dual membership for its members the socialists left the Congress and organized themselves as the socialist Party. It contested the first parliamentary elections held in 1952 and secured the third position. In 1951 another Congress socialist Acharya Jivat Ram Bhagwan Das Kirpalani (1888-1982) formed the Kisan Mazdoor Praja Party. The twin merged together on 12 September 1952 to form the Praja Socialist Party. A faction led by Ram Manohar Lohia left the PSP to form the Socialist Party. Both parties consted the second and third parliamentary elections separately and merged together in May 1964 to form the Samyukt (united) socialist Party (SSP). Simultaneously some socialists gathered to revive the old PSP. The SP and PSP merged together in 1971 and merged with the Bharatiya Lok Dal in 1974. A faction of the socialists led by Raj Narain retainer the title of the SSP and later merged with the Janata Party* on 1 May 1977. That was the end to the Indian socialist movement. A group of former Lohiaites led by Mulayam Singh Yadav which broke away from the Janata Dal* formed a Samajvadi (socialist) Party on 5 November 1992 in Lucknow.

Solicitor-General. Historically, the solicitor-general is in Britain the second law officer of the Crown after the attorney-general, responsible for defending the interests of the Crown before the courts of law. In practice, however, the solicitor-general acts more like a deputy and assistant of the attorney-general than an independent law officer. This status was formalized by an act of parliament passed in 1945. Under the Indian Constitution the Solicitor-General and the additional Solicitor-General have the same status and perform the same duties as the British solicitor-general.

South America is the second continent of the western hemisphere and fourth largest continent of the world. It includes twelve countries: Argentina, Bolivia, Brazil, Chile, Colombia, Ecauador,

South Asia includes the countries of India, Pakistan, Bangladesh, Nepal, Bhutan, Sri Lanka and Maldives.

South Asian Association for Regional Cooperation--SAARC is a regional cooperation forum grouping the regional states of India, Pakistan, Bangladesh, Sri Lanka, Bhutan and Maldives. The idea of South Asian regional cooperation was proposed by President Ziaur Rahman of Bangladesh in 1983. A summit of the heads of state/government of the seven countries of the region was held in 1983 in New Delhi which launched an informal forum by the name of "South Asian Regional Cooperation" (SARC). In 1985 the South Asian Summit held at Dhaka changed the name to the "South Asian Association for Regional Cooperation" (SAARC) and adopted a Charter governing the organisation and functioning of the association. In 1987 a permanent secretariat was established in Kathmandu headed by a Secretary General. The Association is headed by a Chairman elected by its annual summit conference. The annual conference of the foreign ministers is the policy-making organ and the Standing Committee of Secretaries is the executive organ.

South Asian Free Trade Area--SAFTA came into being on 1 January 2006 in pursuance of an agreement entered into by the member-states of the South Asian Association for Regional Cooperation* (SAARC) in their 12th Summit Conference held in Slamabad in 2004. The SAFTA will be built on the principle of progressive elimination of tariffs and other trade barriers and is expected to be fully operative by 2016.

South Pacific Nuclear Free Zone Treaty was adopted by the South Pacific Forum on 6 August 1985 and signed the same day by the representatives of the governments of Australia, Cook Islands, Fiji, Kiribati, New Zealand, Niu, Tuvalu and Western Samoa.

Southeast Asia covers the countries of Brunei, Kampuchea, Indonesia, Laos, Malaysia, the Philippines, Singapore, Thailand and Vietnam.

Southeast Asia Treaty Organization--SEATO was created under a Treaty of Collective Security in Southeast Asia signed on 8 April 1954 in Manila, Philippines, between Australia, France, New Zealand, Pakistan, Philippines, Thailand, the UK and the USA for the defence of South Vietnam and containment of China and communism in this region. After the secession of east Bengal Pakistan left the SEATO in 1972. After the reunification of Vietnam in 1975 the SEATO was formally dissolved in 1977.

Southern Common Market (Mercado Comun Del Sur--Mercosur) was created in 1991 in Montvideo, Uruguay, by Argentina, Brazil, Paraguay and Uruguay (with Bolivia, Chile and Peru as associate members) to create a free-trade zone and a customs union in South America to protect its producers with common external tariffs against non-member imports.

Sovereign (from Latin *superanus* or Italian *soverano* = supreme person) means a supreme ruler or king; In the UK it is the official title of the constitutional monarch (reigning king or queen) who presides over the Crown (executive state).

Sovereignty (supreme power or authority) is an attribute of the modern state. A state is sovereign in the sense that it is independent of any foreign authority and supreme over all individuals and groups within its territory enjoying a monopoly of legitimate use of force to compel obedience from its members. *Popular* sovereignty means that people are the ultimate source of political power and government. The people are the *political* sovereign in the sense that by exercising their right to vote in general elections they transfer their sovereign power to a representative assembly or legislative and executive bodies who govern on their behalf. *Legal* sovereignty means that there should be a person or body of persons or a set of legal rules which is the ultimate source of all legal authority in the state and which is competent to pronounce the final word on all legal controversies arising within its ambit. *Constitutional* sovereignty means that the constitution or the fundamental law is superior to the law made by authorities created by it and in case the acts of subordinate authorities are violative of the constitution they will be declared as null and void by the supreme court. *Parliamentary* sovereignty means that a parliament or legislative body is the sole source of all legal authority. It has absolute and unlimited power of enacting laws (both constitutional and ordinary) in an ordinary fashion. All laws enacted by a sovereign parliament are sovereign and binding until amended, or repealed by it. There is no authority parallel to a sovereign parliament to make law parallel to the law of parliament nor any authority above it (like a supreme court) to override or nullify its laws on any grounds whatever.

Specialized Agencies of the UN have been created for international regulation, coordination and cooperation in diverse functional fields of international life. They are:

1. Universal Postal Union--UPU; founded 1875; hqs. in Berne, Switzerland.
2. International Labour Organization--ILO; founded in 1919; hqs. in Geneva, Switzerland.
3. International Monetary Fund---IMF; founded in 1945; hqs. in Washington, D.C.
4. International Bank for Reconstruction and Development-IBRD; founded in 1945; hqs. in Washington, D.C.
5. Food and Agricultural Organization FAO; founded in 1945; hqs. Rome, Italy.
6. United Nations Educational, Scientific and Cultural Organization; founded in 1946; hqs. in Paris, France.
7. International Civil Aviation Organization ICAO; founded in 1947; hqs. in Montreal, Canada.
8. International Telecommunications Union--ITU; founded in 1947; hqs. in Geneva, Switzerland.
9. World Health Organization--- WHO; founded in 1948; Hqs. in Geneva, Switzerland.
10. World Metereological Organization-- WMO; founded in 1950; hqs. in Geneva, Switzerland.
11. International Finance Corporation-- IFC; founded in 1956; hqs. in Washington, D.C.
12. International Atomic Energy Agency-- IAEA; founded in 1957; hqs. in Vienna, Austria.
13. International Maritime Organization--- IMO; founded in 1959; hqs. in London.
14. International Development Association--IDA; founded in 1960; hqs. in Washington, D.C.
15. United Nations Industrial Development Organization--UNIDO; founded in 1967; hqs. in Vienna, Austria.
16. World intellectual Property Organization--WIPO; founded in 1967; hqs. in Geneva, Switzerland.

17. International Fund for Agricultural Development--IFAD; founded in 1977; hqs. in Rome, Italy.

18. Multilateral Investment Guarantee Agency--MIGA; founded in 1988; hqs. in Washington, D.C.

Span of Control is a common-sense principle of administration meaning that a manager can supervise a limited number of subordinates effectively. If the span of control is stretched too much the result would be lack of control.

Spanish Civil War (1936) was started by some Spanish military officers having fascist tendencies under the leadership of General Francisco Franco when they staged a revolt against the duly elected democratic government in 1936. The civil war ended in 1939 with the triumph of the fascists and Franco became the dictator of Spain.

Special Courts Act, 1979 (India) was enacted by the Janata Party government to empower the Government of India to constitute special courts for speedy trials of persons holding high public offices for committing excesses against the people during emergency rule of indira Gandhi from 25 June 1975 till the withdrawal of the Proclamation of Emergency issued under Clause (l) of Article 352 of the Constitution of India. The Act was passed in the light of the reports of the Commission of Inquiry headed by Justice J.C. Shah. The Act was repealed by the Indira regime in 1982.

Special Drawing Rights SDR's are in the nature of an international monetary reserve created by the International monetary Fund (IMF) in 1970 as a substitute for gold and hard currencies to facilitate international payments. The SDR's augment international liquidity by supplementing hard currencies. The SDR's are allotted to each member's account in proportion to it's quota in the Fund which proportion is determined in proportion to its gross national product (GDP) and the foreign exchange reserves. The value of an SDR is determined in relation to a basket of hard currencies namely the US dollar, the British pound, the Euro, the yen and the Russian rouble. In 2004 the value of one SDR was a little more than US-$ 1.48. The SDR's are freely accepted in settlement of international accounts. Every member of the IMF is given one vote for each 100,000 SDR's held by it plus its normal 250 votes.

Special Economic Zones-- SEZ (India) were established during the decade of 1990's as special economic processing and export zones on the Chinese model to attract foreign capital investment and technologies. Special incentives in the form of physical infrastructure, ancillary facilities and tax incentives are provided to boost India's exports and augment its foreign-exchange earnings.

Spoils System or patronage is the opposite of the merit system of recruitment to public service posts. Appointments were made either on the basis of birth in an aristocratic family or on payment of graft. Recruitment on the basis of merit as determined through competitive examinations open to all was first introduced by Napoleon I in France and from there it was adopted in Britain, USA and other democratic countries.

Spratly Islands are located in the south China Sea; their ownership has been claimed wholly or in part by People's Republic of China, Taiwan and the ASEAN members Brunei, Malaysia, the Philippines and Vietnam.

Stagflation is the combination of stagnation (recessio) and inflation in an economy leading to worsening of social and economic conditions.

Stalinism refers to the particular contribution made by Josef Stalin, the successor of Lenin as the dictator of the USSR, to communist theory and practice. Stalin proclaimed the doctrine of "socialism-in-one-country" (against Trotsky's theory of world revolution); forced collectivization of agriculture; and reliance on coercion and terror to exact obedience at home. In foreign policy he believed in the capitalist encirclement of the USSR, the impossibility of compromise between the compacts of socialism and capitalism; the inevitability of war between the two camps; and hence the compulsion of the USSR to build its military strength and aid anti-imperialist revolutionary movements abroad,

Standstill Agreements (1947). A standstill agreement is signed between a creditor and a debtor country allowing the debtor some time to repay the debt. Similarly, in a conflict situation the disputants may sign a standstill agreement, that is not to do anything till a final settlement is made. The Indian Independence Act, 1947, which provided for transfer of power to two dominions of India and Pakistan on 15 August 947 and declared the lapse of British paramountcy over the Princely States* from that date, gave the rulers of these states the option of acceding either to the dominion of India or the dominion of Pakistan, whichever was contiguous to them, or remain independent. Thereafter some rulers signed standstill agreements with their contiguous dominion to have some time before making a final decision. A standstill agreement continues the normal trade and communications links between the two signatories.

Stare Decisis (Latin for "let the decision stand") is a principle of law requires that a court of law is bound to uphold the past interpretations of the constitution, laws and rules made by the higher courts as well as by itself. Adherence to precedents, unless there is a compelling reason not to do so, ensures uniformity of rulings and facilities judicial decision-making.

State (from Italian *stato* and English *estate* = of high status) is the modem form of political community distinguished from all other earlier forms of political community namely *civitas,* regnum, emirate, kingdom and empire. A modern state or nation-state is a juridical community living in a defined territory and having an organized government which has a monopoly of the use of force to compel obedience from its members and which is independent of foreign control.

State System or international state-system or the community of states came into existence first in Europe under the Treaty of Westphalia (1648) and then spread throughout the world.

The treaty recognized the principles of national independence, territorial integrity and sovereign equality of the new political units in Europe that came into being after the disintegration of the holy Roman empire. Relations among the nation-states are regulated by the norms of international law.

Stateless Persons are persons who are not citizens of any country for the time-being. The legal status of such persons residing in the territory of a state is uncertain and anamolous as they are deprived of the rights and privileges of citizenship of the country of their domicile. Their status is sought to be regulated by two international conventions: the Convention Relating to the Status of Stateless Persons (1954) and the Convention on Reduction of Statelessness (1961).

States Reorganization Act, 1956 (India) reorganized the territory of India into linguistically homogeneous states. The process had started with the Indian National Congress reorganizing its provincial units on a linguistic basis in 1936 and promised to form linguistic provinces in the future to gain the political support of the regional linguistic communities. In 1949 in response to the demands for the fulfilment of that promise the Government of India appointed a Linguistic Provinces Commission which ruled out any linguistic reorganization of the provinces in the interest of national unity. However, the telegu-speaking people started an agitation for the creation of a Telegu-speaking province of Andhra Pradesh. When their agitation turned violent and an ascetic Potto Sriramulu immolated himself by sprinkling kerosene on his body Mr. Nehru promised in April 1953 to appoint a commission to look into the matter and on 1 October 1953 announced the government's decision to create the state of Andhra Pradesh by the merger of Telegu-speaking areas of Hyderabad State and Madras province. The Government of India appointed a States Reorganization Commission on 29 December 1953. The SRC reported in October 1955; and the government passed the States Reorganization Act in 1956 to give effect to the recommendations of the SRC. The main features of the Act were: that it abolished the distinctions between Parts A, B, and C states under the Constitution of India; it abolished the title of *Rajpramukh;* it effected territorial changes and defined the boundaries of the reorganized states mainly on a linguistic basis; provided for the setting up of five Zonal Councils* for inter-state coordination; and provided for safeguards for linguistic minorities left in the territory of the reorganized states.

States Reorganization Commission (India) was appointed by the Government of India on 29 December 1953 with Justice Fazl Ali as chairman and H.N. Kunzuru and K.M. Panikkar as members. The Commission was asked to make their recommendations in the light of certain guiding principles included it its terms of reference: preservation of the national unity and security of India; the reorganized units should be linguistically and culturally homogeneous; economic and administrative viability of the units should be taken into consideration; and reorganized units should be able to take part in the successful implementation of the national development plans. The SRC recommended for the reorganization of the existing Parts A, B, and C States into "States" and "union Territories'*. The report of the SRC was released on 10 October 1955 for eliciting public opinion and countrywide discussion. The Government of India finalized its decisions on 16 January 1956. The states reorganization plan received legislative sanction through a set of three Acts--the States Reorganization Act, 1956; Bihar and Bengal (Transfer of Territories) Act, 1956; and the Constitution (seventh Amendment) Act, 1956. The reorganized states came into being on 1 November 1956. As a result of this reorganization the Indian Union then consisted of 14 states and six union territories.* No territorial change was effected in case of Assam, Orissa, Uttar Pradesh, and Jammu and Kashmir. Tranvancore-Cochin State was renamed as Kerala. The Hyderabad State was entirely merged with Andhra Pradesh.

Statism refers both to a policy of building up a national state as well as a policy of national development through state action.

Status Quo (Latin for the existing state) refers to an existing territorial order or distribution of power at a given time. A policy of preservation of the status quo is called "status quoism" or conservatism. Its opposite is called "revisionism", i.e. a policy of seeking revision of the status quo when it is unfair to some party.

Statute is a bill which having passed the two houses of British Parliament and receiving royal assent is enacted as an Act of Parliament. *Statute law,* as distinguished from *common law* or *customary law* is the law duly enacted by parliament. In British law books, all acts passed by Parliament in a particular session are collectively designated as "statute".

Statute of Westminster (1931) was passed by British Parliament in 1931 granting full internal and external sovereignty to the Dominions of the British Empire. The Statute gave legal effect to the resolutions adopted by the Imperial Conferences of 1929 and 1930. Accordingly, the dominions were given full legislative autonomy including the power to repeal acts of British Parliament concerning them; to make laws having extraterritorial operation; and no future act of British Parliament was to apply to them except at their express request.

Statutory Instruments refer to rules and regulations made by the executive departments under rule-making power delegated to the executive by a parliamentary statute. All such instruments are required to be laid before Parliament for a pacified period of time and unless rejected by Parliament have the same effect as the law of Parliament.

Strategic Arms Reduction Treaty--START (1991) was signed between the USA and the former USSR for reduction of their nuclear weapons and came into force in 1994.

Strategic Defence Initiative (SDI), christened as the "Star Wars", was conceived as a space-based anti-missile defence system during the 1980's by the Administration of President Ronald Reagan. As the nuclear weapons were depoliticized in the wake of the end of the cold war, the SDI receded into the background. However, the idea was revived by the Administration of President George Bush I and put in place by the Administration of President George Bush II as the National Missile Defence System (NMDS), christened as the "son of the Star Wars. Concurrently the USA abrogated the 1972 ABM Treaty in 2001.

Strategic Offensive Reduction Treaty--SORT (2002) was the latest arms reduction measure signed between the USA and Russia under which the parties agreed to reduce the number of their respective nuclear warheads from 6,000-7,000 to 1,700-2,200 by December 2012.

Strategy and Tactics. Strategy refers to long-term goals and objectives or the general plan of war while tactics refer to short-term measures to achieve them or temporary manoeuvres.

Structural Adjustment Programmes (SAP's) refer to a variety of conditions imposed by the International Monetary Fund (IMF) upon states suffering from the balance-of-payments difficulties which must be accepted before the IMF extends its facilities to them to overcome their difficulties. SAP's are conservative measures prescribed for restoring economic health and financial stability in an aided country. The examples are; cutting public expenditure; adopting austerity, measures, increasing public taxation, controlling inflation and devaluating the national currency to boost exports.

Subpoena (Latin for evidence) is a written official order summoning a person to appear before a court of law to give evidence. Hence *subpoenaing* and *subpoenaed.*

Subsidy (from Latin *subsidium* = aid/assistance) was originally aids granted by an act of parliament upon need and necessity. Subsidies of all forms and descriptions may be permanent or temporary. Subsidies are also granted to consumers to lessen their burden and to trade, industry and agriculture to make their goods competitive in international market.

Subversion refers to all types of disruptive activity meant to create disturbance and disorder in a country. The distinguishing feature of subversion is that it is planned, organized, supported or guided from abroad by a hostile power or organization which employs the disaffected or hostile persons within a society for subversive activity to secure it own purposes).

Suez Canal extends from Port Said on the Mediterranean Sea to the Port of Tawfiq in the Gulf of Suez. The 160 km long canal connects the Mediterranean to the Gulf of the Red Sea and the Indian Ocean It was built in 1888 by an Anglo-French Company which owned and operated it till its nationalization by the Egyptian government in 1956 which led to joint invasion by British, French and Israeli forces and occupation of the Canal zone in 1956. The invaders had to withdraw under American pressure and the canal was placed under Egyptian sovereignty and management on payment of compensation to the Anglo-French Company, The canal remained closed from 1967 till 1979 in consequence of Israeli occupation of the Sinai Peninsula, the Golan Heights and the West Bank of Jordan since 6 June 1967 Its legal status is governed by the Constantinople Convention of 1888 which guarantees freedom of passage to all ships whether commercial or military of all nations without any discrimination. The Convention declared that ''No right of war, act of hostility or act having for its purpose to interfere with the free navigation of the Canal, shall be committed in the Canal and its ports of access''.

Sunnites (from Arabic *sunnah* = tradition) are *ahl - i - sunnah* i.e. the mainstream Muslims who follow the teachings of the Holy Quran and the traditions of the Prophet Muhammed and the way of his four rightly - guded successors (Abu Bakr, Umar, Usman and Ali) .. The Sunnites are further divided into *muqallids,* the followers of one of the principal a schools of Islamic Jurisprudence (Maliki, Sha'fe'i, Hanbali, and Hanafi) and *ghair - muqallids* (non - followers), who deny the necessity of following any one of the established schools of law and instead take their guidance directly from the Quran and the teachings of the Prophet.

Super Power was a term coined to designate the post-World War II status of the USA and USSR. A superpower is a global or world power possessing preponderant military power which it can deploy at any point of the globe, with the demise of the USSR in 1991 the USA remains the sole world power.

Surplus Value In Marxist economics the surplus value (profit) is created by the wage-worker's labour spent over and above the value of his labour power. This surplus value rightfully belongs to the workers but is appropriated by the capitalist. If the capitalist wants profit the profit is generated by the exploitation of the workers.

Suzerainty (from French *suzerain* = overlord). The lines between suzerainty, sovereignty and paramountcy are blurred. A suzerain or paramount state, however, is a sovereign state which exercises control over the foreign affairs of a dependent, or vassal or tributary state. A state accepting the suzerainty or paramountcy of another state may be allowed internal self-government but cannot act independently in external matters. The examples are China's suzerainty over and Xinjiang until 1949 and of British India over Bhutan, Nepal and Sikkim until 1947.

Swaraj (Sanskrit for self-rule) was first used by M.K. Gandhi in his pamphelet *Hind Swaraj* (1908); was adopted as a goal of the Indian National Congress in 1920; in 1928 swaraj was interpreted as the attainment of the dominion status* for India within the British Empire; in 1929 swaraj was spelled as *puma swaraj* (complete independence of the British Empire).

Swaraj Party. Following the sudden suspension of the Non-Cooperation Movement by M.K. Gandhi in February 1922

Congress leaders were released from jail, some of them were disappointed by the collapse of the non-cooperation movement and became wary of Gandhian direct action. They favoured council-entry to fight *swaraj* from within. With this aim the prominent liberal leaders C.R. Das (1870-1925) and Motilal Nehru (1861-1931) parted company with the Congress and founded the Swaraj Party to contest council elections. In the elections held that year the Swaraj Party secured 42 of the 101 elective seats in the Imperial Legislative Council, After the All-India Congress Committee session held in June in Ahmedabad Gandhi relinquished his control over the Congress in favour of leaders who advocated council entry. The Swaraj Party faded from the political scene after the death of Das in 1925.

Swastika is hooked- cross like figure used by ancient Aryans as a symbol of power and prosperity. It was used by the German Nazi Party and State as their official embelem.

Swatantara Party was formed by Chakravarty Rajagopalachari (1879-1972) on 4 June 1959 in Madras as a political alternative to the ruling Indian National Congress. It was opposed to Congress' "socialistic pattern of society", economic planning and "quota-permit raj". It advocated a free market economy, private enterprise and a *laissez faire* state. Perceived as a party of the Indian capitalist class it never became a major political force. In the election to the Indian Lok Sabha held in 1971 the party secured only one seat. It merged itself with the Bharatiya Lok Dal* (BLD) in 1974.

Sykes-Picot Agreement (1916) was a secret agreement signed between Sir Mark Sykes on behalf of the British government and Georges Picot on behalf of the French government for dismemberment of the Ottoman Empire after World War I and division of its terrotories between Britain ana France with a minor share to be given to Russia.

Syndicalism (from French *syndicate* = trade union) was an idealistic form of socialism propounded by Georges Sorel in his

Reflections on Violence (1906). Revolutionary syndicalism called for forcible take over of the state apparatus and then management of production, distribution and consumption through a hierarchy of trade unions established at the national and local levels. The doctrine influenced the French General Confederation Labour but lost its appeal because of the improvement of workers' conditions during the early part of the twentieth century.

T

Tabula Rasa (clean slate) theory of state recognition meant that a new state emerging on the political scene of the world starts its career on a clean slate. It, therefore, bears no responsibility for the international commitments and obligations of its predecessors. This theory was applied by the Bolshevik regime in Russia which came to power in 1917. The theory has no standing in international law.

Taiwan Problem. Taiwan is officially the Republic of China with its capital at Taibeh. It is an island with an area of 35,961 sqms located between the East and South China Sea in the Pacific Ocean. It is separated from the southern coast of mainland China by 145 kms wide Strait of Taiwan. Its territory is 35,96 sqms and Its Population in 1995 was 2,15,01,000 persons. The Portugese named it as Ilha Formosa (beautiful island). But Formosa became obsolete and Taiwan

Taiwan was inhabited by the Chinese people in the seventh century AD and ceded by the Chinese Emperor to Japan under a treaty signed in 1895, after the Chinese defeat in the first Sino-Japanese War. After World War II Taiwan was restored to China. In the civil war from 1946 to 1949 between the forces of the Republic of China (ruled by the Kuomintang or the nationalist party) and the guerilla forces of the Chinese Communist Party the nationalist forces were defeated and the People's Republic of China was proclaimed on 1 October 1949 in Beijing. The remnants of the Kumintang regime headed by General Chiang Kai Shek took refuge on the island of Taiwan and operated from there as the Republic of China. The USA and other western powers refused to recognize the PRC as legitimate representative of the Chinese people and continued to recognize the Taiwan regime as the true government of China. In 1954 the US Congress passed the Formosa Resolution authorizing the President to employ the armed forces of the US as he deemed necessary to defend Taiwan and other offshore islands. When the PRC was admitted to the United Nations in 1971 Taiwan was expelled from that body. Most of the western powers withdrew their recognition of Taiwan. In 1980 it was also expelled from the International Monetary Fund and the World Bank. During his 1972 visit to Beijing President Richard M. Nixon acknowledged that Taiwan was a part of China. In 1978 the US severed its formal ties with Taiwan and established diplomatic relations with the PRC on 1 January 1979. At the same time the US Congress passed the Taiwan Relations Act authorizing continued social and economic relations. with Taiwan. The US government also undertook to supply defensive weapons to Taiwan and declared its opposition to any forcible occupation of Taiwan by the PRC. On the other hand, the National People's Congress (parliament) of the PRC passed an anti-secession law on 14 March 2005 authorizing the Chinese government to use force in the event of Taiwan declaring its independence.

Taiwan Strait is a 145 kms wide strech of water separating the island of Taiwan from the mainland China.

Taliban (plural of Arabic *talib* = religious student) were the young and middle-aged Afghan graduates of religious seminaries who undertook a mission of delivering their country from the ravages of a civil war between two rival Afghan formations that started in the wake of the withdrawal of Soviet forces from Afghanistan in 1988. The Taliban defeated both the formations and captured the capital city of Kabul in 1995. They restored the authority of the central government over the whole of Afghanistan and maintained peace and order.

However, misfortune befell them when the Americans, blaming their former ally Osama Bin Laden, who was residing in Afghanistan, for masterminding the attacks on American targets on 11 September 2001 and asked the Taliban to surrender him to Americans. The Taliban refused and faced American sanctions. Then in the face of American invasion they preferred to surrender their power rather than to break their code of honour by surrendering their honoured guest to the Americans. (*Talibans* is incorrect).

Tamil Insurgency. In the Republic of Sri Lanka the Sinhala-speaking Budhists constitute about 77 per cent of the population in 18 out of 25 districts which are also inhabited by Muslim and Christian minorities. The Tamil-speaking Hindus constitute a dominant majority in the seven districts of the northern and eastern provinces of Sri Lanka. Tamil insurgency started in 1976 with the formation of the Tamil United Liberation Front (TULF) which stood for the formation of a separate sovereign Tamil Elam (state) in the Tamil-dominated areas. The movement war later joined by the Tamil Elam Liberation organization (TELO) and the formidable Liberation Tigers of the Tamil Elam (LTTE). An Indo-Sri Lanka peace plan signed in 1987 provided for grant of provincial autonomy to Tamil-dominated areas and disarming of the Tamil guerillas under the supervision of an Indian peacekeeping force. The Tamil fighters rejected this plan and guerilla activity was resumed soon after the withdrawal of the Indian peacekeeping force in 1989. On 22 February 2002 the LTTE and the Sri Lankan government signed a Norwlgian-brokered agreement to cease fire and enter into negotiations for an amicable settlement. The cease-fire was in force till the end of 2005 with sporadic Incidence of violence, with no signs of negotiations between the parties in sight.

Tariffs are taxes and duties levied on imports and exports; also called customs duties. Tariffs may be levied to raise revenue or to protect domestic industry against foreign competition, or retaliatory (which are called anti-dumping duties} or preferential (to advantage to friendly countries).

Tashkent Declaration (1966) was signed between the Indian prime minister Lal Bahadur Shastri and Pakistan's president Field Marshall Muhammad Ayub Khan on 10 January 1966 in Tashkent at the end of their conference arranged by the Soviet premier Alexei Kosygin. The Declaration ended the deadlock created by the India-Pakistan war fought over Jammu and Kashmir in 1965 by restoring the *status quo ante bellum* and withdrawal of the armed forces of the two countries from across the cease-fire line of 1948.

Taylorism, after Frederick W. Taylor, the father of classical American management, refers to a mechanistic and authoritarian approach to management with a view to extract maximum benefit from human labour. Taylorism was replaced by the human relations approach.

Technocracy means the rule by technical experts and specialists, in contrast to bureaucracy or rule by general administrators. Technocracy is oriented towards technological efficiency and goal-achievement.

Telegu Desam Party is a regional political party confined to the State of Andhra Pradesh. It was founded on 29 March 1982 in Hyderabad by N.T. Rama Rao (1923-1996). The party ruled the State of Andhra Pradesh from 1983 till 2004 when it was ousted by the Indian National Congress.

Telengana Problem. Telengana region refers to nine Telegu- speaking districts of the former Hyderabad State which was merged in 1953 with the *Rayalseema,* the Telegu-speaking coastal region of the erstwhile Province of Madras to form Andhra Pradesh. The peasants of Telengana had revolted under the leadership of the communist against grain tax, forced labour and eviction from their lands. The uprising continued till 1952 when it was crushed by the police forces. Ever since 1953 there has been a marked imbalance between the relatively rich and developed *Rayalseema* region and the poor underdeveloped Telengana region. The people from the Telengana region have demanded the creation of a separate Telengana State from time to time. The latest attempt was the formation of the Telengana Rashtra Samiti (Telengana National Committee) in 2003 which supported the Indian National Congress in the national and state elections held in 2004 in lieu of a promise for the creation of a Separate Telengana State.

Telengana Rashtra Samiti--TRS (Telengana National Committee) in 2003 with the avowed purpose of forming a Separate Telengana State out of the present Andhra Pradesh. In the national elections held in 2004 the party won four seats in the Lok Sabha.

Tenth Schedule of the Indian Constitution was originally inserted by a constitutional amendment of 1974 to incorporate the terms and conditions of association of Sikkim (the erstwhile Himalayan protectorate of India) with the Indian Union as an "associate state". It was, however, repealed by the Constitution (36 Amendment) Act, 1975 which provided for outright annexation of Sikkim with the Indian Union. In 1989 the anti-defection legislation of the Rajiv Gandhi regime was housed in the Tenth Schedule. See "Anti-Defection Law".

Territorial Army (India) was first constituted in India under the Territorial Force Act, 1920, on the pattern of the British yeomanry or territorials which are paramilitary units. After independence the Territorial Army Act, 1948 was enacted in supersession of the 1920 Act to empower the Government of India to constitute such a force and manage its recruitment, training and deployment in accordance with rules made under the Act. The Territorial Army was raised in October 1949 to impart military training to the youth in their spare time. The force is deployed during emergencies to maintain public peace and security.

Territorial Waters. According to the UN Convention on the Law of Sea (UNCLOS), which codifies and supplements the customary rules of international law, every littoral (coastal) state has a right to establish the breadth of its territorial sea up to a limit not exceeding twelve nautical miles as measured from the baseline drawn in accordance with the UNCLOS. The contiguous zone of a littoral state extends to a further twelve nautical miles. The continental shelf of a littoral state extends up to 350 nutical miles offshore. In addition, the littoral states are give rights in their exclusive economic zone extending over 200 nautical miles. The littoral states exercise sovereign jurisdiction over their territorial waters and the exclusive economic zones.

Terrorism. Current definitions of terrorism ignore its underlying causes, its motives and its ends and concentrate rather on its outward manifestations. Terrorism may be defined as wanton and indiscriminate use or threatened use of violence to achieve political or ideological objectives'' Characteristic features of terrorism are: spreading of terror and fear among the people ruthlessness; and utter disregard to humanistic values. Some of terroristic methods hitherto employed are; wanton shootings, assassinations, bombings, massacres, hijackings and hostage-taking. For a terrorist the end justifies the means. The terrorists are disgruntled and desperate people not organized as a regular force who are pitted against an stated enemy greater than them in numbers, resources and reach. Not able to engage the enemy face to face they terrorise him by wanton destruction of life and property. Strategies and policies of combating terrorism abound but counterterrorism too ignores the underlying causes and relies on brute force to prevent and punish the terrorists. The recent phenomenon of international terrorism too emanates from ideological causes and needs to be combated ideologically, number of measures have been adopted to strengthen international cooperation to eliminate the menace of terrorism, e.g., the Declaration on Measures to Eliminate International Terrorism adopted by the UN

General Assembly on 9 December 1994; the declaration against international terrorism adopted by the UN Security Council on 12 November 2001 which entrusted the task of exploring ways to combat, terrorism; and a resolution adopted by the UN General Assembly on 12 December 2001 reiterating the measures to be adopted by the international community to eliminate terrorism in all its forms and manifestations.

Terrorist Affected Areas (Special Courts) Act, 1984 was enacted on 31 August 1984 to provide for constitution of special courts for speedy trial of cases in certain terrorist affected areas (i.e. Panjab, Haryana and the Union Territory of Chandigarh). The Act was withdrawn on 23 July 1985.

Terrorist and Disruptive Activities (Prevention) Act. 1985 (TADA) was an extraordinary measure enacted for a period of two years to deal with insurgency in Panjab and terroristic and disruptive activities in other parts of the country. It was extended for two-yearly terms from time to time till 1995 when it was replaced by the Prevention of Terrorism Act (POTA) which was repealed in 2004 and replaced by the Unlawful Activities (Prevetion) Act 2004.

The Indian Union. After the creation of Pakistan and departure of the All-India Muslim League from India the leader of the provincial branch of the Muslim League, Muhammad Ismail renamed the branch as the Indian Union Muslim League with the objectives of promoting loyalty among Indian Muslims towards the Indian Union and to work for the betterment of the Muslim community. Another branch was established in the State of Travancore-Cochin (renamed as Kerala in 1956) The IUML is recognized as a regional political party in these states and takes part in national, state, and local elections. The League is non-existent in north Indian states as it had no social base there after the departure of the Muslim landlord class en *masse* to Pakistan.

Theocracy (theo=god+cracy=rule) means government by the clergy or a religious establishment. In this system sovereignty belongs to God Almighty which is exercised in the name of God by the self-appointed religious authorities over all spiritual and temporal affairs.

Third World was first used by Frantz Fanon in his *The Wretched of the World* (1960) for the poor and underdeveloped countries. The *first world* referred to the developed capitalist countries of North America. Western Europe and Japan; the *second world* to the developed communist countries of the Soviet bloc; and the *third world* to the poor and underdeveloped countries of Asia, Africa and Latin America. In the post cold-war era the first and second worlds are designated as the *north* (symbol of prosperity) and the underdeveloped world is the *south* (symbol of poverty).

Thirty Years' War (1618-48) was a general war in Europe fought between the German princes, Britain, France, Sweden and Denmark on one side and the Holy Roman Emire* as represented by the Hapsburg in Austria, Italy, the Netherlands and Spain on the other. The war ended with the signing of the Treaty of Westphalia* in 1648 which laid the foundation of the modern state system in Europe.

Three-Language Formula (India) was evolved in 1956 by the Central Advisory Board on Education, approved by the Chief Ministers' Conference in 1961, and endorsed by the National Integration Council in 1962. To promote national integration and bring about emotional unity between the people of north and south in India it was agreed that at the secondary level of education in the non-Hindi-speaking states, in addition to the regional language and English, Hindi shall be taught as the third language. Reciprocally, in the Hindi-speaking states, in addition to Hindi and English, any one of the regional languages listed in the Eighth Schedule of the Indian Constitution shall be taught as the third language. The northern states in due course taught Sanskrit as the third language. Following the failure of this formula the Education Commission (1964-66) recommended a graduated three-language formula comprising (1) mother-tongue or the regional language; (2) Hindi or English; and (3) a modern Indian language or a foreign language different from (1) or (2) which is not being used as a medium of instruction. This time also northern states replaced modern Indian languages by Sanskrit.

Tiananmen Square Massacre (1989). The Tiananmen Square is located in the heart of Beijing, People's Republic of China. As a consequence of the policy of economic liberalization and opening up followed by the post-Mao reformist regime in China, the Chinese students started a pro-democracy movement in 1989 demanding political liberalization and freely elected government. The movement was suppressed by force and the students sitting in the Square were massacred.

Tibet Problem. Xizang in Chinese is an Himalayan state with an area of 1, 221.6 sqms and a population of 26,16, 329 (2000) with its capital at Lhasa. Tibet was an authonomous country under suzerainty of the Chinese emperors during the nineteenth century. During the twentieth century it enjoyed self-rule under Dalai Lama till 1950 when the Chinese Red Army occupied it. In 1954 China signed the so-called *panch sheel* agreement over Tibet with India by India voluntarily surrendered to China its extraterritorial rights in Tibet inherited from the British government. The Tibetans revolted against Chinese occupation in 1958 which was suppressed by China and Dalai Lama fled Tibet to Indian where he established a Tibetan government-in-exile at Dharamshala, Himachal Pradesh. Tibet was made an Autonomous Administrative region of China in 1955.

Tokyo Tribunal refers to the International Military Tribunal set up in accordance with the 1945 Potsdam Declaration and the decision of 1945 Moscow conference of the USA, USSR and the UK, to try 28 war criminals of the army of the fascist regime in Japan. The trials were held between May 1946 and November 1948.77 of the war criminals were sentenced to death and the rest to varying terms of imprisonment.

Tort (from Latin *tortum* = wrong) is a wrongful act or infringement of the right of another party in a business transaction (other than breaches of contracts) which may lead to legal action for payment of damages or compensation. Such matters are dealt with by the law of contracts and the law of torts.

Tory was used to describe the members of the royalist party in England during the eighteenth century. The Tory Party changed its name to Conservative Party during the mid-nineteenth century and its members continued to be called Tories. However in general usage the term tory is used for an ultraconservative person opposed to social change.

Totalitarianism was defined by Benito Mussolini in these words: "Everything for the state; nothing outside the state; nothing against the state". Totalitarian ideologies, movements or regimes stand for total subordination of the individual to the collective and total control of all aspects of social life in accordance with the totalitarian creed. Examples are Nazism, Fascism and Communism. Totalitarianism is a system of rule that obliterates the distinction between private and public domains. All preexisting voluntary associations and groups are banned and replaced by state-censored public organizations. The individuals are compelled to join these organizations and submit themselves to the control of the regime.

Trade Union Congress (UK) is the apex body of British trade unions that was founded in 1868 to protect the interests of the workers. Along with the Confederation of British Industry (CBI) it plays an important role in the formation of economic and labour policies of the British government.

Trade-Related Intellectual Property Rights--TRIPS (WTO). The Agreement on Trade-Related Aspects of Intellectual Property Rights (TRIPS) was concluded by the member-states of the GATT in 1995. The agreement adopts uniform standards based on the Paris and Berne Copyright Conventions sponsored by the World Intellectual Property Organization (WIPO). The signatories are now legally bound to protect the intellectual property rights (copyrights, patents, etc.) within their national jurisdiction and punish the violators through their judicial machinery. The Council for Trade-Related Intellectual Property Rights is empowered to monitor the compliance by the signatories with the provisions of the Paris and Berne Conventions.

Trade-Related Investment Measures -- TRIMS. The Agreement on Trade-Related Investment Measures was prepared by a working group appointed by the Singapore Ministerial Conference of the world Trade Organization (WTO) in 1996 and signed at the Doha Ministerial Conference held in 2001. It is one of the multilateral agreements on trade in goods that prohibits trade-related investment measures, such as local content requirements that are inconsistent with the basic provisions of the GATT 1994.

Traditional Society is the opposite of modern society. Traditional societies are mainly agrarian; hierarchical in structure; dominated by ascrptive values and supernatural beliefs; and marked by primordial loyalties.

Transitional Society. is a society which is in a transition between tradition and modernity. It is neither fully traditional for fully modern.

Treason refers to all acts of disloyalty towards one's own country; waging war against it; joining the enemies of the country; or giving enemies aid and support against one's own country. Nobody in the democratic states can be held guilty of treason without due process of law.

Treasury and Exchequer (UK). The Treasury is that department of the UK government that controls the management, collection and expenditure of the public revenue. The Exchequer is responsible to see to it that no money is paid out of the Treasury without the authority of Parliament. The Treasury is headed by the First Lord of the Treasury. The Exchequer is headed by the Chancellor of the Exchequer.

Treaty (from French *traite* = agreement). A treaty is something drawn up or agreed upon by two or more parties. They are called the contracting parties. In international law a treaty is an agreement signed between two or more or their authorized agents Treaties are known by a variety of names like conventions, agreements, pacts, compacts, general acts, charters, statutes, declarations and covenants. The UN Charter prohibits conclusion of secret treaties. Copies of all treaties concluded between member-states are required to be deposited with the UN Secretariat

Treaty of Lausanne (1923) was a peace treaty signed between Turkey, Britain, France, Italy, Japan, Greece, Bulgaria and Yugoslavia on 24 July 1923 in Lausanne, Switzerland, It superseded the Treaty of Severes, 1919, which was imposed upon Turkey after her defeat in World War I by the Allied Powers providing for the division of its territory among the victors. The Treaty of Lausanne recognized Turkey's sovereignty over Istambul, Thrace and Anatolia. The straits of Bosporus and Dardanelles were demilitarized but left under Turkish sovereignty. Turkey's borders with Syria were also defined.

Treaty of Versailles (1919) was signed on 28 June 1919 at Versailles, France, in a peace conference of 27 victoriaous powers of World War I on one side and the defeated powers on the other. Germany was excluded from the deliberations of the conference and invited only to sign the treaty. The Treaty laid down the terms of peace upon defeated Germany and other Central Powers. It also included the Covenant of the League of Nations, drafted by President Woodrow Wilson of the USA, as an appendix.

Tripartite Declaration (1950) was issued jointly by the USA, Britain and France in May 1950 whereby the three great powers guaranteed the borders of Israel resulting from the Armistice Agreements signed between Israel and Arab States in 1949. They committed themselves to act within and without the United Nations to prevent any violation of these borders.

Trotskyism is an offshoot of Russian Marxism; refers to the ideas of Leon Trotsky (1879-1940) who propounded a theory of permanent revolution as against Josef Stalin's theory of socialism in one country.

Truce is in international politics a temporary halting of hostilities on the orders of the UN Security Council. It is less definitive than armistice* e.g. the truce established in Palestine in May-June 1948.

Truman Doctrine (1947) or the doctrine of containment of Soviet expansionism and communist aggression was pronounced by President Harry S. Truman of the USA in a message sent to the US Congress on 12 March 1947 committing the United States to render military and economic assistance to any country in the free world which is threatened by communist aggression from without or communist subversion from within. The immediate step taken was provision of military aid to Turkey to withstand Soviet territorial demands and to Greece to fight the communist guerilla forces.

Trusteeship Council, UN is one of the principal organs of the UN set up in 1945 under its Charter. It was composed of member-states administering the trust territories on behalf of the UN and an equal number of other member-states, including always the five permanent members of the UN Security Council. The Trusteeship Council was responsible for preparing the people of eleven territories inherited as mandates from the League of Nations plus some colonies taken from Italy and Japan during World War II for self-government or independence. The last of these territories, Belau, achieved self-government under an agreement of free association with the USA on 1 October 1994. Thereupon the UNTC formally suspended its operations on 1 November 1994. It cannot be abolished without an amendment of the Charter of the UNO.

Tsarism (after Tsar, emperor of Russia) is synonymous with absolutism and imperialism. Tsar is also spelled as Czar.

Two-Nation Theory (India) was formulated in British India by two opposite political leaders in justification of their own political cause. Vinayak Damodar Savarker, the leader of the All-India Hindu Mahasabha, held that the Hindus constituted a district race and nationality with their distinct religion and culture. Sine they constituted a majority of the Indian population India was a Hindu nation and a Hindu state. On the other hand, Muhammad Ali Jinnah, the leader of the All-India Muslim League, disenchanted with the response of the Indian National Congress to the demands of the Muslim minority in India, formulated in 1940 a thesis that since Hindus and Muslims in India were fundamentally different in many respects they constituted separate nations. Hence Muslims were entitled to the right of self-determination in the Muslim-majority provinces of British India. As opined by M. N. Roy, the Lahore Resolution* (1940) of the Muslim League was a bargaining-counter opened by Jinnah to win political concessions from the majority party, the Indian National Congress. The Congress' reluctance to accept the main League demand for a federal constitution and provincial autonomy ultimately led to the partition of India in 1947.

U

Ulama (plural of Arabic *a'lim* = Muslim theologian/religious scholar) are Islamic theologians and scholars who after graduating from religious seminaries engage in teaching and research in theology; leading prayers for the faithful; rendering other religious services to the community; pronouncing opinions on questions of Islamic law; and settling disputes among the faithful particularly in personal and family matters in accordance with the Islamic *shariat* (the code of ethical laws). *Ulamas* is incorrect.

Ultimatum is the ultimate or final warning or demand issued by one party demanding from another party to do or not to do something. An ultimatum admits of no explanation and allows no remission of time.

Ultra Vires (Latin for "beyond laws") is a principle of law that enables the judicial authorities in a system of constitutional government to declare such executive acts as null and void which are either inconsistent with the law or beyond the legal authority granted to the executive.

UN Charter. See "Charter of the UNO".

UN Conference on Environment and Development (UNCED), also known as the Earth Summit, was held on 3-14 June 1992 in Rio de Janeiro, Brazil. Major documents issued by the summit were:

1. a Declaration on Environment and Development
2. a Statement of Principles for global consensus on

management conservation and sustainable development of forests

3. Agenda 21 (for sustainable development)
4. a Convention of Biological Diversity, and
5. a Convention on Climate Change.

UN Conference on Human Settlement is also called the human habitat conference; the first conference was held in Vancouver, Canada, in 1976 and the second in 1996 in Istanbul, Turkey in 1996; made comprehensive recommendation for improving the human habitat by giving priority to proper housing and sanitation,

UN Conference on Trade and Development-- UNCTAD was established by the UN General Assembly as one of its permanent organs in 1964. Its principal role is to promote international trade* particularly of the developing countries to accelerate their economic development. It has more than 183 states as its members. Its secretariat is located in Geneva, Switzerland. The UNCTAD is held every four years. Between two conferences its work is carried on by the Trade and Development Board of the UNCTAD with its committees and subordinate bodies.

UN Convention on Biological Diversity (1992) was one of the two binding Conventions (the other being the Convention on Climate Change), signed by 153 states attending the UN Conference on Environment and Development (UNCED) in 1992. The Convention aims at preservation of biodiversity and protection of the developing countries from "biopiracy". The Convention came into force after ratification by 30 states but the USA refused to sign it alleging that it was injurious to the interests of the American biotechnology industry. The Rio summit also established the Conference of the Parties to the Convention on Biological Diversity (CBD). 183 states that are parties to the CBD meet from time to time to review the progress of the implementation of the Convention.

UN Convention on Chemical Weapons (1997) was signed by more than 160 countries and came into force in April 1997. It prohibits the manufacture, storage and use of chemical weapons as they are lethal for humanity.

UN Convention on the Law of Sea-- UNCLOS was adopted by the UN Conference On the Law of Sea on 10 December 1982. It codified and modernized the customary principles of the law of sea and created the International Seabed Authority and the Law of the Sea Tribunal. Territorial Sea was defined as twelve nautical miles from the baseline of the littoral state; the contiguous zone as 24 nautical miles from the baseline; the exclusive economic zone was defined as 200 nautical miles from the baseline; and the continental shelf was defined as the seabed and subsoil of the submarine areas that extend beyond the coastal state's territorial sea to the outer edge of the continental margin, or to a distance of 200 nautical miles from the baselines from which the breadth of the territorial sea is measured.

UN Development Programme-- UNDP (1965) was created by the UN General Assembly to help underdeveloped countries in achieving economic growth, sustainable development and preservation of the environment. It reports on its work through the Economic and Social Council (ECOSOC) to the UN General Assembly. Its headquarters is in New York City, NY. Among its publications the most important is the annual *Human Development Report.* It also sponsors the observance of the "international Day for Eradication of Poverty" on 17 October every year.

UN Disarmament Commission was set up in 1978 in pursuance of a decision of the Tenth Special Session of the UN General Assembly on Disarmament. It includes all member-states of the UNO. It is responsible for examining and making recommendations for measures to achieve universal disarmament and supervising the implementation of the decisions and recommendations of the Special Session of the UN General Assembly.

UN Environment Programme--UNEP was created by the UN General Assembly in 1972 to assist in policy development and implementation of policies and programmes relating to conservation of human environment. Its headquarters is in Nairobi, Kenya. Among its publications the most important is the *Global Environment Outlook.*

UN Framework Convention on Climate Change--UNFCCC was adopted at the UNCED in 1992 and came into force in 1994. By 2001 the number of states that became parties to this Convention came to 186. The Convention was followed up by the signing of the *Kyoto Protocol* specially meant to prevent global warming by reducing the emission of greenhouse gases.

UN General Assembly is under the Charter of the UNO the parliament of the United Nations, Its first meeting was convened on 10 January 1946. It is composed of the representatives of all the 191 member-states. Each member-state has one vote. Each member-state can maintain its permanent mission at the UN headquarters composed of maximum five delegates plus their alternates and counsellors and technical experts. The General Assembly elects its President for each annual session. There is a Secretary-General (appointed by the Security Council on the recommendation of the General Assembly) and an Under-Secretary-General. The General Assembly meets in ordinary annual sessions and in extraordinary sessions called at the demand of member-states. It operates through its seven permanent committees, the ECOSOC and its subordinate agencies. Resolutions of the General Assembly are passed by a majority of votes but they are of recommendatory nature and non-binding upon the member-states. Non-member states, non-governmental organizations (NO's) and national liberation movements are given the status of observers

UN General Assembly Main Committees. The UN General Assembly transacts its business through its six permanent Main Committees as well as other ad hoc and sessional committees formed from time to time. The six Main Committees were formed in 1946. They are named numerically, each assigned a particular subject. Each Committee is composed of the representatives of all the member-states of the UN. Each Committee includes an elected chairperson and two vice-chairpersons. The six Main Committees are:

First Committee (Disarmament and International Security)

Second Committee (Economics and Finance)

Third Committee (Social, Humanitarian and Cultural)

Fourth Committee (Special Political and Decolonization)

Fifth Committee (Administration and Budget)

Sixth Committee (Legal).

Besides, there is a General Committee, formed in 1956, which is composed of 28 members including the President of the UN General Assembly, 21 Vice-Presidents, and all the chairpersons of the Main Committees.

UN High Commissioner for Human Rights--UNHCHR is an international officer responsible for monitoring the observance of human rights throughout the world. He reports to the UN Human Rights Commission based in Geneva which in turn reports to the ECOSOC and the UN General Assembly.

UN High Commissioner for Refugees--UNHCR is an international officer responsible for coordinating the work of relief and rehabilitation of refugees throughout the world and for arranging their safe repatriation to their home countries. The office of the UNHCR was created by the UN General Assembly in 1951. He is elected by the UN General Assembly on the nomination of the UN Secretary-General and is responsible for his functioning to the UN General Assembly through the ECOSOC. His seat is in Geneva, Switzerland.

UN Human Settlements Programme (UN Habitat) was established in January 2002 to guide and coordinate activities related to human settlements and sustained urban development. Its headquarters is in Nairobi, Kenya. It is responsible for monitoring the implementation of the decisions of the second UN Conference on Human Settlements (HABITAT-II) held in Istanbul, Turkey, in June 1996.

UN Laissez-Passer is the UN passport which the world body issues to its employees like the international passport issued by the national governments to their citizens. The UN passport is recognized as valid travel document for travel throughout the states which are members of the UN. They may or may not be required to apply for visa.

UN Regional Commissions were established by the ECOSOC of the UN General Assembly for various regions of the world to accelerate their development by assisting the countries of the regions in formulating, implementing, coordinating and monitoring appropriate policies for social and economic development of the regions So far five regional commissions have been established:

1. The Economic Commission for Europe (ECE); founded in 1947; headquarters in Geneva, Switzerland
2. The Economic and Social Commission for Asia and the Pacific (ESCAP); founded in 1947; headquarters in Bangkok, Thailand
3. The Economic Commission for Latin America and the Caribbean (ECLAC); founded in 1948; headquarters in Santiago, Chile
4. The Economic Commission for Africa (ECA); founded in 1958; headquarters in Addis Ababa, Ethiopia
5. The Economic and Social Commission for Western Asia (ESCWA) founded in 1974; headquarters in Beirut, Lebanon.

UN Security Council is the executive organ of the UNO under its Charter. It is composed of five Permanent Members-- the USA, Britain, France, China and Russia, and ten non-permanent members who are elected by the General Assembly every two years giving equitable representation to various geographical regions of the world. The presidency of the Council rotates among the members. The principal function of the Security Council is maintenance of international peace and security and to act to meet a breach of peace or a threat of breach of peace anywhere in the world. Its resolutions are mandatory and binding upon all the member-states. A resolution to be passed by the Security Council requires the affirmative vote of nine out of fifteen members of the Council including the affirmative votes of the five Permanent Members. If any one of them vote in the negative the decision cannot be taken. The Charter of the UNO has enjoined great-power consensus on any matter connected with war and peace. The UNSC is empowered to organize collective measures against the violators of international law and to impose sanctions on them. In case of failure of the UNSC to act the UN GA under the Uniting for Peace Resolution can recommend collective measures to be taken by individual member-states. National Capital Territory of Delhi Act, 1991, with an elected assembly and a council of ministers headed by a chief minister enjoying limited powers of legislation under the control of a Lt. Governor appointed by the central government.

UN Trusteeship Council. see "Trusteeship Council, UN".

UN World Summit on Sustainable Development--WSSD was held from 26 August to 4 September 2002 in Johannesburg, South Africa, and attended by 190 countries. It continued the work done by the 1992 "Earth Summit" held in Rio de Janeiro, Argentina.

Unicameralism, as opposed to bicameralism, is the principle that a legislative assembly should have only one chamber, as, according to Lord Acton, if a second chamber duplicates the work of the first it is superfluous; if it obstructs its work it is mischievous.

Union Territories (India) are directly administered by the central government. These are relatively underdeveloped areas of

India which are sought to be developed and prepared for full statehood by the centre, Originally six union territories were created under the States Reorganization Act, 1956. They are governed in terms of the Government of the Union Territories Act, 1963. The six union territories existing in 2005 are: Andaman & Nicobar, Chandigarh, Dadra Nagar Haveli, Daman & Diu, Lakshyadweep and Pondicherry. The former Union Territory of Delhi was given the status of the National Capital Territory under the Government of the National Capital Territory of Delhi Act, 1991, with an elected assembly and a council of ministers headed by a chief minister enjoying limited powers of legislation under the control of a Lt. Governor appointed by the central government.

Union-State Relations Commission (India) See "Sarkaria Commission".

Union-State Relations Commission II (India) was notified by the Government of India in September 2005. Its terms of reference included the sharing of waters of inter-state rivers; interlinking of rivers; inter-state movement of goods; union-state financial relations; value-added-tax; devolution of more powers to Panchayati Raj bodies; and deployment of central forces in the states, etc. The constitution of the commission was to be announced by the end of December 2005.

United Nations -- UN. The United Nations Organization was created as a universal international organization under a Charter approved by 50 states attending the UN Conference in San Francisco, USA, on 25 June 1945. The principles and purposes of the UNO as mentioned in the Preamble of the Charter include the maintenance of international peace and security, promotion of international cooperation, and protection of human rights throughout the world. The principal organs of the UN are the General Assembly, the Security Council, the International Court of Justice, the Trusteeship Council and the Secretariat headed by a Secretary-General. Besides a large network of institutions and conferences, the

UN has eighteen Specialized Agencies which regulate inter-state relations in diverse fields of international life. Its headquarters is in New York City, USA, and in 2005 it had 191 member-states.

United Progressive Alliance--UPA (India) was formed as a parliamentary coalition between the Indian National Congress (Sonia) and some minor regional parties which formed the government at the centre in the wake of the electoral defeat of the ruling NDA* during the parliamentary elections held in 2004. The UPA government is supported from the outside by the Communist Party of India (Marxist)*, the Communist Party of India*, the Samajvadi Party* and the Bahujan Samaj Party*.

Uniting-for-Peace Resolution (1950) was adopted by the UN General Assembly in November 1950, to empower itself to assume the responsibility of organizing collective action to maintain international security in situations when the UN Security Council was prevented from discharging its primary responsibility of maintaining international peace and security because of the exercise of a negative vote (veto) by one of its permanent members. The main points of the Uniting-for-Peace Resolution were: (1) that in a crisis situation when the UN Security Council is prevented from discharging its primary responsibility of maintaining collective security the matter can be referred to the General Assembly which can be convened within 24 hours to consider it; (2) that the General Assembly can make recommendations to the member-states to take collective measures to preserve peace, including use of armed force, if necessary; (3) that each member-state should maintain within its national armed forces contingents ready for deployment in UN peacekeeping operations at the behest of the UN General Assembly; (4) that a Peace Observation Commission be appointed to observe and report on the situation in any area of tension or conflict; and (5) that a Collective Measures Committee be appointed to study and report on ways and means to strengthen international peace and security in accordance with the UN Charter.

Unlawful Activities (Prevention) Amendment Act, 2004 (India). The original Unlawful Activities (Prevention) Act, 1967, was passed to declare secessionist organizations, particularly the DMK* of Madras, as unlawful. In 2004 the government of the United Progressive Alliance at the centre repealed the draconian 'POTA' enacted by the former National Democratic Alliance government. The UPA thus formally fulfilled its promise to repeal the POTA made to the electorate. But ironically most of the provisions of POTA were incorporated in the Unlawful Activities (Prevention) Amendment Act, 2004. The latter now deals, in addition to secessionist organizations, with the terrorists, terroristic organizations, and persons found guilty of aiding terrorists or terroristic organizations.

Unlawful Assembly is an assembly of persons which is considered to be subversive of law and order or detrimental to public interest and declared as unlawful by a competent lawful authority, Democratic constitutions guarantee the right to assemble and take out processions without bearing arms. Under Section 144 of the Indian Penal Code law - enforcing authorities are empowered to prohibit the assembly of five or more persons for a specified period if they apprehend the breach of peace.

Untouchability is a peculiar phenomenon in a society stratified into *varnas** and castes. It means that the *avarnas* outcastes or untouchables cannot mingle with or interdine or intermarry with the *savarnas* i.e. persons belonging to the higher castes. This ritual impurity and social exclusion was sanctified by religious scriptures and age - old social practice. The liberal constitution of the Indian Republic, however, outlawed untouchability (Article 15) and the Indian parliament passed the Untouchability (Offences) Act, 1955/ Civil Rights Act*, 1976, to enforce this prohibition and to provide for punishment of offenders under this Act.

Uruguay Round refers to multilateral trade negotiations under the GATT* which were started in September 1986 in Penta del

Este, Uruguay, and ended in December 1993 in Geneva. The Uruguay Final Act was signed in April 1994 in Marrakesh, Morocco, which provided for the in a uguration of the World Trade Orgainzation* (WTO) with effect from 1. January 1995. The Act also extended the coverage of the GATT in such fields as agriculture, textiles and clothing, services, and the intellectual property rights till such time as alternative agreements were concluded by multilateral negotiations under the auspices of the WTO.

Utilitarianism or Benthamism is the radical liberal view that morals, law, legislation, justice, and administration etc. should be guided by the pragmatic principle of utility (''the greatest happiness of the greatest number'') in contradiction to the classical liberal advocacy of abstract or metaphysical notions such as natural rights.

Utopianism (from Greek *outopia* = no place). The term Utopia was first used by Sir Thomas Moore for his political satire entitled *Utopia* (1516). Utopianism refers to all idealistic, imaginary, impracticable schemes or blueprints for social reform. Two examples are Plato's ideal state and Marx's ideal communism (or classless and stateless society).

V

Value-added Tax (VAT) is an alternative to the traditional sales tax. It was first implemented in France in 1954; in Britain in 1973; and the European Community (EC) enforced VAT at a uniform rate of 15 per cent throughout the community: India-introduced the VAT from 1 April 2005. The tax has been adopted by around 140 countries. VAT is a taxation of goods and services at every stage of production/provision levied on the basis of "value added". For instance, if trader B bought some goods from trader A he pays the VAT at the requisite rate and then charges it on his output sales. Then he pays the tax to government after deducting his input tax which he had paid to trader A.

Vande Mataram (Sanskrit for "I bow to thee Mother") is the first stanza of Bankim Chandra Chatterji's poem in Sanskrit which is included in his novel in Bengali *Anand Math* (1882). The song has had a peculiar fascination for Hindu nationalists. It has been sung in the meetings of the Indian National Congress since 1896 and the All-India Hindu Mahasabha and the Rashtriya Suyam Sewak Sangh followed suit, on the eve of the inauguration of the Indian Republic on 26 January 1950 while the Constituent Assembly adopted Rabindra Nath Tagore's *Jana Gana Mana* as the national anthem at the suggestion of Jawaharlal Nehru, *Vande Mataram* had to be adopted as the second national anthem on the insistence of the revivalists. Monotheist communities in India have a conscientious objection to this song because of its idolatrous tenor.

Varnashram (from Sanskrit *varna* = colour) refers to the four-fold division of Indo-Vedic society into the categories of Brahmans, Kshatriyas, Vais and Shudra ordered on a scale of superiority and inferiority. Each *varna* in turn is subdivided into numerous hereditary and endogamous castes (jatis) and subcastes (upjatis).

Vatican or the Holy See is 0.16 skms area in the city or Rome in Italy which is recognized as sovereign state. It is the home of the Holy Roman Catholic Church presided over by the Holy Pope who is the spiritual leader of the Roman Catholic community world over. After merge of the papal states in central Italy with newly created kingdom of Italy in 1870, popes authority was limited to the papal place and cathedral in the vatican. The popes never surrendered their sovereignty to the Italian state in 1929, however Italy recognized the reverently of the pope over the vatican.

Vested Interests are powerful persons or groups who have acquired special interests, privileges or entrenched positions to the exclusion of others and would resist any attempts at undermining their entrenched positions. As defined by Thorstein Veblen, a vested interest is "a legitimate right to get something for nothing, usually a prescriptive right to an income which is secured by controlling the traffic at one point or another.

Veto is a negative vote nullifying a decision or blocking a decision from being take. With reference to the voting procedure in the UN Security Council a decision on a substantive matter can be taken by an affirmative vote of none of the fifteen members of the Security Council, including the affirmative votes of the five Permanent Members--the USA, Britain, France, China and Russia. If anyone of them casts a negative vote the decision is blocked. The implicit philosophy of the UN Charter is that on matters of war and peace the great powers must act in concert (unanimously) and implement the decisions collectively. See also "Double Veto")

Veto, absolute (US) refers to the power of the President of the USA under the American Constitution to reject a legislative bill presented for his signature after approval by the two houses of the Congress within a period of ten days of its presentation. The President must state his reasons for rejecting the bill. To overcome the presidential veto the two houses must repass the bill by a two-third majority.''

Veto, Pocket (US) refers to the practice of US President of not formally vetoing a bill presented for his signature towards the fag end of a Congressional session. If the president does not veto the bill within the stipulated ten days but keeps it in his pocket till the Congress adjourns the bill automatically lapses along with all other bills pending with the two houses of Congress.

Via Media means the middle path; a policy of balance; or a moderate stand between two extremes.

Viceregal System refers to any executive system in which authority is concentrated in the person of a single functionary or institution, for example the colonial bureaucratic administration of British India where the entire system revolved around the person of the viceroy and Governor-General or modern Indian universities where all authority is vested in the hands of the vice-chancellors.

Viceroy is the deputy of a king.

Vichy Regime refers to the puppet regime of French collaborators of Nazi occupation forces installed by the Germans after their occupation of France in 1940 at Vichy town, headed by Marshall Philippe Petain. The regime came to an end in 1944.

Vietnam War. The first Vietnam War (1946-1954) was fought between the Vietnamese nationalist forces under Vietminh and the French colonial army. The war ended with the defeat of French forces at Dien Bien Phu in 1954. The American-brokered Geneva, accords of that year led to withdrawal of the French from Indochina and division of

Vietnam into two parts. North Vietnam (People's Republic of Vietnam) was left to the nationalist revolutionary forces while South Vietnam (Rėpublic of China) came to be ruled by American -installed puppet regimes. The second Vietnam War (1957-1974) started with the formation of Viet Cong (National Front) in the south in 1957 and start of guerilla activity against the puppet regime. The insurgency was backed by the north. American military intervention started in 1959 and led to a full-fledged war between the communist and American interventionist forces. The war ended with the signing of a peace accord in 1974 in Paris under which American forces were withdrawn from South Vietnam. In 1375 the North overran the South and the two parts of Vietnam were reunified as the Socialist Republic of Vietnam.

Vishwa Hindu Parishad (World Hindu Council) was created as a united front of orthodox hindu religious and political organizations for the defence of the Hindu religion, by the RSS leaders M.S. Gowalkar, S.S. Apte and Ram Gopal Shalwale. The immediate impetus came from the recent conversion of certain members of the Scheduled Castes in the Meenakshipuram village in the state of Tamil Nadu at the hands of certain maulvis. In retaliation *sadhus* (Hindu godmen) were deployed to convert and reconvert the downtrodden communities to Hinduism. In 1984 the VHP vowed to liberate certain holy places in Ayodhya, Varanasi and Mathura which it claimed to be Hindu temples. In that year it also established the Bajrang Dal, a militant youth wing to be trained as a strike force. The VHP is organized in small local units and central *Marg Darshak Mandals* (guidance groups) which meet twice a year and at the national level there is a *Dharma Sansad* (Parliament of Religion) which is convened on extraordinary occasions to take crucial decisions.

Vote of Credit. Under Article 116 of the Indian Constitution, Parliament is authorized to ''make a grant for meeting an unexpected demand upon the resources of India when on account of the magnitude or the definite character of the service the demand cannot be stated with the details ordinarily given in an annual financial statement'' (budget). Article 206 makes a similar provision in respect of the states. Monies voted in this way are described as votes of credits.

Vote on Account. In India the financial year runs from April to March. The Annual Financial Statement (budget) for the next financial year is usually presented in Parliament in the last week of February. Since it is not possible for Parliament to consider the demands for grants of all departments and pass the requisite appropriation and finance bills before 31 March, Article 116 of the Indian Constitution empowers the Lok Sabha to vote an advance amount to enable the government to meet its expenditure during the three-four months of the next financial year till the regular budget is passed. This is known as a vote on account. This amount is later adjusted against regular grants.

W

Wahhabism refers to a religious reform and purification movement launched by Muhammad ibn Abdul Wahhab (1703-1791) in the Nejd province of Arabia. He attacked all polytheistic accretions to the religion of Islam and exhorted Muslims to return to pure monotheism and religious practices of early believers.

War Crimes were defined in the UN Charter establishing the Nuremberg Tribunal for the trial of Nazi war criminals as "Violations of the laws or customs of war. Such violations shall include, but be limited to murder, ill-treatment or deportation to slave labour or for any other purpose, of civilian population from occupied territories, murder or ill-treatment of the prisoners of war or persons on the seas, killing of hostages or devastations not justified by military necessity". Besides war crimes are mentioned in the Geneva Conventions of 1949, the Geneva Convention on War Crimes of 1958, and other agreements for protection of civilians in a war zone. According to the Convention on Non-Applicability of Statutory Limitations to War Crimes of 1968 war crimes are immune from statutory limitations. The member-states of the UN are enjoined to prosecute, try and bring to justice persons found guilty of committing war crimes or crimes against humanity. Such acts are regulated by the Principles of International Cooperation in the Detection, Arrest, Extradition and Punishment of Persons Guilty of War Crimes and Crimes against Humanity, adopted by the UN General Assembly in 1973. Some of the acts generally recognized as war crimes are: Use of means and methods of warfare prohibited under international law; wanton destruction of towns, cities and human habitats; destruction of monuments and cultural assets; inhuman treatment of the prisoners of war, wounded and sick soldiers and the civilians; plundering and confiscating of public and private property; detention, deportation and ill-treatment of civilian population; and hostage-taking and killing of hostages, etc. So far as apprehension and trial of war criminals is concerned, besides the Nuremberg and Tokyo Tribunals which finished their work in 1946 and were wound up, one International Criminal Tribunal for former Yugoslavia (ICTY) was constituted under a resolution of the UN Security Council passed in May 1993 at the Hague in November 1993 try persons for committing the crimes of ethnic cleansing and genocide in Bosnia-Herzgovina and another International Criminal Tribunal for Rwanda (ICTR) was constituted under a resolution of the UN Security Council adopted in November 1994 at Arusha, Tanzania, for trial of those accused of massacre of the Tutsi people in Rwanda in 1994. The International Criminal Court (ICC) was inaugurated as a permanent international judicial authority in such cases on 11 March 2003.

Warsaw Treaty Organization was a Soviet-sponsored collective self-defence organization created under the mutual assistance treaty signed in Warsaw, Poland, in 1955 between Albania, Bulgaria, Czechoslovakia, German Democratic Republic, Hungary, Poland, Rumania and the USSR. It was the eastern counterpart of the NATO. Albania had withdrawn in 1968. After the end of the cold war and collapse of the USSR the WTO was dissolved in 1991.

WASP is an acronym for the wealthy Anglo-saxon Protestants, the dominant community in the societies of North America.

Wassenaar Arrangement. See "COCOM".

Watergate Affair refers to the break-in and tapping of telephone lines of the Democratic National Committee office located in the Watergate apartments in Washington, DC, by the workers of the rival Republican Party during the presidential election campaign of 1972. The Republican candidate, President Richard Nixon, tried to cover up the scandal but failed and had to resign in the face of impeachment proceedings initiated against him.

Wavell Plan (1945) for transfer of power in India was announced by Lord Wavell, the Viceroy and Governor-General of India, on 19 September 1945. He declared the British determination to establish full responsible government in India; holding of central and provincial legislative elections by the end of 1945 and installation of responsible ministries; convening a Constituent Assembly to frame a constitution for India; and finally transfer of power by means of a treaty to be signed between India and Britain. As an immediate step he proposed to reconstitute his Executive Council by including the nominees of major Indian political parties. The plan failed because of disagreement between the Indian National Congress and the All-India Muslim League.

Weimar Republic was proclaimed on 9 November 1918 in the city of Weimar in eastern Germany. It replaced the German Reich (empire). Similarly the constitution adopted in 1919 in Weimar came be called the Weimar Constitution. The Weimar Republic was replaced by the Nazi state in 1933.

Welfare State may be characterized as institutionalized form of reformed capitalism. It represents a middle path between *laissez faire* liberalism and communistic socialism. If in the non-interventionist state the working principle was: "Everyone for himself and let the hind be taken by the devil", the welfare state takes into consideration those who lag behind in competition or are unable to fend for themselves because of disability, sickness or old age. The essence of a modern capitalist welfare state is that it assumes legal responsibility for providing a comprehensive range of public services, income supplements, and market regulation to maximize security and well-being of all its citizens. Distinction should, however, be made between three types of welfare state: (1) the *positive state* which guarantees citizen welfare by corporate growth and full employment such as the USA; (2) the *social security state* which guarantees minimum/ standards of economic well-being and healthcare such as Britain; and (3) the *social welfare state* which implements policies of economic equality and citizen participation such as Sweden.

Weltanschauung (German for worldview) was defined by Sigmund Freud as an intellectual construction which solves all the problems of existence uniformly on the basis of one overriding hypothesis, which, accordingly, leaves no question unanswered and in which everything that interests us finds its fixed place have been accorded the status of observers and some the status of associate partners. In all 28 countries take part in WEU programmes. Its headquarters is in Brussels. It is visualized to be developed as the security wing of the European Union (EU).

West Asia is a geographic region comprising the countries of the Arab East plus Israel, Iran and Turkey. It is called so because it lies to the west of South Asia. In political usage it is synonymous with the Middle East.

West Bank (Palestine) refers to the Palestinian territory, including East Jerusalem, situated to the west of Jordan River and divided from Israeli territory by the Armistice Line of 1949. The total area of the West Bank is 5, 655 square kilometers and its population (2003) is 1, 873,476 persons. After receiving in 1919 the mandate of the League of Nations to govern Palestine the British Government separated the trans-Jordan eastern part of Palestine from the mandated territory and constituted it as the Hashemite Kingdom of Trans-Jordan (popularly known as Jordan) with Abdullah, the son of British loyalist Sheriff Hussain of Mecca as its king, luring the Arab invasion of Palestine after the proclamation of the State of Israel in 1948 King Abdullah captured the West Bank and East Jerusalem (the area allotted to the proposed

Palestinian State under the UN Partition Plan of 1947) and annexed it to his kingdom in 1950. The Israelis captured this entire in their invasion of June 1967 and placed it under their military administration. In 1988 Jordan renounced its sovereignty over the West Bank and in 1994 concluded a peace treaty with Israel. In 1995 Israel agreed to grant limited self-rule to certain Palestinian areas. (See "Palestine Question"; "Palestinian Authority".

Western European Union--WEU was created in 1935 under the Collective Defence Treaty signed in 1948 in Brussels, Luxembourg. It works in close cooperation with the European Union and NATO. It joins together in a security community: Belgium, Britain, France, Germany, Greece, Italy, Luxembourg, Netherland, Portugal and Spain. Its associate members are: the Czech Republic, Hungary, Iceland, Norway, Poland, and Turkey.

Westminster and Whitehall. The Palace of Westminster house the two chambers of British Parliament. Whitehall is the name of a street in London where most of the important ministries and departments of central government are located. Hence Westminster symbolizes the legislative and the Whitehall the executive branch of British government.

Westminster Model is synonymous with British-style parliamentary democracy* or the system of representative and responsible government.

Whig/Whiggism. The term *whig* is derived from *whiggamore* which literally means robbers. The term was used for the anti-royal English liberals during the eighteenth century. The term stuck to them and their party. The Whigs merged with the Liberal Party when it was founded in the middle of the nineteenth century. The Whigs were opposed to Tories (conservatives). Whiggism is synonymous with liberalism and Toryism with conservatism.

White House (US) is the official residence of the President of the USA located in Washington, D.C.

Wilson's Fourteen Points (1918) were laid down by President Woodrow Wilson of the USA in an address delivered to the US Congress on 8 January 1918, defining the objectives of the USA in entering World War I on the side of the Allies: "(1) Open covenants should be arrived at openly instead of secret treaties negotiated by secret diplomacy; (2) freedom of navigation in the open seas in peace and war alike except as the seas might be closed by international action to enforce international covenants; (3) removal of all barriers to free trade so far as possible; (4) armaments should be reduced to the lowest point consistent with domestic safety; an impartial adjustment of all colonial claims on the principle that the interests of the population must have equal weight with the claims of government; (6) the evacuation of Russian territory and free determination of her own political and national policy; (7) evacuation and restoration of Belgium; (8) evacuation and restoration of the French territory and the righting of wrong done in the matter of Alsace-Lorraine; (9) readjustment of the boundaries of Italy along clearly recognizable line of nationality; (10) opportunity for autonomous development for the peoples of Austria-Hungary; (11) evacuation and restoration of Rumania, Serbia and Montenegro together with access to the sea for Serbia; (12) the Turkish part of the Ottoman Empire to be given secure sovereignty, but the other nationalities to be given an opportunity for autonomous development; and the Dardenelles to be permanently opened to ships of all nations under international guarantees; (13) an independent Poland with free and secure access to the sea; and (14) a general association of nations to be formed to afford mutual guarantees of political independence and territorial integrity to great and small states alike".

World Bank See International Bank for Reconstruction and Development (IBRD).

World Bank Group is composed of the International Bank for Reconstruction and Development (the World Bank),

International Finance Corporation (IFC), International Development Association (IDA), the Multilateral investment Guarantee Agency (MIGA) and the International Centre for the Settlement of Investment Disputes (ICSID).

World Confederation of Labour--WCL was originally founded in 1920 as the International Federation of Christian Trade Unions and was renamed as the WCL in 1968. It affiliates national labour federations in 116 countries.

World Council of Churches was formed in 1948 in Geneva to promote cooperation among Christian churches throughout the world. It has more than 310 churches in more than 120 countries as its members. Vatican is not a member of the WCC but sends its observers to attend its meetings.

World Court. See "International Court of Justice".

World Islamic League *(Rabiteh al-Alam al-Islami)* is a religious foundation established by the late King Faisal of Saudi Arabia in 1962 with its seat in Mecca, Saudi Arabia, to promote exchanges between religious institutions in the Islamic world; to grant scholarships for religious studies; and to propagate the Islamic faith. It should not be confounded with the Organization of Islamic Conference (OIC) which is an intergovernmental organization.

World Politics is a fluid and all-inclusive term to describe the sum of all political interactions between and among both governmental and non-governmental actors, multinational corporations and transnational interest groups, associations and movements, etc. It is distinct from international politics which refers to relations between and among national governments, international intergovernmental organizations and supranational institutions.

World Tourist Council--WTC is an intergovernmental organization created in 1975 under a charter approved in 1910 to replace the non-governmental International Union of Official Tourist Organizations. The headquarters of the WTC is in Madrid,

Spain. Its objective is to promote world peace and prosperity through promotion of tourism throughout the world.

World Trade Organization--WTO is an institutional form of a liberal international economic regime. It was created under the Final Act of the GATT's Uruguay Round of Multilateral Negotiations signed on 15 April 1994 and started functioning in Geneva from 1 January 1995. Its mandate is to create an international free-trade regime by voluntary agreements among the member-states arrived at through multilateral negotiations. In 2005 the WTO had 147 states as its members. The topmost deliberative organ of the WTO is its Ministerial Conference held from time to time and attended by the ministers of the member-states. Below it is the General Council composed of one member from each of the member-state. The General Council also works in two capacities---as the Dispute Settlement Body and as the Trade Policy Review Body. At the bottom is the Secretariat of the WTO headed by a Director-General, with a staff of 1500, which is the administrative organ of the WTO. In 2005 the WTO had 149 member-states and 31 states as observers. The WTO administers and implements more than 29 multilateral agreements in such fields as trade in goods, agriculture, textile and clothing, services, government procurement, rules of origin, and intellectual property rights. Current multilateral negotiations on agriculture and other issues were to be concluded at the Sixth Ministerial Conference convened in Hong Kong on 23 December 2005. The three key issues to be discussed were agriculture and agricultural market access; non-agricultural market access (NAMA); and services. A final broad agreement was hammered out on 29 December 2005.

World Zionist Congress. The political ideology of Zionism was created by Theodor Herzl (1860-1904), a Hungarian who had converted to Judaism, in his book *The Jewish State* (1896). His thesis was that the Jews constituted a separate nation and were entitled to a separate national state of their own. In 1897 Herzl convened the first international Zionist Congress in Basle, Switzerland. The Congress declared that Zionism strives to create for the Jewish people a home in Palestine secured by public law. The Congress formulated a Zionist programme and established a Zionist Organization (which later became the Jewish Agency) to give effect to this programme. The programme consisted of the following measures: (1) promotion on suitable lines of colonization of Palestine by Jewish agricultural and industrial workers; (2) organization and integration of the whole of the Jewish community by means of appropriate institutions, local and international, in accordance with local laws of each country; (3) strengthening and fostering of Jewish national sentiment and consciousness; and (4) preparatory steps towards obtaining governmental consent where necessary towards attainment of the Zionist objectives. Zionist efforts bore fruit in the form of the Balfour Declaration*; the British mandate over Palestine; the establishment of the Jewish Agency as the quasi-official organ to manage Jewish colonization of Palestine; and western military and economic support to Israel since its proclamation in 1948. Since 1948 the World Zionist Congress has played a leading role in garnering international support for Israel's expansionist policies and collecting funds in aid of the Israeli government.

Y

Yalta Agreement (1945) was signed between the Big Three -- President Franklin Roosevelt of the USA, Sir Winston Churchill of the UK, and Josef Stalin of the USSR -- in Yalta (Crimea). They agreed on terms for joint occupation of the defeated Germany; pledged the establishment of a new Poland on a democratic basis; committed themselves to giving joint assistance to countries liberated from Nazi occupation and to enable them to establish their governments through free elections owing responsibility to the will of the people. The Yalta agreement also contained a formula for big-power voting in the proposed UN Security Council and committed the USSR to enter the war against Japan and was promised the return of territories lost to Japan during the Russo-Japanese War of 1904-5.

Yankee (Spanish *yanqui* = an inhabitant of north America) is a term used disparagingly by the inhabitants of south and central America for the people of the USA, e.g. yankee imperialism.

Yaoundé Convention. The first Yaounde Convention signed in 1964 brought eighteen African states into association with the European Community* (EC). A second Yaoundé Convention followed. Then it was replaced by the Lomé Convention* which expanded and consolidated the association of the African, Caribbean and Pacific (ACP) countries, which were former colonies of European states, with the European Community/European Union.

Yavana (Sanskritized form of "Ionians" = Greeks) was the term applied by the ancient Indians to foreigners of all breeds.

Young Turks is applied to any group of radical young reformers within a conservative establishment. The term originated refers to a group of young military officers and intellectuals who formed the Committee of Reform and Progress and revolted against Absolute rule of Sultan Abdul Hamid II. They governed the Ottoman Empire till its defeat in World War I.

Z

Zaibatsu refers to the conglomeration of the Japanese multinational corporations and monopolies which take part in the formulation of Japanese economic policy in close coordination with the Japanese government and form the backbone of the Japanese economy and foreign trade.

Zero-Sum Game is drawn from the mathematical theory of games propounded by J. von Newmann in 1928. It is applied to political and strategic decision-making situations. The two-person zero-sum game assumes that in a game played by two persons with opposite interests the game will inevitably end in gain for one and loss for the other.

Zimmi (Arabic for a protected person) was the term applied to religious minorities under protection of the Islamic state. Islamic *shariat* granted them full religious and cultural freedom and equal rights. The protected persons were also exempted from military service (particularly if a war was to be fought against their coreligionists) on payment of *jizya* (exemption tax). If they joined military service no tax was to be paid.

Zionism (from *Zion,* a hill around Jerusalem) was the political ideology of European Jews propounded by Theodor Herzl (1860-1904), a Hungarian who had converted to Judaism, in his book *The Jewish State* (1896). Herzl called for the creation of a Jewish state in Palestine from where the Jews were expelled by the Romans 1000 years ago and which was now a predominantly Arab country. Herzl convened the first World Zionist Congress in 1897 in Basle and declared the aim of Zionism as the creation of a Jewish national home secured by public law and to take appropriate measures for Jewish colonization of Palestine and bringing world Jewry under a single political organization. The Zionists extracted a promise from the British government (see Balfour Declaration)* towards the creation of a Jewish national home in Palestine. The British who had captured Palestine from the Turks during World War I were given the League of Nations' mandate on 24 July 1922 to govern it. The British administration established a semi-official organization by the name of the **Jewish Agency** which was made responsible for bringing Jews into Palestine and settle them there. The flood of Jewish immigration before and after World War II led to Arab-Jewish conflict. The British referred the Palestine question to the UN General Assembly and announced their decision to withdraw from Palestine in 1948. The UN General Assembly passed a resolution on 29 November 1947 to partition Palestine into an Arab and a Jewish state. When the British withdrew from Palestine in 1948 the Jewish Agency proclaimed the State of Israel in areas allotted to the Jewish state under the UN partition plan. Thereby the Zionist dream was realized.

Zonal Councils (India) were created under the States Reorganization Act, 1956*, to promote inter-state consultation and coordination in the different regions of India. The country was divided into five zones--north, south, east, west and centre. One Zonal Council was created for each of these zones. Each Zonal Council is composed of the Union Home Minister (who is the common chairman of all the Zonal Councils) and the Chief Ministers of states falling within a zone. The chief ministers become vice-chairmen by rotation; a number of officials are also associated in an advisory capacity. A zonal council for the northeastern region was created under the North-Eastern Council Act, 1970.